The German army gained a great ... even more, beginning with its s ... blood.

This is the balance sheet of that gain and loss—during thirteen years of peace and war with the fate of the world in balance.

The German Army 1933-45

"Penetrating analysis based on ten years' work ... revealing important facts hitherto unknown."
—*Reveu des dêux Mondes*

"Lucid, accurate, detailed and instructive." —*Book Choice*

"The value of this book, written in such brilliant style, lies in the author's description of the way in which the army developed, and how this development went hand-in-hand with politico-military considerations and operations in the field. ... The great attraction of the work lies, moreover, in the author's clear judgments on personalities and events, presenting an impressive picture of the political and moral implication of what was going on."—*Historische Zeitschrift*

COLONEL ALBERT SEATON is one of the world's premier authorities on the political and military history of Germany and Russia. Since retiring from the British army, he has worked full time at writing and research. His acclaimed books include *The Russo-German War, 1941–45, The Battle for Moscow, 1941–42, Stalin as Warlord, The Crimean War: A Russian Chronicle,* and *The Fall of Fortress Europe, 1943–45.*

EARLIER BOOKS BY THE AUTHOR

The Russo-German War 1941–45
The Battle for Moscow 1941–42
Stalin as Warlord
The Crimean War – A Russian Chronicle
The Fall of Fortress Europe 1943–45

The German Army 1933-45

Albert Seaton

A MERIDIAN BOOK

NEW AMERICAN LIBRARY

NEW YORK AND SCARBOROUGH, ONTARIO

NAL BOOKS ARE AVAILABLE AT QUANTITY DISCOUNTS WHEN USED TO
PROMOTE PRODUCTS OR SERVICES. FOR INFORMATION PLEASE WRITE
TO PREMIUM MARKETING DIVISION, NEW AMERICAN LIBRARY, 1633
BROADWAY, NEW YORK, NEW YORK 10019.

This is an authorized reprint of a hardcvoer edition published
by St. Martin's Press.

 MERIDIAN TRADEMARK REG. U.S. PAT. OFF. AND FOREIGN COUNTRIES
REGISTERED TRADEMARK—MARCA REGISTRADA
HECHO EN WESTFORD, MASS., U.S.A.

SIGNET, SIGNET CLASSIC, MENTOR, PLUME, MERIDIAN AND
NAL BOOKS are published by New American Library,
1633 Broadway, New York, New York 10019.

Library of Congress Cataloging in Publication Data

Seaton, Albert, 1921-
   The German Army, 1933-45.

   Reprint. Originally published: New York :
St. Martin's Press, c1982.
   Bibliography: p.
   1. Germany. Heer—History—20th century.   I. Title.
UA712.S47   1984   355.3'0943   84-25374
ISBN 0-452-00739-9

First Meridian Printing, March, 1985

1 2 3 4 5 6 7 8 9

*Nondimanco si vede per esperienza ne' nostri tempi,
quelli principi aver fatto gran cose, che della fede
hanno tenuto poco conto, e che hanno saputo con
l'astuzia aggirare i cervelli degli uomini, ed alla fine
hanno superato quelli che si sono fondati en su la
lealtà.*

MACHIAVELLI

Contents

List of Maps

Acknowledgements

I should like to acknowledge my grateful thanks to my publishers: Weidenfeld and Nicolson/Arthur Barker of 91 Clapham High Street, London SW4, Rupert Hart-Davis (Granada Publishing) of 3 Upper James Street, London W1 (and Frogmore, St Albans, Hertfordshire), and B. T. Batsford of 4 Fitzhardinge Street, London W1, for their kind agreement that I should use certain paragraphs that have already appeared in my earlier books: *The Russo-German War 1941–45* (Barker 1970), *The Battle for Moscow 1941–42* (Rupert Hart-Davis 1971), *Stalin as Warlord* (Batsford 1976) and *The Fall of Fortress Europe 1943–45* (Batsford 1981).

I thank most gratefully the authors, editors, translators, publishers and agents for their kind permission to reproduce extracts from their works: *Hitler's Last Days* by Gerhard Boldt, published by Arthur Barker, 91 Clapham High Street, London SW4; *The Final Entries – The Diaries of Joseph Goebbels*, edited by Professor Trevor-Roper and translated by General Barry, published by Secker and Warburg, 54 Poland Street, London W11; *Inside the Third Reich* and *Spandau – The Secret Diaries* by Albert Speer, published by The Macmillan Publishing Co. Inc. of 866 Third Avenue, New York, NY 10022; *The Goebbels Diaries*, edited by Louis P. Lochner, copyright © 1948 by The Fireside Press, Inc. and reprinted by permission of Doubleday and Company Inc., 245 Park Avenue, New York, NY 10017; *Das Heer 1933–45* (three volumes) by General B. Müller-Hillebrand, published by E. S. Mittler und Sohn GmbH, Steintorwall 17, D-4900 Herford and Bonngasse 3, D-5300 Bonn; *Das Kriegstagebuch des Oberkommandos der Wehrmacht 1940–45* (four volumes), edited by Professors Jacobsen, Hillgruber, Hubatsch and Schramm, published by Bernard und Graefe Verlag, Hubertusstrasse 5, D-8000 München; Georg Tessin's *Formationsgeschichte der Wehrmacht 1933–39*, published by Harald Boldt Verlag, Am Alten Sportplatz, D-5407 Boppard am Rhein; Tessin's *Verbände und Truppen der Deutschen Wehrmacht und Waffen SS im Zweiten Weltkrieg 1939–45 (Erster Band)*, published by Biblio Verlag, Jahnstrasse 15, D-4500 Osnabrück; K-J. Müller's *Das Heer und Hitler*, published by Deutsche Verlags-Anstalt, Neckarstrasse 121, D-7000 Stuttgart 1; Foerster's *Ein General Kämpft Gegen den Krieg*, published by Münchener Dom Verlag, D-8000 München; Dorothea Groener-Geyer's *General Groener*, published by the Societäts Verlag, Frankenallee 71–81, D-6000 Frankfurt am Main 1; General Faber du Faur's *Macht und Ohnmacht*, published by Hans E. Gunther Verlag; General Nehring's *Die Geschichte der Deutschen*

Panzerwaffe 1916–1945, published by Propyläen Verlag, Kochstrasse 50, D-1000 Berlin 61; Helmuth Greiner's *Die Oberste Wehrmacht Führung 1939–43*, published by Limes Verlag, Romanstrasse 16, D-8000 München 19; and *Le Operazioni della Unità Italiane nel Settembre-Ottobre 1943*, published by the Ministero della Difesa Stato Maggiore dell'Esercito-Ufficio Storico, Rome (1975).

Notes on Sources and Style

The history of the development of the German Army during the twelve years of the Nazi Third Reich falls into two distinctly separate periods, the six years of peace from 1933 to 1939, and the years of war from 1939 to 1945. Each period poses entirely different problems to the researcher in that the first was marked by discipline and system, while the second was characterized by disorder and confusion that grew more grotesque with the certainty of defeat.

During the first period, that of the peace, the German Army expanded rapidly from the 100,000 professional *Reichsheer* to a conscript standing army of about 730,000 men, with a further 500,000 fully trained reservists, a ground force that was not large by the European standards of the time. Although the expansion was pushed through in feverish haste, it was less eventful than the main drama that was being enacted in Berlin, where Hitler, deliberately and successfully, brought the whole of the *Wehrmacht* under his own tight personal command.

Although the expansion was carried out too hurriedly, it was at least planned and controlled by the commander-in-chief of the army, for there is no evidence of any Führer interference until 1938. And the activity of the general staff can be easily traced by the record. The present-day Bundesarchiv and the Militärgeschichtliches Forschungsamt have already done extensive work in documenting and recounting the detail of the army expansion that took place during this first pre-war period: Tessin's *Formationsgeschichte der Wehrmacht 1933–1939* and Schmidt-Richberg's *Die Generalstäbe in Deutschland 1871–1945* are two such published reference works based on this research. Recently, the Militärgeschichtliches Forschungsamt (the Research Institute of the Bundeswehr) has published the first two (of a projected series of ten) volumes, *Ursachen und Voraussetzungen der deutschen Kriegspolitik* and *Die Errichtung der Hegemonie auf dem europäischen Kontinent*; and, although these are not classified as official German war histories, they will undoubtedly serve that purpose. Professor Messerschmidt has also written and had published his own *Die Wehrmacht im NS-Staat* that forms a companion piece to Professor Klaus-Jürgen Müller's *Das Heer und Hitler, 1933–1940*.

Another most informative and authoritative German source that deals mainly with the military (as opposed to the political) development of the German Army of the period is General Müller-Hillebrand's three volume work *Das Heer 1933–1945*. A former regular officer who, as the military aide to Halder, the chief of the army general staff, sat in his chief's office and attended with him more than a hundred daily military conferences with the dictator before heading the organization *Abteilung* of the general staff, he was particularly well qualified to write such a work even before he began the arduous post-war documentary research necessary to complete it. But although Müller-Hillebrand has a wide and intimate knowledge of the leading German military personalities of the time, these secrets are rarely revealed in his volumes; the book remains a standard and factual work of prime importance with a penchant for organizational and equipment tables produced in meticulous detail.

Of other German learned works covering this period, mention must be made of Beck's *Studien* and of Demeter's and Erfurth's books on the officer corps and the general staff.

There are numerous biographies covering the years of the Nazi peace, written mainly by German generals. One of the most important of these is that written by Groener-Geyer, Groener's daughter; others include published memoirs by Faber du Faur, Hossbach and von Lossberg, von Manstein's *Aus dem Leben eines Soldaten* and autobiographies by Guderian, Nehring and Adam. Even more important are the large collection of military appreciations and essays written, without the benefit of hindsight, during the period from 1934 to 1939 by military leaders already eminent, or yet to become eminent, such as von Seeckt, Guderian, Wetzell, Georg Thomas, Fellgiebel, Adam and Thomsen.

There are relatively few works outside of Germany that deal with the German Army between the years from 1933 to 1939. Benoist-Méchin's many volumed work *Histoire de l'Armée Allemande*, informative though it certainly was at the time of publication, covers the period from the end of the First World War to the end of the Second, and the larger part of it is devoted to European foreign affairs and the political developments within the Reich, rather than to the German Army. Carsten's excellent account finishes in 1933 and Gordon's in 1926. Only Wheeler-Bennett, Craig and O'Neill have covered the period up to 1939 in any detail. Russian and East German histories are too heavily impregnated with dogmatism and propaganda to justify their use; one East German collected work on the Prussian/German General Staff 1640–1965, by Förster, Helmert, Otto and Schnitter, is, however, worthy of note.

For the writing of the second and probably the most important part of this work, that of the war years from 1939 to 1945, there is a superfluity, a conflicting confusion, of material that would require a lifetime to research and reproduce.

The sources used for this part of the book have included documents, many of them unpublished, letters from correspondents, interviews, and published printed material.

Of the official unpublished material a most important and reliable source has been the German order of battle from the *Schematische Kriegs-gliederungen* compiled by the OKH at frequent intervals throughout the whole course of the war. Use has been made of some of the surviving OKH files, and the war diaries of army groups and some armies have been consulted; much less frequently, the war diaries of corps and divisions have been traced, where it has been necessary to check certain details; the very full personal diaries of von Bock and von Weichs have also proved of value; much of this information was obtained during our earlier stays in London and visits to Freiburg, Bonn and Munich, and has been supplemented, over the years, by photostated documents sent from Freiburg, London and Washington.

Of the published German documents, the main sources have been the four volume work *Kriegstagebuch des Oberkommandos der Wehrmacht*, edited by Professors Jacobsen, Hillgruber, Hubatsch and Schramm, Hubatsch's *Hitlers Weisungen für die Kriegführung*, Halder's *Kriegstagebuch* and *Der Zweite Weltkrieg in Chronik und Dokumenten* both edited by Jacobsen, *Nazi–Soviet Relations* and *Nazi Conspiracy and Aggression*.

Tessin has recently completed a second project covering the period between 1939 and 1945, a many volumed work *Verbände und Truppen der deutschen Wehrmacht und Waffen SS*, a monumental reference work that enables the researcher to follow the history of all formations and major units. The most important of these volumes is Volume 1, the volume that was produced last in the series and summarizes the detail contained in the other volumes. Comparison reference works are Müller-Hillebrand's *Das Heer*, Wolf Keilig's *Das Deutsche Heer*, and Klietmann's *Die Waffen SS*. All of these works have been much used in the compilation of this book.

A very large number of German published accounts have been referred to during the writing of this history, particularly where these have been written by primary sources, participants in, or witnesses to, the events they describe. Inevitably, most of these were written after the war by senior officers, Halder, Zeitzler, Guderian, von Manstein, Keitel, Warlimont, von Lossberg, von Ahlfen, Chales de Beaulieu, von Choltitz, Deichmann, Doerr, Friessner, Fretter-Pico, Hoth, Heidkämper, Heim, Hümmelchen, Lange, Lasch, Morzik, von Mackensen, Nehring, Niehoff, Philippi, Plocher, Rendulic, Schwabedissen, Speidel, Teske, von Vormann, Westphal and others. Most of these sources are in German, but in quoting sources that are also available in English translation the English translation has usually been used.

Generally, little use has been made of the other histories of the German Army that have preceded this book and that deal with the war period, if only for the reason that they have been largely superseded by later information from documentary and primary sources.

Surnames have been used throughout this book without initials (except where these are necessary to distinguish between two of the same name), and generally without titles or ranks. These can be found by reference to the index. Place names have been spelt in accordance with the editions of *The Times Atlas* published between the two world wars, even though the transliteration of Russian and Ukrainian names at that time did not necessarily follow the usage of the more modern systems.

Foreword

The subject of this book covers so vast a field that the research, that has been spread over a period of nearly ten years, could not have been carried out without the assistance of a large number of people.

I should like to express my gratitude to government departments, learned organizations, libraries and the many authorities in England, Germany, Italy, France and North America who have given me access to documents and printed material together with assistance or advice in acquiring further source material. In particular: the Department of Documents, the Imperial War Museum; the Institute of Contemporary History and Wiener Library; the British Ministry of Defence Central and Army Library; St Antony's College, Oxford; the Bundesarchiv-Militärarchiv, Freiburg; the Militär-geschichtliches Forschungsamt, Freiburg; the Stato Maggiore dell'Esercito (Ufficio Storico) in Rome; the D. B. Weldon Library of the University of Western Ontario, and the Robarts Library of the University of Toronto; and the Chief of Military History (Department of the Army), Washington. And I acknowledge my very grateful thanks to the Commandant of the Royal Military College of Canada for his permission to use material from the Printed German Collections of the Massey Library, Kingston.

I am grateful also to a number of those German generals and officers who were in key appointments or who served in areas of critical importance, who answered my questions and freely gave me information, either by interview or by correspondence: unless they have wished to remain anonymous their names have been included in the annotated sources.

I should lastly like to thank my wife for typing and retyping the manuscript and for her invaluable help in the German research. Without her support the book could not have been written.

Introduction

Just as the German Army of the Weimar Republic traced the greater part of its development from the imperial army, so was the German Army of the First World War in reality the direct offspring of the Prussian Army, for Prussia, before the creation of the empire, encompassed by far the larger part of Germany, its great mass stretching almost unbroken from the French border to the frontiers of Russia. Even as early as 1869, the Prussian Army had reorganized and absorbed the forces of the states of the North German Confederation, adding them to the Prussian regimental lists and order of battle with a seniority after that of the original Prussian corps. This reinforced Prussian Army accounted for more than eighty per cent of the field strength of the German ground forces at the time of the Franco–Prussian War.

In 1871 the King of Prussia became a dual monarch when he accepted for himself and his heirs the regalia of the new German Empire, an empire that embraced not only Prussia but also the kingdoms of Saxony, Württemberg and Bavaria. Then, from 1874 onwards, the entire German land forces were united as a single army under the command of Wilhelm I, who was both the King of Prussia and the first German Kaiser. By 1914 the authority of the Berlin government had so encroached upon the powers originally held by the twenty-six German member states some forty years before, that Prussia's hegemony seemed complete. Königgrätz and Sedan prussianized most German-speaking peoples outside of Austria, introducing autocracy, reactionary nationalism and anti-Semitism where it had not existed before.

The Kaiser had been the supreme war-lord and the actual, as opposed to the titular, commander-in-chief of the German Army and Navy. Officers and soldiers of the German Army were under an oath of personal allegiance to the King of Prussia, or, in the case of the other kingdoms, to the Kaiser – not necessarily by name or by imperial title but as the Confederate Commander-in-Chief (*Bundesfeldherr*). The military control went directly from the Kaiser to the generals commanding the army corps districts in peace, or to the army groups or armies in war.* To assist him with advice and

* The basic field formation devised by the French at the time of the Revolutionary and Napoleonic Wars and still in use a century later was the infantry division, an all arms grouping usually of four regiments (twelve battalions) of infantry, grouped under two brigades, together with artillery and engineers. The division was said to be basic because it was designed to be capable of operating in isolation and was self-contained and self-supporting, and the military might of a nation was reckoned in the number of divisions it could muster. Several divisions made up a corps and several corps an army; an army group consisted of two or more armies. A corps district was the area allotted to a corps for its peacetime quarters and war reinforcement organization.

to provide the necessary command organization, the Kaiser had a number of army and arms inspectors, together with three separate and independent bodies, the Prussian military cabinet, the Prussian war ministry and the Prussian general staff, these forming a trinity of advisory and executive organs, without themselves, however, having any command authority, for they were there merely to advise and to carry out the Kaiser's orders.[1]

The principles and organization of the Prussian general staff system that had been originated by von Scharnhorst in 1808, were to continue in the German Army virtually unchanged until 1933, except in two important particulars. Raised to its apogee during the period from 1866 to 1883 by the genius and prestige of its chief, the elder von Moltke, the general staff was divided into two parts – the great general staff, housed in the red brick building near the centre of government in the north-east corner of the Tiergarten between the Berlin Königsplatz and the Kronprinzufer, this forming the main thinking and war planning organization of the empire, and the *Truppengeneralstab*, comprising those general staff officers detached from the centre and doing a tour of duty with field formations or with the inspectorates.[2]

The Prussian chiefs of general staff had been responsible to the king or emperor, whose immediate advisers they were on all military war plans excepting those that were the exclusive responsibility of the navy; for in German terminology *Militär*, like the Latin *miles*, referred usually to soldiers.* At the emperor's direction, the chief of general staff, in conjunction with the war ministry, drew up all plans and orders covering mobilization, movement and battle. In peace he was also largely involved, together with the inspectorates and the war ministry, in translating strategic and tactical doctrine into training for war, and in the broader aspects of army organization and equipment; he was entirely responsible for the war academy (the general staff college) and for the selection, training and appointments of all general staff officers. In war the chief of general staff took the field as the chief of general staff of the field army. The chiefs of general staff before von Schlieffen had always been encouraged, and considered it their duty, to express their opinions frankly and to offer, unbidden, advice to the sovereign.[3]

German military thought in the first decades of the twentieth century was deeply influenced, even obsessed, by the actions and writings of the elder von Moltke and of von Schlieffen, the chief of general staff from 1891 to 1906. Von Moltke's successes certainly warranted the closeness of the attention paid to him, provided of course that his methods could be related to the conditions of a rapidly changing world. Whether von Schlieffen's contribution to military science deserved such detailed study and general acceptance, might now, perhaps, be called into question, if only on the

* The Prussian chiefs of general staff after von Moltke the elder were: von Waldersee 1888–91; von Schlieffen 1891–1906; von Moltke the younger 1906–14; von Falkenhayn 1914–16; von Hindenburg 1916–19.

grounds that von Schlieffen's studies concentrated on the Central European politico-military situation of the eighteen-seventies and took insufficient account of the effect of the industrial revolution on the economies of both the Old and the New Worlds. It appears, moreover, that von Schlieffen was in agreement with the prevailing political thought in the German capital at that time, that war, or the threat of war, should be the principal instrument of German imperial diplomacy; and, since the chief of general staff appeared to think that little was impossible to the German soldier, he accepted the hazardous political situations imposed on him by the new emperor, thus shouldering the planning of future military operations so extravagant that they were beyond the German Army's capabilities.

Von Bismarck's policy of a friendly understanding with Russia had spared Prussia the dilemma of a two-front war or of a war against a powerful coalition. But with the first two Kaisers dead and Bismarck dismissed, the statesmen and some of the leading soldiers of the new empire had acquired an overweening confidence in their own armed might.* This led them to discount the diplomacy of negotiation and of *entente*, of finance and of trade. Meanwhile the young Wilhelm II had alienated the major European powers, even his former allies, so that, by the turn of the century, Germany found itself ringed by unfriendly power blocs and potential enemies.

It was in this dangerous political and military situation that von Schlieffen had drawn up the celebrated plan in which he himself eventually had doubts. For although von Schlieffen may have been an out-dated and one-sided strategist, he was undoubtedly clear-minded. The fatal flaw to his character was his reluctance to assert himself against the Kaiser in his advisory role in strategic politico-military matters, for he deferred to the emperor in everything. Like the elder von Moltke, von Schlieffen was taciturn; unlike him, he was sarcastic, with a sphinx-like mask of a face concealing some deficiency of character. Just as Wilhelm II, in demanding implicit obedience from von Schlieffen, became, in effect (as even von Waldersee had said), his own chief of general staff, so was von Schlieffen disinclined to suffer any officer with originality of mind or firmness of purpose to remain in any key position within the great general staff. Officers of the general staff were merely required to carry out von Schlieffen's orders.[4]

The Schlieffen plan, heedless of the Franco–British *entente* and London's interest in Belgian independence, involved the passage of German troops through neutral Belgium and the envelopment of the French armies from the north, it being the intention to force a French capitulation after a lightning campaign of six to eight weeks.[5] The victorious German troops would then be turned rapidly about and moved eastwards against Russia. Von Schlieffen, like Hitler, the latter-day German dictator, found his inspiration from Prussian military history, some of it in the distant past; he still lived in the world of Frederick the Great and Napoleon and of the Franco–Prussian

---

* Von Waldersee, the chief of general staff from 1888 to 1891, had apparently advocated a war against both France and Russia.

War, and he had failed to keep pace with altering social and economic conditions and the changing world of scientific development, industrialization and great power politics. For the fall of Paris, even of France, could not have defeated Britain or Russia, and Germany must eventually have been strangled by the economic blockade. Political, maritime, industrial and economic matters and a world-wide strategy found no part in von Schlieffen's appreciation, and his plan was based on the ill-founded assumption that a great power struggle must of necessity be a short one 'since no nation could bear the material and financial cost of a protracted war'. Von Schlieffen saw Germany as menaced by the Franco–Russian coalition and he had fully accepted that a two-fronted war was inevitable; all was to be staked on the single throw of the dice, it being assumed that France would collapse at the first German onslaught.

Von Schlieffen's plan, his ideas and his methods, were to dominate and to cripple German general staff thinking for nearly half a century; even forty years later the activities of the army general staff rarely rose above the level of grand tactics, so many of its members being content to *operieren* as if in a vacuum, with strategic appreciations being kept within a radius of 200 miles and always halting at the salt water's edge.* Even with the benefit of hindsight, many of its philosophers, Groener and von Seeckt among them, continued to attribute the failure of the Schlieffen plan not to its lack of relevance to the world conditions of 1914 but to the failure of the younger von Moltke and of his assistant von Ludendorff to adhere rigidly to it.†

The German high command from 1914 to 1916 was based, in a large degree, on the experience of the Prussian victories some forty years before, for the detailed organization of the 1914 imperial war headquarters was actually framed on the King of Prussia's campaign headquarters as it had been during the Franco–Prussian War. The command in 1914 centred on the head of state, who did not, however, remain in his capital where he might have used the existing government machinery and communications to their best advantage; instead he took to the field with his general headquarters, attended by the chancellor, the head of the cabinet office, and deputies from

* In 1905 von Schlieffen saw his plan as 'the only solution'; his successor would have preferred not to invade Belgium, since this would bring Britain into the war, but he (and the government) reasoned that 'there was no alternative' if France was to be quickly overthrown. They therefore accepted certain political and strategic disaster in exchange for a possible operative success. In the Second World War the general staff were, according to Faber du Faur, merely 'good technicians, capable of turning out one plan of campaign after another, and then letting fate run its course!'

† According to the original French terminology *strategy* is the art of preparing, mobilizing, concentrating, moving and deploying resources and forces world-wide, between theatres of war, or within a theatre, with a view to success in battle. *Tactics* is the art of fighting the resultant battles in contact with the enemy. German thought interposed *operations*, sometimes known as the operative art (and from which the verb *operieren*) as an intermediate stage between strategy and tactics, since the experience of the Franco–Prussian, Russo–Turkish and Russo–Japanese Wars had shown that separate tactical engagements, instead of being restricted in time and space as they were in Napoleonic times, developed by degrees into prolonged battles covering wide areas and involving large numbers of troops. The preparation and conduct of these major battles were held, according to the Berlin school, to be within the sphere of operations.

the foreign office and other government departments.[6] And this concept of the head of state acting as the commanding general in the field was revived during the Second World War. So it came about that much of the German war effort was controlled for years from out of the way localities, such as Spa in the First World War and Rastenburg in the Second. But whereas the first Kaiser's military suite had been intended for, and indeed was suited to, wars that might be decided by field operations that lasted only a few weeks, latter-day conditions were quite different from those of 1866. And the elder von Moltke's dictum of 'consider carefully and only then dare' (*erst wägen dann wagen*) received scant attention in 1914 or in 1939, for the two world wars so lightheartedly entered upon by Germany were unlikely to have been decided in a few lightning victorious campaigns.

The German high command in the First World War underwent a radical change after the replacement of von Falkenhayn by von Hindenburg in August 1916, in that the Kaiser was finally divorced from real military and, to some extent, political control.[7] Von Hindenburg, recently returned from his victory over the Russians in East Prussia, was venerated throughout the German Army, and his appointment as chief of general staff of the field army met with popular approval everywhere. Yet, according to Groener, who served on his staff, 'the adoration of von Hindenburg showed how misplaced this judgement was; for, although the man's character was most worthy, he was not a high commander and he had not the slightest idea of the affairs of state; without von Ludendorff's ability and energy, von Hindenburg's achievements would hardly have been above average'.[8]

Von Ludendorff, who, as First Quartermaster-General, was von Hindenburg's chief staff officer and deputy, was an unusual personality, out of sympathy with his colleagues on the German general staff. Formerly, when a young major, he had been liked and trusted on account of his frankness and reliability, and his ambition and self-confidence were in no way more than average; but, with the years, his character altered, and he became vehement in manner, obstinate and unwilling to compromise.[9] At times irrational, even unstable, he had little understanding of human nature or of the issues involved in the war. As a war-lord, von Ludendorff showed many characteristics similar to those that were later to be displayed by Adolf Hitler, for he was a military adventurer whose most grievous fault, bequeathed to him by the Prussian military system, was a wilful under-estimating of the enemy.[10] For von Ludendorff had been one of those pre-war officers of the great general staff who, with little sense of what was practicable, were so obsessed by the pre-eminence of the offensive and by what they believed to be the invincibility of German arms, that Grierson, the British military attaché at the time, said of them that 'the minds that put out such theories were unbalanced'.[11] As time progressed von Ludendorff tried to take upon himself the political as well as the military and economic conduct of the war.

On 26 October 1918 Prince Max of Baden, the German chancellor, demanded of the Kaiser that von Ludendorff resign; he was replaced as First Quartermaster-General by Groener. That same day Austro–Hungary sought a separate peace with the allies.

Then came, in quick succession, rioting in the German streets, the Kaiser's flight from Berlin to the safety of the OHL general headquarters at Spa, the naval mutiny at Kiel, and the deposing of the King of Bavaria. The Kaiser, on what was in reality von Hindenburg's advice, fled to Holland, but not until 28 November did he formally renounce his two thrones. By then all the German states had dismissed their hereditary rulers.

It was in this way that the German people had the republic so precipitately thrust upon them. If the threat from the radicals, and in particular from the Spartacist-communists, had not existed, and the form of the future constitution had been allowed to await the election of a constituent assembly as the Social Democrat Ebert had intended that it should – then it is doubtful whether any but a small minority would have wanted a republic. But events outran the direction of the newly responsible politicians, and they, and the German people, faced with a *fait accompli*, settled for the best that they could get, hoping to be free from the triumph of bolshevism.

CHAPTER ONE

The Legacy

Groener's rapid and orderly withdrawal of the three million German troops eastwards across the Rhine has been described as the last great achievement of the old imperial army. Then, like the tsarist Russian Army of the year before, the mass of the rank and file deserted to their homes, often taking their personal weapons with them.[1] The police system had already collapsed and any remaining German Army units were entirely unreliable.[2]

The German revolution then began to follow the pattern of the Russian revolution. The Spartacist-communists and their allies, the Independents, the radicals, as well as some moderates among the Majority Social Democrats, did their utmost to destroy Ebert's provisional government and the remaining vestige of the authority of the OHL general headquarters, of the war ministry and of the army officer. Ebert was forced to agree to the sovietizing of formations and units, that is to say the election of commanders under the control of the soldiers' committees, the abolition of all formality and distinction, including saluting, insignia, badges of rank, epaulets and swords. A citizens' militia was brought into being, and it was urged by both the left and the centre that this should be the permanent replacement for the standing army. Mutinous sailors and armed civilians roamed the Berlin streets and officers were insulted, set upon and sometimes murdered.[3] In the end, the remnants of the imperial army consisted largely of officer and senior non-commissioned officer cadres where the majority of the rank and file had deserted, or of understrength and leaderless bodies of men that had driven away their officers.

The reason that revolutionary Germany did not follow the same path as revolutionary Russia, arriving at its ultimate goal of a soviet republic, was due, in part, to the political and social differences between the two countries. Yet Ebert, who was a moderate with the difficult task of controlling a party that was often more opposed to the military than to the bolsheviks, was a compromiser; left on his own, he might have gone the way of Kerensky and been swept away by the communists. But he owed his survival to the determination of his deputy Noske, and to the good sense and iron nerve of the First Quartermaster-General Groener, who had replaced von Ludendorff as the strongest personality within the OHL. It was due to

1

Noske and to Groener that a new and effective armed force strong enough to suppress both secessionists and left wing revolutionaries was adopted by the new republic.[4]

The new force, known as the *Freikorps*, had been raised from November 1918 onwards by the officer cadres, some on their own volition and others with Noske's encouragement and sanction. These recruiting nuclei were sometimes based on the remnants of a formation or unit of the old imperial army, but more often were raised by individual officers to whom the *Freikorps* members gave their allegiance. Short-term volunteers came from a hard core of soldier adventurers, often without family or property ties, united in their readiness to accept army discipline and combat any elements of the left. At first it proved difficult to recruit officers, let alone the rank and file, and the *Freikorps* were formed haphazardly, without common organization or terms of service and pay, owing loyalty to their own commanders rather than to the newly elected government; then, from early 1919, they were brought into the new military command organization before being committed to action in what was to become a civil war, with all its brutality and atrocity, against Spartacists, Independents, radicals, secessionists, mutineers and freebooters.[5]

On 19 January 1919 the Reich constituent assembly was voted into being and the Social Democrats became the majority party. To ensure that this parliament should not undergo the same fate as the 1917 democratically elected Russian constituent assembly at the hands of the bolsheviks, the new National Assembly was removed from the troubled capital to the more tranquil surroundings of provincial Weimar. Ebert became the first president, with Scheidemann as the chancellor.

Von Hindenburg kept the new government at a distance and his attitude to the dictated Treaty of Versailles was ambiguous. In private he said that he would have no part of it. But just as he had left Groener to act as spokesman when advising the Kaiser to abdicate, so did he leave him with the unpopular task of counselling Ebert to accept the allied demands. Out of this grew the legend of 'the stab in the back'. On 24 June 1919, von Hindenburg went into retirement, leaving Groener as the military adviser to the new government.[6]

The men who were to occupy positions of responsibility in the German Army of the twenties and the thirties were, for the most part, those who happened to be at the political centre in the strife-ridden days of 1918 and 1919; because they were on the spot and because they were acceptable to the Social Democrat government of the time, they were nominated to positions that would not have been theirs by virtue of seniority or experience. Groener, the son of a Württemberg non-commissioned officer and paymaster, was a man of vision in both the military and the political field who had a bond of sympathy and understanding with Ebert and Noske. Although Groener, as a lieutenant-general, had formerly been an outstanding member of the Prussian general staff, he was unlike many of his contemporaries in that he prided himself on being a man of the twentieth century, a realist who had favoured the abolition of the monarchy as the price of German unity, adamantly opposing those generals that wanted to take up arms against the dictated terms of Versailles. Groener was an able man whose principal fault would appear to have been that he clung to office for too long in the thirties and that he had an overtrusting and friendly nature that sometimes clouded his judgement of the characters of others.[7] Von Seeckt, Heye, von Hammerstein-Equord and von Schleicher were among Groener's close friends and protégés.

Ebert had been in favour of retaining Groener on the active list so that he might reconstruct and, if necessary, head the new army – the *Reichsheer*. But although Groener did in fact provide the advice on which much of the future organization was to be based, he was disinclined to remain in the service due to the resentment of part of the officer corps against what it believed to be Groener's responsibility for the Kaiser's abdication, and for Groener's acceptance of the terms of Versailles.[8] That same year the OHL was disbanded and Groener retired from the army to take up the cabinet post of minister for transport.

The last Prussian war minister had been Lieutenant-General von Scheüch, who, in the changed conditions of revolution, had been unwilling to continue in office. The post was assumed by one of his staff, a Colonel Reinhardt, an able Württemberger of such democratic views that many of them were unacceptable – even to Groener. On 1 October 1919, under the requirements of the Treaty of Versailles, the four war ministries of the old empire were abolished and replaced by a single German defence ministry set up in the Berlin Bendlerstrasse under Noske as the minister for defence, comprising the army and admiralty offices (*Heeresleitung** and *Marineleitung*). Colonel Reinhardt was moved from the Prussian war ministry to become the first *Chef der Heeresleitung*, his principal staff deputy being Major-General von Seeckt as the head of the *Truppenamt*† within the *Heeresleitung*.

Groener had been opposed to the appointment of Reinhardt as chief of the army office and wanted von Seeckt to have the post.[9] Reinhardt's position was to prove a particularly difficult one since his responsibilities were not defined *vis-à-vis* Noske, his ministerial superior; nor was it made clear what powers, if any, he had over his military subordinates. His staff subordinate, von Seeckt, sought a very large measure of independence for himself; Reinhardt's field command subordinate, von Lüttwitz, who, by virtue of his former imperial appointment as the commander of III (Berlin) Corps and his present republican post as the commander of the *Freikorps*,

---

* The term *Heeresleitung* in imperial days usually referred to a command, even a field, headquarters (cf. von Hindenburg's *Oberste Heeresleitung* (OHL) in the First World War). At the beginning of the Weimar period the *Heeresleitung* was meant to be an administrative office within the defence ministry, and is translated here as 'office'. Other military and administrative subdivisions below the *Leitung*, in order of seniority, were: *Amt* (directorate), *Amtsgruppe* (branch), *Abteilung* (department), *Gruppe* (section), *Referat* (desk).

† The *Truppenamt* served as the army general staff, the new title being designed to conceal its true function.

exercised operational control over the two new corps group commands, was far senior to Reinhardt and regarded himself as the *de facto* army commander-in-chief. The uncertainties of Reinhardt's position were only resolved by the unsuccessful Kapp *putsch* in which von Lüttwitz headed an armed insurrection against the republican government, with the intention of rejecting the terms of Versailles and the imposed army reductions, and removing Reinhardt from his post. The casualties of the ill-fated *coup* were von Lüttwitz, Noske and Reinhardt.[10] Von Seeckt was eventually appointed to Reinhardt's vacancy, while Gessler, a Democrat, succeeded Noske as minister of defence. Henceforth, until 1926, von Seeckt's leadership in army matters was to be unchallenged.

In the early months of 1919 the German ground forces, of which the larger part was the *Freikorps,* probably numbered over 400,000 men. This force, by a process of amalgamation and reduction, was transformed, firstly into a provisional, then into a transitional, army, and finally into a permanent *Reichsheer* of 100,000 officers and men. About 15,000 officers originally accepted by the government into the provisional *Reichsheer* had become surplus and were compulsorily discharged.[11] Most of them had fought in the streets for the republican government against the government's own radical left, and they left the service as embittered men, particularly when, as was often the case, they saw their places being taken by officers who had sat at home during the civil war. Many of these discharged malcontents were to reappear in later years in the paramilitary forces of the political parties of the extreme right, the SA and the SS, bent on the destruction of the republic that, in their view, had treated them so badly.

By the terms of Article 160 of the Versailles Treaty the new German Army was intended only for border police duties and *to maintain order within the Reich.* The 100,000 *Reichsheer* was to comprise two army corps (the *Gruppenkommandos*) of seven infantry and three cavalry divisions, and was to be without a great general staff, and without heavy artillery, tank, air or chemical warfare branches of the service. Recruiting was to be on a voluntary basis, other ranks being accepted initially for a term of not less than twelve years, a five per cent annual restriction being placed on the recruiting of replacements for those removed from the service by death, sickness or dishonourable discharge. The officer had to serve for a minimum of twenty-five years unless he had prior service in the imperial army, in which case he could be retired after his forty-fifth birthday. The combatant army officer strength was set at 4,000, but this included eighty ordnance officers and 200 officials with officer rank; 300 medical and 200 veterinary officers were permitted in addition to the 4,000 combatant officer ceiling.

The British government of the time had been primarily responsible for the framing of these conditions and had insisted on the retention of only a small long-term professional army without trained reserves; the purpose, of course, was to prevent the rebuilding of a German Army likely to challenge

4

the French ground and air forces in Europe. On the other hand, Foch, who apparently believed that very short-term engagements produced an inefficient standing army and an unsatisfactory reserve, for this reason would have preferred an ineffective 200,000 German Army based on selective recruiting for a short-term engagement, and would have accepted the risk of a repetition of the Prussian *Krümper* system whereby Gneisenau and Scharnhorst had evaded the spirit of Napoleon's dictated Paris Convention of 1808 by using these short-term engagements to build up a very strong military reserve.[12] The British views prevailed, however. A result, unforeseen by the allies, was that the new republican *Reichsheer* would, in the twenties and early thirties, accept and encourage the growth of the paramilitary forces of the political parties of the right, in order that they might serve as the army's emergency reserve. In the event, these paramilitary formations became one of the principal means by which German democracy was destroyed; in the final outcome, in 1944, they supplanted the German Army in control of the armed force of the nation.

The new high command organization that was brought into being after the First World War was to remain without change until the mid thirties. According to the *Reichswehr* law of 18 March 1921, the president was to be the *ex-officio* commander-in-chief, but it was not intended that he should exercise the enormous powers once invested in the Kaiser; any order signed by the president concerning the armed forces had to be countersigned by the minister of defence before it became valid in law, and the actual control of the armed forces was delegated by the president to the defence minister.[13] Yet it is perhaps remarkable that the victorious allies should have deliberately intended that so much power should be concentrated under a single individual, in that the armed forces control organization previously shared between the war ministries of Prussia and the three other kingdoms, between the admiralty, the great general staff and the naval staff and the military and the naval cabinets, were, from 1921, to be centralized in the hands of a single minister of defence. The allies stipulated only that this minister should not be a serving officer. During the twenties, however, the real power did not remain in Gessler's hands, but passed downwards, to his army subordinate von Seeckt.

The chiefs of the army and navy offices, both serving officers, soon acquired, therefore, a wider field of responsibility than that exercised by the former Prussian staff chiefs and the war ministers.[14] In Groener's view, the new organization gave too much authority to the *Leitung* chief, enabling him to control the army with scant attention to ministerial wishes; and Groener had urged in vain that the key army personnel directorate (*Personalamt*), the successor to the imperial military secretary's and adjutant-general's directorates, should be kept independent of the army office and directly under the defence minister. As it was, the minister retained under his own hand only certain specialist bureaux that provided services common to both the army and the navy, and a situation resulted in which the *Reichswehrminister* had

5

little responsibility for military discipline and none for the filling of appointments. Eventually the army and the navy chiefs did very much what they pleased, under cover of the president's approval, to the virtual exclusion of the minister of defence.

Reinhardt had been hampered as *Chef der Heeresleitung* by his lack of seniority and by liberal views that had made him acceptable to the Social Democrats but not to the officer corps. Von Seeckt, on the other hand, with his monocle, his impassive countenance, his thin spidery form, his long silences interspersed with a few curt and caustic comments, seemed to embody the experience and what was held to be the virtues of the old Prussian Army dating back to the elder von Moltke and von Schlieffen; he also brought to his post the authority and prestige of the *Kaiser Alexander Garde-Grenadier-Regiment Nr. 1* and of the senior general staff appointments in the west and in the east, in the Balkans and in Turkey. Von Seeckt was probably more experienced than Reinhardt; he was without a doubt more regressive.

When von Seeckt first took office he warned the officer corps that any kind of political activity within the army would be prohibited – absolute obedience was the requirement, with silence on political matters; officers of the general staff were reminded that they were nameless, performing selfless work and devoting their labours to the whole, and placing cause above personal considerations.[15]

Von Seeckt soon established himself as the senior army authority, and, by the end of 1922, he had extended and consolidated his control over the whole of the army machine, forcing the under-secretary to the minister out of office and taking over the formerly independent army administrative directorate, so that in fact, if not in name, von Seeckt became the commander-in-chief of the *Reichsheer.* The *Truppenamt,* or general staff, under Hasse, had the usual subdivisions for operations, organization, intelligence, training and transportation, the responsibility for training policy coming not under Hasse but directly under von Seeckt. An air planning staff element was set up inside the general staff in contravention of the spirit, if not of the letter, of Versailles. Those general staff officers who were serving outside the *Truppenamt* (officers who in the days of the empire formed the *Truppengeneralstab*), became known as the 'command assistants (*Führergehilfen*)' this name being used to allay the suspicions of the Allied Control Commission. In addition to the *Truppenamt,* the *Heeresleitung* comprised the inspectorates, (which in pre-revolutionary days had been independent and responsible directly to the Kaiser), together with the army administrative directorate, the ordnance directorate and the army personnel directorate. The P3 section of the personnel directorate, responsible for the posting of general staff officers, came directly under Hasse, the chief of the *Truppenamt.*[16]

The two army corps headquarters, known as group headquarters and located in Berlin and Kassel, had a training and inspection (but not a command) responsibility for a total of seven static administrative districts (*Wehrkreise*) in each of which was based an infantry division; the commander of the *Wehrkreis* held in addition the separate field appointment of commander of the infantry division.* The cavalry divisions were usually under the *Wehrkreis* for disciplinary and administrative matters but were directly subordinate to the corps group headquarters for operations and training.†

Von Seeckt attempted to improve his limited resources by decentralizing and farming out responsibilities that, although essential to the future of the army, could be carried out in peacetime by other government or commercial agencies. The war historical section, the war archives and the library of the general staff were civilianized and put under the *Reichsarchiv* in Potsdam, although the responsibility for the evaluation of the military history of the 1914–18 war remained with the ministry of defence. Those aspects of military intelligence that were considered not strictly essential to the intelligence department of the *Truppenamt* (T3 – known to the outside world as 'the statistics section') were handled by the welfare office of the defence ministry. Military, technical and experimental development was centred on the Charlottenburg Polytechnic under General Becker, who worked in conjunction with the research departments of armament suppliers.[17] Numbers of regular officers were transferred to the police. And since the terms of Versailles had provided for an army that was much out of balance, eighteen regiments of cavalry to only twenty-one regiments of infantry, von Seeckt used the cavalry regiments, as well as the divisional motor and horse transport battalions, as a home for infantry and artillery officers and those of the general staff who could not be accommodated elsewhere in the establishment.[18] As the years went by, some cavalry squadrons and the transport battalions were given secondary technical functions such as command and signal squadrons and artillery observation batteries, roles that would certainly not have been permitted by the terms of the treaty. The general staff college (*Kriegsakademie*) had disappeared, but its loss was made good by an alternative and covert system of staff preparation and training devised immediately after the war, whereby students were trained within the divisions and the *Truppenamt*.[19]

Von Seeckt was an avowed monarchist who had been obliged to come to terms with the new republic, but he still lived in the imperial past. Since he attached the greatest importance to what he called tradition, he was undeterred by the reality that the *Reichsheer* was the immediate descendant not of the imperial army but of the *Freikorps,* and that the tracing of the paternity of the eighteen cavalry and twenty-one infantry regiments of the republic

* *Gruppenkommando I* (Berlin) had been allocated: 1 Inf. Div. (Königsberg), 2 Inf. Div. (Stettin), 3 Inf. Div. (Berlin), 4 Inf. Div. (Dresden), 1 Cav. Div. (Frankfurt an der Oder), 2 Cav. Div. (Breslau); *Gruppenkommando II* (Kassel) was responsible for: 5 Inf. Div. (Stuttgart), 6 Inf. Div. (Münster), 7 Inf. Div. (Munich), 3 Cav. Div. (Weimar).

† Whereas an infantry division's peace establishment totalled over 12,000 men, a cavalry division had only half that number.

from the 110 cavalry and 217 foot regiments and forty-five independent infantry battalions of the empire would involve no little ingenuity. However that may be, companies and squadrons of the new army were designated by von Seeckt as the direct successors of regiments of the old, in order to keep the links with veteran associations and to celebrate the history and traditions of all the former imperial regiments.[20] This continued until the coming of the Third Reich swept away such antiquated absurdities.

The new German republic believed itself to be threatened from the west and from the east. The *Reichsheer* could do little against the French Army, but in the east an elaborate and covert paramilitary organization sponsored by the *Heeresleitung* had come into being as the border force *Grenzschutz Ost*, a loose military volunteer organization based on the *Stahlhelm*, the largest ex-servicemen's association at that time. This eastern frontier force was under the control of officers on the active list, known as *Kreiskommissare*, and was equipped with concealed stocks of world war small arms held by the military contrary to the allied restrictions. This volunteer organization was intended for local resistance against Polish irregulars rather than as a reserve of reinforcements for the army. After the 1923 French invasion of the Ruhr, however, the army began the secret and short-term training of small groups of volunteers that were formed into reserve reinforcement units (march battalions) and reservist pools ready to supplement the army in times of crisis, for use both in the east and in the west.

Von Seeckt was opposed to any political or military understanding with the Poles, and this, in any event, would hardly have been possible in the unsettled conditions of the time. Poland was the firm ally of France, and the French government intended to keep a controlling influence in Warsaw against Germany's interest. But von Seeckt did advocate a policy of *rapprochement* to Soviet Russia, with the immediate object of neutralizing the Polish threat to Germany's border areas, and, in the long term, of destroying Poland and restoring to the Fatherland those eastern territories ceded under the Treaty of Versailles. As Moscow appeared to be in favour of such a military understanding, talks began in Berlin in the spring of 1921 between von Seeckt and the Soviet representatives, the German chancellor's agreement having been obtained for a 'limited co-operation' with the Red Army. This led to the funnelling of German defence funds into Russia, a restricted purchase and development of some Russian manufactured armaments, and later to the opening, inside Russia, of a chemical warfare installation and an air and a tank training school for use by the Germans.[21] Such measures were expressly forbidden by Article 179 of the Treaty of Versailles and, in effect, by German law, but this collaboration continued until 1933 with the full knowledge of the successive Weimar democratic governments.

Von Seeckt was one of the most controversial and colourful military figures of the immediate post-war years. His interest in foreign affairs was based on a ready acceptance of the Russo–German Rapallo agreement and on the keeping of the close military connection with Moscow; and yet, at the same time, although he knew Germany was defenceless, he said that 'only a strong and united nation could risk dealing with the Soviet Union'. He stressed his ties of personal allegiance in the oath of loyalty that he had sworn and he affirmed his strict regard for the law, yet he regarded the restrictions of Versailles, and the German jurisdiction that accepted them, as outside the law. Like von Schlieffen, von Seeckt insisted on rigid and unquestioning obedience from his subordinates; yet he, by deliberately absenting himself when he was needed, had declined to support his own superiors, Reinhardt and Noske, against von Lüttwitz at the time of the Kapp *putsch*. He prided himself that he kept the army aloof from party politics, yet he himself tried to influence national policy; he had ordered the new army general staff to be selfless and nameless, yet he himself was politically ambitious, for during the course of his tenure as the *Chef der Heeresleitung* he had seriously considered putting himself forward for the chancellorship and for the presidency.[22] Nor was he guiltless of political intrigue or above using the threat of the army's displeasure, like some Roman praetorian guard, to unseat his political master. For von Seeckt was a man of double standards. He disliked Gessler, the minister of defence, and treated him in cavalier fashion; but, instead of refusing to serve under him and resigning, von Seeckt was determined to remain at his post. He resented Ebert's *ex-officio* appointment as commander-in-chief of the *Reichswehr* because he was a saddler and not a soldier, and he tried to keep both the president and the defence minister away from what he regarded as his own preserve, the army. But when von Hindenburg followed Ebert as president, he, too, earned von Seeckt's resentment, primarily because he *was* a soldier and because the new president confined his audiences with von Seeckt to military matters, keeping clear of all politics; moreover von Hindenburg was not diffident about criticizing von Seeckt's recommendations concerning the army. Von Seeckt was a conceited man who placed an exaggerated importance on the outward form; this was reflected both in his personal behaviour and in the standards that he demanded from the new *Reichsheer*.

In 1919 Groener had been a firm supporter of von Seeckt against Reinhardt, whom Groener disliked. But by the nineteen-thirties Groener had come to see von Seeckt in a different light, regarding him as a political opportunist, courting preferment and favour; Groener said that he had once 'expected better of him'. Von Seeckt's sphinx-like countenance had merely concealed, thought Groener, the weaknesses of the man's spirit and character. At the time of von Seeckt's death, in January 1937, Groener wrote:

I knew Seeckt as no one else did, and I always got on with him, because, in spite of the many shadowy sides of his character, he had a clear and clever head ... But the best about him was his silences on which his fame was based. But as for the building of the *Reichswehr*, others, and in particular Gessler, Otto Hasse, Hammerstein and Schleicher did as much. In difficult situations Seeckt was in no way courageous – he just lapsed into silence.[23]

General Faber du Faur, who had forty years' service in the armies of the empire, the Weimar Republic and the Third Reich, had, in retrospect, a poor opinion of von Seeckt and what Faber called the 'bandbox' 100,000 man army. Von Seeckt, thought Faber, tried to turn back the wheel of progress, and his idea of tradition was not something bequeathed but something artificially created, something 'to keep a certain class in the saddle'. If Reinhardt had remained the *Chef der Heeresleitung*, German history might have taken a different turn in that the armed forces would have been less remote and more popular with the German public, and the officer corps would not have remained a class apart cut off from political and public life. In any event, concluded Faber, the Nazis would have had much of the wind taken out of their sails when, in due course, they set about creating what they called a democratic people's army.[24]

Von Seeckt's *Reichsheer* that lived on until 1933 has been called variously an *élite*, the finest army in the world, and an excellent framework on which to base the expansion of the armed forces later ordered by Hitler. That the 100,000 army did provide a first-rate cadre of drill, weapon training and minor tactics instructors and a ready reserve of trained junior leaders there can be no doubt. Its officer corps produced tacticians of the highest order. But the commentator who looks at armies from the outside is too often impressed with the ornamental trappings, bearing, drill and parade discipline, and does not relate it to what is relevant to modern war. It is likely that von Seeckt's *Reichsheer* was not very different in its composition or standards of efficiency from the small professional armies of that time in Britain and in the United States. For just as the old imperial army, as Faber du Faur has said, 'hooded in its own blinkers lived in the tradition of 1870', so did von Seeckt try to recreate a miniature of the army of 1914.

Von Seeckt's military essays, published in the thirties, throw much light on their author.* Written in a style sometimes polished, but more often artificial and laboured, they are light-weight in content since the writer appears reluctant to deal with concrete facts or situations. And where a military opinion is expressed, time has often proved it to be very wrong, for not even his admirers could have said that von Seeckt was forward-looking or a man of great vision. For von Seeckt was in favour of small highly professional armies, since he stoutly maintained, as von Schlieffen had before him, that 'the provision of an uninterrupted supply of modern weapons for armies of millions was an impossibility'; and he doubted 'those prophets who saw armies transformed into armoured units' and was of the opinion that the days of cavalry were *not* numbered and that 'its lances would still flaunt their pennants with confidence in the winds of the future'. He thought 'the seven English infantry divisions of 1914 to have been excellent' as, according to von Seeckt's standards, they undoubtedly were; and he wanted polo to be introduced into the German Army as training for war.[25] That von Seeckt of

---

* Writing in the 1936 *Militärwissenschaftliche Rundschau (Heft 1)*, von Seeckt said 'war is launched, waged and won by will-power ... strength of will overcomes all difficulties ...'

the twenties was little different from von Seeckt of the thirties was borne out by von Blomberg, the head of the training department of the general staff in 1925. Von Blomberg believed that lances were out of place in the modern age and he proposed that German cavalry should give them up; but von Seeckt refused on the grounds that when he (von Seeckt) had suggested this in the First World War, his idea had been rejected; and so, von Seeckt said, 'as far as he was concerned the cavalry would keep them'. And when von Blomberg had advised that reconnaissance troops should have their bicycles replaced by motor-cycles, von Seeckt had replied: 'Please, if we are to remain friends, let us hear no more of such notions!'[26]

There was some pettiness in von Seeckt's character, for the *Chef der Heeresleitung* was little interested in new ideas that were not his own, and he exercised a repressive influence on his staff and subordinates. He, himself, was a product of the von Schlieffen system, and, like von Schlieffen, he was intolerant of officers of independent views, for he wanted obedience, not advice. Von Seeckt was the last chief who was popular, in that he was a public figure, since those about him were nonentities or unknown, according to Faber, *Inflationsmenschen* 'ruled by appearances and without the courage to cope with realities'. So, after von Seeckt, came others that awoke little trust or confidence, for 'Heye and Hammerstein were anything but Lohengrin figures, each in his way being *satt und zynisch*'.[27]

Von Seeckt afterwards said that he owed his success in creating the new army to the retention of the pre-war officer corps, and to giving preferment in selection to officers of the former general staff, even though many of these had kept clear of the *Freikorps* and the civil war. The majority of the officers taken into the new forces, whether they came from the old nobility or from the *bourgeoisie*, were without means other than their army pay; nearly all, irrespective of their origin, were monarchic and were strongly opposed to the new republic, to socialism and to parliamentary control, and had good cause to remember the treatment meted out to officers by socialists and liberals and the street rabble that these had aroused at the time of the revolution. In imperial times the officer corps, then a highly privileged class well-esteemed by the public, had always been apart from the state and from the people; but it did owe a common allegiance to the Kaiser, as the head of state and commander-in-chief, and it did have some limited contact with the man of the street and of the field through the annual levy of conscripted recruits. Conditions were much different, however, in the 100,000 army; the monarch had gone, together with the imperial black, white and red national colours now replaced by the despised red, black and gold of the 1848 revolutionaries. The Kapp *putsch* had increased the distrust between the officer corps and the Weimar politicians, and the situation was not improved by the unprovoked, bitter or sneering attacks, on both officer and soldier, made by parliamentary speakers, even from the more moderate centre parties.[28]

The officers of von Seeckt's army had all had war service, and the

11

majority of them, including the junior ranks, had received their commissions from the Kaiser before 1914; the number of imperial regular officers who had been former long-service other ranks was small. The post-war intake of officers – the candidates for commissions – came from volunteers of good education under the age of twenty-one, preference being given to those with a certificate of higher education; these candidates, on acceptance, were taken into regiments as other ranks. After fifteen months service, and if still considered suitable, the candidate took a junior ensign's (*Fahnenjunker*) examination and was promoted to first-class private (*Gefreiter*); then, in due course, whatever his arm of service, he attended a corporal's course at the infantry school at Dresden. After passing an officer's examination, the aspirant was promoted to senior ensign (*Oberfähnrich*) and, though still an other rank, he joined the officers' mess of the regiment of his choice. There he was on approval and was subjected to rigid mess discipline by the unmarried officers of the regiment – he could speak only when spoken to, otherwise he had to keep silent. Then, *between four or five years from the date of his original enlistment,* and with the permission of his commanding officer, he was accepted, or rejected, for commissioned rank, by the vote of the officers of the regiment. This post-war system of training and selection was somewhat similar to that formerly in use in the imperial army, except that it was far more spartan and far more exacting.*

A foreign military attaché, reporting on the 100,000 man *Reichsheer* in 1928, thought that the officers were little different from those of the old army, except that they knew and mixed with their men to an extent unheard of before the war; and the relationship between officer and enlisted man, it was noted, was particularly good. The enlisted other ranks in the 100,000 army were not, however, the cross-section of the nation that had been conscripted into the army in 1913, and were by no means representative, in their background or in their outlook and political views, of German youth between the two world wars.

The recruiting of other ranks for the *Reichsheer* took place twice a year from unmarried German nationals between the age of seventeen and twenty-one years. The acceptance standards were high, and recruits had to be medically fit and not less than five feet five inches in height; any record of imprisonment or of any illegal political activity, or a police conviction for begging or vagrancy, automatically debarred recruitment; the candidate had to produce his birth certificate, police identity card, employers' references and school reports. Recruiting was carried out on an allotted territorial basis, advertisements being inserted in the local press inviting applications in advance; the responsibility for acceptance was delegated to squadron, company or battery commanders, who, being in effect their own recruiting

* In 1913 graduates from the Corps of Cadets were commissioned directly; if, on the other hand, the aspirant came straight from school or university, then he entered the ranks as a *Fahnenjunker*, taking his meals in the officers' mess and being allowed to sleep out of barracks in private accommodation after the first six weeks of his service. He then went on to a military academy (*Kriegsschule*).

officers, showed a keen interest in seeing that they got the best men available. Recruits were preferred from rural rather than from industrial urban areas since they were generally fitter physically and were considered to be more conservative mentally. Often the recruit was little removed, in his political views, from the officer that recruited him.[29] Discipline in the service was strict, but generally fair, and certainly not as rigid as that of 1913, in that stress was laid on the fostering of initiative. The abuse of soldiers by non-commissioned officers that had reached such scandalous proportions before 1914 was comparatively rare in the new army; the non-commissioned officers were of a high standard and this was probably due to the close supervision exercised by the officers.

All members of the army, both officers and other ranks, required official permission before they could get married and this was not usually granted until after their twenty-seventh birthday; all applications had to have the final approval of the ministry of defence. It was the duty of the commanding officer to satisfy himself, before recommending the soldier's application, that the future wife was free from debt and had 'an unblemished reputation and came of a respectable family'. It is against this requirement for the prospective wives of other ranks that the marriage of von Blomberg, the latter-day minister of defence, a serving officer and a field-marshal, should be judged.

It was von Seeckt's greatest achievement that he took what others had salvaged from the demoralized and disorderly remnants of the imperial army and, keeping it clear of the political struggles of the day that might have torn it asunder, gave it stability and order. But the new *Reichsheer,* even in 1933, was little more than a *gendarmerie* with a light artillery component, barely able to maintain internal security and certainly incapable of defending Germany's frontiers, even against Poland. And this was exactly how Germany's former enemies intended that it should be. Von Seeckt had done his utmost to circumvent the restrictions imposed by the terms of the Treaty of Versailles and had spent all that he could afford on weapon research and development both at home and abroad.

It has been said that the allies restricted the new *Reichsheer* in its size and armament but could not succeed in chaining the military thoughts of its leaders, since the German generals of the future were free to create concepts for war that were intellectually and technically much in advance of those propounded by their former enemies. Yet the evidence of the existence of such concepts among those in authority appears to be scanty, for von Seeckt looked backwards to the period between 1906 and 1918. Although he stressed the value of mobility in any war of the future, he had not progressed beyond von Schlieffen's ideas of cavalry and hard-marching infantry, backed by the use of railways. He wanted, of course, the support of heavy artillery and gas, together with aircraft and armoured cars for reconnaissance; and he was prepared to allocate money for research into the use of tanks as a supporting arm. But all these had been proved and accepted in the First

World War. And von Seeckt was apparently convinced that the wars of the future would be won by a small professional long-service German Army of cavalry and dismounted infantry, relying on its marching mobility, striking deep into enemy territory and enveloping its foes, while the defence of the homeland was entrusted to second line short-service militia conscripts. If von Seeckt had remained responsible for the development of the German Army during the thirties, even if he had been given all the funds and manpower that he might have required, it is doubtful whether his pattern *Reichsheer* could have overthrown the French Army of 1940.

Von Seeckt had succeeded in keeping together the army general staff and in restoring some of its earlier privilege. But it was no longer the great general staff, the main adviser and executive of the head of state and of the commander-in-chief, but was merely an organ of von Seeckt's *Heeresleitung* with no authority over the other directorates; and von Seeckt was responsible to the minister of defence who was himself under the head of state. The army general staff's influence, even on von Seeckt, was certainly not great, for the autocratic and touchy general was not generally susceptible to new ideas or receptive to advice; subordinates had to be kept in their place, and a representation or a seemingly justified complaint by a member of the general staff could be met with a harsh punishment or a lasting penalty.[30]

Von Seeckt continued to recruit young officers for the new army general staff, but, contrary to the imperial practice where regimental officers applied *on their own volition* for permission to take the examination for admission to the *Kriegsakademie* staff college, von Seeckt decided that he would recruit the general staff from the best brains in the army. So, from 1921 onwards, it was made compulsory for all lieutenants of middle seniority, irrespective of whether or not they wanted to become members of the general staff, to prepare for, and to take, the written staff examination. Each candidate had the anonymity of a number and each paper was marked by several examiners, the paper being finally credited with the average of the marks variously awarded. Those candidates at the top of the mark list were then taken for training. Whereas, in 1913, the officer's record of service and his recommendation were of great weight in the selection of candidates, from 1921 to 1933 recommendation and character assessment were of only minor importance; the thing that mattered was examination marks. In consequence, many an unenthusiastic officer whose main qualification was that he was good at examinations edged out another of character and ability for whom the general staff would have been a calling.[31] The system, as modified by von Seeckt, undoubtedly produced excellent staff technicians; that the selection might have been improved by attaching more weight to recommendation, character and record of service, is possible. However this may be, there can be no doubt that there were men of outstanding character and integrity among both the pre-war and post-war graduates of the general staff selection system; whether they would reach the highest ranks and fill the key appointments was entirely another matter. If their ideas or personalities were in conflict with those of von Seeckt it is unlikely that they would have been allowed to remain in the *Heeresleitung*; the officers who prospered under von Seeckt were those who agreed with him; those subsequently singled out for the highest appointments were, for the most part, men of von Seeckt's personal staff with long service at the centre, sometimes with little field or command experience.* Among von Seeckt's principal lieutenants were Heye, von Blomberg, von Fritsch, von Brauchitsch and von Schleicher. Von Schleicher was out of the ordinary, and it was with von Schleicher that difficulties first arose.

Von Schleicher's meteoric rise had started when, as a major of the Third Foot Guards (a regiment that had once had among its officers the two von Hindenburgs, von Hammerstein-Equord, von Brauchitsch and von Manstein), he joined, in 1913, the railways department of the great general staff under Groener. The association between the two men was close and von Schleicher rose, as it were, at Groener's coat-tails. At the time of the troubles and the formation of the *Freikorps,* von Schleicher, still in the centre at Groener's side, had shown courage and good judgement; then, in 1919, he formed a *Referent* for political matters touching upon the army, further developing this little organization, with himself at its head, as a political and public relations office responsible firstly to Groener and then to von Seeckt; from 1926 onwards, when his office was moved from the *Heeresleitung* and made subordinate to the minister, he came directly under Gessler. Von Schleicher was talented, hardworking and experienced in the tactics of negotiation, and he was also on close terms with industrial, banking and political circles in Berlin. According to Groener's daughter, 'fate had always made life too easy for von Schleicher in that he had never shouldered any responsibility – he lived with a rich aunt, had no financial worries or the burden of a family; he was as a ship with too little ballast'. Wilhelm Keil, the President of the Württemberg *Landtag* called him frivolous (*verspielt*). Gambling was a family trait, but von Schleicher did not gamble with dice or cards, but with people. He had a finger in every pie and was a born intriguer. His wit and humour made him a welcome guest in Berlin society, but his talk was increasingly tinged with sarcasm and cynicism; although he was not a malicious man, his careless and hurting comments lost him friends and won him enemies.[32] But then friendship meant nothing to him and he was not to be trusted.

Von Schleicher had dissimulated under the lash of von Seeckt's caustic tongue but, in 1926, the same year that his office was removed from the *Heeresleitung* and put under Gessler, von Schleicher cultivated the new president and the president's son, Oskar von Hindenburg, his former regimental colleague. When von Seeckt, in answer to a request from the exiled Crown Princess, with whom he was in correspondence, permitted the

---

* The successive chiefs of the *Truppenamt* were: Heye (1920–2), Hasse (1922–6), Wetzell (1926–7), von Blomberg (1927–9) and von Hammerstein-Equord (1929–30).

Kaiser's grandson, Prince William of Prussia, to attend the army manoeuvres in the uniform of the old imperial First Foot Guards, without first informing or obtaining the permission of the minister or of the government, the public outcry was such that Gessler and the cabinet determined that von Seeckt should be dismissed. Von Seeckt did not want to go; and, it is said, such was the *Kadettenanstalt* mentality of the man, that he suggested that the offence might be atoned for 'by the award of a punishment of room arrest', as though he were a Lichterfelde cadet to be confined to barracks. Gessler, who had been sorely tried and badly used by von Seeckt during his term of office, would tolerate his haughtiness no longer, and the cabinet informed the president of its intention to resign if von Seeckt were permitted to remain at his post. Von Hindenburg, who said privately that 'von Seeckt's insufferable conceit was ruining the army', did not intend to help him and asked for his resignation. Although Gessler later denied that this was so, von Seeckt always regarded his downfall as von Schleicher's work; if von Schleicher did not bring von Seeckt down, he certainly did nothing to help him, and he afterwards said that 'if anyone treated him as von Seeckt had done, then he [von Schleicher] showed his teeth'.[33]

Although von Seeckt was regarded as a difficult and unlikeable character by those closely associated with him, he was at least a familiar figure to the regimental officers and men. Heye, von Seeckt's nominee and successor, was virtually unknown. Heye had been part of Groener's OHL staff in 1918 and 1919 and then had served directly under von Seeckt from 1920 to 1923, both as the *Chef des Truppenamts* and as head of the *Personalamt*, before becoming the commander of *Wehrkreis I* in East Prussia. Known among the officers as 'Papa Heye' or 'Uncle', he was a moderate, a kind-hearted and genial character lacking in confidence, who, after a three year tenure, left von Seeckt's army very much as he had found it.

Heye had been entirely dwarfed by President Hindenburg, who 'stood out like a rock in the ocean', the titan with the stern countenance and nerves of iron 'whom nothing would shake since he saw himself answerable in the final outcome only to God'. This popularity was to last less than five years, and by 1932, according to Faber, von Hindenburg was no longer held in great esteem by the army, for 'von Ludendorff had seen to it that youth was quite clear as to who was the real victor at Tannenberg; and without Tannenberg von Hindenburg was worth little'.[34]

At the end of 1927 Gessler was driven from office by the political clamour aroused by the scandalous revelations of the misuse of, and speculation in, service funds by his subordinates. On 18 January 1928, Groener, the former lieutenant-general of the old army, was brought back to office as a civilian by von Hindenburg, it is said at von Schleicher's suggestion, to be minister of defence. When Groener took over his post he found much of which he disapproved. The British and French had intended that the defence minister should be the *de facto* commander-in-chief responsible to the president and the cabinet, the channel of command running directly from him to the

16

commanders of the *Wehrkreise*. But under Article 5 of the ministry standing orders the command of the *Wehrkreise* was shown directly under the *Chef der Heeresleitung*, and this, presumably, had been von Seeckt's doing. The new defence minister had virtually no control over discipline or appointments.[35] Yet Groener himself was to take little action to restore the situation to that intended by the Treaty of Versailles – his daughter said that it was already too late and beyond his power to do so.

Groener's position was admittedly a difficult one. According to the constitution he was supposed to be the *de facto* commander-in-chief, exercising an authority delegated to him by the president. But Groener, like Heye, found himself overshadowed by the president, who was a field-marshal; and von Hindenburg, or so it would appear, had come to regard himself not as the *ex-officio* commander-in-chief but as *the* commanding general. The situation was further complicated by the president's military record and prestige, for this carried, at least in the early days, particular weight with the officer corps of the *Reichsheer*. The new president assumed some of the attributes of a monarch in that the officers felt themselves bound by loyalty, not to the indefinite and shadowy concept of a constitution and a parliamentary republic, but by a personal allegiance to their military president. It was said that 'he who controlled the *Reichswehr*, controlled the state'; but, as it so transpired, he who had the power in the land was not he who had the *Reichswehr*, but he who had von Hindenburg's ear. For Groener realized only too late how fickle (*wandlungsfähig*) was the apparently stolid old man.[36] And this was where von Schleicher came into his own.

The principal members of Groener's old staff in the 1918 OHL were by now in the leading positions within the defence ministry and the *Reichsheer*, and, according to Groener's daughter, the new minister of defence assumed, somewhat naïvely, that they were still his subordinate colleagues and dependent friends.[37] And there is little doubt that von Schleicher, outwardly at least, treated Groener with marked deference. Groener trusted von Schleicher implicitly and relied on his advice in both political and military matters, making no secret of the fact that political dealings were entrusted to him whom he called his '*Kardinal in politicis*'.

By 1929 von Schleicher's influence had so grown that he was, in his own words, the recognized representative of the defence minister and the armed forces 'in all questions that have no connection with military matters, and in all military matters of a purely political nature'. He was already a major-general and his office had become a *Ministeramt*; since, as Groener's representative, he was in constant touch with parliamentarians and the cabinet, he was already in effect an under-secretary of state. But his sphere of activity soon extended far beyond ministerial matters and the politics of the armed forces. Although Groener may have been inhibited about regaining his rightful ministerial control over the army, von Schleicher was not so diffident, for he began to meddle in the preserves of the *Reichsheer* so that even the easy-going Heye protested that his own position and that of the

Heeresleitung was being undermined. And von Schleicher formed a small but powerful clique based on himself, von Bredow, who was his own deputy and staff head of the *Ministeramt*, Joachim von Stülpnagel and *Freiherr* von dem Bussche-Ippenburg, the successive heads of the *Heeresleitung Personalamt* between 1927 and 1933; this cabal dominated both Groener and Heye. Von Blomberg, who had in 1927 been promoted within the general staff to replace Wetzell as the chief of the *Truppenamt,* was outside of this group and was on particularly bad terms with von Schleicher. So it came about that when, in 1930, von Blomberg was posted to command *Wehrkreis I* in East Prussia, he was replaced by von Hammerstein-Equord, von Schleicher's friend and former comrade from the Third Foot Guards. Although von Hammerstein-Equord had only been promoted to major-general the year before, he was advanced again in rank to lieutenant-general. Meanwhile von dem Bussche-Ippenburg and Joachim von Stülpnagel had been promoted major-generals.[38]

Criticism was openly voiced by the officers within the 100,000 German Army that the last imperial high command was again at the helm, those same people 'who had once before steered the ship on to the rocks'; and the highest appointments were apparently being reserved for those at the centre or for their friends. Certain it is that von Schleicher, who had no experience at all in high command, appears to have had a particularly powerful influence in the filling of the key appointments within the *Heeresleitung.* Meanwhile able and experienced general officers in the corps headquarters and the *Wehrkreise*, forecast, with some cynicism, that Joachim von Stülpnagel, a colonel in 1928, would replace Heye as the chief of the army command. The British military attaché commented in 1930 that the army was 'passing under the control of a group of young and pushing generals who tolerate the Weimar republic for only so long as the field-marshal [Hindenburg] should live'.[39]

Von Stülpnagel, whom Faber du Faur called 'the next-to-come' (*Joachim der Zukünftige*), considered himself an obvious contender for Heye's post.[40] But it was on von Schleicher that so much depended, and it was von Schleicher alone who had Groener's ear, in addition to access to the presidential palace. Some believed that von Schleicher coveted the minister's post for himself and wanted to strengthen his personal position by filling the key appointments in the *Reichsheer* with his own placemen. Whatever his motives, he told von Stülpnagel that 'Groener had decided in favour of von Hammerstein-Equord'; to others von Schleicher said that he would have preferred von Stülpnagel, but was 'unable to oppose' his old friend von Hammerstein. Adam succeeded von Hammerstein as chief of the *Truppenamt.*

It was on this and on other accounts that Groener and von Schleicher were most unpopular both inside and outside of the German Army. Groener's belief that all war veterans were now of a healthy and sensible pacificism was very wide of the mark, for 'the spirit of the front-fighter' had spread through all the right wing parties. Groener made well-intentioned efforts to broaden the political education of the officers (an activity that von Schleicher regarded with indifference), and he solemnly warned the armed forces, in his circular of 22 January 1930, of the twin dangers of communism and national-socialism to both the armed forces and to the state; there was, according to Groener, nothing to choose between them except that one had a national and the other an international basis.[41] For these efforts Groener was bitterly attacked, not only by the Communists and the National-Socialists, but also by the right and centre parties that accused him, variously, of 'an unwarranted meddling with the attitude of the officers, all of whom were expected to be above party politics'; he was also censured for attracting the officers into freemasonry, and for attempting to introduce republicanism, democracy and left wing views into the *Reichswehr*. Many senior officers regarded Groener's efforts with strong disapproval. Among the junior-officers a minority had already been attracted by the extravagant propaganda of Hitlerism.*

In December 1929 a 2nd Lieutenant Scheringer of *Artillerie Regiment Nr. 5* at Fulda attempted to recruit another officer into a movement aimed at preventing 'the continual drift of the leading elements of the army towards the left', it being the movement's intention that the *Reichsheer* should remain impassive 'and not shoot' should the National-Socialists stage a *coup* against the government. Three junior officers of the regiment were brought to trial three months later on a charge of conspiring to commit high treason. The incident in itself was relatively unimportant except that both Adolf Hitler and Ludwig Beck, the colonel commanding *Artillerie Regiment Nr. 5*, appeared before the court as witnesses for the defence of the three accused. Hitler used the box as an election platform to promise that he would advance the army's interest as soon as he came to power. Beck went beyond what might have been expected of a commanding officer, in that he did not restrict himself to evidence of character but showed that he was in sympathy with some of Scheringer's and, by extension, with some of Hitler's, ideas. Beck came away from the trial much impressed by what he had seen and heard of Nazism, and he recommended Hitler to von Schleicher by word of mouth of Eugen Ott, the *Chef der Wehrmachtabteilung*. Ott was depressed about Beck's attitude; von Schleicher condemned Beck as being politically naïve. Hitler's impressions of Beck at this first meeting are unknown, but only nine months after Hitler came to power, Beck, who, unlike von Blomberg, von Fritsch and von Brauchitsch, had never been at the centre, was brought from outside to succeed Adam as the *Chef des Truppenamts* and subsequently to become the first chief of the army general staff of the Third Reich.[42]

Groener's reaction, immediately after the trial of the young officers, was one of indignation, and he wanted to have Beck retired from the army. On 6

* Some of those who were later to become activists in the July 1944 bomb plot were staunch supporters of Hitler between 1930 and 1936; they included von Stauffenberg, von Tresckow, von Hase and Mertz von Quirnheim. (Cf. Teske, *Die Silbernen Spiegel*, p. 31)

19

October 1930 Groener issued an order concerning the trial, to be read to all officers, saying that any soldier who had first to agree with his orders before he carried them out was worthless, for such thoughts were 'the harbingers of mutiny, of disintegration of the *Reichswehr,* and of civil war'. Any officer, said Groener, who did not agree with the order should leave the service.[43] About a fortnight later, in a talk to the *Wehrkreis* commanders after the autumn manoeuvres, Groener said that he had no sympathy with the three accused officers; he was, moreover, indignant that it should be thought that he was 'steering a left-oriented course'. He had 'one aim only, the freeing of Germany [from the restrictions of Versailles]', but he could not 'shout this from the housetops'. According to the latter-day account of General Heinrici, these views were heard in icy silence, 'not because the officer audiences were Nazi supporters, but simply because they could not understand why Groener and von Schleicher did not assert themselves against the Social Democrats, a party that appeared to be completely disinterested in the defence of Germany and in the armed forces'. And there can be no doubt that this army criticism was justified, for the whole country knew that the parties of the centre were moving steadily towards the left; and with over five million unemployed in Germany at the end of 1931, the influence of the radicals and extremists was growing rapidly. Even the moderate Groener, although by now complacent with age, could detect an undercurrent of bolshevism in the teachings of both the schools and the churches.

The German high command and the officer corps of the *Reichsheer* were divided and deeply disturbed by the political and domestic issues of the day, hating and fearing the radicals of the left and despising the parties of the centre. There appeared to be no army general of force and vigour in the Bendlerstrasse and there was no unifying figure left to whom the officers could owe allegiance and in whom they could place their trust, except the aged von Hindenburg, their only link with the imperial past.

CHAPTER TWO

In the Grip of Fear

Following the 1925 Locarno Treaty, after which Germany had entered the League of Nations and the Allied Disarmament Control Commission had been withdrawn from the Reich, the internal situation within Germany deteriorated rapidly once more with a second bout of inflation, industrial depression and rising unemployment. Street violence had again erupted with the main political parties raising uniformed private armies to protect their own organizations and terrorize or destroy those of their opponents.

In 1925 Hitler's National Socialist Party (NSDAP) had been of no political importance, but, in the next few years, it grew rapidly in that it skilfully turned the nation's ills to its own advantage. It gave promise of a clear and reactionary programme when the other parties appeared to have no programme at all. Its nationalistic and anti-Jewish foundation proved to be popular with all classes and with old and young alike, for Hitler promised all things to all members of German society. Much of the money necessary for the very existence of the party had been contributed by German industrialists.

In the 1930 *Reichstag* elections the National-Socialists secured 107 seats, forming, with the forty-one German Nationalists, the rightist block in the house. On the left there were 220 Social Democrats and Communists, while the centre consisted of 198 members owing allegiance to seven different parties. Since this centre was not sufficiently strong to maintain Brüning, the new chancellor, in power, Brüning was obliged to rule by decree, being tolerated by parliament but rarely enjoying its actual support; this ruling by decree in itself helped pave the way for the latter-day dictatorship. Groener remained as the minister of defence and, in October of the next year at von Hindenburg's suggestion, he also became the minister of the interior, responsible for the maintenance of law and order, at a time when the major parties had already mobilized their own private armies to fight it out on the streets.*

The violence had reached such proportions that the police seemed

---

* The private armies (and ex-servicemen's associations) were the NSDAP brown-shirted SA and the German Nationalist *Stahlhelm* forming the *Harzburger Front,* while the left polarized *Eisener Front* could call on the Socialist *Reichsbanner* and the Communist *Rotfrontorganisation.*

powerless, even unwilling, to deal with the worsening situation; no action had, as yet, been taken to use the army in support of the civil authorities, and the army leaders, following the example given earlier by von Seeckt, viewed this task with disfavour. Groener wanted to suppress the paramilitary organizations of all the parties, at least in so far as he proposed to forbid the wearing of uniforms, but he was inhibited by von Hindenburg's refusal to dissolve the *Stahlhelm,* and by his own reluctance to re-establish law and order by battling against both the forces of the extreme right and the radical left, since he feared that the police and army might be overwhelmed.[1] At von Schleicher's suggestion Groener had held exploratory talks with Hitler to see whether some compromise might be possible with the right at the price of including some National-Socialists in the cabinet, and von Schleicher had, in January 1931, issued a secret instruction cancelling an earlier order forbidding the German Army from co-operating with Hitler's NSDAP.[2] In reality von Schleicher was not interested in an honest partnership with Hitler – he intended merely to use him. In the final outcome he was himself used and outwitted.

At the beginning of 1932 Groener, in a letter to his friend Gleich, and probably quoting von Schleicher's views, said that he did not fear a *Hitlerei* armed *coup* because he was sure that Hitler himself understood that any such attempt would be put down ruthlessly, for 'the *Reichswehr* could be relied upon without question in such a situation, and Hammerstein – unlike Seeckt in 1923–4 – was just the man to use brutal force'. What Groener did fear was the arrival of the Nazi 'wolf in sheep's clothing – in the guise of loyalty – for this would be highly dangerous to the *Reichswehr*'.[3] The more that Groener saw of the Nazis the more untrustworthy they appeared to be.

That same year, Hitler came second to von Hindenburg in the cast of votes for the presidential election. During the election campaign Hitler sent a letter to his opponent von Hindenburg – having first released its contents to the foreign press – appealing that 'the principles of knightly conduct be observed', and that the Nazi Party be protected from the attacks of the Socialists; at which Groener, replying in his capacity as minister of the interior, could only marvel at Hitler's tender susceptibilities, particularly when one recalled the treatment that the Nazis had meted out to their opponents everywhere in Germany over the space of many years. When Severing, the minister of the interior for Prussia, warned that 'he who votes for Hitler votes for war', Hitler seized on the remark to complain again to von Hindenburg. In all, said Groener, 'the chameleon-like skill with which Hitler, according to circumstances, changed from being the watchdog of the constitution to the revolutionary destroyer of the state, made it difficult to combat him.'[4] Or, as the lawyer von Brauchitsch remarked, 'although Hitler had said in the Ulm trial of the young artillery officers, in September 1930, that he was pursuing his political aims only on a strictly legal path, it could be shown by the NSDAP press that the party was committed to the violent overthrow of the existing state and was fully engaged in the psychological preparation of the public with that end in view.'

By the beginning of April 1932 Brüning and Severing believed that a Nazi armed *coup* and a seizure of the government reserve stock of weapons were imminent; Groener summoned von Hammerstein and Raeder for a briefing, von Schleicher being present.* Von Schleicher suggested that the SA and the communist *Rotfront* should be banned, and von Hammerstein emphatically agreed with him. Raeder seemed to think that the Social Democrat *Reichsbanner* should also be outlawed, but, as von Schleicher thought that this was without point since the *Reichsbanner* was no immediate threat, the matter was dropped. All those present at the meeting went away fully agreed that action should be taken by a government decree to dissolve the two most violent of the organizations, the SA and the *Rotfront*.[5]

Groener had some time before been warned by his friend Gleich of the untrustworthiness of von Schleicher, but he had chosen to disregard the advice. Von Hammerstein's words and attitude at the meeting had indicated that he was entirely resolute and there had been no hint of any doubt as to the German Army's reliability or readiness to carry out his orders against the SA, when the time came to give them out. Von Hindenburg, too, appeared to be completely in favour of the total ban on the SA. But then, on the evening of 10 April at the chancellery meeting attended by Groener and von Schleicher, it became obvious to Brüning that von Schleicher had apparently changed his ground and wanted to spare the SA, and the chancellor began to suspect that von Schleicher had formed a conspiracy against Groener.[6] Von Schleicher was in truth at the centre of a number of intrigues. He was in touch with both Hitler and Röhm, the chief of staff of the SA, and he was trying to split Hitler from the SA and Röhm, and to separate Hitler from his own colleague Gregor Strasser; he also intended to overthrow Groener by a personal alliance with von Hammerstein and the *Reichsheer* and by undermining Groener's understanding and past friendship with von Hindenburg.

On 13 April the cabinet voted without dissension in favour of the emergency measure and this action was agreed by the ministries of the interior of the provincial *Länder*. The police then shut down the SA headquarters throughout the country and the wearing of the brown-shirt storm trooper uniform was forbidden.

An outcry immediately broke out against Groener, both in the German national press and in the presidential palace, where what became known as the 'extra-parliamentary government' consisting of the leaders of the Fatherland Front and several *Reichsheer* generals, including von Hammerstein and von Schleicher, put the aging president under severe pressure in that they censured Groener behind his back and offered advice contrary to that agreed on earlier. Von Hindenburg did not want the NSDAP in power, but he disagreed that they should be singled out for police action and he began to demand the dissolution of the Socialist *Reichsbanner*; it soon became

* Admiral Raeder was the *Chef der Kriegsmarineleitung*.

obvious that the president was acting contrary to practice and to law in that he was accepting advice, and documents, directly from von Schleicher's office, given to him by von Hammerstein without Groener's sanction or knowledge.

Many of the economic and military measures for which Hitler later gained the credit had already been prepared by Brüning.[7] The Lausanne conference that was to bring German reparations to an end had been postponed from January to June 1932, and Brüning and Groener had worked out a plan, for presentation to the Geneva disarmament conference that April, whereby the period of other rank army enlistment should be reduced from twelve to five years; this would have allowed the army to accumulate a reserve. They intended to propose, moreover, that the standing army of 100,000 should be doubled by the addition of a militia of 100,000 men and that heavy weapons should be added to its equipment tables. Brüning, however, got nothing out of the Geneva conference because France would not attend, the French ambassador in Berlin apparently having been tipped off by von Schleicher, two days before, that Brüning's government was about to fall! And, as Groener's daughter has said, what the allies had refused to allow to the moderate Brüning 'they were later forced to countenance by yet a hundredfold to the charlatan Hitler'.

The Hindenburg clique was determined to get both Brüning and Groener out of office. When, on 10 May, Groener defended his action in dissolving the SA, saying that 'for the first time in years Germany had order in the streets', he found that he was nearly alone and that the opposition had been joined by von Schleicher and von Hammerstein who, according to state secretary Meissner, were both demanding Groener's resignation, saying that 'he had lost the confidence and support of the German Army'. In a subsequent letter to Gleich, on 22 May, Groener wrote:

> Schleicher is not interested in getting the Nazis to power – he wants it for himself through Hindenburg and his close friend Oskar [Hindenburg's son] who has the greatest of influence there. Meissner is Schleicher's willing assistant ... Schleicher does not want to become chancellor or defence minister yet. Hindenburg revealed to me without any shame that he wants a chancellor who will carry out the Hindenburg line ... Schleicher has for some time been harbouring the notion to govern [the country] without the *Reichstag* but with the support of the *Reichswehr*; his plans, which he certainly did not divulge to me, are quite unclear, but perhaps the Nazis are superior to him in cunning. It would have been quite easy to have dealt effectively with [the German Army] opposition to me and Brüning, if Schleicher had wanted to do so, because Admiral Raeder certainly managed it within the fleet. Hammerstein follows his friend Schleicher around like a well-trained lapdog ... now the generals must take care that the army does not become Schiklgruber's [*sic*] property.[8]

Some of what Groener wrote at that time has since proved to be prophetic; yet Groener himself was still deceived both in von Schleicher and in von Hammerstein. For Groener harboured a somewhat pathetic confidence that, in the end, both of these newly promoted generals would prove a match for Hitler, and many of Groener's assumptions – even after the rift with von

Schleicher and von Hammerstein – were only a reflection of von Schleicher's views, many of which were entirely erroneous. For von Schleicher had become convinced that *he* talked with the concurrence and support of the German Army – a force that was supposed to be politically neutral – and that, with its aid, he would, behind the scenes, nominate and control the future governments of the Reich with scant attention to the wishes of parliament or people. And von Schleicher believed that, in addition, he enjoyed the full confidence of the president. Von Schleicher was a man so besotted by his own conceit and cleverness that his views had become unrealistic, and he had come to believe, according to Schäfer, that, if necessary, he, von Hammerstein and the *Reichswehr* could jointly prevent the Nazis from coming to power. In truth of course no German political party would give von Schleicher trust or support; the *Reichsheer* generals did not want him; von Blomberg, as an enemy of von Schleicher's, had already found his way to Hitler, and von Reichenau, von Blomberg's chief of staff, was impatiently waiting for von Schleicher's post in the *Ministeramt.*

Although Brüning's government was still in being, von Schleicher was secretly negotiating behind the scenes the dissolution of the *Reichstag* and the appointment of a new chancellor; his choice fell on von Papen, a member of the Prussian Diet, who was described by Groener as being von Schleicher's puppet. The selection of the new chancellor was, apparently, made entirely by von Schleicher who found little difficulty in persuading von Hindenburg to his way of thinking, and he convinced von Papen that 'the offer of the chancellorship [to von Papen] represented the vote of the army'. This argument, false though it was, was apparently regarded by von Papen as sufficient grounds and legality for assuming office.[9] Von Schleicher had meanwhile done a deal with Hitler promising, amongst other things, that, if the Nazis tolerated von Papen, the SA could have its uniform and freedom of action restored to it. Von Hindenburg then dismissed Brüning's government. The ministers in von Papen's cabinet, as the new chancellor ingenuously said, had 'been chosen well by von Schleicher'. Groener's place as minister of defence was taken by von Schleicher.

In the 31 July 1932 election the Nazi vote increased from six million to over thirteen million with a total of 230 seats in the *Reichstag,* so that they formed the key party; without their support no other party could be assured of a parliamentary majority. Göring was elected as the Speaker in the *Reichstag.* Hitler demanded the chancellorship but von Hindenburg, von Schleicher and von Papen contrived to withhold it from him. Von Papen's government was defeated in a parliamentary vote and new elections were held, the Nazis being returned once more as the strongest party in the house, although with slightly diminished numbers. Hitler remained adamant that the NSDAP would refuse to take any office in coalition with the other parties unless he himself headed the government as chancellor. Von Papen wanted to remain in office ruling by presidential decree during a declared state of emergency 'doing without the *Reichstag* for a short period'. It was von Schleicher's ambition to take over the government himself, and he continued his efforts to split the Nazi Party by offering Gregor Strasser and his friends cabinet office but excluding Hitler from any post.

Von Schleicher had for some time been undermining von Papen's position within his own cabinet, warning the other ministers that 'a continuation of von Papen's policies must bring about civil war at a time when the *Reichswehr*, because of its lack of strength, would be unable to intervene effectively in support of the government'; and, added von Schleicher, 'a great number of the younger officers were known to sympathize with the National Socialists, and he [von Schleicher] was not prepared to accept the possible consequences'. This was news to von Papen and was certainly contrary to what von Schleicher had said previously both to the president and to Groener at the time he had unseated Brüning. In the final outcome von Schleicher produced his own general staff officer, Eugen Ott, to give an exposition to the cabinet, warning of the consequences of a general strike and of the situation that might arise if the police and the *Reichswehr* had to combat both the Nazis and the communists; and Ott concluded that the government resources were entirely inadequate to do this. Von Hindenburg was hastily told of the new turn of events, this causing him to drop von Papen immediately and 'let Schleicher try his luck'.[10] Von Schleicher had, in anticipation of von Papen's removal, already been in touch with Hitler and other political leaders soliciting support for himself. At the beginning of December 1932 von Schleicher was appointed chancellor.

Von Schleicher had come to power because of his newly found conviction that Germany could not be ruled by the declaration of a state of emergency and the president's and chancellor's dictatorial form of government. But no sooner had he been given the chancellorship than he found that he was unable to interest the Nazis or any of the other major parties in supporting him. By the last week in January von Schleicher was asking the president for 'the declaration of a state of emergency and the dissolution of the *Reichstag*'. Having declined, at von Schleicher's insistence, to do this for von Papen, von Hindenburg could see no good reason why the situation could have changed so radically, only six weeks later, to permit him to act in this way for von Schleicher. Von Schleicher then resigned, but he apparently continued to negotiate with Hitler in the hope that he might be included as the minister for defence in any new Hitler-led cabinet. Von Papen, meanwhile (he later said with von Hindenburg's concurrence), had negotiated with Hitler for his own place (and that of other conservatives) in what was to be a Nazi dominated cabinet.[11]

At this point it was rumoured and feared that von Schleicher might use his post as minister of defence, a post from which he had not yet been officially relieved, to 'mobilize the Potsdam Garrison and isolate the president', from whom he was now estranged; this rumour may have been deliberately fed to Oskar von Hindenburg and to von Papen by Göring. It was believed to be important therefore to appoint a new minister of defence immediately so as to safeguard the president, and the choice fell on von Blomberg, a serving general commanding *Wehrkreis I*, for von Blomberg was known to dislike both von Schleicher and von Hammerstein: he was sent for by telegram with orders to report direct to the president.[12]

At 11 a.m. on 30 January 1933 Hitler, von Papen and members of a new cabinet were summoned by von Hindenburg preparatory to taking office. Hitler had, at last, come to power.

The victorious allies had intended that the *Reichsheer* should be nothing more than an internal security organization to support the German police and the authority of the central government. But the successive chiefs of the *Heeresleitung* had adamantly set their faces against the use of the small professional German Army in a policing or in an internal security role, and they looked forward to the day when the armed forces could be expanded and re-equipped to match the armies of their continental neighbours; consequently the training and the education of the troops had been directed to that end. The basis of military preparation, preparation that for the moment could not be translated into action, had been to plan the reorganization and the re-equipment of the army after having made a thorough examination of the experiences of the last world war.

In 1926 the first plans had been produced to strengthen the 100,000 man army, should Germany be threatened by its neighbours, these measures being purely defensive in that the seven infantry and three cavalry divisions were to be brought to a war footing by taking in volunteers from those German citizens who had had military service before 1918. Further volunteers had already been earmarked for the *Grenzschutz Ost*, the clandestine border organization for the defence of the frontiers against Poland and Czecho-Slovakia. The concealed stocks of world war weapons had been further augmented by new arms that had been secretly purchased by funds accrued as a result of hidden economies in the army budget; these monies, known as *A (Aufstellung) Vorhaben*, gave rise to the use of the terms *A-Plan* and *A-Heer*, meaning in fact the emergency or mobilization army. This was the first step to a planned and organized expansion of the 100,000 man *Reichsheer*. These plans had originated and had been developed by successive chiefs of the general staff *Truppenamt*.[13]

From January 1930, when Groener was still minister for defence, a mobilization plan had been put in hand that had as its object the tripling of the existing standing army from seven to twenty-one infantry divisions to meet the country's defence need in an emergency, for Groener, no less than his subordinates, was anxious to form an *A-Heer* or reserve army. The plan, however, existed largely on paper, since the Versailles restrictions still put obstacles in its way, and only sufficient armament was available to provide the first equipping of an additional seven divisions: much of this existing equipment was out of date and there were no maintenance stocks at all for the replacement of losses. There was, moreover, no mobilization or requisitioning organization set up within the Reich to embody the volunteers or conscripts that would form nearly two-thirds of the new *A-Heer*, or take in the enormous numbers of horses and carts from street and field to form the artillery and transport echelons of the new force.

Since the existing equipment was entirely inadequate both in scale and in design, the first step was to produce or purchase new. In 1932 the situation was reviewed and what was known as 'the Second Armament Programme' was produced, having as its object the equipping or re-equipping of twenty-one infantry divisions in the five years from April 1933. This was what later came to be called the Black Rearmament, a clandestine programme that was approved of not only by the government but also by the leaders of the main centre parties and by the Social Democrats. The number of people who knew of the plan was, however, restricted by the need for secrecy, and this later gave rise to many false conceptions.

The first problem was to find the 484 million Reichsmarks to finance the project and this was done by an annual budget saving of just under a hundred million marks a year; this saving, that had to be concealed from abroad, had to be included in separate vote lists known as the *X*, *L* or *I-Haushalt*; these funds remained, however, subject to special audit and to parliamentary control. The limited amount of funds available restricted the planned size of the emergency *A-Heer*, and forced the extension of the preparations over a space of five years. A particularly expensive cost factor was the laying up of a reserve of maintenance stocks of ammunition, and there was sufficient money for less than eight weeks' battle consumption rates for the full force. Even so, money was only one of the difficulties to be overcome. The Reich munition industry could not be made ready within three months of the start of hostilities to meet even part of the maintenance demand for equipment, particularly since the Saar, the Ruhr and the Upper Silesian industrial centres were ringed or occupied by Germany's neighbours.[14]

These mobilization preparations, comprehensive though they were on paper, did not in fact amount to very much in terms of men or equipment that could be made ready for battle. Each of the twenty-one peacetime infantry regiments was to be transformed into a division in war.* But the *war* establishment for the 1938 division would have been very little different to the 1933 *peace* establishment of 12,000 men for an infantry and 6,000 men for a cavalry division, except that each infantry division would have had an additional war complement of twenty-four anti-tank guns and a further six medium guns added to the field guns of the divisional artillery. Some thirty medium and heavy batteries were to be raised as army artillery, together with about thirty light and thirty heavy anti-aircraft batteries.† Only one panzer battalion of fifty-five light tanks was to be raised by 1938.

---

* The post-war German infantry division had been reduced from four to three infantry regiments and the brigade organization had been done away with.

† Army artillery is that artillery directly under the control of the army commanders, to be allocated temporarily, at their discretion, to corps or divisions.

The *A-Plan* or *Not-Plan* covered the raising of the additional fourteen divisions and the conversion of the whole of the German Army to a war footing. But it was obviously impossible to form and train the numbers of medium, heavy, anti-tank and anti-aircraft batteries – let alone a new air arm – required to support a field army on mobilization, since such units did not exist in peace. The first step therefore was to raise specialist artillery and air force units as part of the standing army, and the *A-Plan* had thus to go hand in hand with a concomitant plan known as 'the new peacetime army', involving the changing of the structure of the 100,000 army.

It has often been said that the latter-day *Luftwaffe* was spirited out of nothing, but this, however, is not entirely true, for a small air element had been kept alive within the *Reichsheer* and the *Reichsmarine*, and von Seeckt had always shown a keen interest in the retention of the air arm. About 180 flying officers of the First World War had been taken into the 100,000 man *Reichsheer* at its inception, and a Colonel von Thomsen, the last chief of air staff, together with his aide, a Captain Wilberg, set up the tiny air defence *Referat (TA(L))* within von Seeckt's *Truppenamt*, to form the main air force department within the German Army.[15] A flying officer was accredited to T1 (Operations) while information on foreign air forces was farmed out to T3 (Intelligence); technical air force questions were dealt with by another desk* under a Captain Student, attached to the army arms and equipment inspectorate.

From 1923 to 1927, Wilberg, with a staff of two, headed the TA(L), sometimes as an independent desk of the *Truppenamt*, sometimes as an element within the T2 (Organization), during a lively period of air development. In 1923 100 first-class Fokker D XIII fighters were secretly bought from Holland, it being the original intention to use them against the French in the Ruhr. Afterwards these were sent off in crates to the German fighter school at Lipetsk in Russia that formed the *Flugzentrum*, firstly under Thomsen and then under von Niedermayer. The first courses to be trained there consisted of the former war fighter pilots undergoing refresher training, and these were followed by officers and potential officer cadets who had already gained a civil pilot's licence but had no military flying experience, the serving officers being sent into Russia in civilian clothing and with passports made out with false names. In all, 130 army fighter pilots and eighty air observers were trained at Lipetsk between 1925 and 1933, together with a few navy fliers.

The German air industry was encouraged, often by *Reichswehr* purchases or subsidies, to keep alive its warplane trials and development and to transfer some of its production abroad, Junkers to Sweden (in addition to its Russian factory at Fili), Rohrbach to the Netherlands and Dornier to Switzerland. Gliding, too, was sponsored as a sport inside Germany with the use

* A *Referat* is the equivalent of a US 'desk' and might consist of one or two officers and clerks.

29

of *Reichswehr* funds, in order to attract, not only youth, but both serving and former officers.

One of the main props of the *Reichswehr* air effort, clandestine and restricted though this was, was provided by the civil air transport ministry (RVM). At von Seeckt's instigation, Brandenburg, a former war pilot, became its director in 1924: and it was due to Brandenburg that civil air transport was developed with an eye to the future requirements of the military. The RVM also provided an additional source of funding for the *Reichswehr* secret air actitivies. In 1925 the 'Black' *Reichsheer* air fund from all sources totalled ten million marks; in addition the *Reichsmarine* at that time was spending about a quarter of a million on air development.

In 1926, at the direction of the RVM, the Lufthansa (DLH) was formed by an amalgam of Aero–Lloyd and Junkers–Luftverkehr AG under a former officer, a Captain Milch. Wilberg's interest had been concentrated on fighters rather than on bombers or reconnaissance aircraft, since it was believed at that time that bombing and air reconnaissance missions could be carried out by modified civil transport, intercommunication or trainer aircraft. With the formation of the Lufthansa, an air transport and a permanent ground support organization had been brought into being that could form a military reserve of pilots, technical staff and aircraft, together with a ready-made training organization for military personnel. In 1927 Wilberg was replaced as head of the TA(L) by Sperrle who, in 1929, was relieved by Felmy. Not before 29 November 1930 was it agreed, at a meeting presided over by Groener and attended by Brandenburg and by von Mittelberger (the arms inspector with a responsibility for the air arm), that German military aircraft were to be acquired, kept on German soil, and secretly flown in the Reich air space, these aircraft being apart from the civil aircraft operated by Lufthansa.

In the First World War, air operations and air defences, except for those at sea and on the coastal approaches, had been the responsibility of a special command of the German Army; a large proportion of the anti-aircraft resources had been allotted to this special command. The acceptance of this traditional arrangement had been continued in the *Reichswehr*. So it came about that, when, on 11 July 1932, Adam, the head of the *Truppenamt*, had made a presentation to von Schleicher, at that time minister for defence, seeking the minister's permission to raise a peacetime air component of the standing army, to consist of six fighter, three night bomber and thirteen reconnaissance squadrons, together with seven reserve flying units (in all about 140 first line aircraft and 630 officers and 4,000 men), this proposed flying organization was linked to a further request for permission to raise in peace a number of light and heavy anti-aircraft batteries to form the nucleus of the air defence force for the Reich. And, although this air defence organization was to be brought into existence in peacetime, it was to be funded out of the secret allocation for the *A-Heer*. Adam's proposals had been accepted by von Schleicher and were ordered to be completed by 1936.

At the beginning of 1933, however, there was a radical change in policy, for, on 21 February, von Blomberg, the newly appointed minister for defence in Hitler's cabinet, signed the orders for the setting up of an air defence directorate (*LS Amt*) directly responsible to himself, so removing the responsibility for the air arm from the *Reichsheer*. This directorate was headed by a Colonel Bohnstedt, with a naval officer as his chief of staff, it being agreed that the army and the navy should henceforth share these appointments. The new directorate was responsible to von Blomberg for the raising, training, equipping, manning and funding of the new air arm (*Luftwaffe*), and also for the anti-aircraft defence required both for the *A-Heer* and for the security of the homeland. This Blomberg order laid the foundation for what was to become a fully independent *Luftwaffe*, eventually independent not only of the army and navy but, under Göring, virtually independent of von Blomberg himself.

On 27 April 1933 von Hindenburg authorized the setting up of a 'Reich Air Ministry' (RLM) from the former *Luftfahrt-Reichskommissariat* of Minister Göring and his deputy *Staatssekretär* Milch, this RLM to be 'under the Defence Minister von Blomberg'. Satisfied with this arrangement, in which he had presumably had a hand, von Blomberg, on 10 May 1933, ordered that Bohnstedt's air defence directorate, just recently made part of the defence ministry, should be transferred to the RLM under Göring. The *LS Amt* was later redesignated as the *Luftkommandoamt (LA)*. [16]

The high command and the military chain of responsibility was now much confused in that the command of the new air arm and anti-aircraft artillery, all manned by army personnel and forming part of the *Reichsheer*, was exercised by what was still supposed to be a civil ministry, headed by Göring, theoretically under von Blomberg as minister for defence. The *Truppenamt* no longer had operational responsibility for these troops and none for their future use and development, although the *Reichsheer* still had to command and discipline them. Within a month, the army general staff had cause to regret von Blomberg's decision, and it remonstrated that all flying and anti-aircraft formations intended for the support of the field army should be returned to the command of the *Chef der Heeresleitung*, the operational (T1) and training (T4) departments emphasizing that this step was essential for discipline, control and training. Only Colonel Keitel, the head of the organization directorate (T2), although he had been formerly entirely against the setting up of an independent *Luftwaffe*, now temporized and suggested 'waiting to see how things would turn out'. [17]

The *Luftwaffe*, at the time that it was separated from the *Reichsheer*, was a purely defensive organization based largely on a study of the world press and on intelligence on the development of foreign air forces. From 1926 onwards there had been some study of the *operative*, that is to say the deep tactical role of the German air force, but this had never been expanded to the realms of strategic air warfare. Douhet's ideas of the massive air offensive, with the air force operating as an independent war-winning armed service, had not been seriously considered by the general staffs in the Bendlerstrasse. Admittedly, there had been objections by some of the flying members of the army general staff to any idea that the air force was no more than a supporting arm or a particularly versatile form of field branch artillery, for they preferred to see themselves as a main arm, co-equal with infantry, or as the modern successors to the cavalry within the *Reichsheer* structure: but none had gone so far as to imagine that the air force would be a third service completely independent of the army.[18]

That the *Luftwaffe* was soon to become independent of the *Reichsheer* and the *Kriegsmarine*, to such an extent that the requirements of the two older services were held to be of secondary account by this new arm of the service, was to be illustrated during the first months of 1933. For the expansion programme for the air arm was drawn up by Milch and his staffs in June 1933 without consultation with the *Heeres-* or the *Marineleitung*, so that Adam protested against the way the air force leadership was setting to work. The army, said Adam, was dissatisfied with the number of air reconnaissance squadrons planned for allocation to the ground forces, and wanted its own army air arm; and, continued Adam, all of the six fighter squadrons then being formed by the air command should be part of the army order of battle, being expanded by 1938 to fifteen squadrons in five fighter wings, one for the *Heeresleitung* and one for each of the four new army headquarters that were to be raised. For the *Truppenamt* still saw the air force fire and reconnaissance support of the field forces as an integral part of the organization of the German Army.

Adam's views, and those of the *Truppenamt*, were, however, treated as largely irrelevant, for the development of the *Luftwaffe* was now in the hands of the non-professional soldiers, Göring and Milch. Even the *Truppenamt* plans for the *A-Heer* were no longer applicable. Adam's 1932 project had been agreed and authorized by the German government of the time in expectation of some early relaxation of the Versailles restrictions; it was accepted that the new manpower coverage would be much in excess of the 100,000 ceiling and preparations were made for the officer and non-commissioned officer training establishments to double their output.[19] All these innovations had, however, hardly been commenced when Hitler's taking office as chancellor created an entirely new situation and put to an end an unsatisfactory method of creating an emergency mobilization army by stealth, an army that would have been inadequately trained, both individually and collectively, largely unequipped, and without the industrial capacity to support it even in a short war. For the peacetime *Reichsheer* by itself was too small and had too narrow a basis to have formed the framework of the national field army and *Luftwaffe* that would have to be raised on mobilization.[20]

The politics and the fulcrum of power within the high command changed radically during the time that Groener was minister for defence. The

Ministeramt had become a power centre largely outside of the minister's control, for von Schleicher was the permanent deputy to the minister and attended to his ministerial and political duties: he was also responsible for the control and co-ordination of all other bodies within the ministry of defence and had taken upon himself a good deal of political and personnel manoeuvring within the *Heeresleitung*, this being done largely at Heye's and .von Hammerstein's expense, for their powers were not to be compared with those that von Seeckt had once arrogated to himself. And, as a newly promoted general, von Schleicher had interposed himself between the *Chef der Heeresleitung* and the defence minister. When von Schleicher succeeded Groener in June 1932, he retained under his own hand the control of the armed forces, so that this had the effect of restoring the status of the minister. In December, von Schleicher was both defence minister and chancellor; this was the situation when he gave up his ministerial post to von Blomberg at the end of January.

Under von Blomberg, however, the balance of power was to shift yet again. Von Blomberg, contrary to the restriction of Versailles, remained a serving general on the active list: von Blomberg certainly intended to keep the military control centralized in his own office. But since von Blomberg's character was insufficiently strong to withstand von Hindenburg's interference in detailed military matters, and his emotions insufficiently stable to resist the pressures, cajolery and charms of the new chancellor, he soon found himself unable to insist that both von Hindenburg and Hitler should recognize that the *Kriegsmarine* and the newly developing *Luftwaffe* were directly subordinate to von Blomberg alone. The main loser came to be von Hammerstein, the *Chef der Heeresleitung*. For whereas Göring and Raeder relied on their direct access to von Hindenburg and what came to be the closeness of their relationship with Hitler to ignore von Blomberg's pretensions, von Hammerstein, lazy and passive, now found himself without the support of von Schleicher's intrigues and of von Hindenburg's friendship; for von Schleicher was in retirement and von Hindenburg had taken offence; and there was no trust between von Hammerstein and Hitler. The German Army itself, notwithstanding its experience and its great size compared with the small *Kriegsmarine* and the tiny *Luftwaffe*, was the arm of service most directly threatened, on the one side by the interference of von Hindenburg and the pretensions of von Blomberg, and on the other by the ambitions of Röhm, the chief of staff of the SA. And it was the German Army that was least able to defend itself.

In 1933 von Blomberg was promoted colonel-general and was officially designated as commander-in-chief of the *Wehrmacht*. But although von Blomberg was to use this to the full in the demands that he made on the *Heeresleitung*, being convinced that, in the event of war, he would personally command all the forces in the field and at home, his title was in fact without substance since the three chiefs of the *Leitungen* retained their own command responsibilities for their own arms; so it was that von Blomberg had no right to issue a single order direct to any land or air formation or to any of the war fleets on the high seas. Nor did he have any form of *Wehrmacht* defence staff qualified to assist him in framing directives, even to his subordinate *Chefs der Leitungen.*[21] Von Blomberg's appointment was in no way that of a Generalissimo; rather was his post a legacy of Versailles and Weimar.

Von Hammerstein, on the other hand, had a ready-made command and staff headquarters, within the ministry of defence, that could be transformed into a suitable apparatus for command and *operative*, that is to say grand tactical, planning. But he was unequipped and ill-placed to cope with strategic planning for general war because he had not an all arms head-quarters and because he was too far removed from the political, economic and financial centre of government. The primary task of the *Heeresleitung*, and that of the *Marineleitung*, as the new Nazi chancellor was soon to make clear, was to create, equip and train a machine for fighting by land and by sea. For this, war planning staffs were hardly required, particularly as Hitler gave them no political or planning guidelines or indeed a firm timetable to replace the assumptions on which they had worked before he came to power. Organization and mobilization staffs, and inspectors at the head of each arm, would have been sufficient to have carried out the peacetime role that Hitler expected of the commanders-in-chief.[22]

At the beginning of 1933 the *Heeresleitung* was made up of the arms inspectors and five separate directorates (*Ämter*): the *Personalamt (PA)* controlling officer administration, the *Verwaltungsamt (VA)* dealing with quartermaster matters, finance and accommodation, the *Waffenamt (WaA)* for weapon and equipment development and provision, and the *Wehramt (WA)* that controlled the army vote and funds, other rank administration, and looked after the inspectorates for the various arms. The arms inspectors themselves came directly under the *Chef der Heeresleitung*. The functions of the general staff were performed by the *Truppenamt* with its departments for operations, organization, intelligence and training; the chief of the *Truppenamt* was the first among equals with the other *Amt* leaders (over whom he exercised no control), but he could, if need be, state his view to the *Chef der Heeresleitung* on any affairs dealt with by the other *Ämter*. Keitel, Jodl, Krebs, Model and von Manstein were all part of the *Trup-penamt*; von Brauchitsch was the inspector of artillery, while Guderian was the equivalent of chief of staff to Lutz, the inspector of transport troops.[23]

There was, as yet, no *Kriegsakademie* and no officially recognized output of general staff officers. But, from October 1932, all the trainees for the general staff had been concentrated as the 'Officers' Course Berlin' in the court building in the Lehrterstrasse, so that, in fact, a clandestine centralized staff college was again in existence.

At the beginning of 1933, therefore, the foundations had been sketched out for the future expansion of the German Army, even though the framework on which it had to be built was not in being. But the war planning

34

and the war command organization required for the waging of a general European or a world war did not exist either for the German Army or for the *Wehrmacht* as a whole.

Some latter-day critics of the Weimar German Army have censured its leaders for allowing Hitler to come to power in January 1933. And it has been said, on rather doubtful evidence, that von Schleicher, von Hammerstein and even von Reichenau had discussed among themselves whether they should arrest von Hindenburg (presumably to prevent the aged president calling on Hitler to head a government), but had failed to put their plan into action. But such criticism of the inertia of the army leaders in January 1933 is ill-considered. Hitler and his *Reichstag* deputies had been legally elected, and precedent and political conditions were such that it was proper that he should have been offered the chancellery. Admittedly, an army *putsch* to exclude Hitler from power would have been well-advised in view of what happened thereafter, but such a step would have been entirely illegal in January 1933 and might have been lawfully resisted, not only by Hitler's storm troopers but also by the German public. Hitler's true personality was largely unknown, and it was commonplace at that time to dismiss his writings and speeches as the outpourings of a demagogue who would soon be tamed by the hard realities of office. Moreover Hitler's new coalition cabinet, with von Papen as the vice-chancellor and the conservatives outnumbering the National-Socialists, offered, so it was assumed, an adequate safeguard against any Nazi excess.

An army *putsch* could, in any case, never have been attempted with any hope of success unless it had been led by a popular figure, sufficiently independent and sufficiently determined to act with complete ruthlessness, well knowing that his action might lead to civil war. There was at that time no such leader to be found in the presidency, the ministry of defence or in the German Army, for German generals, having been indoctrinated by von Seeckt, prided themselves on being apolitical and on their readiness to obey. Moreover, there is no means of knowing whether, in January 1933, the 100,000 *Reichsheer* would have obeyed a general's unlawful orders to act against the Nazi party; without von Hindenburg's sanction, it might not have done so.

Hitler, however, far from being tamed by the realities of office, had no intention of straying from the path that he had set himself. He had come to office by legal precedent: he intended to stay in power by any means, legal or illegal.* Although he kept the extent of his aims and ambitions carefully concealed, he set to work systematically, and at once, on the first steps towards a complete dictatorship. On 27 February, only four weeks after assuming office and at the climax of the new election campaign, came the

---

* Admittedly, Hitler later clouded the change of government by calling his legal assumption of power the *Machtübernahme* 'the taking over of power', or better still the *Machtergreifung* 'the seizure of power', this being intended as a sop to his own extremists and to emphasize the revolutionary nature of his party.

35

Reichstag fire that was used by Hitler deliberately to provoke an atmosphere of emergency, the Red scare serving as an excuse to suppress the communists and their allies. The following morning von Hindenburg acted on Hitler's advice and suspended the basic rights of the constitution, including protection from arbitrary and illegal arrest, secrecy of correspondence, and freedom of the press and assembly. Socialist newspapers were banned. In the newly elected parliament the Nazis and their allies had lost ground, obtaining just over fifty per cent of the votes, but their overall position was soon improved by the outlawing of the eighty communist deputies. Two days later, when the *Reichstag* met in a Berlin opera house, Hitler demanded the sanction of an Enabling Law that would permit him to make and apply laws without the consent of parliament, including laws that were contrary to the Weimar constitution, Hitler assuring his listeners that he had no intention of encroaching upon the rights of the *Reichstag*, the upper chamber *Reichsrat*, or of the *Länder* or of the president. Germany was already in the grip of the Nazi street terror, and all the main parties, including those of the centre, voted the new chancellor the powers that he demanded, thus underwriting all Hitler's actions for a complete and a final dictatorship.

Hitler then broke the promises he had just made to the *Reichstag*, for within a few months the *Länder* had ceased to exist, their sovereign rights being taken over by the Reich central government. All trade unions were dissolved and their property was sequestered by the party Labour Front, a compulsory organization comprising both employees and employers. The coalition cabinet lasted barely six months and the NSDAP was then proclaimed as Germany's 'only political party'; the former trade unionists and opposition party leaders were harassed, beaten-up or arrested, and the *Stahlhelm* was incorporated into the SA. The Prussian police, now under Göring, was purged of all elements hostile to the Nazis and the more senior posts were filled by party men; the SA was enrolled as the official police reserve so that it might better pursue its course of lawlessness and violence, for the SA was the principal instrument of the Nazi terror. The violence, that was previously directed against Jews and communists, was used, during that spring and summer, to include anyone that was not a wholehearted and vociferous supporter of the new régime. And, as Golo Mann has said, 'the fight was fought by one side alone, the blows, symbolic and real, falling on a people who did not defend themselves; such was the state of the nation only three months after 30 January.'[24]

The first racial laws came into force at the beginning of April, and Jews were declared to be unfit for government service; this meant that all Jews and persons of mixed non-Aryan parentage were dismissed from the civil service, the judiciary, universities, schools and even orchestras. Jewish shops were picquetted and looted, the Jews, and the Germans that dared to be seen in their company, being intimidated and assaulted by brown-shirted ruffians, many of them convicted criminals. And in Munich, as early as 1933, 'people told hair-raising stories about the treatment of prisoners in the nearby

36

Dachau concentration camp'.[25] Nor was the German Army excluded from this atmosphere of general fear, for Faber du Faur has said, together with many of his military fellows, that 1932 was the last year in which he dared to speak his mind openly.[26]

Only a few days after Hitler had become chancellor he was invited to dinner at von Hammerstein's apartment to meet a number of senior army officers; and, however unprepossessing they may have found his manner and his talk, Hitler told them much that they wanted to hear, and this in a most convincing way. He denounced what he called the Utopian Weimar democracy that sapped the energy of the nation, and he proposed to replace party politics by *his* authoritarian rule. In exchange for this rule, that he called 'the rebirth of Germany', Hitler would restructure and re-equip the armed forces, absolute priority being given to the needs of the military. The new chancellor said that he rejected any form of a militia, either on Italian lines or in the form of a short service auxiliary force that had once been favoured by von Seeckt and by von Schleicher – for he was convinced that a strong standing army was required. 'With the help of the generals', Hitler said, he had no doubt that he would achieve this ultimate goal. Less than a week later, when addressing the principal military commanders in the defence ministry, Hitler added, to the obvious relief of many of those present, that 'the army would never be called upon to subdue internal conflict – because for that he had other means at his disposal'.[27] Hitler had trimmed his address to the needs of his listeners and he had been at pains to keep his proposals palatable.* The implications of what was involved were obviously lost on those present, and, condoning the principle of dictatorship, they willingly abandoned to the lawlessness of the irregular paramilitary party gangs one of the primary and basic roles of the military forces of any nation – supporting the civil police in the maintenance of law and order.

Von Blomberg had been appointed to the defence ministry the day before Hitler had assumed the chancellorship, and it is widely, and probably rightly, thought that the choice of defence minister must have been von Hindenburg's. Von Blomberg was one of the foremost of Germany's soldiers and his personality was pleasing to the president. How much von Blomberg's inclination to National-Socialism and his known animosity to von Schleicher and von Hammerstein weighed in the selection, may never be known, although it was believed at the time that he had been appointed in haste in order that von Schleicher should be quickly removed from the office of minister for defence. As was customary in the German Army, the incoming general brought with him his own chief of staff, von Reichenau, who replaced von Bredow at the *Ministeramt* at the beginning of February 1933; the energetic and unconventional von Reichenau was already widely known as a thorough-going supporter of Nazism.† With von Blomberg's assumption of

---

* Hitler was not sparing in his public praise of the army, lauding its discipline, its tradition and its glorious past. (K-J. Müller, *Das Heer und Hitler*, p. 35)

† The *Ministeramt* became the *Wehrmachtamt* in February 1934.

office it was obvious that von Hammerstein's days were numbered and that his appointment would not be extended.

Freiherr von Hammerstein-Equord was mistrusted both inside and outside of the army, for he owed his position to, and was too deeply entangled with, von Schleicher. Groener had written him off as von Schleicher's *'Jagdhund'*, and his part in the dismissal of Brüning and Groener in the previous year was unlikely to be forgotten by a politician of any hue; his daughter was said to be a communist and he himself was believed to have very marked socialist tendencies.[28] Although von Manstein, his former regimental colleague in the Third Foot Guards, was later to say that he regarded von Hammerstein 'as brilliant', he showed very little leadership during his tenure as *Chef der Heeresleitung*. In his defence it can be said that he mistrusted, and was opposed to, Hitler, and that he was the only German general who had the courage to defy the party and army order that no German officer should attend either von Schleicher's or Groener's funerals. When in office, however, he seemed unwilling, or too indifferent, to resist von Blomberg's irregular interference in the day to day running of the army, for von Blomberg and von Reichenau often ignored the very existence of the *Chef der Heeresleitung* and dealt directly with the heads or even the departments of von Hammerstein's subordinate *Ämter*.[29] Von Hammerstein had already lost von Hindenburg's ear and sympathy, and von Blomberg saw to it, as far as he was able, that von Hammerstein no longer had the direct access to the president that he had had under Groener and von Schleicher. The defence minister was the only armed forces representative on the newly formed defence council, and this too served to divorce von Hammerstein from the political centre. Nor was Adam, von Hammerstein's chief of the *Truppenamt*, more popular with von Blomberg, possibly on account of his outspoken criticism of the proposed raising of an independent *Luftwaffe*. In any event, both von Hammerstein and Adam were shortly to come to the end of their tour of office.

Beck, the commander of 1 Cavalry Division, had, according to one witness, been noted by Hitler as worthy of a senior post and he was expressly recommended to von Blomberg by the Chancellor. Von Blomberg, too, had a high opinion of Beck, and, that October, when Adam was posted as the commander of *Wehrkreis VII* in Munich, Beck was appointed as his replacement. Von Hammerstein was scheduled for retirement in the following February, and the choice of his replacement became the subject of a difference of opinion between von Hindenburg and von Blomberg. Von Blomberg – one assumes with Hitler's approval – wanted to appoint his *Chef des Wehrmachtamts*, von Reichenau, to the *Heeresleitung*. Von Hindenburg refused to countenance this, because, so he said, of von Reichenau's lack of command experience; in reality, according to von Papen, the president had been much irritated by Hitler, who had pressed von Reichenau's case. Von Papen himself had suggested to the president the name of von Fritsch, who was a personal friend of von Papen's; they had attended the staff college together before the First World War.[30] Since von Fritsch was the commander of *Wehrkreis III* in Berlin and was known to von Hindenburg, von Fritsch's nomination was confirmed by the president.

Von Blomberg took exception to the substitution of a candidate against his own and the chancellor's wishes; and he was particularly irritated that the suggestion had come from von Papen, who was regarded as a light-weight in the political circles of the day. Von Blomberg then threatened resignation if von Reichenau were not appointed; he was summoned by the president who told him that 'he was free to resign on political grounds but not to challenge on political grounds a presidential decision in military matters', for this, in von Hindenburg's opinion, 'was insubordination'.[31]

Von Hindenburg's somewhat nonsensical views, as voiced on this occasion, were entirely contrary to his own legal position under the old Weimar constitution. The executive military power was meant to be concentrated in the hands of the minister of defence rather than in those of the president, for the president could not, in law, sign a decree concerning military matters that was not first signed by the minister of defence. But von Hindenburg had, for some years past, been assuming military powers that were not his by law, and had, in 1932, encroached on the civil liberties of the state when he had ordered von Rundstedt, the general commanding *Gruppenkommando I* in Berlin, to use military force to suspend and to disperse the elected government of Prussia; and the president had himself appointed von Papen as 'the Commissioner for Prussia' to act in its stead, a breach of the constitution for which von Hindenburg later feared that the Nazis would indict him. And von Hindenburg had lately begun to act as though the military establishment were a regiment, with himself at its head, the minister of defence being no more than von Hindenburg's second-in-command or adjutant. As a serving officer, von Blomberg himself was, according to the Weimar law, illegally a member of the government, since he should have been a civilian – automatically retired on the day of his appointment. In any event, von Blomberg could not have been responsible to the chancellor and the cabinet, to the *Reichstag* and to the president, according to the requirements of his office and the constitution, and at the same time have been subject by military law to what von Hindenburg, the titular commander-in-chief, was pleased to call military orders, orders that infringed on the constitution and the rights of the minister of defence.

What is most noteworthy about this incident is that von Blomberg did not resign in protest; and with the president threatening that *he* would resign if von Fritsch were not appointed, Hitler did not yet feel sufficiently secure to have challenged the president on this issue.[32] And so von Fritsch was appointed in February 1934, as he later said, 'against the wishes of Hitler and von Blomberg', to a post that he accepted with misgiving and reluctance.

Von Fritsch and Beck were to occupy the most influential positions in the German Army from 1934 to 1938 at a critical time during its expansion and development, and both, as seen in retrospect and from a political and personal standpoint, may be judged as unsuitable candidates for the posts they occupied. *Freiherr* von Fritsch came from the impecunious nobility of the Rhineland, where his father had been a lieutenant-general. Originally commissioned in the artillery, von Fritsch was considered to have had outstanding ability as a general staff officer; his general education, however, like that of the German officer of the time, was very narrow, and his knowledge of political, social and economic matters was very restricted.[33] The little that he wrote showed an anti-Semitism and a hatred of the Social Democrats worthy of any confirmed Nazi.[34] Yet von Fritsch was believed to be modern and progressive in his approach to military development and there is no doubt that he enjoyed the respect of his fellow generals both for his ability and for his character. He knew the new defence minister well since he had previously headed the T1 department of the *Truppenamt* directly under von Blomberg when the latter was the *Chef des Truppenamts*, and yet he was to prove entirely incapable of defending the German Army against von Blomberg's pretensions. In the final outcome, he was so passive that he could not even defend himself. A bachelor, his taciturn and haughty bearing – von Blomberg called him 'a cold fish' – reckoned at that time to be 'in the tradition of von Schlieffen and von Seeckt', probably cloaked the shyness of the man. Like von Blomberg and von Brauchitsch (who was to succeed him) he thought his function was to obey, 'limiting himself to the military field alone and keeping himself apart from any political activity'. His role was to be an inglorious one.

Beck, the new chief of the *Truppenamt*, was an entirely different type of character. A Rhinelander, and an artilleryman like von Fritsch, he had become a widower during the First World War. His service had alternated between staff and artillery appointments and he had come to Hitler's attention when in command of *Artillerie Regiment Nr. 5* at the time that the party leader had given his propaganda evidence at the trial of the three young artillery officers on a charge of conspiracy to commit high treason.[35] Beck had then gone on to higher appointments, to be the artillery commander in *Wehrkreis IV*, then, in October 1932, to the command of 1 Cavalry Division, and finally, a year later, to head the *Truppenamt*, firstly under von Hammerstein and then under von Fritsch.

When Beck took over his appointment he did so with cheerfulness and optimism. He apparently had some respect for von Blomberg and, dismissing his predecessor Adam's forebodings, he was convinced that Hitler would in due course 'develop into a real statesman'.[36] The previous year, when on a visit to Italy, Beck had become an admirer of Mussolini, and this had confirmed him in his view that Germany's future lay in being rid of parliamentary government.

Like von Fritsch, Beck was austere, even harsh, and his character was tempered with not a little vanity. Most of the senior generals appear to have felt the need to model themselves on one of their illustrious predecessors, and Beck tried to follow in the footsteps of the elder von Moltke, with whom he liked to hear himself compared. Much of his spare time, particularly later in life, he was to devote to military study and to writings, and he came to be regarded in Germany as one of the foremost military thinkers of the time.

Von Manstein thought that Beck's operative ability was of a very high order, and he based this opinion on the chief of the army general staff's preparation and supervision of war games and exercises. Yet Beck was no man of action, but a procrastinator, and, at times, a needling faultfinder who sorely tried the patience of his subordinates with his seemingly endless revision of plans and directives, often arriving back at the draft originally submitted by his staff and rejected by him.* On operative battle-fighting matters he was very conservative, looking backwards to the last century rather than to the present or to the future.† Unlike von Fritsch, Beck was not generally receptive to new ideas: he underestimated the role of the *Luftwaffe*, even in support of ground operations, and he saw little place in war for the German Navy.

Beck's abilities were never put to the test, but, in all probability, he would have been inferior in the operative field not only to Halder, but also to the higher commanders, such as von Brauchitsch, von Bock and von Manstein; in the sphere of tactics he would have been outclassed by the armoured specialists, Guderian, von Kleist, Hoepner and Hoth. But Beck's greatest quality, and in this he appears to have been so outstanding as to have been almost alone among his contemporaries, was in his understanding of the greater problems that would beset Germany in fighting a European and a world war; for Beck had a clear conception of the real meaning of politico-military strategy in modern times, of the proper relationship between diplomacy and the armed struggle, and of the moral and material sinews of war. Much of what Beck wrote in his last months in office and in the three years prior to 1941 had a particularly prophetic ring.

By 1938, when German armed expansion and rearmament were well under way, Beck noted that Germany was already able to defend itself against the aggression of any state; on the other hand, said Beck, Germany was unable to force its will on any foreign country except by armed force, for Germany had no alternative means at its disposal. Germany's only real asset, compared with the world powers, was in its highly trained and disciplined manpower, for its other resources were limited. And since Germany lacked strong and reliable allies, it must of necessity stand or fall by its own endeavours.[37] While there were many ways in which Germany could lose a war, said Beck, there was only one in which it could win one, *by force of*

---

* An exasperated staff officer (Heusinger) once pointed this out to Beck, who, nothing abashed, replied, with a wintry smile, that 'that proved that together they had examined and carefully considered all aspects of the problem'. (Cit. K-J. Müller, *Das Heer und Hitler*, p. 222, note 86)

† He chided his deputy Halder for his dealings with Guderian (who was pressing on Hitler, and on the general staff, his views on the primacy of armoured and mechanized operations) saying, 'Why do you want to have anything to do with those *arrivistes*?' Guderian, for his part, saw Beck 'as a paralyzing influence wherever he appeared'. (Guderian, *Panzer Leader*, pp. 30–2)

arms, and this success could come only by ground warfare. Skilled diplomacy and the proper conduct of foreign affairs were essential in creating and in maintaining political conditions favourable to the waging of war, for they all went hand in hand. Germany's leaders should remember that their foreign ambitions must be limited by the capabilities of the German armed forces. And the *Wehrmacht* itself depended on the German economy, on the ability of the nation to feed and provide for itself, and on the inner morale of the people; should one of these pillars fall, then the *Wehrmacht* must collapse.[38] Beck disagreed with von Ludendorff's contention that the government control and the military command should be concentrated in the hands of one man, for, like Wetzell, an earlier *Chef des Truppenamts*, Beck was certain that the burden was too enormous for one man to carry, and that the political, economic and military tensions and competing priorities were impossible for one man to regulate.[39] Such Ludendorff ideas, said Beck, were feasible only at the time of Frederick the Great. The head of the government, the *Regierungschef*, might, and probably would, become the war leader, the *Kriegsherr*, but the *Regierungschef* should never become the military chief, the *Feldherr*; and the military, just like other organs of state, must, in the final outcome, be responsible to the *Regierungschef*, the state, and the people.

Beck, and this opinion was shared by von Fritsch, was in no doubt that any German aggression in Central Europe would probably, and immediately, develop into a European and a world war. And he saw this war as a total war, not merely as a succession of battles (*Waffenkrieg*). For he was certain that Germany's potential enemies intended that war should be total, so that they could develop to the full those telling advantages they enjoyed over Germany – time, space and the inexhaustible reserves of a boundless hinterland. The armed forces of these potential enemies were the least of the factors threatening Germany. It was always possible, thought Beck, that the great world powers would actually avoid any great armed clashes with Germany in the early part of a war, until they had developed and mobilized their strength.[40] They would then attack with final and decisive war-winning blows. Such a world war would determine Germany's very existence. These factors, according to Beck, restricted Germany to a European rather than a world power role.

Yet Beck was ambitious, and his readings of von Moltke caused him to relive those times, when the monarch was the *de facto* commander-in-chief and the chief of the great general staff his principal military adviser and executive. Soon Beck became dissatisfied with the way that the German high command was evolving in the Third Reich, with its three independent armed services all equal in status and theoretically under the command of a *Wehrmacht* commander-in-chief.

Beck's conclusion that the German Army must be the main, if not the only, defender of Germany's future, led him to recommend that Germany's war planning staff must necessarily be based on the general staff of the army, since no other military staff was capable of undertaking the task; and this war planning staff should ideally work under the direct control of the head of state who was responsible for all foreign and home policy. Moreover the head of this war planning organization must be the main, indeed probably the only, permanent military adviser to such a head of state. In fact Beck, by no great process of reasoning, had returned to the functions and status of the elder von Moltke's great general staff.[41]

The organization of the high command was undoubtedly highly unsatisfactory, and would, in all probability, have led to a breakdown in time of war. In Beck's view there were two possible ways in which the situation could be rectified. Either von Fritsch's post as the *de facto* commander-in-chief of the ground forces should be done away with, and the army general staff should be taken into von Blomberg's command organization with additional command, planning and executive responsibilities *over* the German Navy and *Luftwaffe*; or, as an alternative, von Blomberg's ministry should be abolished and the other two armed services brought under the *Chef der Heeresleitung*. These views were to bring Beck into conflict with both von Fritsch and von Blomberg.

Meanwhile, however, a far graver threat had arisen, not to the army's role in peace or in war, but to its very existence, for von Blomberg and von Reichenau appeared to be willing to sacrifice the German Army's interests for the benefit of good relations with the Nazi Party and the SA.[42] The SA had for long been demanding a major role not only in what it was pleased to call the maintenance of internal security but also in border control and in national defence. A series of meetings took place at various levels between the party and the army to discuss the SA demands. On 13 August 1933, Hitler, at one of these conferences, had made it clear that wherever the SA might be used it would be under the control of the army. Such pronouncements widened the growing split between the chancellor and Röhm, the chief of staff of the SA, for Röhm, a former army captain, an able organizer but a very violent man, was dissatisfied with Hitler's leadership that seemed to him to be too accommodating to the Germany Army and to the government establishment. For Röhm sought a real revolution with the destruction of the establishment and its institutions and not the pallid *Machtübernahme* of 30 January; he wanted the standing professional army replaced by a militia, commanded and organized by the SA, with himself at its head, for he apparently coveted von Blomberg's ministerial post and his recently acquired title as 'Commander-in-Chief of the *Wehrmacht*'; and he demanded that all pre-military training, whether this was carried out in the form of labour service or by other means, and the organization of reserves and reservist refresher training, should be under the control of the SA. According to Röhm's ideas, the role for the German Army was to be a diminishing one, that is to say the training of the SA cadres to a professionally acceptable standard to meet the military demands of the task. The SA had for some time past been used by the army as an auxiliary force on the eastern frontier, and regular, though limited, training of the SA was being carried out by the army.

The army was already suffering the consequences of its own folly in its tacit acceptance of the new chancellor's declaration that 'never again would the army be called upon to subdue internal conflict'. By the autumn of 1933 the attitude of the *Heeresleitung* had become ambivalent. In October, and again in February 1934, Beck was insisting that the German Army must be the sole bearer of arms *and the basis of government power* in the new Reich.[43] And yet, even as late as 7 December 1933, the documentary evidence shows that Beck was fully in favour of von Reichenau's ideas that the SA should form part of the armed defence of the nation.[44] Von Fritsch did not take over his appointment until 3 February, and his condemnation of von Reichenau's earlier attitude to the SA was voiced, for the most part, several years after the event.

Von Blomberg's and von Reichenau's actions were certainly remarkable, although these actions do not appear to have excited hostile comment from the leading generals at that time.[45] Unpleasant incidents and some violence were becoming increasingly widespread throughout Germany between German officers and other ranks on the one side, and the SA on the other, most of the trouble being deliberately provoked by the SA. The SA was demanding, and was being granted, the equivalent privileges and status as the German Army throughout the Reich, and it was already rapidly assuming an official and permanent existence as a government body of troops, trained and capable of bearing arms. In September 1933, von Blomberg, in what was apparently an effort to appease the SA and lessen the possibility of clashes, ordered that soldiers should salute members of the SA, SS, and other party formations, when both were in uniform and out of doors, and that SA colours and formed bodies of men should be saluted in the same fashion as if they belonged to the military.[46] The Nazi salute, with the raised arm, had to be used on all occasions when the soldier was not wearing headgear, *even when he was saluting another soldier.* * In joint parades, the SA was permitted to march in front of the army, thereby, in some measure, acknowledging its precedence. In February 1934, by von Blomberg's order, the Nazi party's *Hoheit* emblem of the swastika carried by an eagle with outstretched wings was to be worn on the uniforms of all members of the armed services. The political and legal implications of such a monstrous order, with its apparent acceptance that the NSDAP, the only remaining party in Germany, would stay in power for all time, and that the army owed allegiance not to the constitution but to this political party, was presumably lost on both von Blomberg and von Reichenau.

Von Fritsch's attitude was largely passive. Von Papen, as vice-chancellor, uneasy at the rapid consolidation of Hitler's personal power and the further violence threatened by the party's radicals, tried to approach the *Heeresleitung* for some assurance of support, but his former colleague von Fritsch

* NCOs with officers' swordknot (*Feldwebel* and above) were saluted by inferior ranks.

wanted to keep himself and the army clear of party strife and political entanglements. Von Fritsch appears to have done little to check the flow of orders that were to identify the army with the party and to enmesh it with the SA, for it had been agreed that volunteer recruits for the army, to be enlisted for one year only, should be found from the ranks of the SA, and that, once conscription had been introduced, the SA should be responsible for pre-military and reserve training.* Von Blomberg had ordered that the anti-Semitic (non Aryan) laws should be applied to the armed forces, this leading to the discharge of a number of officers and other ranks; and it would appear, according to the directives that were sent out over von Fritsch's own signature, that von Fritsch fully agreed with these measures, measures that were in the main approved of at that time by the German officer corps and by the rank and file.[47] Nor did Beck see fit to raise any objections.

Von Reichenau, who had once been an officer of the imperial guard artillery, was, notwithstanding, progressive in his thinking; intellectually superior to von Blomberg, he was hard, decisive, clever, many-sided and flexible, yet with some wantonness in his attitude in that he was a staunch supporter of Hitler and determined to fit the army into the National-Socialist State. Yet he quickly recognized the danger posed by Röhm, and, in November 1933, instructed that army officers attached to the SA were to keep him informed of any apparent danger from that quarter, 'for if things go wrong we will really be in trouble'.[48]

At the beginning of February 1934 there came an open breach between Röhm and von Blomberg. Röhm had already been given a seat in the cabinet and had been made a member of the newly formed Reich defence council where he sat side by side with von Blomberg, and, on 1 February, he gave to von Blomberg the Röhm plan for the SA to take over from the German Army the responsibilities for defence. The following day von Blomberg hastily summoned an army conference of *Wehrkreis* commanders in which it was agreed that the earlier policy of close co-operation with the SA should be reversed – the SA being held at arm's length – von Blomberg warning the army leaders against too sudden and too obvious a reversal 'in case this should lead to open fighting'. While this meeting was in progress a letter for von Blomberg arrived from Röhm, saying that he (Röhm) regarded the *Reichswehr* as no more than a training school, since the conduct of war, 'and therefore of mobilization as well', would in future be the task of the SA.[49]

Von Blomberg presumably hurried to the chancellor with the letter, for Hitler called together what was afterwards called 'a peacemaking confer-ence' of the heads of the SA and the *Reichswehr*. This meeting, presided over by Hitler, was held in the Bendlerstrasse on 28 February.[50] Hitler told those present that the time of internal revolution was over and that *the time of external strife was approaching*; he rejected Röhm's ideas of further revolution or of a SA militia; a militia was inadequate for defence and he

---

* The one year enlistments, in defiance of the Versailles restriction, represented the first stage of the expansion of the army prior to conscription.

himself wanted a people's army* that would be built out of the *Reichsheer* on the lines of the old imperial army. This new army, continued Hitler, must be ready for defence in five years' time, and for an offensive war in eight years' time, rigorously trained and equipped with the most modern weapons, ready to strike short sharp decisive blows in east and west to ensure Germany's *Lebensraum*. Meanwhile Hitler 'was agreed with the *Reichswehrminister*' that the SA should be employed in the interim in frontier protection and pre-military training.

Hitler had had a protocol drawn up, roughly following what he had decreed at the meeting, and he required Röhm and von Blomberg to sign this protocol as an acknowledgement and acceptance of the situation. Although Röhm signed without demur, he immediately afterwards made it clear within his own circle that he had no intention of abiding by the agreement. He referred to Hitler as an ignorant first-class private (*Gefreiter*) of world war vintage, and said that 'if he (Röhm) could not go along with him then he would go against him'. These remarks were immediately taken by one of the SA present back to Hitler.[51]

Von Blomberg and the German Army leaders were entirely satisfied with the action taken by the chancellor against Röhm on their behalf, and, in return, von Blomberg lost no opportunity in repeatedly and publicly emphasizing the *Wehrmacht* support for Hitler. The chancellor's talk of offensive war in the next eight years was not taken too seriously, particularly as it contradicted his vehement public protestations that he only wanted peace. But the army continued to fear a Röhm SA *putsch* and revolution, and its commanders were ordered to prepare contingency plans against it. Röhm meanwhile had not come out in the open, but he continued secretly to ferment friction against the army in the *Wehrkreise*. Von Reichenau, in his turn, countered by placing his own confidence men in the SA training organization and started secret negotiations with Himmler, the head of the SS. Röhm, so it is said, already had his spies within the *Reichsheer*. On 7 May, von Fritsch was so bold as to tell the generals that they must not stand for insults from the SA, but he tempered this advice with the demand that henceforth 'they show a more positive attitude' to the National-Socialist state than they had done hitherto.

Hitler had been biding his time. On 7 June he persuaded Röhm to send all the SA on a month's leave from Sunday 1 July, preparatory to a strenuous autumn programme. Röhm had no understanding of the man with whom he was dealing, and, in agreeing, Röhm might as well have signed his own death warrant.

That Röhm intended the removal of Hitler, by fair means or by foul, is probable. But it is most unlikely that he had as yet formed any plan as to how this was to be done; and he misjudged Hitler in that he underestimated his ability and his ruthlessness, for Röhm could not have considered himself to

---

* By a people's army Hitler meant a regular conscript army with close political and social links with the party and people.

be in any immediate danger, otherwise he would not have agreed to send the SA on leave. Hitler on the other hand saw himself and his leadership directly threatened. Some years before he had taken over the command of the SA, but, in the interim, he had allowed Röhm, its chief of staff, to assume the actual control of the 400,000 strong force. Some of the SA leaders would have supported Röhm, rather than Hitler. Hitler could count only on his *élite* bodyguard, what was eventually to become Himmler's *Waffen SS*; but although trained in the use of arms the SS comprised as yet only a small mobile reserve.* Since the SA was still, for the most part, unarmed, the German Army remained the most powerful force in the country. And contrary to what the chancellor may have said a year before, that the task of the army was to be restricted to external defence, it is certain that he intended to rely on the armed support of the German Army while he dealt, in his own fashion, with the internal threat from the SA.

On 16 June Hitler met once more with the leaders of the SA and the army to stress that the SA was to be subordinate to the *Wehrmacht*; this gave rise to expressions of dissent from members of the SA who held Hitler responsible for what they believed to be a lack of leadership. The next day the tension within the cabinet and party was heightened after von Papen, in a public speech at Marburg, attacked the radicals in the Nazi party on account of their notions of perpetual revolution, and he expressed his fears at the rapidly disappearing freedom of the press and of political and private life in Germany.[52] This speech marked the end of von Papen as vice-chancellor in Hitler's government and marked down for murder two of von Papen's secretaries who had prepared the speech.

In the last week in June the SS and *Sicherheitsdienst (SD)* leaders had been called to Berlin where they were briefed by Himmler and Heydrich on the imminence of a Röhm-planned SA revolution; the SS was instructed to liaise with the German Army *Wehrkreise* to obtain the loan of rifles and accommodation (that could also serve as a refuge from the SA, for the SS was no more popular with the SA than was the army). The army had meanwhile been put on the alert, an infantry regiment being held at stand-to near Döberitz, while a company was detached to protect the ministry of defence buildings in the Bendlerstrasse, care being taken to avoid exciting the suspicions of the SA. Beck had meanwhile ordered that officers in the *Heeresleitung* should always have their personal weapons ready in case of attack. Von Fritsch had already had orders issued to the military districts, parallel to those issued to the SS, that they should, if asked to do so, arm the SS and the police, and should take special precautions for the defence of all army barracks.

Hitler had visited the president at Neudeck in mid June, presumably to brief him on the internal situation. It seems likely that the chancellor

---

* Himmler was theoretically subordinate to Röhm but he sought to have his force removed from any association with the SA and have himself placed directly under Hitler. This was done immediately following the purge of the SA.

concluded that he was unlikely to meet interference from the presidential circle, for thereafter his attitude against the SA hardened and there was increased activity behind the scenes; Sauer has said that the SS and SD deliberately provoked and heightened the hostility between the SA and the army, in order to justify the murders that were planned for the Saturday night of 30 June. On 28 June a suspicion that this was happening occurred to von Kleist, the commander of the Breslau cavalry division; for, according to von Kleist's latter-day account, Heines, the SA *Obergruppenführer* in Silesia, told him of the SA foreboding that the army might attack them; this feeling, according to Heines, was common everywhere in Germany. After their talk, von Kleist and Heines came to believe that the tension was being deliberately provoked 'by unseen hands at the highest level'.[53] Von Kleist flew to Berlin to inform von Fritsch and Beck, but when von Reichenau was briefed concerning the matter he is said to have made the pregnant reply that 'it may be so but it is too late now'.[54]

Other incidents are alleged to have occurred, but they afford no firm proof of the complicity, that is to say the foreknowledge, of any members of the German Army in the conspiracy to murder. It has been hinted that von Reichenau's contacts with Himmler may have led him to know that something was afoot; and so they might: Beck is said to have sent a friendly warning to von Schleicher to be on his guard, and von Fritsch and Beck, perhaps in the fashion of von Seeckt at the time of the Kapp *putsch*, were not available on the night of 30 June; this may indicate some foreknowledge of the intended action.[55] But the most damaging and justifiable charge that can be levelled against the German Army, and also against responsible German politicians and officials from the president downwards, was the bland acceptance – in many cases the open approval – of the murders of Röhm and perhaps a hundred of his close SA associates, these, without any form of charge or trial by law, being shot or bludgeoned to death on the spot by detachments acting under the personal direction of Hitler, Göring and Himmler.* Others, too, were murdered who had nothing to do with the SA but had been put on Hitler's list because they had opposed him or his movement at some earlier time, and these included General von Schleicher and his newly married wife, General von Bredow, von Reichenau's predecessor at the *Ministeramt*, two of von Papen's secretaries, and others against whom Hitler bore a grudge.† The night of the long knives gave to the

---

* Hitler later justified his action partly on the grounds that those murdered were themselves murderers. For the SA, at the direction of the party elements and with the connivance of the German police, had previously set up their own interrogation centres and prisons in which those they illegally detained were often tortured and murdered. That the SA should have been brought to account for these crimes by the due process of law there can be no doubt. But Hitler had countenanced if not instigated these SA crimes and his ordering that the SA leaders be murdered was, by any standards, as criminal as the original crimes committed by many of these people; and their deaths had in reality been ordered only because they threatened Hitler's personal position as party leader.

† Among Hitler's other victims were: Kahr, who had disassociated himself from Hitler in 1923 at the time of the abortive march on the Munich Feldherrnhalle; Gregor Strasser, whom von Streicher had attempted to set against Hitler within the party; and Klausener, a leader of the Roman Catholics.

chancellor his first taste of personal revenge. In a brazen and cleverly worded speech to the *Reichstag* on 13 July Hitler justified these murders by claiming that he was 'protecting the integrity of the German Army', and he involved the president in his action in that he said that his 'promise to *him* [von Hindenburg] to preserve the army as a non political instrument of the nation' was as binding to the chancellor from innermost conviction as from his pledged word.

The ailing von Hindenburg, from his isolation at Neudeck, sent the chancellor a telegram of congratulation based 'on the facts made known to him'. The previous day, on 1 July, von Blomberg, in a *Wehrmacht* order of the day, praised Hitler's courage 'in personally breaking the revolt', and two days later, at a cabinet meeting, expressed his 'absolute gratitude'; he further forbade any members of the *Wehrmacht* to attend von Schleicher's funeral. Von Witzleben, at that time one of the *Wehrkreis* commanders, the same von Witzleben who was later to be tried and executed for his part in the 20 July 1944 bomb plot, when told of the shooting of the SA leaders on 30 June, reportedly said that 'he was delighted and only wished that he had been there'.[56] Von Fritsch, as usual, remained passively silent, 'waiting for orders from above' so he subsequently said. Beck, according to his biographer, began to have doubts. A few protests were made by some serving and retired officers against the murders of von Schleicher and von Bredow, but they had to satisfy themselves with the official explanation that 'the personal honour of the two officers had not been involved, but that they had chosen paths that were regarded as hostile to the government; these thereby led to fateful consequences ... the deaths of these two men being regarded as in the interests of the state'. The lame and belated *Schlieffen-Verein Ehren-erklärung* for the two murdered generals could only be circulated privately and in secret, in typed copy and by hand.

The regimental officers and the rank and file of the *Wehrmacht* did not know what was going on, and what it was told was misrepresented and false. The generals, on the other hand, heard von Blomberg's explanations with some scepticism, although many allowed their doubts to be set at rest by von Hindenburg's congratulatory telegram.[57] Von Blomberg and von Reichenau may have had no prior knowledge of Hitler's exact intentions, but von Blomberg was party to a conspiracy by which von Schleicher's murder was first reported as justifiable homicide, in that von Schleicher was said to have been killed resisting arrest with a pistol in his hand. And both von Reichenau and von Fritsch would appear to have been fully aware of the murders at the time that they were being committed, because the 'wild shootings' were immediately reported from Dresden and Munich by both List and Adam.[58]

The whole of Germany was already in a grip of fear, and this applied to the generals, both serving and retired. On 30 June Brüning had warned Groener to go into hiding. And, shortly after the murders, Groener, only one of many, was, at party instigation, subjected to indignities by both the civil and military authorities. His native town of Ludwigsburg took away from him his honorary citizenship, while General von Sodenstern, the last commander of the *Regiment-Kaiser-Friederich*, demanded that Groener resign from the regimental association 'on account of the events of 21 March'.[59] Von Ludendorff, too, became the object of some party harassment and police control. All of the senior officers knew that their private mail was subject to interception and none dared express openly any criticism of the party or of the régime.

The German Army had long been passive in a climate of disorder and when faced by provocations and by the lawless conduct of a legally elected government. Its political neutrality, inspired by von Seeckt and approved by von Hindenburg, had made it difficult for it to interfere in the Hitler period of government before 30 June 1934: the occasion, and even a clear justification, were lacking. The night of the long knives was to afford the first – and the last – occasion, when the German Army should have acted to have prevented these crimes – or to have brought the criminals to trial. In its acquiescence, in the selfish furtherance of what it considered to be its own interests, the German Army thought that it had bound Hitler to itself. In fact it had bound itself to Hitler. Hitler alone was the master as together they set off on their path of tyranny, violence and atrocity, that was to destroy thirty million people, maim countless more, and transform the face of the world. And that other grim dictator, Stalin, closely watching the events of the 30 June from his Moscow Kremlin, immediately came to the rightful conclusion that Hitler was the sole power in Germany, and that henceforth the Soviet Union could discount any idea of the existence of a German opposition or of an *eminence grise*, civil or military, standing in the German chancellor's shadow.

CHAPTER THREE

From Reichsheer to German Army

Towards the end of July 1934 arrangements had been made for army parades to be held throughout the country to celebrate, on 2 August, the twentieth anniversary of the 1914 mobilization day for the First World War. But then, early on the morning of 2 August, the death of von Hindenburg was announced, and the opportunity was seized upon to use the occasion of the parade to have all ranks swear a new oath of allegiance. The new form of oath was entirely different from that used in the life of the Weimar Republic, for in the old *Reichswehr* the troops had sworn fealty 'to the Reich constitution, the Reich and its lawful institutions', with obedience to the holder of the presidential office and to the soldiers' superior officers. Then in December 1933, under Hitler's chancellorship, the old Weimar oath had been revised so that the recruit swore allegiance merely to 'the people and Fatherland', all mention of president, constitution, institutions and superior officers having been dropped. The death of the president should not have made it necessary to readminister the oath, except that Hitler meant to bind the armed forces to himself. For the August 1934 oath was far-reaching and momentous, the officers and men being *ordered* to swear *unconditional* obedience not to an office or to a constitution but to the person of Adolf Hitler, 'the Führer of the German Reich and Commander-in-Chief of the *Wehrmacht*'.[1]

The death of the aged president had not been unexpected. But the fact that the orders were issued throughout the whole German Army in the space of a few hours would appear to indicate that the chancellor was ready with his plan to abolish the president's office and to substitute for it a newly created appointment of Führer, embodying that of president and chancellor, at the same time nominating himself to fill that office. It has been said that the idea and the framing of the oath had been entirely von Reichenau's work, an impulsive and impetuous gesture to prove the loyalty of himself, his chief, and that of the *Wehrmacht*, to the new dictator.[2] But a change to the oath of such enormous significance could not have been made without von Reichenau and von Blomberg first having obtained Hitler's agreement; von Papen has said that all action was indeed instigated or approved by Hitler. And although witnesses have subsequently stated that von Reichenau

51

dictated the form of oath on 2 August, with all the appearance of spontaneity, it is more likely that it was an act calculated for effect, and the oath had already been framed by Hitler many weeks before.*

The oath violated German law and military precedent in that the basis of the military engagements of the whole of the standing army and fleet rested solely on the original Weimar oath taken by the officer or soldier. No warning had been given to the troops of the intention to administer the new oath so that the soldier might have time for reflection, nor of course was the soldier allowed the option of declining the oath and either serving out his engagement under his old oath or of leaving the service immediately. The personalized form of oath and the promise of unconditional obedience turned the armed forces into Hitler's instrument and property, to use according to his will.[3]

Hitler's abolition of the presidency and creation of his own post as Führer was submitted for the approval of a German plebiscite, and subsequently a law was passed retroactively legalizing the changes.

That month von Blomberg proposed to Hitler, and the chancellor accepted, that henceforth 'he be addressed by the Wehrmacht as "Mein Führer"'.[4] Der deutsche Gruss, or raised arm fascist salute and the 'Heil Hitler', was not yet obligatory in the army, although it was becoming increasingly used. On 20 August Hitler wrote a letter to von Blomberg that was made public, a letter in which the ambiguity was such that it might be inferred that the officers and soldiers of the Wehrmacht had voluntarily bound themselves to the new state 'in my person'; in return, the Führer said that he would always regard it as his 'highest duty to defend the existence and inviolability of the Wehrmacht and ensure that the army would form the bedrock of the nation as the sole bearer of arms', a reminder to von Blomberg of the debt he owed to Hitler for the dictator's destruction of Röhm's SA leadership.[5] In reality, of course, Hitler had no intention of allowing the army to remain as the sole bearer of arms, for, shortly afterwards, the SS Verfügungstruppe was established as a fully armed and independent standing body of political troops entirely separated from the SA. The SS was, by now, no less hostile to the German Army than Röhm's SA had been. Insults and violence against the army were instigated by the SS leadership, this developing, from mid 1935 onwards, as a deliberate campaign directed from the centre, slandering the army generals and impugning their loyalty.[6] Hitler was content to play a double game, because he could, if he had so wished, have stamped out this internal strife immediately.†

---

* In common with other tyrants in history, Hitler frequently pretended that his actions were in accordance with the popular will or at the pressing invitation of the armed forces. Similarly he used generals to remove other generals less compliant to his will, and, in 1944, to deliver generals to the vengeance of the so-called 'people's courts'.

† The NSDAP was aware of the danger that army officers might challenge SS members to a duel. For in 1934 it appeared as if duelling, suppressed by the late empire and the republic, might again be revived; it was therefore forbidden by laws of 1938 and 1939. (Kitchen, p. 52 and Messerschmidt, p. 87). In 1938, von Fritsch did in fact challenge Himmler to a duel.

Within the *Heeresleitung* von Fritsch and Beck soon found that they had little cause for satisfaction in the destruction of the threat from the SA. Von Fritsch could not get on with von Blomberg and found him difficult to work for, and, behind his back, he raged against the minister's naivety and lack of backbone. Yet von Fritsch did little on his own account to protect the army, nor did he resign in protest. In Hitler's presence von Fritsch was dumb. Both von Fritsch and Beck saw the *SS Verfügungstruppe* as a new threat, and they wanted to limit its size, but they did not tell Hitler this, and Beck's letters of protest were never sent. Beck, according to his biographers, now had grave misgivings not only about the 30 June murders of the SA but also about the oath of allegiance that he himself had taken.[7] Yet some idea of Beck's outlook may be gauged from his reaction to the order that would remove Jewish war veterans from the old comrades' associations, for Beck thought that these Jews should resign of their own accord 'to avoid unpleasantness'. Nor would Beck believe that Hitler had anything to do with the odious conspiracies that were being deliberately mounted against the army, for Beck thought 'that Hitler was too high-minded for that'; and when asked by Holtzmann why Hitler did not simply order the intrigues to stop, Beck answered that 'Hitler could not always do as he pleased'.[8] For Beck, as von Hammerstein said, was still completely under Hitler's spell.

In January 1935 Hitler had addressed the leaders of the *Reichswehr*, the SS and the party, telling them that he 'did not believe the rumours of treason that were being put about against the army high command'.[9] That Hitler should have made so outrageous a statement, virtually in public, might be regarded as an intention not to quell rumours and heal dissension, but to keep alive the suspicions and add to the uneasiness of the generals; for the matter should have been settled by disciplining the SS. But Himmler, unlike Röhm, was no threat to the dictator; the German generals, however, still might be. Yet the speech was very well received by the military. Then, in June 1936, Hitler appointed Himmler as *Reichsführer SS* and Chief of the German Police in the Ministry of the Interior. Again, surprising though it may seem, this rapid expansion of the powers of the SS was at first welcomed within the German Army, since it was believed that the change would strengthen the hands of the police and remove from the army any possible future commitment of assisting the police in maintaining internal security. This being done, the German Army, so its leaders thought, could then devote itself to the task of its own expansion and the problem of external defence.

Five million Germans voted against Hitler and thirty-eight million gave him their approval – or were officially said to have done so – at the plebiscite: and so the bulk of the nation, covering all classes of society, accepted one man and one party dictatorship with its total disregard of law and order and its increasing terror, knowing that once confirmed in power the Führer could never be removed. In this way they placed themselves and the nation in the hands of a political adventurer and murderer. The brutal evidence was there for all to see and hear, in the violence of the police auxiliaries, in the known atrocities of the concentration camps and SA prisons; no German was entirely ignorant of what was going on around him, and even the man in the street at the time of the plebiscite should have had some foreboding of what the future held, even if he had no idea of the new Führer's world-wide political ambitions and the wholesale slaughter that the leader deliberately intended to provoke – for Hitler kept many of his designs to himself, concealing their true extent and direction from the German people and the outside world. Many Germans did not think; others were afraid to think; most were lulled by the Führer's speeches and interviews, that played on the fears, the hopes and the emotions of his listeners, that reassured them by words that they wanted to hear, and that were suited to the occasion, being militant, patriotic, emotional, pathetic and pacific in turn, calculated to enlist widespread support while at the same time exploiting the differences between individuals, factions or foreign states.

Hitler had no time for the League of Nations, and the Japanese withdrawal from the League and from the disarmament conference in March of 1933 had shown Hitler the way he must take. In October 1933 Germany left the League to a chorus of Berlin protests about the unfairness of the treatment it had received, and a clamour of Hitler assurances of his desire for world peace. Less than three months afterwards, Hitler had quietened Poland, his noisy and threatening neighbour, by concluding with that country a ten-year pact. This manoeuvre, regarded with dismay by the Soviet Union and by many of the top ranking German generals, was intended by Hitler merely to create a schism between Poland and France and to safeguard his rear while he prepared to face the western powers. Yet the pact was welcomed both in Warsaw and in the capitals of most democratic states as evidence of Hitler's good intentions. In 1933, at Stalin's demand, the Russo–German military collaboration ended.

Hitler then turned his attention to the west, and sought, and obtained, the naval agreement with London. In retrospect it can be said that Britain was the loser, particularly since the agreement weakened any remaining Franco–British resolution that Germany should be made to adhere to the military restrictions of the Treaty of Versailles. The waning authority of the League of Nations was further shaken when Mussolini attacked Abyssinia, and Britain and France were again in disarray; and Hitler sowed further confusion by his protestations of good faith and peaceful intentions, for war, he told the world, was madness.

Hitler lived, as Golo Mann has said, by a few simple ideas. Life is a struggle that in the final outcome can be improved only by war. Just like a predatory animal, a great nation can live only at the expense of others; what it wants it must take, and, finally, it must destroy its neighbours as political and military powers, lying and breaking treaties and sacrificing its allies where it is to its advantage to do so. Compassion, charity, truthfulness and loyalty to persons or to obligations meant nothing to Hitler; it was this form of nihilism, a total rejection of decency, trust and faith, that was to prevail in German foreign and domestic policy and in all walks of German public life. Hitler made no secret of his intention to free Germany from the fetters of Versailles, since this was a very popular, plausible and, indeed, as seen even by many foreigners, a patriotic and praiseworthy aim. Hitler was, for the time being, however, less open in his secondary and tertiary aims, the formation of a pan-German state including Austria and Bohemia and those German territories lost following the First World War, and a further expansion eastwards at the expense of Poland and Russia, with the establishing of a *Herrenvolk*, a people that would rule the world, with himself at their head, destroying all remaining vestiges of Jewry and bolshevism. France would have to be brought under subjection or neutralized, and he aimed to do this by splitting it from its British ally; for Hitler favoured coming to some arrangement with Britain, at least for the time being, in exchange for a free hand in Europe and Western Asia. Hitler was little preoccupied with the United States or with the New World, and it would appear that he regarded them as negligible quantities. All these ideas had been developed in *Mein Kampf*, first published in 1925, and Hitler did not stray from them in any major particular for the next twenty years.[10] Some eighty million German people were to be the instrument that this Austrian proposed to use in the furtherance of his own personal demonic ambition.

Hitler's instructions to von Fritsch, on the taking-up of his appointment as *Chef der Heeresleitung* in February 1933, had been of a very general nature: 'to create an army of the greatest possible strength, inner resolution and unity, on the basis of thorough formation training'; this was in line with the dictator's attitude to rearmament and to army expansion in his first few years of office.[11] For he wanted merely 'more' and 'faster' and was careless of the details, being ready to leave these to the military specialists. Such military directives that were submitted to him he was content to sign, unread, once he had had the purport explained to him. And he did not attempt to influence the selection of military officers to the higher appointments.

The situation was, however, by no means entirely satisfactory to the military planners. Their plans and financial economies to bring about a covert expansion, made before the Nazis came to power, now meant little. Henceforth, money, manpower, equipment and training facilities were no longer to be the problem that had beset them in the latter days of the Weimar Republic. But since Hitler had laid down no strategic aims or guidelines, preferring for the moment to keep his political and foreign ambitions to himself, von Fritsch and Beck were left to their own devices, having been instructed merely, and as a first step, to implement in peace the expansion from seven to twenty-one infantry divisions. As they saw it, they were building a new German Army that would guarantee the defence of the Reich and this could best be done by tripling the number of standing infantry divisions preparatory to the reintroduction of conscription; then, as more manpower and equipment became available, these twenty-one divisions could, if need be, be used as the basis for the expansion to a wartime army. Not until August 1936, in a memorandum for his Four Year Plan, did Hitler, and this still in general terms, demand that he should have 'the best army in the world' in the shortest possible time, 'in order to provide the military solution against bolshevism'.

The necessary political and military guidance should have been provided by the defence council that had been formed in April 1933, which was supposed to convene under Hitler's chairmanship. But since von Blomberg, the defence minister and, from autumn 1933, the commander-in-chief of *Wehrmacht*, was the only military representative there, and since the council did not meet regularly, it proved to be of little value.[12] Even its steering committee was to be of no help, since its chairmanship, originally to be filled by Beck, was assumed by von Reichenau. And so von Fritsch and Beck had to be content with planning in a political vacuum while they grappled with the gigantic task of raising the new German Army at what was to prove headlong speed.

At the beginning of 1933 *Gruppenkommando I* in Berlin, at that time something between a field inspectorate and a corps headquarters, was commanded by von Rundstedt; *Gruppenkommando II* at Kassel was under von Leeb. The seven *Wehrkreise* forming the static headquarters and the administrative area for each of the seven infantry divisions, were, in numerical sequence, commanded by von Brauchitsch (Königsberg), von Bock (Stettin), von Witzleben (Berlin), List (Dresden), Liebmann (Stuttgart), Fleck (Münster) and Adam (Munich); the three cavalry divisions came under Feige, von Kleist and von Weichs.

The expansion proceeded systematically and logically, it being the intention first to double the number of infantry divisions in the spring of 1934 so that the strength of the standing army would rise from just over 100,000 to about 240,000 officers and men, and then to triple the strength in 1935. Eleven new corps headquarters (*Generalkommandos*) were to be raised before 1935. Seven of these were found simply by converting the existing *Wehrkreis* headquarters to corps headquarters, most of the divisional commanders being reappointed as commanders of the new corps and being known merely by the covert designation of *Wehrkreis* commander (*Befehlshaber im Wehrkreis*). A further two corps headquarters were formed in 1935 in Breslau and Kassel, and, in 1936, another two in Hamburg and Hanover (*Wkr XI*). For the time being these newly raised corps were disguised as 'headquarters army installations'.[13] A twelfth army corps at Wiesbaden followed in 1936.*

The seven infantry divisions had to be increased threefold, and the first

* In 1935 the *Wehrkreise* were: *I* Königsberg (von Brauchitsch); *II* Stettin (Blaskowitz); *III* Berlin (von Witzleben); *IV* Dresden (List); *V* Stuttgart (Geyer); *VI* Münster (von Kluge); *VII* Munich (von Reichenau); *VIII* Breslau (von Kleist); *IX* Kassel (Dollmann); *X* Hamburg (Knochenhauer). The *Gruppenkommandos* were: *I* Berlin (von Rundstedt) responsible for *Wkr I, II, III, V, VIII*; *II* Kassel (von Leeb) responsible for *Wkr V, VI, IX*; *III* Dresden (von Bock) responsible for *Wkr IV, VII, X*.

step was to create three *Gauleitungen* in each *Wehrkreis* (four in *Wehrkreise II* and *III*), each *Gau* forming the territorial basis of a division. As the seven divisional headquarters had been raised to the status of corps, the lieutenant-generals commanding the divisions becoming the new corps commanders, a further twenty-one commanders and headquarters of division were required. Since each of the old *Reichsheer* divisions had had an infantry commander and an artillery commander, major-generals or colonels, each with his own headquarters, acting as the deputy to the divisional commander on matters concerning his particular arm and, where necessary, exercising command on the divisional commander's behalf, there were fourteen potential divisional commanders and headquarters already in existence, leaving only another seven to be formed. As a temporary deception measure the new divisions were known by the former appointments of their commanders, e.g. *Infanterieführer I* or *Artillerieführer VI* or, in the case of the seven newly created divisional headquarters, given a territorial designation such as *Kommandant Ulm*.[14]

The covert increase continued on this logical and systematic basis. The twenty-one infantry regiments of the *Reichsheer* had no direct lineage from the infantry of the imperial army, for the affiliations thought up by von Seeckt were entirely artificial. Nor, contrary to what Wheeler-Bennett has said, were these affiliations of any use in the expansion. Infantry Regiments 1 to 5 and 7 to 9 bore the name 'Prussian' simply because they were based inside Prussia; similarly 10 and 11 were Saxon because they were located in Saxony, 13 was Württemburger, 14 was from Baden, while 19–21 were Bavarian, and this for the same reason; the remaining regiments were mixed and in this case battalions within the regiment sometimes bore a *Land* designation.[15] Some battalions had, in addition, the light infantry designation *Jäger*, but this was merely an honorific title since *Jäger* battalions were in no way different from the battalions of the line.* All three battalions of the regiment prior to 1934 had three rifle companies and one machine-gun company, being numbered consecutively throughout the regiment from 1 to 12: 13 Company was the regimental mortar company while 14, 15 and 16 Companies were the training companies forming part of the training battalion that was in fact the fourth depot battalion of the regiment.

The 1932 *Reichswehr* plan for the creation of the emergency *A-Heer* had envisaged the doubling of the numbers of infantry regiments in the first phase, and then tripling them in the second, and this was the plan that was used in 1934 and 1935. In the first phase the twenty-one new regiments, numbered consecutively from 22 to 42, were formed simply out of the third battalion and the training depot battalion of each of the *Reichsheer* infantry regiments, *Infanterie-Regiment 1* providing the cadre for the new *Infanterie-Regiment 22* and so on.[16] Each of the original regiments then

---

* The arms colour (as worn on uniform piping) was white for all infantry, the new machine-gun battalions carrying in addition the letter 'M'. Battalions in infantry regiments bearing the honorific title of *Jäger* wore light green piping as did the newly formed mountain troops (*Gebirgsjäger*).

created new battalions to replace those they had given up, while the new two-battalion regiments raised their own third and sometimes a fourth battalion so that, by the end of the year, the overall infantry strength, including that of the training schools, stood at forty-three regiments and 165 battalions, the increase in strength being largely made up of the recently inducted one year volunteers.

In the second 1935 phase the old and the new infantry regiments, parent and offspring (e.g. *Regiment 1* and *Regiment 22*), were both to give up their training battalions, together to form a third generation regiment (this being *Regiment 43* in the case of *Regimenter 1 und 22*), so that these three regiments had a common origin; the third and newest regiment was increased from two to three battalions by the transfer of the armed *Landespolizei* to the German Army. It was intended that all regiments should be made up of three battalions each of four companies together with a regimental mortar (13) and an anti-tank (14) company – the designation 'training' battalion or 'training' company within the regiments having fallen into disuse. In fact, however, eighteen of the regiments had, for the time being, only two battalions.

In the early stages of the expansion the training of recruits was not to present a great problem. The reintroduction of compulsory general service was not to be announced until March 1935, becoming law two months later, and the first conscripts (the class born in 1914) were not due to join the colours until the autumn of 1935. The first step, before conscription should be enacted, was to increase the army by inducting one year volunteers, many through the SA, preference being given to those who had already had some form of military service or who had served in the army in the First World War. The other source of reinforcement, the police officers and other ranks (that had been brought under the centralized Reich government on 30 January 1934 as the *Landespolizei*) were the former barrack *gendarmerie* or *Kasernierte Polizei* that had already received some training in the use of small arms; in 1933, although they were still police battalions, they had been reorganized and re-equipped on complete infantry pattern so that, from 1935 onwards, the *Landespolizei* battalions were ready for assimilation into the German Army as complete battalions, little or no reorganization being necessary, except that the men changed their police green uniforms for field grey, and were issued with steel helmets.

During 1935, even before conscription had begun, the *A-Heer* expansion had already been exceeded and the German Army was on its way to a peacetime strength, newly set by the dictator, of thirty-six divisions and 110 infantry regiments. And, in order that the annual classes from 1901 to 1913 (the so-called 'white groups' that had been too young for call-up in the world war but were above the 1935 conscription age) should not escape military service, training battalions (*Ergänzungsbataillone*) were raised – fifty-eight for the infantry alone – preparatory to providing short term training for these men, so that they might form a supplementary reserve.

The organization of the new infantry divisions and regiments was at first close to that of the old *Reichsheer* except where temporary shortages left appointments unfilled or units still missing. One minor departure from the *Reichsheer* infantry organization was the formation of motorized heavy machine-gun battalions trained in the use of long-range indirect fire. By 1935 nine such battalions had been formed from men drafted from infantry and motor-cycle battalions; each of these battalions had three companies each of sixteen heavy machine-guns.[17]

The artillery in the Weimar *Reichsheer* had been made up of seven divisional regiments each of three battalions (*Abteilungen*) of three batteries (each of four guns), with three further battalions intended to provide artillery support for the cavalry divisions being attached to Artillery Regiments 3 and 6. The expansion of the artillery followed the same pattern as that of the infantry, the seven divisional artillery regiments being expanded to twenty-one, most of the new regiments taking the numerical designation of the division of which they formed part. The threefold expansion was accomplished simply by turning each of the three existing battalions (of three batteries each of four guns) of the 1933 regiments into a 1934 divisional artillery regiment with a new organization of four battalions each of two batteries each of three guns. The 1934 regiment, therefore, had a strength of twenty-four guns against the 1933 establishment of thirty-six guns to a regiment. In the early days of the expansion, numerical designations were not used for the new regiments in order to disguise the rate of the army expansion, and they took their titles from their geographical locations. All artillerymen continued to wear their distinctive arm of service bright red piping.

There were some variations in the divisional artillery organization, but the first three battalions in each divisional regiment were equipped with horse-drawn field guns while *Abteilung IV* had horse-drawn medium guns. Some divisions had a fifth battalion of motor-drawn medium guns. In 1935, with the continued expansion from twenty-one to thirty-six divisions, the organization was changed again in that the medium guns were withdrawn from the divisional organizations, all the divisional field regiments then being numbered from 1 to 36 in accordance with the most recent divisional order of battle, while the medium and heavy artillery were centralized in thirty-six heavy regiments numbered from 37 to 72; each of the heavy regiments consisted in fact of two medium artillery battalions removed from the divisional artillery.[18]

The *Reichsheer* had a separate arm of administrative troops known as the *Fahrtruppe*, and these were the horse-transport troops equipped with horses and carts who, being the experts in horse-driving and horse-mastership, trained the driving instructors of all other arms at their Hanover riding school. Although the *Fahrtruppe* were a separate service arm wearing their own light blue piping on their shoulder straps, they had always been closely linked with the artillery since one of their principal tasks in war was the carriage of ammunition. Each of the seven infantry divisions had a *Fahrtruppe* battalion of seventeen officers and 400 men, and this formed part of the divisional artillery coming under the tactical and administrative control of the *Artillerieführer*. Some of the *Fahrtruppe* officers had indeed been artillery officers in the old imperial army, but, whatever their origin, von Seeckt and his successors had insisted that all ranks of the divisional *Fahrtruppe* should be thoroughly trained in field artillery duties so that they could, if the need arose, be used as first reinforcements for the artillery batteries. For no highly trained young *Reichsheer* soldier could be wasted on purely administrative duties that could be performed by more elderly reservists.

The *Reichswehr* had been forbidden by the Treaty of Versailles to have anti-aircraft artillery or chemical and smoke troops; but the latter-day promise of a relaxation in the restrictions encouraged the *Reichsheer* to set up training cadre headquarters in Döberitz and Jüterbog to develop these branches, the *Fahrtruppe* providing much of the manpower required for anti-aircraft and artillery observation batteries and chemical warfare and smoke troops. By 1932 the first anti-aircraft battalion was in being at Berlin-Lankwitz, having been formed from the nucleus of a motorized battery and from horse-transport troops; for the time being it was still disguised under its former designation of *Fahrabteilung 3*.[19]

The *Reichsheer* had been very strong in mounted troops, having eighteen regiments, in all about fifteen thousand cavalrymen. Yet, surprising though it may seem for a *Heeresleitung* that eventually raised a very powerful tank force, the cavalry was not used as the main framework for this new arm. Three cavalry regiments, it is true, were turned into panzer regiments, *Reiter-Regiment 12* in Dresden to *Panzer-Regiment 3*, *Reiter-Regiment 4* in Potsdam as the cadre for *Panzer-Regiment 6* in Zossen, and *Reiter-Regiment 7* in Breslau as the cadre for *Panzer-Regiment 2* in Eisenach; in addition *Reiter-Regimenter 11 und 16* were converted, the first to two regiments of motorized riflemen to support the tanks of the new panzer divisions and the second to three motor-cycle battalions. Four cavalry regiments had thus disappeared; the fifth (*Reiter-Regiment 4*) was kept in existence by using the *Landespolizei* to make up its depleted ranks. The three cavalry division headquarters were shortly to be disbanded, but the remaining fourteen horsed cavalry regiments remained in being, two forming a cavalry brigade in East Prussia while each of the other regiments was allotted to an army corps for reconnaissance duties.[20]

Unlike many of the British and French military theorists of the time, von Fritsch and Beck were unable to support, in its entirety, the view that the days of horsed cavalry were over. Germany's agriculture was still based on the use of the horse, and the number of horses in the Reich, about 3,400,000, was greater even than it had been in 1873. With this large number of horses went both horse-drawn carts and the men from town or country that were experienced and knowledgeable in the care and training of the animals;

these formed a national asset that could not be ignored, particularly since motor vehicles and motor fuels were in short supply. Von Fritsch, the horse artilleryman, and Beck, the former cavalry division commander, and their cavalry advisers, believed, moreover, that mechanized troops must of necessity be tied to roads, and that there were still huge tracts of country, particularly in the east, where the mobility of the horseman would be invaluable in reconnaissance tasks.

In the final outcome, however, their successors determined to make the best of both worlds, and, in the autumn of 1938, the cavalry regiments were reorganized each into two cavalry battalions, one of five horse squadrons and the other of three motor-cycle squadrons and one anti-tank and one light gun support squadron. On mobilization in 1939, these horsed and motorized squadrons were allotted to the infantry divisions as the divisional reconnaissance troops, and the parent cavalry regimental headquarters were disbanded.

The new German panzer arm came to be based not on the cavalry but on the seven motor transport battalions (*Kraftfahrabteilungen*) of the Weimar *Reichsheer*. These battalions formed the divisional trucking units and were essentially the service troops that the Versailles victors had intended that they should be. But because they operated and maintained motor vehicles the *Kraftfahrtruppe* were regarded in the twenties as a technical arm, with its own distinctive pink piping, being entirely separate from the horse and wagon *Fahrtruppe* battalion with its light blue piping that came under the divisional artillery commander.* Admittedly, designations in the old *Reichsheer* were often merely designed to deceive. But in this case the word *Kraftfahrtruppe* truthfully described the organization and purpose of the troops.

In the early days, under von Seeckt, there had been no intention of developing the *Kraftfahrtruppe* as a main fighting arm, although it numbered among its officers many who had distinguished records in other arms in the world war. Like the cavalry and the *Fahrtruppe*, it was at first a resting place, a niche in which officers could be held on the active list. On the other hand, the service of some *Kraftfahrtruppe* officers, like that of Major Lutz, who was at that time commanding *Kraftfahrabteilung 7* in Bavaria, had always been in railways and mechanized transport.

Von Seeckt saw the future of mechanized troops as a separate main arm, in addition to infantry and cavalry; but he did nothing to bring this about. It was left to the first inspector of transport troops, General Erich

---

* Originally in the early days of the *Reichsheer* both the *Kraftfahrtruppe* and the *Fahrtruppe* came under the *Inspektion der Verkehrstruppe* within the defence ministry, with two chiefs of staff, one for MT troops and the other for the horsed troops. Long before 1933, however, it was clear that they were to be regarded as fighting troops, one joining the armoured forces and the other the artillery. Later, in February 1935, a new supply and transport organization (*Nachschubabteilung*) was brought into being to replace the old *Reichsheer* men; then, from 1937 onwards, all service transport troops, whether motorized or horse-drawn, were known as *Fahrtruppe* and took the light blue service piping, the old *Reichsheer Fahrtruppe* having already been absorbed by the artillery (or *Luftwaffe*) and having taken the red piping of the artillery arm.

von Tschischwitz, together with his staff officer, a Captain Guderian, to attempt to alter the use of the seven motor battalions away from service tasks in favour of tactical experiments. At that time Guderian's only experience with mechanized troops had been an attachment, during 1922, to Lutz's *Kraftfahrabteilung 7*. But then, in 1924, came a check when von Natzmer succeeded von Tschischwitz, for the new inspector decided that the purpose of the *Kraftfahrtruppe* was to carry flour.* Guderian left for Stettin to become a military history instructor for staff aspirants.[21]

In 1925 the German armoured school opened in Russia at Kazan on the Kama, and among the students who attended there were von Thoma and Harpe. The first post-war tanks to be manufactured in Germany were six heavies, weighing 23 tons, equipped with 75 mm guns and powered by 300 hp BMW aircraft engines, and three mediums, of 12 tons, mounting a 37 mm gun; these were sent to Kama in 1928.

Von Natzmer was succeeded as inspector in October 1926 by von Vollard-Bockelberg who reversed his predecessor's decision about the tactical employment of the MT troops; and to stress this, von Vollard-Bockelberg coined the word *Kraftfahrkampftruppe* (MT battle troops), although this designation could not be revealed to the public. It was von Vollard-Bockelberg who was mainly responsible for beginning regular instruction of the *Kraftfahrtruppe* officers in the theory of armoured and mechanized war, basing this on a translation of the British official pamphlet 'Provisional Instructions for Armoured Vehicles 1927'.[22] Practical exercises in mechanized warfare, using dummy mock-ups, were also arranged with 3 (Spandau) Battalion of *Infanterie-Regiment 9*, the commander of which was a Lieutenant-Colonel Busch and the adjutant a Lieutenant Walther Wenck. In 1929 von Vollard-Bockelberg went to the *Heeres-Waffenamt (WaA)* inside the *Heeresleitung* where he remained until December 1933, becoming responsible for the introduction of motorization into the German Army. It was at this time, in 1929–31, that motor-cycle and mechanized reconnaissance companies began to be formed, and the Mk I and Mk II tanks were designed.†

Guderian, a former infantry captain who had never seen a tank, had been promoted major of the transport corps in 1927 and began to give lectures on panzer tactics. He soon fell foul of Major-General Otto von Stülpnagel, the inspector of *Kraftfahrtruppe*, who, although entirely in favour of developing the MT troops as an armoured fighting arm, forbade Guderian to spread his ideas on large armoured formations; for von Stülpnagel condemned the conception of panzer divisions as being Utopian. At the beginning of 1930 Guderian went to Berlin-Lankwitz to command the MT trucking battalion of 3 Infantry Division, returning to the ministry of defence in late 1931 to become chief of staff to the new inspector of *Kraftfahrtruppe (In 6)* Major-

---

* The new inspector was reputed to have said: '*Zum Teufel mit der Kampftruppe! Mehl sollt Ihr fahren.*'

† In 1929 the inspector of *Kraftfahrtruppe*, in conjunction with the inspector of cavalry, set up a motorized reconnaissance element under Munzel within *Reiter-Regiment 4*.

General Lutz. Among Guderian's own staff were Nehring, Breith and Chales de Beaulieu, together with Kempf who designed the first six-wheeled armoured car.

Much of the groundwork for the development of the panzer arm and motorized troops had been done by von Tschischwitz, von Vollard-Bockelberg and by Otto von Stülpnagel. But it was Lutz and Guderian who determined on the *operative* use of tanks in large formations, Guderian providing many of the advanced ideas which Lutz transformed into practical projects. Lutz was fortunate in that he had little opposition from the inspector of cavalry, in that Major-General *Freiherr* von Hirschberg was doubtful as to the future of motorized troops and left their development to the *Kraftfahrtruppe*. Within other branches of the *Heeresleitung*, however, Lutz was to find a lack of knowledge and sometimes a lack of interest in armour. The *Truppenamt* itself was ready to accept the introduction of tanks as a supporting arm to infantry (very much as the French had done), but was not prepared to go further; and some of its more prominent members, said Guderian, 'did not trust the drivers of supply vehicles to have any useful ideas in the field of tactics or of operations'.[23]

In 1932 the first motor reconnaissance exercise was held in Silesia, but the equipment was restricted to the motor-cycle and the general service lorry and to the wooden anti-tank gun and wood and canvas dummy tank. Some realism was given to the development of the training of anti-tank gunners when a Captain Hildebrandt discovered that the flight path of the bullet from the standard 1898 pattern rifle was exactly the same as a shot projectile from the 37 mm anti-tank gun that had yet to come into service, so that rifles could be converted as sighting weapons for the wooden anti-tank gun dummies.[24]

From 1933 onwards, however, Lutz and Guderian began to receive support from outside of the *Heeresleitung* in that Hitler, von Blomberg and von Reichenau were all intensely interested in motorization; and although Guderian talked to Hitler only two or three times before the war, there was, according to Nehring, some form of understanding between Guderian and von Reichenau, for they got on very well together.[25] Within the *Heeresleitung*, von Fritsch was receptive to new developments and lent a ready ear to what was to become the panzer inspectorate. Beck, 'that clever staff officer of the old school', opposed Guderian and his ideas, for the men differed radically in their opinions and characters; Fromm, the chief of the *Wehramt* (*WA* later the *AHA*) within the *Heeresleitung*, was also against Guderian; Model, the principal technical general staff officer within the *Truppenamt*, firstly in T4 and then in T8, was on the side of Guderian and the panzer arm, as opposed to his assistant Mieth (who became the assistant chief of general staff at the beginning of the war) who was against them. But many of the decisions of critical importance concerning the reorganization of the German Army were being made not by von Fritsch and the *Heeresleitung* but by von Blomberg and von Reichenau; for in April 1934 Nehring, (acting

63

in Guderian's temporary absence), was sent for by von Reichenau, who was apparently making a final recommendation as to whether the *Kraftfahrtruppe* or the cavalry should be the founding arm of the new panzer troops. By 1 June the decision had been promulgated in favour of the *Kraftfahrtruppe* and Lutz's responsibilities were widened in that, in addition to his appointment as inspector (*In 6*), Lutz was given, in September 1935, a field armoured command headquarters responsible for co-ordinating and controlling the panzer units as they came into being. Guderian left the *Heeresleitung* to become Lutz's chief of staff within this *Kommando der Panzertruppe*, his place as chief of staff within the inspectorate being taken by Paulus, who had formerly been in command of *Kraftfahrabteilung 3.**

The reorganization of the motorized field troops actually dated from 1 October 1934 when two brigade headquarters were formed in Berlin with another at Kassel, these being called *Kraftfahrkommandos* for the purpose of deception. One of these brigades was intended for the raising and command of panzer regiments while the other was to form anti-tank and reconnaissance battalions, for it was proposed that these should all be part of the panzer arm. A year later, in October 1935, further brigade headquarters had been raised, including three panzer brigades, each to command two panzer regiments, these forming the armoured basis for the three newly raised panzer divisions.†

The nucleus of the new units came from the original seven divisional trucking battalions of the *Kraftfahrtruppe*, numbering in all not more than 3,000 men, and from these were formed, in October 1934, fourteen anti-tank battalions and seven motorized reconnaissance battalions, these battalions being grouped in two brigades under a controlling and temporary 'motorized-cavalry' corps. The first panzer regiments (1 and 2) based on *Kraftfahrtruppe* cadres were raised that month at Zossen and Ohrdruf.[26] To the outside world, however, the units were still known as MT troops, and they continued to wear their rose pink piping, the piping that was eventually to be used until the end of the Second World War by all panzer, anti-tank, motor-cycle and reconnaissance troops not forming part of the cavalry.

The feverish and headlong expansion from the old *Reichsheer* of the twenties to the new German Army of the thirties had temporarily destroyed the army as an effective fighting force, for, after October 1934, the cohesion of the old organizations had disappeared. After 1935 sixty-one battalions of the *Landespolizei* had gone the same way and into the same melting pot, leaving only twenty-eight battalions under police control. And what

---

* Guderian himself wore two hats, being both the chief of staff of Lutz's *Panzerkommando* (which became XVI Panzer Corps in February 1938) and the Commander of 2 Panzer Division (one of the three panzer divisions within that *Kommando*).

† The three panzer divisions were: 1 Pz. Div. (Weimar), commanded by von Weichs (from cavalry) with general staff officer Bachsler (from infantry and MT troops); 2 Pz. Div. (Würzburg), Guderian (from infantry and MT troops) with Chales de Beaulieu (from artillery and cavalry); 3 Pz. Div. (Berlin), Fessmann (from cavalry and MT troops) with Röttiger (from artillery and MT troops). (Nehring, *Die Geschichte der Deutschen Panzerwaffe 1916–45*, p. 89 *et seq.*)

remained of the *Reichsheer* appeared to be a continually moving mass of men, the proportion of the trained and experienced becoming progressively less as they were all but submerged by the great numbers of the newly inducted, who were either insufficiently trained or were unfamiliar with their recently acquired equipment and changed fighting arm. No time was allowed for formations or units to absorb and properly retrain their incoming drafts before they were required to split, and split again, continually throwing off new units and cadres.

The situation was bad enough for the infantry and artillery, but their expansion did at least proceed by a systematic and recognized pattern, and their trained officers and men were in no doubt as to what was required of them as they strove to organize and train the latest arrivals. The newly raised motorized troops on the other hand were working in a vacuum, without established and tried organization and methods, and often without equipment or proper instruction. Some idea of the confusion that must have existed at that time can be gained by tracing the forming of the first six panzer regiments that made up the three panzer divisions. *Panzer-Regimenter 1* and *2* were formed on *Kraftfahrkampftruppe* cadres, their numbers being made up to establishment by the addition of officer and other rank drafts from the cavalry. *Panzer-Regiment 3* had its first battalion based on officers and men transferred from *Reiter-Regiment 12*; its second battalion was formed from drafts from six other cavalry regiments. Within a year, however, *Panzer-Regiment 1* broke up to form *Panzer-Regiment 5* and, together with the main body of *Reiter-Regiment 4*, formed *Panzer-Regiment 6*. *Panzer-Regiment 2* was renamed as the new *Panzer-Regiment 1*, but it threw off a framework so that *Panzer-Regiment 2* should continue in existence, most of the officers and other ranks for the new *Panzer-Regiment 2* coming from *Reiter-Regiment 7*.[27] Then Panzer Regiments 1, 2 and 3 gave up drafts to form a new *Panzer-Regiment 4*. This process continued during 1936 and 1937, *Panzer-Regiment 7* being formed from further drafts from Panzer Regiments 1, 2 and 4, and *Panzer-Regiment 8* from 3, 5 and 6. And so it went on, with little apparent stability anywhere.*

It was intended to raise a motorized rifle brigade of two rifle regiments for each of the new panzer divisions.† In battle a tank crew can see and hear very little of what is going on outside, and the task of the motorized rifleman was to provide close infantry support for the tanks, to act as their eyes and ears, assist them forward, hold ground for them and protect them from anti-tank weapons and close-quarter attack; these rifle regiments were of course additional to the divisional motor-cycle battalions (formed from the cavalry) that provided the medium reconnaissance for the formation. The new motorized rifle regiments were created according to the customary formula of 'first create, then split and then split again'. The first motorized rifle

---

* Nehring said subsequently '*Es ist erstaunlich, was man der neuen Waffengattung zumuten konnte, ohne ihre Zusammenhalt zu gefährden*'.

† In fact, except for 5 Pz. Div., each division had only one rifle regiment.

regiment was formed from a cavalry regiment (*Reiter-Regiment 11*) while the second was formed almost exclusively from infantry from two different line battalions. Then the first phase of the splitting began with a third motorized regiment being put together by drafts from the first two regiments.[28]

The process of raising mobile and armoured troops was anything but straightforward since the ministry of defence and *Heeresleitung* were by no means certain of what they were trying to do; the army leadership itself could not be clear as to the place or form of mobile operations in a war of the future, and, since the need for haste was being pressed on them by the political leadership and the sudden introduction of conscription, the motorized force was rapidly coming into being before extensive field experiments and training could take place.* Basic differences of opinion and attempts to preserve vested interests led to further dissension. Lutz and Guderian championed the *Kraftfahrtruppe*, the arm of which they formed part in the Weimar days, but the infantry and cavalry inspectorates, now taking a belated interest in what was going on, began to press their own views.

The infantry not only wanted a hand in the new organizations but it wanted to retain for its own use what it regarded as a proper share of motor vehicles and anti-tank guns as soon as these should come into service. It also wanted to be sure that sufficient panzer brigades were going to be raised outside of the organization of the panzer divisions, and that their immediate tactical control should be retained by infantry formation commanders, so that foot soldiers, in their hour of need, might be given the close support of tanks in the infantry battle.† The armoured men, on the other hand, condemned such infantry thinking, arguing that this role was a prostitution of the true characteristics of the tank and a wasteful dispersion of tank resources; tanks, they said, should be used *en masse* and in a purely mobile role, in deep operative penetrations and encirclements.[29] If the matter had been left to Guderian then the infantry would indeed have got nothing; Guderian, however, had quitted the *In 6* inspectorate and was not present when the important decisions were taken; he was later to blame Fromm and

---

* A number of armoured manoeuvres were of course held, although some of these were little more than demonstrations or publicity exercises. In July 1935 the new tank arm was viewed by Hitler in a joint exercise with an infantry regiment and a dive-bomber (*Stuka*) squadron at the Zossen training ground. The next month there was a larger exercise at Munsterlage, conducted by von Weichs and von Greim and attended by von Fritsch; this exercise was to have concluded with a successful deep penetration by panzer troops, but then von Fritsch, uninvited and without warning, and in order to test the tank troops in surprise situations, continued the exercise beyond its planned duration by introducing new (and imaginary) enemy forces that attacked the panzer penetration in the flanks. Von Fritsch was apparently satisfied with the counter measures taken by the panzer arm. The 1937 autumn manoeuvres held at Neustrelitz and attended by Hitler, Mussolini, Badoglio and the British chief of general staff, were, however, near disastrous, according to Nehring: about 800 tanks were deployed under Guderian and many of them broke down or ran out of fuel so that the German Army spectators of high rank had much to say that was uncomplimentary about the panzer arm. (Nehring, pp. 88 and 93–4)

† General of Artillery Ulex, summing up the 1938 Lüneburg exercises, said of Nehring: 'What the *Herr Oberst* says may be well and true, but if ever we use these tanks in action, we will do so in the way we think fit.' (Nehring, p. 100)

his adversary Beck and others within the army command; nor did Guderian spare his old chief Lutz and his own successor, Paulus, in that they allowed additional panzer brigades to be raised from 1936 onwards 'for the purpose of providing close support for infantry'.[30]

At the same time, at the urging of the cavalry inspectorate, the decision was taken to form light divisions of two motorized regiments and one tank battalion to carry out the tasks of motorized reconnaissance and protection, ahead and to the flanks of the main formations, the role that had formerly been carried out by horsed cavalry. But the cavalry could not find the men for these new cavalry sponsored divisions unless they disbanded more of the horsed regiments, and, in consequence, the new regiments for these light divisions (known as cavalry rifle regiments) had originally to be found from the infantry, the *Kraftfahrtruppe* and the motor-cycle battalions, the officers and men of this mixed force being transferred to the cavalry in 1938.[31] Within eighteen months this pattern of light division was done away with since it was found that the role could be better performed by the panzer divisions already in being: the cavalry light divisions were later reformed as normal panzer divisions.*

The panzer division, theoretically based on a paired organization of a panzer and a motorized rifle brigade, each of two regiments, each of two battalions, remained virtually unaltered for nearly five years, except that the second rifle regiment was not always included.[32] But, as the general staff insisted, and rightly, that there was a need for further mobile divisions of motorized infantry to work with and give close support to the panzer divisions (since panzer divisions by themselves cannot hold ground), four existing infantry divisions (2, 13, 20 and 29) were motorized to meet this need and were eventually to be grouped together as motorized corps.†

In 1934, according to Nehring, German tanks had no radio, and all control was by visual signalling flags. In 1934 and 1935 many of the tank companies had few tanks, the training being carried out on Rubezahl tractors and Carden-Lloyd tracked carriers, or, if the companies were fortunate, on the 23 ton tanks returned from Kama, and on Krupp-Wanne tracked chassis (the driver training models based on the Pz I tank).‡

* They became 6, 7, 8 and 9 Panzer Divisions. These many and frequent changes were confusing, even to the troops themselves. Generally, all tank and anti-tank troops belonged to panzer troops and wore the pink (*rosa*) piping of the old *Kraftfahrtruppe* (although there were, much later, to be occasional exceptions: e.g. 1 Cavalry Division converted in 1942 to 24 Panzer Division was permitted to retain cavalry gold piping for its panzer and rifle troops). Reconnaissance troops first wore the gold of the cavalry, then, becoming an independent corps, its own brown piping, before being transferred to the panzer arm (pink) in 1943. The riflemen in the short-lived light divisions had worn cavalry gold; the riflemen in the motor-cycle troops in the panzer divisions had the traditional *Jäger* light infantry green piping. The four motorized infantry divisions retained their former white infantry piping.

† By January 1938 three motorized corps were in being: XVI Motorized (later Panzer) Corps under Lutz, made up of panzer divisions; XIV Motorized Corps under von Wietersheim consisting of motorized infantry divisions; XV Motorized Corps of cavalry light divisions; these motorized corps were not based on *Wehrkreise* but had been grouped directly under *Heeresgruppenkommando IV* (then commanded by von Brauchitsch).

‡ Tanks were known either as Mk I or Pz I.

Von Vollard-Bockelberg's *Heereswaffenamt* within the *Heeresleitung* was responsible for the design and provision of the motorized equipment for the new arm, though its fighting vehicle specialists (*Wa Prüf 6*) had necessarily to defer to Lutz, to Beck and, of course, to von Fritsch. Following Lutz's and Guderian's visit to Russia, an order had been placed in the spring of 1934 with the firm Rheinmetall for a 25 ton tank, mounting, in the early Russian fashion, a 75 mm and a 37 mm gun, together with five machine-guns; this needed a crew of seven men. A few tanks of this type were produced, but thereafter the project was discontinued, for it was decided to rely on the earlier La S (Pz I) light tank ordered from Krupp in the spring of 1931, much of the design being based on the British Carden-Lloyd. The Pz I was a two man tank, weighing about six tons, with two machine-guns mounted in the turret. A prototype had been quickly produced and the unarmoured models for driver training appeared in the summer of 1934. By the end of that year the tanks were in mass production and by the end of 1936, 3,000 Mk I tanks were already with the units. These fighting vehicles were, however, entirely outmatched by the tanks in service in the French and Red Armies, and it was essential to put heavier models into production without delay.

The first of these heavier series was the La S 100 (the Pz II) manufactured by the firm MAN, a tank weighing about 11 tons, manned by a crew of three, with a 20 mm gun and a single machine-gun, the prototype appearing in the spring of 1935. The representative of the technical inspectorate of *Wa Prüf 6* raised many justifiable reasons why this new tank should not be put into mass production, but, as Nehring has said, even though the tanks were unsatisfactory in some respects, they were adequate for the task and they were the only ones readily available. Such was the pressure for a rapid expansion of the tank arm that Guderian took the *Wa Prüf 6* representative aside, saying 'Don't you raise difficulties – I *must* have those tanks.' And so the Pz II went into production.

From 1934 onwards, however, even heavier tanks were being designed, and the firm Maybach was given orders for the 300 hp engine that was eventually to power both the Pz III and the Pz IV. The general staff had originally objected to the projected weight of these new models (18 tons), but finally this was exceeded when the first Pz III appeared in 1937, equipped with a 37 mm gun and weighing over 20 tons; in the following year a few Pz IV were in service, having the short-barrelled 75 mm gun as the main armament and weighing nearly 25 tons: the Pz III and Pz IV were produced by Krupp, Daimler and MAN. A super heavy tank – what was to become the 1942 57 ton Pz VI Tiger – had already been planned and was being designed by the firm Henschel as early as 1936.[33]

The mechanical design of all these models was of a high order and the optical and radio ancilliary equipment that was being received from 1937 onwards was of first-class quality. The weaknesses in the early tanks were that they were usually under-weight, under-gunned and under-armoured, and that there was an inadequate understanding on the part of the German designers of the effect of angle on the efficiency of armour.* These deficiencies were only appreciated after 1941 when the new class of Russian tanks that had come into service proved superior to the German models.

The most serious difficulties faced by the armoured troops in the early days, in addition to the lack of stability resulting from the rapid expansion, were the problems of training caused by inexperience, shortage of equipment, and the lack of facilities. At the formation and ministry levels there was the struggle of conflicting interests and ideas. For although Lutz had been gazetted as the first general of panzer troops as early as November 1935, there was still much uncertainty not only as to the role and likely development of the new arm but even as to its future existence in the new German Army.

One of the first problems that arose in the rapid expansion of the German Army as a whole was in the shortage of officers, for the increase from seven to twenty-one and then to thirty-six divisions meant that at least 20,000 more officers would be required for the active army, while a further 10,000 would be needed to put these divisions on to a war footing. The reduction of the training period for officer cadets from over four years down to barely two and a half years, and an increase in the number of candidates admitted (2,000 in 1938 as against 180 in 1933), provided only junior officers without former commissioned service for the bottom of the rank structure pyramid, and these could not fill any of the vacancies in the intermediate ranks. About 2,500 officers were taken in with the *Landespolizei* and a further 1,500 *Reichsheer* non-commissioned officers had been raised to officer rank. And, in addition, 1,800 former officers of the *Reichsheer* or of the imperial army had returned to the service, the First World War officers being held on a separate supplementary list known as *Ergänzungsoffiziere* and serving mainly in administrative posts.[34] But all these formed only a small fraction of the numbers required to command the new army. The lack of non-commissioned officers was even more acute, and many thousands of vacancies on the establishment remained unfilled.

The situation with the intake of men, however, was much more favourable. The last annual intake for military training in the *Kaiserheer* had been the eighteen year olds born in the year 1900, who were about thirty-five years of age in 1935. In consequence, therefore, large numbers of men above the age of thirty-five had already had a thorough basic military training and these were rapidly listed and organized into a paper reserve, the *Landwehr* up to the age of forty-five, and the *Landsturm* from over that age, these men becoming liable for recall for military refresher training if required. These

* A 60 mm plate at 60 degrees angle of slope offers the same thickness of steel to the path of a solid shot projectile as does 120 mm at the vertical; but in fact, because of the deflecting (ricochet) effect of its slope, it affords considerably more protection than that given by the double thickness plate.

reserves and their responsibilities were defined in the defence law of 21 May 1935, the same law that re-established compulsory military service for all German youth. In the autumn of that year the twenty-one year old 1914 class was called up, originally for one year with the colours, although this term was later extended, on 24 August 1936, to two years, this being done before the original one year draft already under training had been released. Each conscripted annual intake could be expected to bring 300,000 men into the army for training, with a reduction to 250,000 men for the classes from 1916 to 1918. When these conscripts completed their military service and returned to civilian life they were to form the Class I Reserve, the youngest, the fittest, and the most recently trained reserve.[35]

This left only the so-called 'white years', those born between 1901 and 1913, who had had no previous military training at all, and were too old for the conscription call-up. These were listed into a Class II Reserve, it being intended to call them up for military courses of up to three months each year; then, after undergoing an aggregate of nine months' full-time training, they would be transferred to the Class I Reserve. In fact, however, by 1939 very few had been trained, since much of the training organization was used for other purposes, particularly for running short refresher courses for non-commissioned officers and for those men who had served in the First World War, in order to prepare them for mobilization service in the *Grenzwacht* or the *Landwehr* on the eastern frontier. Hitler never forgave von Fritsch for 'his failure' to train all the 'white years' and continually harped on this subject years after the event.

A new territorial administrative organization had been hurriedly formed to prepare for the call-up of the conscript classes and to compile the lists for the other reserves. The actual notification of call-up to the individual, and its enforcement, was the task of the local police, according to the directions of the ministry of the interior, which itself acted on the information and requirements provided by the *Wehrmacht*. The instructions concerning the call-up and the new reserves were the responsibility of the OKH *Heeresamt* acting not only for the army, but also for the navy and the *Luftwaffe*.* The executive organs for the OKH were, of course, the *Wehrkreiskommandos*, each of which had a number of call-up inspectorates controlling the district *Bezirkskommandos* responsible for keeping up to date the address rolls and for the holding of personal papers for reserve officers and officer aspirants. The actual call-up was done by subordinate call-up offices (*Meldeämter*) in conjunction with a police representative. This call-up organization also undertook the requisition of horses and transport for the armed forces.[36]

It was on this hastily raised OKH and *Wehrkreis* organization that the expansion and mobilization of the German armed forces were to depend, for

---

* In 1937 Keitel and Jodl had proposed that the *Wehrkreise* should be removed from the OKH and put under the OKW; thereupon von Fritsch had threatened to resign. (Jodl's diary entries 27 January and 15 July)

there was, until the outbreak of war, no Replacement Army (*Ersatzheer*) in existence.

In 1926 the *Reichsheer* had tried to keep contact with the industrial economy in order to obtain the war equipment that might be needed to expand the army. The ordnance directorate (*Waffenamt*) within the *Heeresleitung* had set up what it called an industrial statistics company (*Stega*) with a headquarters in Berlin and regional commissioners accredited to each *Wehrkreis*. These worked through subordinate officer representatives (*Wirtschaftsoffiziere*) in order to collate information regarding industrial armament capacity, and the work they did provided a good basis for the 1933 expansion and rearmament. The information drawn up by *Stega* was so advanced by 1933 that the military had enough data to work on without taking German industry into their fullest confidence, for the need for secrecy made it preferable that information regarding the rearmament programme should not go beyond the *Heereswaffenamt* and the *Marineleitung*. From 1934 onwards, in spite of the lack of an established armament industry of any size, war equipment started to become available almost immediately.[37]

The plans for the creation of a war economy and armament industry had originally been made by the German Army, but von Blomberg decided that his own ministry must assume a controlling and co-ordinating role and present the armed forces interests and needs as a whole to the minister for the economy. In order to do this he formed inside the *Wehrmachtamt* a branch for the military economy to be known as the *Wehrwirtschaftsstab* (*W. Stb*), the nucleus for this staff being transferred in November 1934 from the army's *Heereswaffenamt*; and he used this staff as his advisory body, whose task it was to decide on priorities and the allocation of materials. In war the duties of the *W. Stb* were to cover both the war economy and economic warfare. However, the responsibility for the planning of its own requirements of equipment remained with each of the armed services, and in the army this was still done by the *Heereswaffenamt*; great freedom was permitted to the *Heeresleitung* and the *Marineleitung* to deal directly with, and even to develop, their supporting associated armament industry.

In 1935 the German Army further improved its existing ground organization for armament liaison, attaching an *Inspektion* to each *Wehrkreiskommando* in which the former *Wirtschaftsoffizier* was incorporated. The next year the military economic organization was extended down to the level of the *Bezirk*. But although the German economy proved able to provide much of the equipment for the first thirty-six divisions, and that at break-neck speed, many problems associated with the rearmament remained unsolved: and the rearmament itself had raised yet further economic difficulties. Admittedly, the relative and temporary stability of the Reichsmark, the rearmament programme, conscription and the compulsory labour service, did much to reduce the level of German unemployment. But the world economic crisis, the fluctuating world monetary standards, and the narrow basis of the Reich economy with its shortage of raw materials, food and foreign exchange, together with the high cost of rearmament, put the balance of the German economy and the overseas value of the Reichsmark on a delicate knife-edge balance that required all of Schacht's ingenuity to stabilize. The food difficulties led to the setting up of a raw materials and foreign exchange control in October 1936 in order to direct labour, improve the raw material situation and cut down on the importing of food. This control body worked in conjunction with the organization for the Four Years' Plan that was under Göring's direction.[38] All these factors militated against the German Army and the *Wehrmacht* as a whole from getting the equipment and the support of the industrial base that it required to fit itself for a protracted war.*

Hitler, no less than Schacht, had to do the best he could on the materials available; and, since he courted the popularity of the man in the street and claimed to be improving German living standards, he could not make a drastic cut in consumer production. But the dictator appears to have assumed that he had sufficient war industry capacity for his purpose; and either he did not recognize the importance of a rearmament in depth – and not merely in breadth – or he did not consider it necessary to create an industrial and economic base of sufficient size to maintain the Reich and its armed forces during a world war that might last a number of years. In the light of subsequent and post-war evidence it seems more probable that Hitler believed that he would achieve many of his aggressive aims by bluff and intimidation; should those fail to get him what he demanded he would then use the German armed forces to destroy his opponents, one after the other, delivering sudden and massive blows in short whirlwind campaigns.

Until 1 March 1935 the emerging *Luftwaffe* remained, at least as far as the outside world was concerned, part German Army and part of what was supposed to be a civil ministry, the *Reichsministerium für die Luftfahrt*. This ministry had, however, already taken in much of the military air command, adding it to its existing civil organization, so that it came to comprise a curious *mélange* of directorates: the *A-Amt* or air staff operations under Wever; the *B-Amt* responsible for civil aircraft under the *Ministerdirektor* Fisch; the *C-Amt* responsible for air force development and production under Wimmer; the *D-Amt* under Kesselring that handled the construction of airfields and barracks and general administration; the *P-Amt* for personnel administration under Stumpff and later the *E-Amt* for *Luftwaffe* supply under the control of Kitzinger.[39] Many of the officers that founded the *Luftwaffe* came from the army, some of them being non-flying personnel compulsorily transferred; but, as the military air organization expanded, the larger part of the early *Luftwaffe* officer corps was made up of *E-Offiziere*,

---

* In 1937, for example, out of a Reich monthly steel production of 1.8 million tons the *Wehrmacht* asked for an allocation of three quarters of a million: it received hardly forty per cent of this figure. (Müller-Hillebrand, *Das Heer*, Vol. 1, p. 37 *et seq.*)

men direct from civilian life who had formerly held commissions, usually in wartime or on the former reserve.*

Göring had already planned the dividing of the territory of the Reich into air force *Luftkreise*; the boundaries of these did not, however, coincide with those of the army *Wehrkreise*: *Luftkreis I* (Schweickhard) was in Königsberg, *II* (Kaupisch) in Berlin, *III* (Wachenfeld) in Dresden, *IV* (Halm) in Münster, *V* (Eberth, later Sperrle) in Munich, a coastal *Luftkreis VI* (Zander) was in Kiel, and a later *Luftkreis VII* (Felmy) in Brunswick.[40] Then, following the death of Wever in an air accident, there were some further staff and command changes: firstly Kesselring, and then Stumpff, succeeded Wever; Wimmer went to Dresden and was replaced by Udet in the *C-Amt*; Volkmann and then Bogatsch took over the *D-Amt*; and von Greim succeeded to the *P-Amt*. Kühl became inspector-general and Rüdel chief of air defence, although his responsibilities seem to have been connected with supply and general equipment (other than aircraft); the responsibility for the training organization was firstly Jeschonnek's and then Foerster's. And since Göring had come to the conclusion that he, like von Blomberg, must have his own personal secretariat in the form of a *Ministeramt*, Bodenschatz was nominated for this appointment. Many of these officers rose to prominence during the Second World War, some of them working closely with the dictator and being present in the Berlin bunker in the last days of his life.

The *Luftkreis* organization was not to endure, however, for in 1938 the *Luftkreise* were amalgamated in *Luftwaffengruppen*, *Luftwaffengruppe 1 (Ost)* under Kesselring being based on Berlin, *2 (West)* under Felmy in Brunswick, while *3 (Süd)* under Sperrle was in Munich. When the *Luftkreis* organization was done away with, its territorial responsibilities were taken over by the *Luftgaue* each bearing the same number as its army and host *Wehrkreis*. Groupings of *Luftgaue* were commanded by a *Luftwaffengruppe*.† Whereas the *Luftwaffengruppen* dealt with the main offensive and defensive operations, the commanders of the *Luftgaue* were responsible for the ground organization, anti-aircraft and local fighter defence, signal and supply installations and civil air raid defence.

The German Army had to find not only the senior officers that were to provide the framework for the new *Luftwaffe* but also a number of other ranks to form the basis of the ground organization: and it continued to be responsible, though in a reducing measure, for the basic military training of *Luftwaffe* officers and men. Then, in April 1935, it had to transfer to Göring all anti-aircraft units (in all eleven heavy and one light *Abteilungen*) formed mainly from the *Reichsheer Fahrtruppe* and field artillery. This was done against the wishes of the German Army leaders, and many of the officers and men in the flak units were unwilling to change the field grey they had worn so long for the new pattern open-necked and short blue-grey tunic of the

---

* Among those compulsorily retired and transferred in 1933 to the *Luftwaffe* (in the first instance as a civilian) was Kesselring. (*Soldat bis zum letzten Tag*, p. 25)

† In February 1939 the *Luftwaffengruppen* became *Luftflotten*.

Luftwaffe, even though they were permitted to retain the bright red artillery colours in their collar patches.[41]

There is little doubt that there was some logic in putting the flak artillery under the operational control of the *Luftwaffe* in matters of air defence; this had already been done in Germany during the First World War and it was obviously essential that anti-aircraft artillery should be closely co-ordinated with the air arm. But such command arrangements could properly apply only to those flak formations that could be used solely for air defence, and, depending on the circumstances, possibly only to those within the homeland. Whether it was necessary actually to transfer those troops from the army to the air force may, perhaps, be questioned, since gunnery is the province of the artilleryman. And when, in 1936, 88 mm batteries were sent to Spain as part of the Condor Legion under Sperrle, it was soon found that this flak equipment had many uses that were not originally envisaged by its designers, since its high muzzle velocity, range, accuracy and rapid rate of fire made it an excellent weapon for use against tanks and bunkers; it could also be used, if necessary, for the close support of infantry. All these weapon characteristics argued against the use of the 88 mm gun solely by units of the *Luftwaffe* and solely in an anti-aircraft role. Eventually the German Army was obliged to rely in war on these *Luftwaffe* flak formations, when they were allotted, not only for its air defence but also to buttress the framework of its anti-tank deployment.

Already by 1935, even before the many uses of the 88 mm flak gun had been appreciated, there was much army opposition, voiced in the military press, against the removal of these flak units from the army organization, for the German Army would, according to all appearances, have to take the field without having the anti-aircraft equipment or units for its own defence against air attack. Not before the autumn of 1938 was the army able to convert a few machine-gun battalions to a light anti-aircraft role, and this in the face of strong opposition from the *Luftwaffe*. And not before the middle years of the Second World War, and then much too late, were army manned 88 mm flak regiments added to the German Army order of battle.

But this was not the limit of *Luftwaffe* pretensions. Göring wanted his own private body of *élite* ground fighting troops that would carry his name and owe allegiance to himself, a need that became more pressing when he lost the control of the Prussian police force to Himmler. He had therefore earmarked the Prussian police battalion Wecke to be transferred as a body to the *Luftwaffe*, eventually to be expanded into *Das Jäger-Regiment General Göring* and consisting of a heavy and a light flak *Abteilung*, a light infantry battalion for guard and ceremonial duties in the capital, and a parachute battalion.[42] This small formation was a portent of Göring's military ambitions that eventually were to lead to the creation of whole *Luftwaffe* ground armies entirely separate from and independent of the German Army.

Von Blomberg, meanwhile, had other difficulties within his defence ministry. He was disliked by Himmler and Göring who, so said Bodenschatz, coveted von Blomberg's appointment.* It was partly von Blomberg's doing that the air arm had been separated from the German Army, but having successfully achieved this major surgery he found he was unable to command Göring or his *Luftwaffe*, for Göring had no intention of subordinating himself to von Blomberg. Raeder continued to deal directly with Hitler on all naval matters of any importance. There was only the German Army left to control and, since he had been appointed both defence minister and the commander-in-chief of the *Wehrmacht*, von Blomberg saw himself in time of war as the commander of the field army, in the appointment that properly belonged to von Fritsch; if he were not to be the field commander, he told von Fritsch, he would have nothing to do in time of war and 'just as well might shoot himself'.[43] He no longer had von Reichenau's support, for the unorthodox von Reichenau had proved a difficult subordinate and von Blomberg had found it convenient to post him to Munich to replace Adam in command of *Wehrkreis VII*. Von Reichenau had been relieved in October 1935 at the *Wehrmachtamt* by Keitel. Keitel, like von Reichenau, was an enthusiastic Nazi supporter, but he was entirely without von Reichenau's independence and strength of character, for he could be relied upon to do exactly what he was told. And there was a family connection with the defence minister in that Keitel's son was engaged to be married to von Blomberg's daughter.

Von Blomberg was impulsive, emotional, impractical, and without political and military stability: he liked to be thought 'forward-looking' but he lacked depth and, according to von Fritsch, he was filled with such romantic and fantastic notions that von Fritsch said that he found it easier to deal with Hitler than with von Blomberg.† Von Blomberg probably disliked von Fritsch just as he had disliked von Schleicher, and it is said that he may have created mischief in carrying tales to Hitler.[44] Von Blomberg's relationship with Beck, that had once been good, cooled rapidly as the dispute continued as to the future of the German high command. Von Blomberg was soon left without friends or allies within the party or the armed services, and he came to rely increasingly on the personal support of the German dictator.

Of von Fritsch, Guderian has said that he had charm and humour, although this was not always apparent to many of those who met him. He was an introverted man, with a haughty, taciturn, even morose, exterior, who was considered highly by his fellow generals, not only for his military ability

---

* According to von Rundstedt's post-war evidence, at a time when it was fashionable to blame von Blomberg for all the army's ills, von Blomberg was unpopular, too, with many of the senior officers of the army, for, said von Rundstedt, very few of them 'could stand him'.

† Speer, citing Brückner, said that von Blomberg 'burst into tears from sheer emotion' on listening to Hitler's 1937 Party Rally speech. (*Inside the Third Reich*, p. 116). Faber thought him 'a prima donna of touchy sensitiveness when faced with situations that demanded more than faith in the Führer'. (Faber du Faur, p. 158)

but also for his integrity and strength of character; those few who were suspicious of the Führer thought that von Fritsch and the army could be the counter-weight to the Nazis and the possible saviour of the nation should Hitler's ambitions get out of hand. This trust was to prove entirely misplaced.

Under von Fritsch the army expansion continued rapidly and efficiently, but before long the commander-in-chief of the German Army was to be charged by Hitler with being too cautious for the task. Von Fritsch was on poor terms with Göring and his relationship with Beck in the early days of his office was no closer than formal. For von Fritsch saw his functions being reduced on the one side by von Blomberg and on the other by Beck, so that he risked finally ending up with an honorary appointment in which his duties would be, as he expressed it, no more than 'making a few speeches and laying a few wreaths'.[45] Von Fritsch was politically naïve. From the few letters that he has left behind, we know that he feared that his personal correspondence was being intercepted by the Gestapo; even so, he was not obliged to echo the party line as he did; his views were illiberal; in addition to hating socialists and despising Jews, he appears to have held the Führer in high regard.

Both von Fritsch and Beck were ambitious men; and the reservations they might later have had about the nature of the Nazi régime were insufficiently strong to have made them disinclined to serve it; and indeed, when the one had been dismissed and the other had resigned from his post (but not from the army) both went into compulsory retirement, resentful that they had not been offered the further military appointments that they sought. Under Beck, the staff college, the *Kriegsakademie*, that had been covertly re-established in 1932, included in its course political lectures on Aryanism, racial biology, *Rassenhygiene*, the Jewish question and the organization of the National-Socialist state.

Beck prided himself, with justification, on being a military philosopher and strategist. Yet he thought only on the highest military plane, being 'more of a Clausewitz than a Blücher', more of a historian than a general staff planner for Germany's immediate military needs; for he was incapable of projecting himself into the future tactical employment of troops or of appreciating the military application of scientific and technological development. Beck was ultra conservative and had little conception of the proper place of the air and tank arm in the war of the future, and he did his best to resist the pretensions of the protagonists of these new arms. His military thinking was sound but outdated, just as Guderian's was sound but one-sided; Beck and Guderian, as Nehring has said, were both right in their different ways, but each had solutions to different problems in different settings; neither could see an overall picture; Guderian was insistent on the mobility of armour; Beck, on the other hand, could not envisage armoured formations as battle winning factors by themselves – even in the short term – and he concentrated solely on the mobility of the infantry corps, mobility in all its aspects – not only by motorization but by fire power and by an obstacle-crossing capability.[46]

Beck did not fear Czecho-Slovakia or, as German Army expansion got under way, Poland. But he did view France with misgiving, particularly as the German military attaché in France, and Karl-Heinrich von Stülpnagel, the head of army intelligence, rated the French Army highly. For the moment Beck does not seem to have regarded a war with the Soviet Union as an immediate possibility, but he thought that war against a combination of the Anglo-Saxon powers could only end in disaster for Germany. However that may be, Beck's views on political and strategic questions had no bearing on Germany's future since Hitler had already plotted his own path. Nor did Beck have any particular influence over von Fritsch or von Blomberg, for both of these men were more flexible and probably more clear-sighted than Beck on tactical questions, in that they intended to move ahead with the development of large armoured formations; and von Fritsch had already approved the continuation of the artillery rocket development that eventually produced the V–2. But there was little wholehearted co-operation, unity or loyalty within the high command. Von Blomberg, without friends, was blindly loyal to the Führer and was his obedient subordinate; von Fritsch threatened resignation because von Blomberg neglected to consult him; and Beck, penning his memoranda of protest that were never sent, inspired little confidence in those around him.*

Von Blomberg proceeded to widen the basis of his own office. In January 1935 he had replaced Beck as the chairman of the defence council steering committee by von Reichenau, and he attempted to restrict Beck's liaison activities with other ministries: Beck's only reply was to forbid his subordinates to deal directly with von Blomberg and Keitel and to offer his own man, Jodl, to Keitel to serve as Keitel's principal staff officer; this transfer availed Beck nothing since Jodl soon became a fanatical supporter of the principle of *Wehrmacht* command. Von Blomberg then increased the *Wehrmachtamt* by including in it a new army general staff cell for his own use, and he began to think in terms of a combined-arms general staff that led to the setting up, in 1935, of a joint staff college (*Wehrmacht-Akademie*) with Adam as its first and its last commandant; for, after von Blomberg had departed, it shut down after running but two courses.[47] Both the navy and the *Luftwaffe* resisted providing students, and Göring eventually persuaded the Führer that his *Luftwaffe* officers had more important things to do.

In July 1934 the Austrian National-Socialists, with covert German support, tried to overthrow the Dollfuss government by an armed uprising; Mussolini, by way of counter to Hitler's threat, concentrated his troops on the Austrian border, so that the German dictator was forced to give way and pretend that the Reich government was in no way involved. Hitler then

---

* On 20.4.36 von Fritsch and Raeder were given the cabinet rank of minister but this did not in effect improve von Fritsch's position in any way.

proclaimed his friendship for Italy, declaring, in July 1936, that he recognized the full sovereignty of Austria and undertook not to exert any influence, directly or indirectly, over Austrian affairs, an undertaking that he had no intention of honouring. Italy had been suffering from the League of Nations' half-hearted and ill-applied economic sanctions imposed because of Mussolini's aggression in Abyssinia, and the Italian relationship with Britain and France was poor. Like Japan, Italy was isolated, and Hitler hastened to align himself with these two nations: Germany joined Italy in supporting Franco's revolt against the Spanish republican government and, in November 1936, signed the Anti-Comintern Pact with Japan. One year later Italy also subscribed to the pact and the Fascist Axis had come into being. Meanwhile the Soviet Union had joined the League of Nations and, in 1935, entered into a defensive alliance with France.

On 14 March 1935 Hitler told his military aide Colonel Hossbach that he intended to renounce Versailles and publicly proclaim, what had already been happening, the expansion and rearmament of the German Army; at the same time he said that he would announce the introduction of conscripted military service. Hossbach himself suggested, so he subsequently said, that the figure for the peacetime standing army should be broadcast 'at thirty-six divisions'.[48] Two days later the defence law was made public: the *Reichswehr* had become the *Wehrmacht*. A few months later, on 1 June 1935, the defence minister was renamed as the minister for war: von Fritsch, instead of being the *Chef der Heeresleitung*, had become the Commander-in-Chief of the Army, and the *Heeresleitung* was redesignated as the army high command (OKH) while the *Truppenamt* became the army general staff. That summer the German government publicly admitted that the general staff *Kriegsakademie* and a *Luftwaffe* (independent from the army since March 1935) were already in existence.

Von Fritsch and Beck were alarmed at the German rearmament being announced in this fashion, and the figure of thirty-six divisions apparently took them by surprise. Von Fritsch would have preferred to expand more slowly so that at least part of the new army might have been kept near battle readiness; Beck and Karl-Heinrich von Stülpnagel believed that, with its armed forces in disarray, Germany was in no condition to fight a war of any sort, and Beck noted that 'it is not what we do but the way that we do it that is so bad'.[49] On 30 March 1935 von Reichenau, when still with the *Wehrmachtamt*, had signed a memorandum enumerating circumstances in which a surprise attack might be required against Czecho-Slovakia. Then, on 2 May (the same day as the signing of the Franco–Soviet treaty promising mutual aid to Czecho-Slovakia), von Blomberg asked von Fritsch for his views on *Schulung*, a plan embracing a surprise attack by Germany on Czecho-Slovakia, von Fritsch being told to ignore the disorganized state of the German Army and its incomplete rearmament, since 'improvements at a later date would make such an attack feasible'. Beck was not necessarily against such action if the international situation should be favourable and the political and military objectives clear; but in May 1935 he feared that Germany would become involved in a war that it was unready to fight. On 3 May he told von Fritsch that if the intention of von Blomberg's *Schulung* directive was to prepare for war, then he (Beck) could not shoulder this responsibility and must ask to be relieved of his post.[50] Beck noted, moreover, that the minister's directive was unclear in its scope and lacked direction, particularly in so far as it contained nothing about the military objectives for the army, 'without which no strategic or tactical studies could begin'.* Nothing, however, came of Beck's objections, nor did he resign. Hitler himself was both surprised and disappointed at the generals' attitude to his bold announcements and energetic policies, for he appears to have thought that, as military men, they would have welcomed the opportunity to go campaigning.

In that same summer the Anglo–German naval treaty had been concluded by which Germany was to have a surface war fleet of one third of the size of the British, and a parity in submarines. This treaty, too, was to be abrogated by Hitler as soon as it suited him, but, for the moment, it served for use as a political wedge between the British and the French and to quieten the diplomatic outcry against the earlier proclamation of the rearmament defence law.

Beck had described von Blomberg's *Schulung* proposal for a surprise attack against Czecho-Slovakia as an act of desperation that could only end in defeat; the plan had then been left in abeyance. A new plan, *Aufmarsch Rot*, mainly defensive in its character, was then drawn up late in 1935; its purpose was to defeat a possible French invasion and, at the same time, hold the Czechs back on the south-east frontier, and to do this, three German armies were to be deployed on the west while a fourth was to be responsible for the east and south-east. By 1937, however, Beck had authorized the preparation of *Aufmarsch Grün*, a *pre-emptive* blow at the Czechs before a French offensive could be developed, although he himself was said to have considered the concept to be absurd since it would have ensured not only French, but British, intervention as well.

On 24 June 1937 von Blomberg issued a comprehensive directive with a deviously worded preamble that said that the army must be ready 'in case of outside attacks, to exploit, by military means, favourable political opportunities'. Von Blomberg listed possible eventualities, to be added to *Aufmarsch Rot* and *Grün*; and these were – an attack against Austria (*Sonderfall Otto* – said to be against a possible Hapsburg restoration), action against Republican Spain (*Sonderfall Richard*), and a possible extension of *Rot* and *Grün* in case Britain, Poland and Lithuania should also intervene. For there should be no illusions, said von Blomberg, about the path that

---

* This appears to have been the first of many ministry for war and *Wehrmacht* high command directives issued between 1935 and 1945, many of which were careless of world-wide conditions and unclear as to politico-strategic aims and objectives, and this largely because they were dictated orders emanating from one man and not a directive arrived at by study and joint consultation.

Britain would take. No action was, however, taken by the army high command on *Otto* or on the possible extension of *Rot* and *Grün*.[51]

This June 1937 directive, although drafted by von Blomberg, was unlikely to have been prepared without prior consultation with Hitler. Indeed the words in the preamble were undoubtedly Hitler's own. By the middle of 1937 Hitler had still not immersed himself in the detail of military affairs, and the direction was left in von Blomberg's hands, except that von Blomberg was required to consult the chancellor on matters of importance. The important directives and orders still originated from the war ministry, usually on the initiative of the minister, but only after consultation between von Blomberg and Hitler. As in the days of the Weimar Republic, the orders were first countersigned by the minister and were then sent to the head of state for signature. After 1937, however, the situation changed radically in that Hitler began to take a close and personal interest in the details of rearmament and in the preparation of military directives and plans; part of the reason for this was Hitler's increasing lack of confidence in the high-ranking generals of the army, for he doubted their determination and loyalty to his person and their unstinted readiness blindly to obey his orders.

At the beginning of 1936 Hitler had decided that the next treaty to be unilaterally abrogated would be the Locarno Pact that had provided for the demilitarization of Germany's western frontier. On 12 February 1936 Hitler told von Fritsch (in von Blomberg's absence) to prepare to send German troops into the Rhineland in the near future, and he later mentioned the matter to von Blomberg 'in an off-hand manner', as though the business was an afterthought and of no consequence. Von Blomberg, von Fritsch and Beck were strongly against the idea but, on 7 March 1936, after some last minute vacillation, Hitler ordered three infantry battalions to march into the Rhineland amid the acclaim of the German population and against the protests of the western world.[52]

The rift between Hitler and von Blomberg began at about this time. When Geyr von Schweppenburg, the German military attaché to Britain, warned von Blomberg of the gravity of the situation as viewed in London and what he believed to be the imminence of British action against Germany, von Blomberg suggested to Hitler that the German troops be withdrawn. The dictator, after a moment's hesitation, held firm.* 'Everything', as von Stülpnagel said, 'was wrecked by von Blomberg, who just drifted helplessly.' Thereafter, both Hitler and Beck came to doubt von Blomberg's leadership, although for different reasons; Hitler, because of von Blomberg's lack of enthusiasm in carrying out orders, and Beck, because von Blomberg weakly acquiesced to anything that Hitler wanted. Meanwhile Faupel, Hitler's ambassador to Franco, was asking for three divisions for Spain, a proposal that horrified Beck since he knew that von Blomberg would not resist it. Hitler, however, on his own account decided against it, and the German

---

* Hitler well knew that the German Army could not have resisted French intervention.

assistance to Franco, which was not extensive, was shouldered mainly by the *Luftwaffe.**

In the autumn of 1937 von Blomberg had asked Hitler to convene an inter-service conference to discuss the allocation of raw materials, and this developed into the 5 November chancellery meeting that came to be regarded as a landmark in Hitler's progress towards the Second World War. Hitler intended to raise much wider issues, for he was much dissatisfied with von Fritsch, whom he regarded as hesitant and dilatory, and with the slow rate of expansion of the German Army.

The conference was attended by von Blomberg, von Fritsch, Göring, Raeder and von Neurath, the Foreign Minister; no record appears to have been made, although Hossbach, Hitler's military aide, made notes after the conference as to what had been said. In addressing the meeting Hitler said that the rearmament of the Reich would be completed shortly after 1943, and thereafter the equipment now being issued to the German Army would become outdated; in the same period German initiative relative to other European powers might decline with the run-down in dynamism of the Nazi party movement; and the foreign exchange situation might cause further problems. Although the National-Socialist government had always been at great pains publicly to declare that the *Wehrmacht* was meant only for the defence of the Reich against attack, its real purpose, said Hitler, was to exploit any opportunity that might offer itself in Europe: this might take the form of internal trouble in France or of a Franco–Italian war, for the war in Spain, the dictator thought, might go on yet for years.† It was essential to secure the south-eastern (Austrian and Czech) flank and to neutralize Russia through Japan; even though the Soviet Union and Poland might want to challenge Germany, they were bound to move slowly and, for this reason, they must be presented with a *fait accompli.* Hitler left his audience in no doubt that he intended to accept the risks of a world war in the furtherance of his expansionist political aims.[53]

Von Blomberg and von Fritsch then spoke out to the Führer against any idea of war with France and Britain, and von Blomberg drew attention to the strength of the defences in Northern Bohemia. Göring said little, although he came under attack during the meeting from both von Blomberg and von Fritsch, in criticism that Hitler listened to without making any comment; yet there are some grounds for believing that Göring, too, was uncomfortable at the dictator's speech and that much of it was new to him. All the listeners were oppressed with a sense of emergency: Göring suggested that the *Luftwaffe* troops in Spain should be withdrawn to the homeland and von Fritsch thought that his own forthcoming leave to Egypt should be cancelled. Hitler, however, said that all this was in the future and that there was no

---

* The army assistance to Franco consisted of little more than training cadres, among which was *Panzer Abteilung 88* of three companies of Pz I and Pz II tanks under von Thoma's command.

† At this meeting Hitler voiced entirely unrealistic views on what he termed the high fighting value of the Italian armed forces.

pressing urgency about any of these matters; no special action need be taken for the moment.

Afterwards von Fritsch, Beck and von Neurath met in the Bendlerstrasse to discuss this ominous chancellery meeting; von Fritsch and von Neurath then asked separately for an interview with the chancellor. Hitler declined to see von Fritsch and purposely delayed the interview with von Neurath, an interview that was shortly to lead to von Neurath's removal and the dismissal of von Blomberg and von Fritsch.

On 12 January 1938 the widower von Blomberg married a woman who, it was later alleged, had a police record of conviction for immorality, the marriage taking place in the war ministry with Hitler and Göring being present as witnesses. What von Blomberg knew of his bride's past life can never be proved. Immediately after the wedding, however, the chief of the Berlin police showed the new Frau von Blomberg's police record to Keitel, who sent him on to Göring. By 24 January the file was in Hitler's hands, together with another dossier, produced by Göring and Himmler, alleging homosexual practices against von Fritsch. The whole business was very convenient to Hitler, Göring and Himmler. Von Blomberg was prevailed upon to resign and take himself and his wife to Italy, using exchange currency funds made available to him by the Führer. Von Fritsch, although he was answerable to military and not to civil jurisdiction, had been summoned for interrogation by the Gestapo that began rounding up von Fritsch's orderlies in their quest for incriminating evidence. Since the dossier on von Fritsch had been in existence for a long time and is said to have been seen by Hitler some two years before, the charge against von Fritsch was patently a conspiracy between Himmler, Göring and Hitler.[54]

Göring wanted von Blomberg removed, but, at the same time, intended to ensure that von Fritsch did not get the coveted post of minister for war. Hitler wanted to be rid of von Blomberg and von Fritsch, together with Beck, a man who, according to what the dictator said in 1944, 'busied himself with the most incredibly petty plans'.[55] Von Blomberg had suggested Göring to the dictator as his successor, but Hitler did not favour the idea; von Blomberg then proposed that the Führer should himself become the de facto commander-in-chief. On 27 January, after von Blomberg had taken his departure, Hitler discussed with Keitel, probably only as a matter of form, the question of von Blomberg's replacement.[56] Von der Schulenburg, von Rundstedt, von Stülpnagel, von Leeb and von Reichenau were proposed in turn and rejected.[57] The von Fritsch case, too, appears to have been gone over at this meeting; it was apparently accepted that von Fritsch was in fact guilty, for, on Keitel's return to the Bendlerstrasse, Keitel told Jodl that von Fritsch would have to go, and he (Keitel) claimed to have known for two years that von Fritsch was a pervert. The matter of his replacement had been discussed between Keitel and Hitler, and it was apparently at Keitel's suggestion that von Brauchitsch was selected as von Fritsch's successor.

Von Brauchitsch, at that time commanding Heeresgruppe IV, was ordered to report directly to Keitel in the capital, and negotiations began between the two as to the terms under which Hitler would be prepared to accept von Brauchitsch as von Fritsch's replacement, Keitel acting, so it would appear, as Hitler's intermediary and spokesman.* Von Brauchitsch would be required to integrate the German Army with National-Socialism and to work with a new chief of army general staff. Von Brauchitsch, however, had his own personal problems that had brought him to the point of asking to be retired; for some years he had been living apart from his wife who declined to divorce him unless she could be assured of a substantial financial settlement; the impecunious von Brauchitsch wanted to remarry, and it was therefore suggested that the money for the settlement should be provided for him from the Führer's privy purse.† At length von Brauchitsch agreed to the Führer's terms.[58]

Von Brauchitsch was interviewed by Hitler in von Rundstedt's presence and he accepted the post that was not yet vacant. Once again the matter of a successor for von Blomberg was ventilated and von Rundstedt opposed any suggestion of appointing von Reichenau. It was then that Hitler announced that 'with Keitel's help' he would himself become the *de facto* commander-in-chief of the *Wehrmacht* with Keitel filling the post of *Chef der OKW*.‡

On 31 January von Rundstedt was again received by Hitler who wanted his opinion on a number of generals. The significance of this move was lost on von Rundstedt, but the next day Keitel appeared in Beck's office with a list of senior officer changes that had presumably been decided upon by Hitler the previous day, changes that may have reflected some of von Brauchitsch's wishes. In his haste to depart Keitel inadvertently left the list behind him, and on it Beck saw his own name, with Halder noted as his replacement.[59] On 3 February Hitler required von Fritsch to resign and on 4 February all the army retirements were announced publicly, together with other new government and diplomatic appointments, for, as Jodl said, the Führer wanted to divert public attention, at home and abroad, away from the *Wehrmacht*, by heading the changes with those of ministerial rank. Schacht made way for Funk and von Neurath for von Ribbentrop; the ambassadors von Hassell and Dirksen were replaced by von Mackensen and Ott. Keitel was given the ministerial rank of the departed von Blomberg. Beck, however, was left in his appointment for the time being in order that the army moves should not take on the appearance of a purge. Among the generals to be removed or retired were von Schwedler, the head of the Army Personnel Department (who was succeeded by Keitel's younger brother Bodewin), von Leeb the commander of *Heeresgruppe II* and, to the surprise of all, Lutz, the commander of panzer troops, who was to make way for Guderian.

* The new *Gruppenkommando IV* was formed in Leipzig in 1937; in 1938 (*Gr Kdo*) *II* moved from Kassel to Frankfurt a.M., and *V* and *VI* were formed in Vienna and Hanover: all *Gr Kdos* were then renamed as *Heeresgruppenkommandos*.

† After the war von Brauchitsch denied that he received such money. (Cf. K-J. Müller, *Das Heer und Hitler*, p. 268 note 65).

‡ Buchheit considers that Hitler may have been following Mussolini's lead in assuming such a post.

At the time of the announcement Hitler addressed the senior officers in the main hall of the war ministry, during which he attacked the departed von Blomberg and described the absent von Fritsch in so poor a light that he made clear his own opinion that von Fritsch was guilty and that there could be no question of giving him another appointment. Once again he reassured his listeners by giving what he called his sacred pledge against SS encroachments, saying that he would not appoint a non professional man to a military post; but at the same time he made it clear that he regarded the generals themselves as being entirely responsible for the present state of affairs. The *Wehrmacht*, he said, 'was hardly worthy of his efforts to hide its shame by reorganizing the entire government'; the 100,000 army had failed to produce any great leaders, and henceforth he, Hitler, would concern himself with personnel matters and ensure that the right appointments were made.[60] Neither von Rundstedt nor Beck nor any of the other generals made any objection or remonstrance; to many of those present the revelations concerning von Blomberg and von Fritsch were new and unexpected, and left them in stunned silence.[61] Hitler's political and moral stature had by now grown in their eyes to such proportions that the generals were obliged to think that there must be some basis for what he said. After the meeting Hitler was said to have sneered to his SA stalwarts that 'the army's generals were either cowards or fools'.[62]

During the previous week, at the time of von Fritsch's interrogation by the Gestapo, there had, according to von Manstein, been a stormy meeting between Halder and Beck in which, reputedly, Halder said that the army commander-in-chief was being deposed and that the time had come to march on the Gestapo headquarters in Prinz Albrechtstrasse.[63] Beck called Halder's proposal 'revolution and mutiny'. And when, on 28 January, List, the commander of *Wehrkreis IV* in Leipzig, at Goerdeler's insistence, drove to Berlin to see Beck, he found him vacillating and without purpose or clear ideas.[64] Adam said that Beck complained to him after Hitler's address of 4 February that Hitler 'had not kept his promise to take no action without first seeking the opinion of the chief of the army general staff'. To which Adam, according to his own version, had replied, 'You are a fool.'[65]

Von Fritsch was to be tried by court martial, but this was delayed by Hitler's occupation of Austria. The court martial reconvened on 17 March and von Fritsch was acquitted two days later, largely due to the energy and skill of his defence counsel who had himself unearthed evidence that refuted the accusation, evidence long before known to the Gestapo. Within the month von Fritsch wrote to Hitler asking 'for the public restoration of his honour and the disciplining of the SS'. Hitler did not reply.[66] Von Fritsch then went into retirement resentful not only at the treatment that he had suffered but also because he had not been offered another appointment. Hitler justified his action to the army saying that *he* (not von Fritsch) had been the victim of a shameless deception, though he rejected any charge that the SS accusations had been brought frivolously. The villain of course, said

Hitler, was the false witness Schmidt: and since the law could only award imprisonment for perjury, he (Hitler), who regarded himself as above that law, 'had ordered him to be shot'.

No general had supported Hitler more enthusiastically and faithfully than von Blomberg, and no general, except Keitel, was more despised by the dictator.* Over those generals 'who were with him' the Führer exercised patronage mingled with contempt; for those that were against him he reserved his hatred. Yet all the generals, including those few who had reservations as to the nature of his government, were deeply conscious of the debt that they owed this man in raising the nation to political and military equality with the rest of the world, and they were grateful for the expansion and re-equipping of the army and for the improvement in their own prospects and fortunes. Hitler himself was determined to increase his personal control over the German Army, a control that was to become tighter with each successive year, and this determination became unmistakeable from the end of 1937. The soldiers' and officers' loyalty was already vested in his person by the oath of August 1934.

Hitler intended that the *Luftwaffe* should be taken away from the German Army not because he was persuaded of the correctness of operational and tactical doctrines that would demand such a separation, but because he wanted this new arm as a counterweight to the army. Its command had been entrusted not to an army general but to Göring, a junior fighter pilot of the First World War, a captain appointed almost directly to general rank and then to field-marshal. The *Waffen SS* had replaced the SA as the army's main rival, and it was at first cautiously and then rapidly expanded into an *élite* arm entirely independent of the army. And notwithstanding the restoration by Hitler on 12 May 1933 of the traditional and much prized right of the army to try its own offenders and award its own punishments for crimes against both the military and the civil code (*Militärgerichtsbarkeit*), the Fritsch case had demonstrated that Himmler could remove even the commander-in-chief from the security of his Bendlerstrasse office and subject him to Gestapo interrogation.†

That von Blomberg should have entered into his unfortunate second marriage sheds some light on the mentality of the man. The marriage was certainly so opportune for Hitler that one might be tempted to suspect a SS intrigue, although there appears to be no evidence that this was so. The Fritsch case, on the other hand, was a Hitler directed conspiracy, for Hitler was determined to be rid of von Fritsch as well as von Blomberg. He

* Hitler despised von Blomberg for his naïvety and his 'lack of nerve'; yet in his own circle, and at a later date, he acknowledged von Blomberg's aid 'in ridding the army of a great number of reactionaries and in silencing the others'. (Cf. K-J. Müller, *Das Heer und Hitler*, p. 256 note 11, and Messerschmidt, p. 210 note 746)

† Under the Weimar Republic there were no courts martial, and all crimes, including the more serious military offences, had to be tried by the civil courts, a member of the Judge-Advocate's Department (*Heeresanwaltschaft*) acting as prosecutor. (At the same time as the abolition of civil jurisdiction, the elected men's welfare and messing representatives, the *Vertrauensleute* introduced in 1921, were discontinued; these were regarded as a relic of the revolutionary soldiers' councils.)

wanted a commander-in-chief of the army who was in his personal debt, who would bring the army closer to National-Socialism and who would do what he was told, particularly in the matter of general appointments. Hossbach, Hitler's army aide, had disobeyed instructions given to him by Hitler that von Fritsch should not be forewarned as to the charges being made against him: Hossbach was replaced by Major Schmundt, an officer who had formerly been Keitel's adjutant when Keitel commanded an artillery regiment; he had no special loyalty to von Brauchitsch and showed himself to be devoted to the Führer.* The Army Personnel Office had been purged of von Schwedler and his two principal deputies and entrusted to Keitel's brother. The army chiefs that were displeasing to the Führer or inconvenient to von Brauchitsch began to be retired from that February of 1938, and the more senior generals who were promoted thereafter were usually the personally loyal (*treu ergeben*) or the technicians (*Nursoldaten*), those without political or personal views but who could be counted upon to carry out the dictator's orders.

* So much so that he soon became known among the general staff as 'His Master's Voice'. (Messerschmidt, p. 311)

CHAPTER FOUR

Towards a War Army

To mobilize an army the high command has to convert peacetime troops in their garrison stations, usually on restricted establishments and light scales of equipment, to a fully mobile and independent force that can operate and maintain itself in the field; in modern times it has also meant the call-up of large numbers of reserve formations to be added to the peacetime field force – being ready for field service on, or shortly after, mobilization day – and the stockpiling of reserves of equipment.

Germany, however, had to start almost from scratch, and was faced by apparently insuperable problems. The expansion of a peacetime army from seven to thirty-six divisions and beyond did not provide Germany with a field army that could be mobilized at short notice ready to match the armed forces of France or the Soviet Union. And, whatever the peacetime strength, a large reserve and a replacement army were required in addition, together with stockpiled munitions and equipment, not only to mobilize the army but also to keep it in the field; and the build-up of men and materials for this would have involved the diversion of enormous resources of manpower, supplies and production capacity. Since Germany could not rely on sea imports in war, or indeed in any period of acute international tension before such a war, it was essential that supplies and raw materials should be accumulated in the Reich in time of peace.

The military planners were further bedevilled by a lack of political direction as to what sort of army would be needed after the German frontiers had been made secure against a possible Polish or Czech invasion. Consequently the mobilization preparations became a hastily contrived and incomplete patchwork that suffered not only from a lack of resources but also from the necessity of keeping the mobilization plans attuned to Hitler's demand that the whole system should be sufficiently flexible to allow the dictator political freedom in international affairs. So it came about that the mobilization plans had to take account of a number of possible political and military situations, largely of Hitler's making, that were to involve the German Army in partial mobilization measures, some affecting only the peacetime army, and some only certain border *Wehrkreise*. For Hitler required that the mobilization scheme should be so organized that mobilization could progress by stages, some secret and some overt; it also had to allow for a full as well as a partial mobilization, with or without public proclamation; or, if it so suited Hitler, mobilization could be ordered without any pre-mobilization preparation having been done at all.[1] In addition, mobilization could merely mean the bringing of peacetime field formations to battle readiness without any movement of troops towards the frontiers or other emergency measures being taken.

From 1935 onwards, the planning began for the raising of a war army (*Kriegsheer*) that was to consist of the peacetime field army (*Feldheer*) divisions raised to war strength by the intake of mobilization reinforcements and equipment, and of a new reserve army to be found by the embodiment of reserve divisions yet to be formed. Then, in addition to organizing a full *Kriegsheer*, plans were to be made in peace for a Replacement Army (*Ersatzheer*), a formation that would exist only after mobilization. Both the *Kriegsheer* and the Replacement Army were to be based on the existing *Wehrkreise*, which were in reality corps districts, for, when the mobilization of the *Feldheer* was complete, the *Wehrkreiskommandos* would take the field as corps headquarters, and they and the field army divisions would move away from their peace locations. Their place would then be taken by deputy *Wehrkreis* commanders, appointed in peacetime, with replacement headquarters and formation and unit rear echelons occupying the now vacant accommodation, and these would all form part of the Replacement Army. The commander of the Replacement Army would command not only the replacement *Wehrkreise* but he would also be responsible to the OKH for the reinforcement, manning, equipping and basic training of the new formations and units of the home army and for the general control of the home administrative units and depots.

The first requirement, however, before the building of the framework of the *Kriegsheer*, and before even the *Reichsheer* had arrived at its figure of twenty-one peacetime divisions, was to strengthen the border defences, particularly in the east. At the beginning of 1934, all border defence planning still dealt only with the east, with the menace of Poland and Czecho-Slovakia, and other frontiers were ignored. A partially disguised military organization, the *Grenzschutz Ost*, had been set up on the Polish and Czecho-Slovak frontiers, based on static regimental headquarters located at Deutsch-Krone, Neustettin, Küstrin, Breslau, Glogau, Oppeln, Schweidnitz, Dresden and Regensburg, these being known, as a deceptive measure, as garrison headquarters (*Kommandanturen*).[2] At the end of 1935 this organization, that had since been redesignated the border guard (*Grenzwacht*), was reformed, in that the *Kommandanturen* were redesignated as army stations (*Heeresdienststellen*); the headquarters at Küstrin, Breslau and Glogau were disbanded but four new stations were sited, for the first time, in the west and south of Germany, at Stuttgart, Giessen, Dortmund and Munich, in order to cover the borders with France and Austria. Then, after the occupation of the Rhine demilitarized zone in March 1936, a new station was set up in Heidelberg while the others in the west were moved nearer to the French frontier at Freiburg, Koblenz and Cologne. In 1938, as the Reich frontier expanded yet again into Austria, the *Heeresdienststellen* were deployed even further afield, to Aussig, Innsbruck, Klagenfurt and Krems.

The border guard continued, for the time being, to use administrative and non-tactical descriptions for its headquarters and formations. The regiment was known as the sector (*Abschnitt*) and the battalion as the *Unterabschnitt*: the commanders and staffs of these formations were permanent regular officers, and the officers and men to form the battalions were earmarked from the readily available reserve at the frontier – the paramilitary border and customs police that came under the Reich finance minister, reinforced by conscripted army reservists living near the borders.* This border and customs police organization was to become part of the army border guard on mobilization. The static frontier *Grenzwacht* organization could be further reinforced on mobilization by construction battalions from the labour service working in the area; these consisted of militarily untrained conscripts doing their six months' labour service before entering the *Wehrmacht*.

The *Grenzwacht* organization covered all borders (except those adjacent to Denmark, Switzerland and, later, Slovakia), and its basic sub-unit was the standard infantry company. Sometimes, however, anti-tank and pioneer troops were allotted in support, and the *Grenzwacht* also commanded the strong points within the border zone, these being equipped with artillery and manned on mobilization by the older age-group *Landwehrpflichtige* from the nearby population.[3]

Later on, as war became imminent, it was felt that this static *Grenzwacht* reserve force was inadequate for its task, and separate *Grenztruppen* were raised, from autumn 1938 onwards, for the defences on the West Wall and on the Oder–Warthe bend in the east, these forming a regular part of the active army and being made up of all arms groups. At the end of the summer of 1939, these were given the same organization as regular infantry divisions, being fully mobile and capable of taking the field. The East Prussian fortress troops in Königsberg and Lötzen that were to be raised on mobilization were organized as reserve infantry divisions.

In 1939 the expansion of the border command organization gave some indication of the way that Germany might fight a European war, in that these mainly defensive measures now took place only on Germany's western frontier. On 1 March two new border corps headquarters (*Generalkommandos Eifel und Oberrhein*), in Bonn and Baden-Baden respectively, were added to the existing single corps headquarters (*Saarpfalz*) in Kaiserslautern, these three border corps headquarters being entirely independent of the *Wehrkreise* in which they were located.[4]

* The *Zollgrenzschutz* border/customs police could, if need be, be reinforced before mobilization in times of crisis by conscripts from the local border population to become the VGAD (*Verstärkter Grenz-Aufsicht Dienst*). On mobilization the VGAD joined the army.

The mobilization strength of all border troops numbered almost a quarter of a million men, about 100,000 being allocated to the west, nearly 60,000 against Poland and over 30,000 covering East Prussia.

Meanwhile the creation of the new peacetime army had continued apace. In October 1936, with the forming of *Wehrkreis XI* in Hanover and *Wehrkreis XII* in Wiesbaden, the twelve army corps scheduled in the rearmament defence law of the previous year had already been raised. After this, the expansion continued without any further public announcement being made.

During 1937 a *Wehrkreis XIII* was formed in Nuremberg and, at the beginning of 1938, three motorized corps (XIV, XV and XVI at Magdeburg, Jena and Berlin) were raised to command, respectively, the motorized, the light and the panzer divisions; these differed from the previous corps in that they had no territorial (*Wehrkreis*) basis.* Then, with the Austrian *Anschluss* occupation and the incorporation of the Austrian armed forces into the *Wehrmacht*, two further corps *Wehrkreise* came into being in April 1938, *Wehrkreis XVII* in Vienna (later in Linz) and *Wehrkreis XVIII* in Salzburg.† Then in the summer of 1939 a XIX Corps was raised in Vienna to command the panzer and the light division there, this motorized corps having no territorial responsibility.[5]

After the occupation of the demilitarized zone the German Army received a substantial reinforcement by the transfer of a further twenty-eight battalions of Rhineland armed police. These had always been counted as a military asset, even before the occupation of the zone, and they had been secretly instructed to hold themselves in readiness to join the German Army in the event of war, even though they retained the green police uniform without the steel helmet and had no artillery support. And the police inspectorate for the demilitarized zone had kept in close touch with the *Heeresdienststellen* recently set up in the west, with an exchange of key personnel between the Rhineland and Brandenburg, so that the Rhineland police military training was already standardized with that of the German Army. Then, from March 1936, after the occupation of the Rhineland and when the need for deception no longer existed, the Rhine *Landespolizei* changed its uniforms and was incorporated into the German Army, forming eight new regiments, the main body of 25, 26, 33 and 34 Infantry Divisions.[6]

There were comparatively few formations raised during 1937. The divisional numbers from 37 to 43 had been left open and it was originally

---

* The German Army of the Republic and of the Third Reich followed the system of the old imperial army in the numbering of its formations, this being done by alternating arabic and roman figures: e.g., armies were numbered in arabic figures, corps were roman, and divisions were arabic; brigades (no longer in being inside infantry divisions after 1919) were roman, but regimental numbering was arabic; battalions were roman and companies arabic. In this book, and in accordance with more modern German military usage, all corps designations after September 1939 (at which time they were separated from the *Wehrkreise*), will be shown in arabic numbering.

† The Austrian armed forces at the beginning of 1938 had consisted of seven infantry or alpine divisions, one motorized division, and two air regiments.

intended that these sequences should be taken by the three panzer divisions, the mountain division and the three light divisions in the course of being raised. With the take-over of the Austrian Army in April 1938, two Austrian infantry divisions took the numbers of 44 and 45, and two Austrian alpine divisions became 2 and 3 Mountain Divisions, and the Austrian motorized division became 4 Light Division of the German Army. In the autumn of 1938 the new 4 and 5 Panzer Divisions were raised in Würzburg and Oppeln, and 46 Infantry Division in Karlsbad. This was the final regular division to be formed by the German Army in peacetime and was the last formation of the *Friedensheer*. The incorporation of units of the Austrian *Bundesheer* and the raising of additional battalions to complete some of the regiments to their full three battalion establishment, raised the German infantry strength during 1938 to 124 regiments of 336 battalions and eleven battalions of border guard troops. The number of infantry training and reinforcement (*Ergänzung*) battalions had meanwhile increased to 129.[7]

The infantry divisions kept very much to the organization of the old *Reichsheer* without returning to the brigade establishment of the imperial army, the brigade being retained only for some armoured, cavalry, and mountain troops. The infantry divisions had three regiments of three battalions, each of three rifle companies and a machine-gun company.* The mountain *Jägerregiment* was similar in its organization except that each battalion was designed to be self supporting should it be out of range, out of touch, or away from its parent regiment.†

Some of the infantry regiments had reinforcement companies for specialists (infantry and anti-tank gunners and signallers) as part of their organization, these taking the company numbering within the regiment from 15 to 17. In addition to the reinforcement companies there were the 129 reinforcement infantry battalions, distributed in peacetime one or two to each infantry regiment. Since they did not form an integral and permanent part of the parent regiment their companies had their own system of numbering.

Motorized machine-gun battalions were raised from the end of 1935 onwards and consisted of three companies each of sixteen heavy machine-guns. From 1937 a fourth anti-tank company was added to these

---

* The rifle company had nine light and two heavy machine-guns and three light mortars, while the machine-gun company, which in reality was a support-weapons company, had eight heavy machine-guns and six medium mortars. The companies were numbered in sequence throughout the regiment, the machine-gun companies taking the numbers 4, 8 and 12. Directly under the regimental headquarters came an infantry signals platoon and a horse-mounted platoon together with the heavy mortar company (13) that, from 1936 onwards, became the infantry-gun company equipped with two short-range 150 mm and six light 75 mm infantry-guns: 14 Company was the anti-tank company with twelve 37 mm anti-tank guns. The infantry-gun, manned by infantrymen, was in fact a gun/howitzer used not only for direct (line of sight) fire at close ranges but also for normal artillery supporting fire in both the lower and the upper registers. The 75 mm fired a 12 lb shell up to a range of 4,000 yards; the 150 mm gun fired an 80 lb shell about 5,000 yards. The infantry-gun company afforded the infantry regimental commander his own short-range artillery support without calling on divisional artillery resources.

† The *Jägerregiment* had therefore five companies, No. 4 being an infantry-gun and mortar company and No. 5 the machine-gun and infantry pioneer company. Only the No. 16 anti-tank company remained directly under the regiment.

machine-gun battalions. Then, in 1938, steps were taken to convert the machine-gun battalions to a dual role so that they might also be used to engage low flying aircraft. However, since this role could, officially, be undertaken only by the *Luftwaffe*, their anti-aircraft employment could not be admitted at an inter-service level and they still retained their official MG designation. It had been intended that each infantry division should have its organic machine-gun battalion, but, by 1939, only twenty-five such battalions were in existence.[8]

On 1 April 1937 the first German Army parachute infantry company was raised at Stendal, where it was to do its parachute training with the nearby *Luftwaffe* parachuting school. Meanwhile Göring had formed his own parachute battalion from the police battalion Wecke, part of the *Jäger/Flakartillerie-Regiment General Göring*. On 1 April 1938 this battalion provided the nucleus of the *Luftwaffe Fallschirmjäger-Regiment 1*, also stationed at Stendal, and there then developed the tug-of-war between the *Luftwaffe* and the German Army as to which of the two services should own the airborne troops. Göring won the day. On 1 January the army element, that had meanwhile been increased to a battalion, was transferred to the *Luftwaffe* as the second battalion of Göring's regiment. By the beginning of the war this *Luftwaffe* parachute regiment had been increased to four battalions.[9]

The original general staff commitment for the year 1935–6 had been to reach a figure of thirty-one peacetime divisions. During 1936, however, the emphasis had been changed in that the planners began to design an army for wartime, a *Kriegsheer* to be made up of a 1938 peace establishment expanded from thirty-one to forty-one regular divisions, plus a further twenty-five cadre divisions of the reserve that were to be embodied and brought up to strength on mobilization.

Four of these twenty-five reserve divisions were to be newly raised formations based on Class I (and some Class II) reservists, the divisions being formed on cadres thrown off by regular formations and operating on reduced scales of weapons and mechanical transport. The other twenty-one reserve divisions were to be *Landwehr* divisions formed from those classes prior to 1901, men of thirty-five and older who had last served in the First World War. These *Landwehr* divisions were to be equipped with the obsolescent weapons removed from the regular army and were to have only one artillery battalion and very little mechanical transport. The *Landwehr* divisional and regimental commanders were appointed in peace together with small regular staffs.[10]

The mobilization strength of the *Kriegsheer* by the end of 1937 stood at thirty-six infantry and three panzer divisions, one mountain and one cavalry brigade, all of the active army, and four reserve and twenty-one *Landwehr* divisions, a total of sixty-six formations. By 1938 this figure had improved to forty-two peacetime formations and eight reserve divisions making seventy-one formations in all. The real situation, however, was not as favourable to the *Wehrmacht* as these formation figures might suggest. Army headquarters, army troops, and many of the support and administrative services for this order of battle did not exist in peace. The mobilization of the force would have required, in the space of a few days, the addition of nearly 3,000,000 men, 400,000 horses and 200,000 trucks and carts; and because of the transportation difficulties within the Reich it was considered essential that the mobilization reinforcements should be taken from reservists who lived in the same area as the formation to which they were to be allotted in war.

There were two main reasons why the German Army was still unfitted for a major European war in early 1938. In the first instance the shortage of trained personnel was the immediate obstacle to the rapid deployment of a force fit and ready for battle; and although each successive six months was to show an improvement in the general state of individual training and an increase in the numbers of trained reservists, Germany would not, in time of peace, have approached the standard of overall efficiency desired by its military leaders until some time after 1943. The second and more important deficiency was in a lack of stockpiled resources and of an industrial armament capacity sufficient to sustain its armed forces in the prolonged action of a major European or of a world war.

It was estimated at the time that a *Kriegsheer* of seventy-one divisions would have required an armed strength of 3,300,000 men.* Against this requirement, the peace army numbered only 550,000 and the personnel earmarked for the *Landwehr* divisions another 300,000; the total Class I and II reservists still stood at only 400,000, making an overall deficiency of about two million men. If war had come at the beginning of 1938, the shortfall could have been filled by the only partially trained reserve available, the older men of the *Landwehr* reserve, men who had not shouldered a rifle since 1918.[11] The requirements of armaments needed to equip and maintain this force could never have been found.

The whole situation was, as both von Fritsch and Beck knew full well, militarily unsound. It would have taken several years to train and accumulate a war-ready mobilization reserve and to have produced a workable mobilization system that could have operated smoothly at short notice. The active army might indeed have mobilized in a few days, but all its new headquarters and its many new support units could not possibly have done so. In 1937 the reserve and *Landwehr* divisions had been ordered to prepare mobilization plans that would have enabled them to be ready for battle in six days. In fact they would have been lucky to have done so in six weeks, and this only provided that some preparatory mobilization measures had already

---

* The field army required 1,600,000 and the continued support of 500,000 *Bautruppen* (for construction and fortifications); 300,000 were needed within the framework of the *Ersatzheer* and 900,000 recruits would be inducted immediately to form not only the field army's first replacements but also to fill vacancies on the war establishment.

taken place; otherwise they still would not have been ready after three months.[12] The whole mobilization plan was in fact a face-saver, a paper scheme that would have been difficult, if not impossible, to enact, a plan forced on the OKH by political expediency, since Hitler required a window-front *Kriegsheer* rich in numbers of divisions; the technical difficulties were made known to the dictator and he understood and fully accepted, so he said, the weakness of Germany's military position should war with France erupt at this time.

Hitler's military aggressions in 1938 and 1939 overcame some of the weaknesses in the original general staff mobilization plans in that the whole German Army was spared a sudden and complete mobilization from a peace to a war army. With the deteriorating European situation, mobilization came about gradually and in stages, often by stealth. It is true of course that Hitler's orders for partial mobilization sometimes caught the OKH by surprise in that no plans existed for such unusual measures. In March 1938, for example, Hitler ordered, preparatory to the occupation of Austria, the mobilization of two corps districts, the southern border *Wehrkreise VII* and *XIII*. This gave rise to formidable difficulties that were represented to Hitler by the OKH; and once again he quietened the military protesters by telling them that he understood the problems and accepted the risks involved. If mobilization had been extended to the whole army at this time it would, said Müller-Hillebrand, have led to irrevocable confusion, particularly as the civil government was not in gear with the military.[13] But this apparently negative *Anschluss* exercise proved to be a most valuable and useful lesson for the future, in that it confirmed that the only military units that could be relied upon at short notice were those peacetime formations already in existence.

So it came about that, in the autumn of 1938, a large part of the active army was deployed ready for use against Czecho-Slovakia; several months had been set aside to prepare the standing army for such a task. The formations had been reinforced and brought up to near war strength by trained reservists called up for continuation training, and the necessary army group and army troop units were raised in peace by the same process. Seven of the eight reserve divisions had been embodied for training and were at exercise readiness that September, deployed near the western frontier of the Reich.

It was customary to amend and reissue the mobilization orders for the German Army in the autumn of each year in order to take into account changes in the strengths of reserves and any alteration that might be demanded by the political situation. In the autumn of 1938, however, due to the Munich crisis and the occupation of the Sudetenland, a new mobilization plan was not put in hand, and the old autumn 1937 plan remained in force until March 1939.[14] The army general staff was in any case fully engaged in incorporating the Austrian *Bundesheer* into the German Army and raising a further infantry division in the Sudetenland. In March 1939 there followed the occupation of the rump of Czecho-Slovakia, although this did not call for any further mobilization or for the calling up of reserves, since only regular troops were involved; headquarters, signal and administrative troops were improvised from the standing army. Again the risk was accepted by Hitler that the whole of the German Army would not be able to mobilize at short notice should Germany be brought to war, since a large part of the army was away from its peace stations and fully employed on other duties, doubling up on and reinforcing other formations and finding headquarters and support troops.

On 1 March 1939 began the new mobilization term covered by a plan that should have lasted until the spring of 1940 and this was the plan on which Germany went to war. By mid 1939 the general mobilization position had much improved since the spring of 1938: the German armament output had increased to produce enough equipment to fit out twelve new divisions a year, without, however, being able to add anything to the maintenance reserve essential for protracted war. The acquisition of the Czech heavy and armament industries had made the overall position a little easier, and the booty taken from the Czech Army was used to outfit the low category German divisions. The personnel deficiency on mobilization had been reduced in that additional reserves had become available as more conscripts completed their service, and by some further short term training of the 'white years'. By 1939 the *Feldheer*, which included not only the field divisions but also the border troops and the construction troops, had a war establishment of 2,750,000 men: the planned establishment of the *Ersatzheer* remaining within the Reich had been reduced to just under a million men.* Against this establishment liability of 3,750,000, the trained assets were 730,000 in the active army, 500,000 Class I and 600,000 Class II reservists, about half the numbers required.[15] The remainder would still have to come from the *Landwehr*.

––––––––

By midsummer 1939 the field army order of battle stood at the imposing total of 103 divisions, an increase of thirty-two since the spring of 1938. Of this increase five were Austrian divisions, eight were new reserve divisions and fourteen were to be formed on mobilization, at Hitler's express demand, from the 279 peacetime reinforcement battalion (*Ergänzungsbataillon*) cadres.[16] The trained manpower available could not have staffed more than half of this total of 103 divisions, and, since the reinforcement battalions were to disappear into the new divisions, a war that involved immediate and heavy sustained fighting might have led to grave difficulties in the training and reinforcement system. But this was the pattern on which the Hitler Army of the future was to be based, with a *Feldheer* so strong in numbers of divisions that it outbalanced the support resources available to maintain it.

* There had been an increase to 200,000 in the numbers of *Wachtruppen* (older age groups for internal guard duties forming forty-five *Landesschützenregimenter*) but a reduction in the recruits from 900,000 to 500,000.

The motorized, panzer, mountain and cavalry formations were organized in peace as they would be in war and required only war first reinforcements and services to fit them out for battle. All motorized troops were held at virtual stand-to and had to be at twelve hours' readiness to move so that they could, if need be, be mobilized well ahead of the rest of the army. The remaining eighty-six infantry divisions had been divided into mobilization, organization and equipment categories known as waves (*Wellen*), and this category pattern was to remain in force for all infantry divisions until 1945. The thirty-five regular infantry divisions were all classified as category 1 and had to be ready for war by 48 hours after mobilization (*Mob X*) day. But although these regular divisions represented the most reliable and battleworthy formations of the German Army, even they would have to cope with deficiencies, for they would require thirty-one infantry battalions and five artillery *Abteilungen*, together with administrative and rear services to complete their order of battle. But this was only a part of their problem, since all category 1 divisions were required not just to mobilize themselves but, in addition, to throw off regular cadres on the first day of mobilization to provide the framework for the forming of the sixteen reserve divisions of category 2. The gaps in the regular divisions left by the departure of these cadres had to be filled by reservists. The main part of the strength of the sixteen reserve divisions of category 2 was to be made up of reservists I and II and *Landwehrpflichtige*; according to the optimistic orders of the time, mobilization of the category 2 divisions was to be complete by four days after M day. The twenty-one category 3 divisions of the *Landwehr* were to be mobilized with no help from the active army; embodiment was to be complete six days after mobilization day and they were expected to be operational after a further several weeks' training.[17] The fourteen infantry divisions of category 4 were those to be raised from the reinforcement battalions from the active army.*

The Replacement Army training and reinforcement system was to be organized so that it would foster regimental and territorial loyalties, in that all reinforcements would be closely associated with the unit to which they were being despatched and would come from the same home area; and in order to strengthen the regimental and unit association between the field and the Replacement Army, each field formation and unit was directly linked with its own reinforcement and training source.[18] In *Wehrkreis VI* for

---

* Regular personnel formed about eighty per cent of the category 1 divisions but less than ten per cent of the categories 2 and 4 divisions. Class I reservists formed over eighty per cent of the category 2 reserve divisions while Class II reservists filled nearly fifty per cent of the ranks in the category 3 and 4 divisions. The *Landwehr I* reservists provided only forty per cent of the men for the category 3 *Landwehr* divisions but about twenty-five per cent of those in the category 4 divisions. Whereas the peace establishment was less than 13,000, the infantry divisional war establishment tables varied, by category, from 15,000 to 18,000 men; a large number of war establishment appointments remained unfilled, however, and there was always a deficiency in motor vehicles, both in numbers and in types, so that it was by no means unusual to see anti-tank guns being towed by small civilian pattern saloon cars. The infantry divisional numbering gave an indication as to category and origin since the category 1 were numbered from 1 to 46, category 2 from 52 to 87, category 3 from 206 to 246 and category 4 from 251 to 269.

example, in the north-west corner of the Reich, the category 1 regular infantry divisions due to take the field on mobilization had the numbers 6, 16 and 26. In each of the divisional *Wehrgaue* an infantry *Ersatzregiment* was to be formed on mobilization bearing the same number as the division it was to reinforce; this replacement regiment was to have three battalions each bearing the number of the regiment to which it was linked. Other arms were dealt with in exactly the same fashion. The Replacement Army reinforcement organization was responsible not only for the category 1 peacetime divisions, but for all formations brought into existence on or after mobilization; it was also to channel back to their original units the sick and casualties returning to duty from the base hospitals.*

All schools and experimental units were to come under the command of the Replacement Army except for the general staff college and the senior war schools. The allocation and the movement of officer reinforcements were to be dealt with by the OKH *Personalamt* and not by the *Ersatzheer*.

The organization of the German Army command system in 1938 had not altered significantly since the days of the First World War. The higher control organization (*die obere Führung*) was said to comprise the command of all formations down to and including divisional headquarters, the control of regimental formations and units within the division being known as *die untere Führung*.[19] The preparation and conduct of major battles within a theatre were held, according to German military science, to be within the sphere of *operations*, a technical military term that has no meaning outside of Germany and the Soviet Union. At a risk of over-simplification it may be said that the Germans regarded the warlike activities of divisions and corps as tactical, while armies and army groups were more likely to be employed on *operational* tasks; the co-ordination and control of two or more army groups came within the definition of strategy. The distinction between strategy, operations and tactics was admitted to be very fine, however, since this depended not only on the size of the forces involved but also on frontages, depth, the time element and the nature of the task. For example, tactical formations such as the army and the corps could perform roles that had an operative significance, particularly when they received independent missions at critical moments of an action.

The six peacetime *Heeresgruppen* were only training inspectorates: on mobilization four were to become army headquarters while two only were scheduled to become wartime *Heeresgruppen* (army groups), the highest operative headquarters in the field with full command (but no supply) responsibility for its subordinate formations.† An army headquarters could have operational or tactical duties and was entirely responsible for the supply of all formations under its command. No army headquarters existed

---

* These *Ersatzregimenter* were grouped for control under *Wehrkreis Ersatzdivisionen* that took their numbering from 141 to 200.

† *Hr Gr Kdo II* became *Hr Gr C* in the west; *Hr Gr Kdo I* first became *A O K 2* then *Hr Gr Nord* in Poland.

in peace, and it was intended, on mobilization, to raise ten such headquarters from the nuclei of other staffs, these new army headquarters being numbered from 1 to 5, 7, 8, 10, 12 and 14.[20]

The corps headquarters was purely a small tactical command grouping, that was, nevertheless, of great importance in the battle: like the *Heeresgruppen* it had no supply or administrative responsibility for the divisions it commanded. Nineteen corps headquarters were in existence in peace and a further four were to be raised on mobilization. The field divisional headquarters were responsible for all aspects of command including their own reinforcement and supply.

The command and staff system was uniform and simple; appointment designations, though not necessarily ranks corresponding to those designations, were standardized. The commander of an army group was the *Oberbefehlshaber*, and of the army the *Befehlshaber*, the commander of the corps was the *Kommandierender General* while that of the division was simply the *Divisionskommandeur*. The commander's staff was subdivided basically into operations (*Führung*), quartermaster (*Quartiermeister*) and personnel and reinforcements (*Adjutantur*); to these three staff branches were added, as the need arose, arms and specialist departments.[21]

Since, at the beginning of 1939, there were, out of a total of 19,400 army officers on the active list, only 272 fully trained general staff officers, to which could be added a further 147 'assigned' officers (*kommandiert zum Generalstab*), it was intended that only the key staff appointments should be filled by general staff officers.[22] The most important staff branches were held to be operations, intelligence and supply, and the key appointments were of course those controlling those branches. All staff branches were designated by type with a common number, operations being known as *Ia*, quartermaster (supply) as *Ib*, and intelligence as *Ic*; the officer in charge of the operations branch was usually known as the 'first general staff officer', the chief of the *Quartiermeister* department was the 'second' while the principal intelligence officer was called the 'third general staff officer', these designations being independent of rank or the level of headquarters; alternatively, these officers might simply be referred to as *Ia*, *Ib* or *Ic*. In the field division there were, at the most, only two officers of the general staff, the *Ia*, who was usually a lieutenant-colonel, and the *Ib*, a major. The *Adjutantur* (*IIa,b* or *c*) had no general staff officers allotted to it.

Military authority was vested in the appointed commander and not in his staff, and there was only one command channel except for those of the counter-intelligence and the justice department. All headquarters above that of division had a chief of general staff whose task it was to represent the commander during his absence and co-ordinate the work of the rest of the staff. On all major operational or tactical decisions the commander was *obliged* to listen to his chief of staff's recommendations before coming to his own decision, and it was the right and the duty of the chief of staff to state that opinion. The decision, however, once made, was the responsibility of the commander and, from 1939 onwards, the chief of staff could no longer record his dissenting opinion and forward it to the next superior head-quarters, as had formerly been the rule. Close confidence was of course necessary between the commander and his chief of general staff, and many chiefs of staff moved with their commanders to new appointments, a change of commander usually signifying a change of chief of general staff. At divisional level the first general staff officer (*Ia*), although he was not a chief of general staff, carried out many of the same duties. The readiness of these general staff officers to think ahead and assume great responsibility was one of the reasons for German tactical flexibility in the early days of the war.[23]

The general staff operations departments of the bigger headquarters were headed by the first general staff officer (*Ia*) who deputized for the chief of staff in his absence; the *Ic* was his immediate assistant. At army group and army there were in addition a 'fourth general staff officer (*Id*)' who dealt with training matters and a counter-intelligence *Abwehr* officer. And although the army groups and corps had no executive role in the German replenishment system, both headquarters had a *Ib* representative whose duty it was to keep his commander briefed as to the overall supply position. The second general staff officer at army group and division was known simply as *Ib*, but at corps and army he sometimes took the designation of '*Quartiermeister*' or '*Oberquartiermeister*'.

At the higher headquarters, specialist *Luftwaffe*, artillery, anti-tank, engineer (*Pionier*) and signals advisers were permanently allotted to the formation, but at the level of division and corps the commander and *Ia* frequently made use of commanders of the supporting arms in the dual role as arms advisers. The service specialist branches forming part of the head-quarters were co-ordinated by the *Ib*.*

The *Heeresleitung* that became the OKH had been made up of five main directorates (*Ämter*) all of them directly under the *Chef* who became the German Army commander-in-chief. From the spring of 1935 these directo-rates began to expand rapidly.

The *Truppenamt* (later the general staff of the army) was multiplied threefold in that its original four departments grew to twelve.† Then from 1 January 1936 the general staff (*Abt. 7*) began to publish the general staff military review (*die Militärwissenschaftliche Rundschau*), and measures

* The main service branches under *Ib* were: Arms and Equipment (*W* and *WuG*); Intendance (*IVa*); Medical (*IVb*); Veterinary (*IVc*); Motor Transport (*V*); Supply (*Nachschubtruppe*).

† The former T1 operations department, now *Abteilung 1*, threw off a new department 5 for rail and canal transport and a new *Abteilung 6* for supply, this approximating to the British Q (Ops and Plans); from *Abt. 6* was to be developed General Wagner's wartime appointment as *Generalquartiermeister*. On 1 July there followed two more departments, *Abt. 7* for the study of military theory and *Abt. 8* for technical development (in conjunction with the *Heereswaffenamt*). In the spring of 1936 *Abteilung 1* was thinned out again to form a further two departments, 9 for cartography and survey and 10 for fortifications. Early in the following year, the intelligence *Abteilung 3* (Foreign Armies) was reorganized as *Abt. 3* (*West*) and *Abt. 12* (*Ost*) with a separate *Attaché Gruppe* that was later upgraded to an *Abteilung*. Then, during that same spring of 1937, *Abt. 4* (training) was subdivided into *Abt. 4* (troop training) and *Abt. 11* (general staff training).

were taken to reassemble the copious military record and library facilities that had been dispersed after 1919. On 1 April 1937 the war history study institute was reformed from part of the Reich archives, and it was placed directly under the general staff; and the army archives in Potsdam were expanded by acquisitions from the Reich archives and by the addition of the files of Prussian military history from the Prussian *Staatsarchiv* in Dahlem.[24]

In order to reduce the burden that this expansion entailed, the chief of army staff was provided, from July 1935 onwards, with a number of deputies, general officers who took the name of *Oberquartiermeister*, this having no quartermaster connotation but being linked to the distant past with the chiefs of staff (*Generalquartiermeister*) of the Prussian Electors. Three such posts were created in 1935.*

Another important change that took place in July 1935 was the transfer to the general staff of the *P3 Gruppe* of the *Personalamt*, this coming under the *Zentralabteilung* under Major (later Colonel) Hossbach who, in addition to holding this appointment, was also the senior military aide to Hitler. This central co-ordinating department was responsible for the selection and posting of general staff officers and the posting, on mobilization, of all commanders up to those of the rank of divisional commander; its leader Hossbach (and later Schmundt) provided such permanent liaison links as there were between Hitler and the commander-in-chief of the army; Hossbach also saw, at fairly regular intervals, Keitel, Jodl and Beck.[25]

The chief of the army general staff was the principal adviser to the commander-in-chief of the army and represented him during short periods of absence; he also had a co-ordinating role with the other OKH directorates and any drafts of particular importance meant for the commander-in-chief were usually first seen by him. The chief of general staff was the only staff officer who retained the *Aktenkundig* right officially to record his opinion for posterity in the event of any difference with his superior.[26] Yet, in spite of the increase in his responsibilities and organization, he had been given no additional powers or status and he still ranked only as an equal with the other four *Ämter* chiefs; and his appointment remained a comparatively subordinate one in the military hierarchy, as proof of which may be cited that, during the important five years of rearmament, Beck saw Hitler only twice, and then when he was representing the absent commander-in-chief of the army. Nor did Beck often come into contact with von Blomberg.

The *Heerespersonalamt (PA)*, originally under von dem Bussche-Ippenburg and then, from 1934 to 1938, under von Schwedler, before it

---

* The *O Qu I* was the first deputy to Beck and, from 1936, this key appointment was filled by von Manstein who was promoted to it from *Abteilung 1*; the *O Qu I* directly controlled five of the main general staff departments, those that had originally belonged to T1. The *O Qu II* (Halder) was responsible for all training departments while the *O Qu III* was to be responsible for organization. In the autumn of 1937 an *O Qu IV* (Karl-Heinrich von Stülpnagel) was appointed to take over the two intelligence departments and then, in late 1938, a *O Qu V* was introduced to be responsible for *Abteilung 7* and all military libraries and archives.

passed to the younger Keitel, dealt only with officers, and had consisted of four sections, one of which (P3) had been transferred in July 1935 to the general staff.* The head of the *Personalamt* was most influential in that he controlled the development of the officer corps and dealt not only with the regimental careers of officers but also with the highest command appointments, so that he was in effect both military-secretary and adjutant-general to the commander-in-chief of the army. And at the time of von Hammerstein-Equord's replacement, von Schwedler had actually been directly in touch with von Blomberg concerning the selection of a new commander-in-chief for the army. When von Fritsch fell, von Schwedler and two of his principal staff officers were removed from their appointments, partly because they were unacceptable to von Brauchitsch and partly because of advice proferred to him by Wilhelm Keitel.[27]

The *Allgemeines Heeresamt* (*AHA*) under Fromm was the third of the OKH main directorates and was formed in 1934 from the *Wehramt*. As the German Army expanded, the AHA eventually took over from the general staff much of the detail of army organization and build-up. The AHA function was similar to that of the OKW armed forces office (AWA), and its designation, which means 'general army directorate', was apt in that it was a resting place for a number of important though unrelated OKH branches and departments grouped together for convenience of administration. Like most directorates it had a *Zentralabteilung* responsible for general coordination. Within the directorate organization it had a branch for the administration of the army budget and a department for the judge-advocates, and it included the administration of the twelve arms inspectorates, although the inspectors themselves came directly under the commander-in-chief of the army and dealt closely with the chief of army staff concerning matters of their arm. Another part of the AHA was a branch that had the same responsibility for other ranks as the army personnel office had towards officers, except that it did not concern itself with the detail of individual personal administration.† The AHA uniform department controlled uniform design and replacement.

The fourth pillar of the OKH was the army administration directorate (*Heeresverwaltungsamt* (*VA*)) under Karmann, responsible for rations, clothing, pay, and accommodation for the army (and sometimes for the remainder of the *Wehrmacht*), for accounting and for the personal administration of the military officials that formed part of the military establishment, and for the civilian workers employed by the armed forces. These armed forces officials (*Wehrmachtbeamte*), who had always formed a most important part of the German Army, were members of the civil service recruited from the professions and trades or from former regular long-service non-commissioned officers who had qualified for acceptance. They were either

---

* P1 dealt with officer administration, P2 with education and welfare while P4 was for replacements and reinforcements.

† *Amtsgruppe Ersatz- und Heereswesen.*

'military', in which case they wore uniforms and were graded as officers or other ranks, wearing badges of rank similar to, though distinctive from, those worn by combatant troops, or they were 'civilian'. Intendants, senior apothecaries and paymasters formed most of the officer grade 'military' official ranks, while the other ranks were armourers, saddlers, clerks, and hospital workers. The 'civilian' officials were not attached to units of the army but were employed in administrative offices and bases within the Reich.

The fifth directorate of the OKH was the army ordnance directorate (*Heereswaffenamt (WaA)*) under Liese, responsible for the design, testing, development and acceptance of all ordnance equipment. One of its two main branches covered development and testing, and the other industrial development and supply, its function being to place orders with industry; other departments included organizations for research, administration and regulations.[28]

The chief of the army justice department and the inspectorate of war schools (*In 1*) had a separate existence outside the five main directorates of the OKH and were responsible directly to the commander-in-chief of the army.

All the arms inspectors were in reality the chiefs of their respective arms and were responsible for the technical training of their troops and for recommending to the *Heerespersonalamt* the departmental appointments affecting their arm. The panzer troops were already in a special category that distinguished them from the other main arms, for Lutz, the inspector of panzer troops, as the commander of the *Panzerkommando* was also a commanding general in the field. At some time after he had succeeded Lutz, Guderian was shown a paper prepared by von Brauchitsch proposing the setting up of a new arm of mobile troops (*Schnelle Truppen*) embracing all tank and anti-tank troops, reconnaissance troops and all motorized rifles, motorized infantry and cavalry.* This reorganization was brought into being during the autumn of 1938. Thereafter, until September 1939, Guderian, as *Chef der Schnellen Truppen*, was on a different plane and had far greater resources than the other arms inspectors, in that not only did he have a command function with his own headquarters independent of Fromm's AHA, but all the mobile troops schools were directly under him and he was able to carry out his own experiments in the use of his new arm.[29] And Guderian continued to be represented within the OKH and AHA by his own inspectorate (*In 6*).† Although this *Schnelle Truppen Kommando* was to last for only a year, since it was disbanded at the beginning of the war, it is

---

* Although von Brauchitsch said that it was his own paper, the idea and the direction came entirely from Hitler. It was apparently at Hitler's insistence also that Guderian had replaced Lutz and that Guderian was selected to head the *Schnelle Truppen* rather than von Kluge. (Cf. Nehring, *Die Geschichte der Deutschen Panzerwaffe 1916–45*, p. 101)

† The last annual exercise (*Übungsreise*) that took place under the chief of army general staff in the spring of 1939 had as its object the testing of the employment of mobile troops and their function within the framework of the army. The follow-up exercises with troops scheduled for the autumn never took place.

worthy of note in that the organization was revived in 1943, at Guderian's instigation, with even greater scope and independence.

By late 1938, before Beck had departed from his office, the OKH had already taken the form in which it would go to war. Its main function was to provide a command organization for war, both in the field and at home, and to establish in peace the framework of a wartime Replacement Army that would maintain the *Feldheer* in men, materials, labour and money, and also provide many of the common-user items required by the rest of the *Wehrmacht*.

On mobilization it was intended that the OKH should split itself into three parts – main, rear and Replacement Army headquarters. The main headquarters, reduced to a skeleton insofar as numbers were concerned, was to consist of the commander-in-chief of the army accompanied by the younger Keitel (but not by the *Personalamt* itself), and by the chief of the army general staff. The general staff in this main headquarters would consist of only the *O Qu I* (Operations) and *O Qu IV* (Intelligence), together with the organization and training departments and the *Zentralabteilung* responsible for general staff appointments. In addition there was to be a newly appointed *Generalquartiermeister* (Wagner) to advise the commander-in-chief and chief of army general staff on supply matters and to co-ordinate supply planning; the main OKH headquarters was also to include OKW intelligence and *Abwehr* representatives, a *Luftwaffe* general, a chief signal officer (Fellgiebel) and chief transport officer (Gercke), both of whom had a dual responsibility to both the OKW and OKH.[30]

The posts of the *O Qu II* and *III* were to be disbanded in time of war and the *O Qu V* was to remain in the Berlin area with the task of supervising and co-ordinating the rump of the OKH headquarters left behind. This consisted of the second echelon of the general staff departments deployed in the forward area and those general staff branches not required in the main headquarters with the commander-in-chief.

Split though they were in two different locations, only the general staff and the *Personalamt* remained more or less as they had been in peacetime within the framework of the OKH. For the arms inspectors and the other *Ämter* of the OKH were all to be amalgamated under a single commander of the Replacement Army; Fromm, of the *Allgemeines Heeresamt*, was the officer nominated for this most important mobilization appointment.* Fromm was to be directly responsible to the commander-in-chief of the army, exactly as he had been before, but his responsibilities were to be enormously increased in that the *Waffenamt* and *Verwaltungsamt* would be part of his headquarters and that the Home Army, that is to say the static *Wehrkreise* (less the *Feldheer* already in the field) would be directly under his command.

Although the German Army before 1933 had been a potential political force within the Reich, it had been kept small and lacking in modern equipment by

* The suggestion that Joachim von Stülpnagel should head the *Ersatzheer* had been rejected by Hitler.

both external and internal politics and by a shortage of money. The rank and file, no less than the officers, were divorced from the German people, for, unlike the imperial army, the Weimar *Reichsheer* had never been popular with the man in the street. All of the officer corps held the republic in contempt, and the difference between generals and lieutenants was only in the intensity of their condemnation.[31] The *Reichsheer* generals and field officers, on the whole, had been suspicious of Nazism, although some of the young lieutenants had begun to support Hitler and voice dissatisfaction with their own seniors and high command.

By 1938, however, the situation had changed in that the senior officers, except for some generals in close contact with the dictator, were now admirers of Hitler, for, as von Blomberg said after the war, 'he gave them what they wanted'. The officer corps as a whole, whether they were lieutenants or lieutenant-colonels, had, for the most part, come from civilian life, either through the police, or as *Ergänzungsoffiziere*, or from the greatly increased junior officer intake. Many of the younger officers had been members of the Hitler Youth. The political indoctrination of officers, begun by von Blomberg, increased in momentum year by year.* The conscripted rank and file had similarly come into the army through the compulsory six month labour service, as former members of the Hitler Youth or of one of the SA organizations. Hitler was immensely popular everywhere. The army had become the dictator's instrument for he had always said that the old *Reichsheer* had been a foreign body within the nation and that this could only be corrected by the creation of a truly national army closely identified with the people; such an army, according to Hitler, would then serve as the political educator of the young German citizen.

With von Blomberg gone and with the army strongly behind Hitler, and the dictator himself having assumed the appointment as the Commander-in-Chief of the *Wehrmacht*, it might have been expected that von Brauchitsch's position would have become immeasurably stronger than that of his predecessor von Fritsch. The reorganization of the high command brought von Brauchitsch into immediate contact with the Führer; and, if Keitel were disregarded, von Brauchitsch should have been in a strong, if not unassailable, position as the only army adviser to, and the executive of, a commander-in-chief who was entirely without command or staff experience and knew comparatively little about the German Army. This did not happen, however.

Von Brauchitsch had begun his service in the Third Foot Guards and had had an outstanding military record in the First World War in the artillery; he then served in the *Truppenamt* under Heye and Hasse from 1922 to 1925, showing himself, according to one authority, 'in the forefront of military

---

* General Renondeau, the French military attaché, wrote as early as 23 January 1934: *Le parti est en train de s'emparer de la Reichswehr; il la conquiert du sommet à la base; l'armée perd sa neutralité.*

thought, using motorized troops with aircraft on manoeuvres'.* In 1930 he headed T4 (Training) and in 1932 became inspector of artillery, from whence he went, in 1933, to command *Wehrkreis I* in East Prussia, and then, in 1937, to the newly formed *Gruppenkommando IV* in Leipzig. Unhappily married and without any private financial resources, he supported a wife and four children: his only refuge was in his work; for the previous five years he had been separated from his wife, and he could be found at all hours in his office 'working like an ox'.[32] His political views and his support for the party at this time were tinged with cynicism and may have been based on expediency, for he appears to have lacked the exuberant and genuine political enthusiasm of the naïve von Blomberg, at least until he came under the influence of his second wife.† Von Brauchitsch was, moreover, under a personal debt to Hitler and, in part, to Keitel for his appointment; there was some doubt about his divorce. Von Brauchitsch was said to have a high opinion of Beck but was apparently in favour of having the chief of army staff removed from his appointment, either because he, von Brauchitsch, himself wished it, or in deference to the views of the Führer and Keitel.

On 4 February 1938 when Hitler had announced to the generals assembled in the chancellery the cases and charges against von Blomberg and von Fritsch, he had told them that he himself proposed to take von Blomberg's post; this move was to be seen, he said, not as an attack on the armed forces, but as a centralization of authority. Beck was, according to Hossbach, disturbed by von Brauchitsch's acceptance of the situation described by Hitler and by his readiness to take a post that was not yet vacant. It was unlikely, therefore, that Beck and von Brauchitsch could work in close accord.

On the morning of 10 March 1938 von Brauchitsch happened to be absent from the Tirpitzufer and Beck and von Manstein answered a Führer summons to the chancellery.‡ Hitler wanted German troops to move into Austria in forty-eight hours' time and the necessary orders had to be prepared within a space of five hours. Beck protested to Keitel against the political dangers involved in the occupation, and Keitel told Beck that he would represent the army case to the dictator, without, however, having the slightest intention of doing so.[33] No sooner had Austria been annexed, than Hitler moved on to his next excess, telling Keitel, on 21 April, of the political principles 'that would govern a German attack on Czecho-Slovakia'. The army general staff were then instructed to revise and bring up to date *Aufmarsch Grün*, the plan that had been intended for a pre-emptive attack to the south-east before France should have the opportunity to intervene in the west.

* O'Neill, p. 143. According to Faber, however, von Brauchitsch became a motor enthusiast when it was fashionable to do so and when Hitler was already its champion.

† Von Brauchitsch was apt to sneer at party enthusiasts, including those young officers who greeted him with the Fascist salute, telling Faber that he had no wish to run the risk of having his eyes poked out.

‡ Von Manstein had remained temporarily at his post as *O Qu 1* after the removal of von Fritsch, until relieved by Halder.

Beck returned once more to the writing of his memoranda of protest, memoranda that rarely got beyond von Brauchitsch. On 7 May he placed before von Brauchitsch a written appreciation of the situation, dealing mainly with the politico-military dangers inherent in the Führer's foreign policy. Beck regarded Soviet Russia as a possible threat in that it might 'intervene with its air force and navy', and in doing so he must have been one of the few German military planners who even considered the likelihood of Soviet intervention as being a factor of importance. If France should take up arms in accordance with its obligations to Czecho-Slovakia, then, said Beck, Britain would side with France. The final outcome of such a war, thought Beck, could not be in doubt, 'even though the United States support [to France] might be limited to the supply of *matériel*'. Germany's enemies, continued Beck, had 'rearmed to a considerable degree' whereas the German armed forces were not ready for war, and the very lack of living space would make it impossible for Germany to endure a long war.

Von Brauchitsch presumably took no action to present Beck's appreciation to the Führer.* But the gist of Beck's doubts apparently filtered back to the dictator by way of the OKW staff. On 28 May Hitler spoke once more to his military leaders, emphasizing that the political and military situation demanded lightning action – the British rearmament had only recently begun and would not be effective until 1941–2. The right moment, said Hitler, had to be grasped. Beck, unconvinced by what he had heard, returned to his own theme the next day, writing in a memorandum to von Brauchitsch that Hitler's earlier foreign policy victories were no guarantee that similar action would be successful in the future. For Germany, continued Beck, either alone or with Italy's help, could not overcome France or Britain. Beck was ready to concede that Czecho-Slovakia could be conquered, but this, he said, would not determine the outcome of a general war, for Germany's enemies had time, space and resources on their side. Beck's memorandum was presented to von Brauchitsch on the following day, two days after Hitler had already signed the revised orders for *Aufmarsch Grün*, beginning with the words: 'It is my unalterable decision to smash Czecho-Slovakia in the near future by military action.'[34] On 30 May, during his talk to army leaders at Jüterbog, Hitler had defined 'the near future' as 'by 1 October'.†

The personal relationship between von Brauchitsch and Beck worsened rapidly and there was friction between the general staff and Bodewin Keitel's army personnel office. Von Brauchitsch began to ignore Beck and deal directly with Halder.[35]

On 16 July Beck put yet another memorandum before von Brauchitsch in which he said that the German people and the German Army did not want a

---

* It was in fact discussed with Keitel, who advised von Brauchitsch to suppress all but the military content; when Hitler was apprised of this part he angrily dismissed it with the remark: 'What sort of generals are these that I have to force into war!'

† Jodl's diary entry for 30 May reads: 'The Führer's intention [is] that we must do it this year; the army, on the other hand, believes that we are not yet strong enough.'

war, and that the outcome of a European or a world war would be cata-
strophic.[36] Beck felt himself obliged, he said, to request that the preparations
for war be halted and that the intention to solve the Czecho-Slovakian
question by force be postponed until the military situation should be basically changed. Beck wanted von Brauchitsch to sound the senior army
leaders and Raeder and Göring for their opinions. He continued:

History will burden those leaders with blood guilt . . . military obedience has a limit
where knowledge, conscience and a sense of responsibility forbid the execution of a
command. If their warnings receive no hearing then they have the right and duty to
resign . . . if they all act with resolution a policy of war is impossible . . . Extraordinary
times demand extraordinary measures.[37]

Beck pressed for action against the SS and 'boss rule' (*Bonzokratie*) and,
on 19 July, he told von Brauchitsch that this was the last opportunity to free
Germany 'and even Hitler himself' from the tyranny of a Soviet type *Cheka*
and the oppression by the party bosses, for Germany had to return to the rule
of law and a cessation of the persecution of the churches.[38]
Although von Brauchitsch had no intention of presenting these views
directly to Hitler, he was, presumably, much influenced by the cautionary
words of his subordinate. During the first week in August he read to the
assembled senior generals a memorandum, that von Weichs, who was
present, suspected had been written by Beck, in which it was propounded
that the problem of the Sudetenland did not justify the risk to the nation of a
general war; von Brauchitsch asked that 'the generals should stress this point
to Hitler', a duty, it might be supposed, that rested solely with von
Brauchitsch. Such was obviously von Reichenau's view, since he said that,
from his personal experience, more would be achieved by the approach to
Hitler of an individual than by a mass confrontation. Busch thought that
soldiers did not understand politics and should keep clear of them. Von
Brauchitsch ended the meeting by prophesying that war 'would mean the
end of German civilization'. After the meeting von Weichs overheard von
Rundstedt advising von Brauchitsch to be cautious in the way he put these
views to Hitler: and this advice reveals much of the character of von
Rundstedt.[39]
The gist of what had been said found its way to Hitler's ears, for, according
to Keitel, both von Reichenau and Guderian were always ready to intrigue
against von Brauchitsch.[40] Hitler's immediate reaction was to go behind the
backs of the senior commanders and, on 10 August, invite to the Berghof
their chiefs of staff and those earmarked to become army commanders in
war, the dictator confiding to them some of his plans and objectives. His
listeners appeared sceptical and unconvinced. Von Wietersheim told Hitler
of Adam's opinion that the western fortifications of the Reich could not be
held against the French for more than three weeks, and this was answered by
an explosion of rage from the dictator 'that they would, if necessary, be held
for three years'. Jodl, already echoing his master, noted in his diary the

defeatist attitude of the generals 'that was seeping down and could affect the morale of the troops'.[41]

On 15 August Hitler attended an exercise at Jüterbog and he made use of the meeting to confront his senior army commanders. He told them that he was going to solve the Czech question by force, reminding his listeners of 'his prophetic gifts' and saying that as long as Chamberlain and Daladier were in power there would be no general European war. During the address Hitler made a point of attacking the army general staff. After the meeting Beck asked to resign, and his resignation was accepted by the Führer on 21 August on the condition that news of his going should not be revealed until Hitler decided that it was opportune; for the dictator did not want the world to know that there was any dissension within the OKH at a time when the German Army was on the point of invading Czecho-Slovakia.

Beck undoubtedly played into Hitler's hands when he agreed to remain silent on his resignation, but it would appear that he may have been influenced by the promise of a further field command that was temptingly held out to him. Between August and October he rotated between the Tirpitzufer and the newly forming 1 Army cadre in the west.[42] But then, in the middle of October, when Hitler had already secured the Sudetenland for Germany, the dictator declined to re-employ Beck and he was placed on the retired list. Beck was promoted on retirement to colonel-general. At the time of his retirement from the army he ordered, as a Parthian shot, that a postscript should be added to his official memorandum of 16 July, that 'he would like to record the fact that he refused to countenance any adventurist National-Socialist wars'.[43] Then, after he had been retired, Beck complained, as did Fritsch, that Hitler had treated him shabbily, and that he (Beck) had been betrayed by his army colleagues.[44]

Beck's short term and pessimistic predictions, particularly as to the relative efficiency of the German and French armed forces, proved to be wrong; yet his long term strategic forecast was entirely correct. In his understanding of the reality of power within the National-Socialist state he was extraordinarily naïve. According to his own memoranda he was in agreement with many of Hitler's political aims, that Germany needed *Lebensraum*, that Czecho-Slovakia in its present form 'was intolerable' and eventually must be removed, and that Germany, in the final outcome, would also have to deal with France. But, having already aligned himself so closely with Hitler's main aims, he could not, or would not, bring himself to express his newly found dissatisfaction and doubts directly to the dictator, but, instead, he complained to von Brauchitsch and to his own subordinates, and blamed the OKW. But, in any event, Beck's opinions were of no consequence to the dictator.

That August Beck had given way to Halder, an even more controversial and complicated character. It was said that Halder was reluctant to take the appointment, particularly since he had apparently been drawn into a conspiracy 'to arrest Hitler and put him on trial should he order the attack on

Czecho-Slovakia'. But take the appointment he did. Halder was a Bavarian and a Roman Catholic, able, indefatigable and stubborn, a sceptic who was doubtful of the wisdom of Hitler's headlong rush. These uncertainties had already been discussed within the OKH with Beck, Karl-Heinrich von Stülpnagel (who followed Halder as *O Qu I*) and Wagner, with von Hammerstein, with Thomas of the OKW, and with Canaris, Oster, Gisevius, Groscurth, and Dohnanyi (all from the OKW *Abwehr*). Senior commanders on the fringe of the plot included von Witzleben, von Brockdorff-Ahlefeld (of the Potsdam garrison) and Hoepner, commanding, first a light division and then XVI Motorized Corps. Among the dissidents outside the armed forces were Goerdeler, Popitz, Schacht, Hassell and Giessen. Nearly all of these men were involved in some way in the subsequent July 1944 conspiracy, and all of them were moved by grave fears as to the destruction that Hitler's foreign policies might visit on Germany should a general war break out. But, in the main, they disapproved not so much of the man's aims but of the way he was carrying them out. The extent and efficiency of the conspiracy, or indeed the seriousness of the plotters' intentions at that time cannot be judged. For the time being von Brauchitsch was excluded from their critical discussions.

The unfortunate von Brauchitsch was meanwhile between many fires. Glad to be rid of Beck, he found that his new chief of general staff was another doubter. Von Brauchitsch was not only under a debt to Hitler but he was morally afraid of him; he had, as we have said, something of an obligation to Keitel; his own *Chef des Personalamts* who should have been his right hand man and confidant, was Keitel's brother; Keitel and Jodl were already Hitler's men; von Brauchitsch did not trust Hossbach's successor, Schmundt, who was also firmly in the Keitel camp, and he appointed Engel as a supernumerary army aide to the Führer in order that von Brauchitsch's own interests might be better served. The new army commander-in-chief was under pressure, too, from some of the more cautious commanders of the *Heeresgruppenkommandos* and corps districts, who would have preferred that some sail be taken in from the ship of state. Nor was von Brauchitsch himself convinced that the Führer was necessarily right and that he understood the risks that he was running, and in his heart he continued to doubt the dictator's political and military direction in spite of Germany's political victories. Von Brauchitsch, like some twentieth century Faust, had already sealed his bargain and his fate.

Von Brauchitsch began, however, to voice his reluctance and his fears, although probably half-heartedly, both to Hitler and to Keitel. With Hitler, anyone with reservations as to the dictator's policies was counted as against him, and Hitler was soon moved, first to disenchantment and then to anger. And when von Brauchitsch, apparently at von Rundstedt's urging, made a further representation to Hitler on 3 September 1938, he became the object of a tirade of personal abuse. Six days later, after von Brauchitsch and Halder had gone to Nuremberg for an audience with the dictator, Keitel complained to Jodl that he was 'bitterly disappointed in von Brauchitsch – in whose appointment he [Keitel] had played so great a part'.[45] Jodl, in his turn, told his staff that the Führer was already aware that the army commander-in-chief had asked his army commanders to support him against the Führer's ideas, so that now von Brauchitsch had no influence with Hitler, their relationship being cool – even frosty. It was tragic, thought Jodl, that the Führer should have the whole nation behind him but not the generals; there was in fact only one refractory element in the army, that is to say the generals, who had neither confidence nor discipline 'because they were unable to recognize the Führer's genius'.

By the last week in September the plans were ready for the attack on Czecho-Slovakia; although only the peacetime army was to be used, those formations earmarked for entry into the Sudetenland had been brought to mobilization strength by the call-up of reserves for continuation training and by the addition of support units.[46] Concentration was to be complete by the end of the month. Then, on the afternoon of 28 September, Chamberlain announced that he was ready to go to Munich and, on 1 October, the German troops, already poised for attack, moved in to occupy the Sudetenland.

Hitler had proved to his own and to the German people's satisfaction that he was right once again, and this deepened his mistrust of – even contempt for – the army leadership. Von Rundstedt was retired, so he afterwards said, at his own request. Beck's retirement was announced on 31 October, and Keitel was promoted to colonel-general. Von Brauchitsch's reaction was an order to the German Army, on 18 December, stressing the Führer's great gifts and demanding from the army its loyalty to the leader – the officer corps in particular was not to allow anyone to surpass it in the purity or strength of its National-Socialist thought.[47]

After Hitler's Munich success, Göring was instructed by the dictator 'to put some courage into the army generals' and run a special course for them in Berlin on the merits of National-Socialism. Göring openly reproached the generals with faintheartedness, while Hitler himself emphasized the necessity to build 'a new upper class'.

Halder afterwards blamed the British, and Chamberlain in particular, in that they had ignored Halder's emissary (Böhm-Tettelbach) to London. Chamberlain's Munich visit, so Halder said subsequently, put an end to the conspiracy against Hitler, for the whole Reich, except for a few senior officers in Berlin, appeared to be solidly behind the Führer, rejoicing that he could recover German territories and, at the same time, avoid war. Whether in fact the 1938 German Army would have supported Halder against the Führer, even before Munich, is questionable, for it was a vastly different army from that in 1934; the old officer corps, except in the more senior ranks and in the general staff, had virtually disappeared, and with it the old imperial cohesion and tradition; the new body of officers was already largely National-Socialist by political persuasion, and they owed their loyalty to the

Führer and not to von Brauchitsch; with the rank and file the change was even more marked. So it came about that, after Munich, Halder shelved his plots and restricted himself to his duties.

Thereafter Europe moved rapidly towards war. On 15 and 16 March 1939 Czecho-Slovakia, virtually defenceless after the loss of the Sudetenland, was occupied by peacetime formations of the German Army without any further reinforcement, and the puppet state of Slovakia and the protectorate of Bohemia were brought into being. Memelland was entered by German troops a week later. During these events that were accepted in Britain and France as confirmation of what had long been feared – that war with Germany was not to be avoided and could not be far away – Hitler was said to have told the German Navy that there was no sacrifice that he would not make to avoid war with Britain. Yet, within a matter of days, he told von Brauchitsch that he had decided to use force against Poland in order to gain 'control of Danzig and a German land-bridge' between Pomerania and East Prussia; planning for *Fall Weiss*, said Hitler, should therefore begin straightaway. And, immediately after signing the Pact of Steel with Italy on 22 May 1939, Hitler summoned his service chiefs to the chancellery to give them his reasons for the intended attack on Poland; during this meeting the dictator mentioned the possibility of war against the West and actually stressed the need for occupying the Low Countries, both to protect German industry in the west and to provide an assault base for operations against the United Kingdom. At the time of this meeting von Brauchitsch and Halder presented the army plan for the war against Poland, and, according to Warlimont, these were heard for the first time by Keitel, the representative of the OKW.[48] At about this time Thomas of the OKW is said to have warned Keitel that lightning war was an illusion and that Germany was without the industrial sinews to sustain it in a general European conflagration.

In the summer of 1939 Beck, retired but still intent on stemming German aggression, turned once more to Halder. But, according to Gisevius, Halder was in favour of the return of Danzig to Germany, and he was too busy with the preparation of military plans to give Beck his serious attention: there would be time enough to depose Hitler, Halder was supposed to have said, after the Polish question had been settled.*

By the end of that summer Britain and France had guaranteed the territorial integrity of Poland, a political move that Hitler countered by entering into a non-aggression pact with the Soviet Union, to which pact a secret protocol provided that Poland was to be attacked and partitioned by both Germany and the Soviet Union. On 22 August Hitler addressed the senior officers of the armed forces at the Berghof, telling them that the intention was to crush Poland, even though war with the West might result. A long peace was not

---

* If true, a surprising attitude to have taken when, according to Speer, even Göring and Goebbels were firmly against this new war. As K-J. Müller has said, when Beck was chief, Halder pressed him in vain; now that Halder was chief, Beck concluded that *he* lacked the will.

good, he said, for any nation, for war was fought by men and not by machines, and Germany had the better men. The Führer could not predict what Britain or France's actions might be, but he did not think that they would come into the war in view of the recently signed Russo–German Pact. In any event, what was important was not that right should be on Germany's side, but that Germany should be victorious. Never, said the dictator, had any German statesman had the whole of the German people so solidly behind him, for he, Hitler, had authority the like of which had not been seen before. The rulers on the other side were beset by difficulties. For Germany the choice was simple, for Germany had little to lose by war, and Göring would confirm that the existing economic situation was so difficult that Germany could only continue on its present course. It was, moreover, he continued, necessary that the new German *Wehrmacht* should be tried out in a limited conflict before it came to a trial of strength with the victorious powers of the World War, and this would be of importance not only for the confidence of the troops themselves but also for the sake of public opinion.

The German attack on Poland, Hitler went on, naturally involved risks, but he was fully convinced that this stroke of daring would come off. England could not afford a war in view of its many world-wide commitments and its falling birthrate; it was just putting on a bolder front than it had done in 1938. England and France were powerless to help Poland: if they tried an economic blockade Germany would just expand to the east; they could not attack Germany from the west without first invading Belgium and Holland. The very worst case would be if England tried to overcome Germany by a long war of attrition, but even for that Germany was still prepared, since its 1939 production capacity was far better than it had been in 1918.[49]

The initiative for the Russo–German Pact, said the dictator, had come from Moscow. Stalin was not interested in preserving Poland or in dealing with the English, and he knew full well that war between Germany and Russia would mean the end of his régime. This new pact meant the beginning of the end of Britain's hegemony. Now that he, Hitler, had made all the political preparations, the way was open for the soldier.

With this strange recitation of truths, half-truths, deliberate untruths and wild misconceptions still in their ears, Hitler's generals left the Berghof for their battle posts and mobilization appointments.*

---

* What Hitler's senior generals really made of the situation is unclear, since their private reaction has for the most part been recorded only after the war. Von Witzleben and von Sodenstern thought war with the west inevitable and von Rundstedt is said to have told his chief of staff: 'That crackpot (*Narr*) wants war.' Von Reichenau reportedly said: 'The man is in the greatest of error if he thinks the war will be over in six weeks; it will last six years!' (Krausnick, cit. K-J. Müller, *Das Heer und Hitler*, p. 411)

CHAPTER FIVE

Poland and Moral Degeneration

Beck, like Adam, had considered that the fortifications in the west would take ten years to develop before they could be effective against an invasion by the French Army. When this view came to Hitler's ears in 1938 he had General Förster, the Chief Engineer and Inspector of Fortifications, removed from his post and had the responsibility for the building of the West Wall transferred to Dr Todt as *Generalinspekteur für das Bauwesen.*[1]

From April 1939 onwards, partial mobilization and secret preparations for war continued to bring the army to readiness for an invasion of Poland before 1 September.* Most of the officers recently retired were recalled to the service. The category 2 and 3 infantry divisions were embodied by the call-up of reservists for what was described as autumn manoeuvres, and the panzer formations were moved into training areas near the Polish frontier. The military preparations for the twenty-fifth celebration of the anniversary of Tannenberg were used as a cover for further reinforcement, particularly in East Prussia, and, at the suggestion of the OKH, a number of regular divisions were moved up to the eastern border to carry out what the general staff called defensive works, in reality the preparation of concentration areas and jumping off positions for the new war. Then, after the OKH general staff outline plan for the Polish war had been presented to Hitler and altered by him in at least one important particular, Halder set off on the annual summer general staff training ride in order to complete the planning.

About sixty-two divisions had been allocated to the campaign against Poland, consisting of forty regular divisions, including the equivalent of sixteen panzer, motorized and light formations, and a further fifteen infantry divisions of categories 2 and 3. The defence in the west was entrusted to *Ritter* von Leeb's Army Group C of three armies, Liebmann's 5 Army, von Witzleben's 1 Army and Dollmann's 7 Army, with a total of forty-four infantry divisions of which twelve were regular, twenty-two were category 2

---

* In July 1939 the peacetime command was as follows: *Heeresgruppenkommandos – I* (von Bock), *II* (von Witzleben), *III* (Blaskowitz), *IV* (von Reichenau), *V* (List), *VI* (von Kluge); *Wehrkreise – I* (von Küchler), *II* (Strauss), *III* (Haase), *IV* (von Schwedler), *V* (Geyer), *VI* (Förster), *VII* (von Schobert), *VIII* (Busch), *IX* (Dollmann), *X* (Knochenhauer), *XI* (Ulex), *XII* (Schrott), *XIII* (von Weichs), *XIV* (von Wietersheim), *XV* (Hoth), *XVI* (Hoepner), *XVII* (Kienitz), *XVIII* (Bayer), *XIX* (Guderian). *XIV, XV, XVI* and *XIX* were in reality motorized corps.

and 3, and the remaining nine were the most recent category 4 formations.[2] The strength in the west amounted to 750,000 men with a further 60,000 conscripts in the labour service and 160,000 other workers of the Todt organization.*

The OKH plan was to destroy the main body of the enemy by a double envelopment of the large Polish Army grouping lying in the great Vistula bend between Cracow and Bromberg, by two main thrusts, one from Silesia and Slovakia northwards to meet a second German penetration coming south from East Prussia. The strongest of these thrusts was to be that from the south made by the thirty-six divisions of von Rundstedt's Army Group South: the main formation there was von Reichenau's 10 Army with a strong panzer and motorized element, its flanks being covered by List's 14 Army on the right and Blaskowitz's 8 Army on the left. The axis of Army Group South lay in a north-easterly direction towards Warsaw.†

Army Group North, under von Bock, consisted of only two armies, von Kluge's 4 Army in Pomerania and von Küchler's 3 Army in East Prussia, separated by the free international port of Danzig and the Polish corridor to Gdynia. The first task of these two armies, as envisaged by von Brauchitsch and Halder, was to overrun the Polish corridor from east and west, before turning south-eastwards and jointly thrusting on Warsaw. Von Bock's force had twenty-one divisions.‡ According to the OKW war diarist Greiner, when this part of the plan was presented to Hitler he disagreed with it entirely since he maintained that von Kluge's 4 Army in Pomerania was strong enough to overrun the corridor without any help from von Küchler's troops in East Prussia. Von Küchler's main and primary task, he said, was to attack out of the East Prussian enclave and move south-east in the direction of Warsaw on the first day of the war without waiting for von Kluge: for the essence of the plan, he continued, must be surprise and mobility.[3] This Führer-directed change was written into the final plan of battle.§

The war was set to begin at 0430 hours on 26 August. On 22 August the London government informed Berlin that the British undertaking to Poland would stand, irrespective of any action that the Soviet Union might take; the partial mobilization of the British armed forces began. The following day Hitler threatened that should any further British mobilization take place he would counter by the immediate mobilization of the *Wehrmacht*, although it

---

* The Reich labour service formed 220 battalions of *Bautruppen*; in 1939 these had been given field grey uniforms with light brown piping to distinguish them from army pioneers (who wore black engineer piping).

† Army Group South (chief of staff von Manstein) had been formed from *AOK 12*. Army Group North (chief of staff von Salmuth) was from *AOK 2* (formerly *Hr Gr Kdo I* in Berlin); Army Group C was from *Hr Gr Kdo II* in Frankfurt am Main: the other peacetime *Hr Gr Kdos, III* (Dresden), *IV* (Leipzig), *V* (Vienna) and *VI* (Hanover) became respectively *AOKs 8, 10, 14* and *4*.

‡ Von Bock had Panzer Group Kempf (East Prussia) and Guderian's 19 Motorized Corps (Pomerania) with three panzer and two motorized divisions. Von Rundstedt had four motorized corps (14, 15, 16 and 22 under von Wietersheim, Hoth, Hoepner and von Kleist) with four panzer and six motorized or light divisions.

§ Kesselring's *Luftflotte 1* was to be in support of *Heeresgruppe Nord* and Löhr's *Luftflotte 4* in support of *Heeresgruppe Süd*. All headquarters down to infantry corps and panzer divisions had a *Luftwaffe* reconnaissance squadron, and twenty-six *Luftwaffe* flak battalions under army command.

had in truth already been secretly and partly mobilized; and the dictator blamed the British attitude in that it 'incited the Poles to terror acts against the German minorities'. At 1330 hours on 25 August the dictator handed further German proposals to the British ambassador in Berlin.[4] Hitler emphasized that he was determined in any case to settle the Danzig and the corridor question and put an end to 'the Macedonian situation' on the eastern borders, by which it could be inferred that he intended to settle his differences with Poland by force. But he proposed to London, with not a little condescension, that he was prepared to enter into an agreement 'to guarantee the British Empire with the might of the Reich after the limited German colonial demands [on Britain] had been satisfied': it was his irreversible decision, he said, 'never again to go to war with Russia'. On the other hand, Hitler added, he was ready to enter into any reasonable arms limitation agreement with Britain, and Britain could be assured that 'he was not interested in [Germany's] problems in the west and that any change in [Germany's] western borders was outside any such considerations'. These last words were meaningless and were intended to raise the hopes of the appeasers; the dictator was convinced in his own mind that Britain would not go to war and he wanted merely to sow further doubts and dissension in London.

According to the original timetable for *Fall Weiss*, Hitler had to issue the order for war by noon on 25 August if the offensive was to begin at dawn on 26 August. At midday on 25 August he asked the OKH for the time beyond which the order could not be delayed, and he was told that the final limit was 1500 hours. So, shortly after handing to the British ambassador Germany's latest proposals, Hitler ordered the offensive to begin, as previously arranged, at 0430 hours the next morning. But then, at about 1730 hours, the dictator heard through the news service in London that the Polish–British pact had been formally signed and ratified, and this so surprised him that he ordered the postponing of the attack on Poland, 'although the [German] mobilization and troop concentration should continue uninterrupted'. The commanders-in-chief were to report to the chancellery at 1900 hours that evening. By then the field command element of the OKH was already moving out of Berlin on its way to Zossen and Wunsdorf.*

By 25 August the *Grenzwacht* was already mobilized and in position; the army mobilization in East Prussia had been practically completed since 16 August, in that all formations were at exercise readiness and had been joined by part of the army and corps troops.[5] In Pomerania and Silesia, however, it had originally been intended to sacrifice the advantages of strength that a full mobilization would have brought, in favour of a flying-start surprise offensive with an incompletely mobilized army. And so it had been ordered that the first day of full mobilization (*X Tag*), on 26 August, should coincide with

---

* Speer, who was not at the centre at that time, associated Hitler's indecision with Mussolini's refusal to go to war. The OKW war diarist, Greiner, on the other hand, says that it was the events in London that caused the check.

the first day of the offensive (*Y Tag*). This would have meant that the troops that were to cross the Polish frontier on the 26 August would have been the motorized divisions and part of the regular category 1 infantry divisions that stood at near-war readiness. The remaining formations would then move up to the frontier concentration areas as they were made ready, anything from three to seven days after the start of the war; the only exception to this pattern of concentration was that the movement into Slovakia, on the far southern flank, would have to be delayed until after the start of the war, because of the shortage of roads and railways there and because of the difficulty in maintaining secrecy under the eyes of a foreign population.

When, in the early evening of 25 August, Hitler revised the plan so that the full mobilization should begin on the next day but that the invasion *Y Tag* should be postponed, this had the effect of alerting the Poles. On the other hand it had the advantage, from the German point of view, that a much greater force would be concentrated and ready for battle by the time that *Y Tag* was finally ordered.

In the next few days Hitler's political demands hardened. The British reply to his note of 25 August declined some of his proposals and questioned others: it did, however, urge direct negotiations between Germany and Poland. Hitler seized on this part of the reply to tell London that he agreed with 'the British proposal that a Polish plenipotentiary be sent to the German capital', and he demanded the attendance of the Polish representative in Berlin 'within twenty-four hours'. After some reflection the Chamberlain government, knowing what had happened to Schuschnigg and Hacha, gave its support to the Polish government request that direct negotiations should be through normal diplomatic channels and not through a Polish plenipotentiary in Berlin, who, they knew, would be subjected to Hitler's bullying. Hitler, however, was by now determined on war, presumably, as he himself said, because he wanted to give his new *Wehrmacht* battle experience: it seemed unlikely that he would this time be able to impose his own dictated solution without recourse to war, and the offer of negotiations was intended merely to place Germany's case in a better light.* Then, on the afternoon of 28 August, von Brauchitsch told Hitler that a decision on the invasion must be given without further delay since the build-up of army formations on the Polish frontier could not be continued indefinitely: the troops must either cross the frontier or be dispersed to their peacetime locations.[6]

Hitler temporized once more: on 28 August he set the invasion for 1 September but wanted the arrangements kept flexible so that he could, if need be, alter *Y Tag*, telling von Brauchitsch that his principal political objective was to force Poland into a weak bargaining position and show Warsaw up to be in the wrong. Late on 30 August a warning order was sent

---

* Hitler said, in the presence of his interpreter Schmidt: '*Ich brauchte ein Alibi, vor allem dem deutschen Volk gegenüber, um ihm zu zeigen, dasz ich alles getan hatte, den Frieden zu erhalten.*'

to the *Wehrmacht* saying that the attacks should begin at 0430 hours on 1 September, but that 'if there should be another postponement then this would not be beyond 2 September' as the autumn rains would break up the roads and tracks in Poland and seriously slow down all movement. On 31 August, at about 1600 hours, Hitler gave the final order for the war to start at 0445 hours the next day; at the same time he strictly forbade any offensive action, or indeed anything that might be taken as a provocation, on the western frontiers with France or with the neutral states.[7]

In his address to his generals at Obersalzberg on 22 August, Hitler had said that he would provide the propaganda *casus belli* that would unleash hostilities, 'however incredible the incident might appear – for the victor was unlikely to be questioned afterwards as to what was the truth'.* On the night of 31 August the German radio station near the Silesian border town of Gleiwitz was said to have been attacked by a number of men dressed in Polish army uniform and with Polish arms and documents; afterwards foreign correspondents were conducted over the area to view the dead bodies. This provocation, approved by Hitler, had been stage-managed by the SS, and the corpses put on display were those of murdered concentration camp prisoners.†

On 3 September, immediately after making an address to the *Reichstag*, Hitler boarded his special train bound for the Polish theatre, accompanied by the first *Führerhauptquartier*, a very small one compared with those that afterwards took the field: for it consisted of Keitel, Jodl and an army OKW staff officer, Schmundt and the Führer's *Wehrmacht* adjutants and liaison officers from the *Luftwaffe*, SS, SA and foreign office, Bormann, the chief of the party chancellery, the dictator's personal physicians, Morell and Brandt, and Hoffmann, the Führer's official photographer. The defence of this headquarters was entrusted to a small *SS-Leibwache*, a motorized flak battalion and the Führer guard battalion commanded by Major-General Rommel, this being a mixed force of armoured cars, tanks and motorized infantry. The headquarters took up a position just inside the Polish border and finished the war at the Kasino-Hotel in Zoppot.

At this time the Führer's headquarters with its attached OKW element did not function as a general or as a field headquarters in any sense of the word. The main element of the OKW, including its *Landesverteidigung Abteilung* under Warlimont, remained in the Bendlerstrasse, and it was Warlimont's main task to compile the overall war situation report each day, these being sent by teleprint each morning to the Führer's train. The few OKW directives issued over Hitler's signature were also edited by Warlimont, as directed in messages or telephoned instructions from Keitel

---

* 'Propagandistische Massnahmen würden die Auslösung des Krieges durch polnische Provokation bewirken. Auf mehr oder weniger Glaubhaftigkeit kommt es dabei nicht an. Es geht nicht um Recht, sondern um Sieg.'

† At first a Lieutenant-Colonel Steinmetz of 8 Corps refused to obey a Jodl-transmitted Führer order that the army in this sector was to put itself under Himmler's orders. (Von Lossberg, p. 36)

or Jodl. This proved a very difficult method of exercising higher command, particularly since the OKH was in Zossen, with the OKM in Berlin and the OKL at 'Kurfürst' at the Wildpark *Luftwaffe* academy near Potsdam. None of the three commanders-in-chief of the *Wehrmacht* were in close contact with the Führer headquarters.[8]

During the course of the lightning campaign Hitler made no attempt to interfere with the conduct of operations and he left von Brauchitsch to get on with his own business. In fact the dictator occupied his time in making aircraft and vehicle trips from his railway train base to different parts of the front, accompanied by a surprisingly large number of party functionaries, all sporting their party uniforms, jostling for seats and position even in the motor cavalcades. Von Lossberg has told how astounded he was at the scene near the San when List briefed Hitler on the military situation, with all the noisy party hangers-on swarming around to look at the map boards and trying to have themselves photographed close to the Führer. And Hitler himself seemed entirely untroubled by such unseemly behaviour, since it was apparently part of his design to emphasize, through the photographs taken at the time, his closeness to the people.[9] This, also, was von Manstein's conclusion, when, near Warsaw, Hitler abruptly and rudely refused to meet the commanders of the victorious German troops, preferring, or so it appeared, to take a few spoonfuls of soup outside with the troops at a field kitchen.[10]

The forty divisions of the Polish Army fought with tenacity and spirit but their defeat was inevitable due to the overwhelming German armoured strength and air power. When, on 17 September, the Red Army invaded Poland from the east, the Polish Army disintegrated. The German losses had been surprisingly small, in all less than 17,000 dead and missing, leaving Hitler so enthusiastic for the tactics of the *Blitzfeldzug*, that thereafter, air bombing, the panzer breakthrough and the deep motorized envelopment became, in his view, all there was to be learned about the waging of war.

By 27 September Warsaw had fallen and, the next day, a Russo–German agreement was drawn up modifying the earlier secret protocol of 23 August; an agreement as to borders was finally reached on 4 October, whereby Stalin renounced his interest in ethnic Poland (but not in Belorussian or Ukrainian Poland) in exchange for the inclusion of Lithuania in the Soviet sphere of interest. In this way the borders of the Reich were pushed eastwards to include not merely the provinces of West Prussia and Posen that had formerly been in the empire, but were extended even further, beyond the Prosna and the Warthe, taking in Lodz (henceforth to be known as Litzmannstadt). This new Warthegau, although its population was largely of Polish origin, was to be Germanized, while the area to the south and south-east of Warsaw that centred on Cracow, Radom and Lublin as far east as the new Russian border of the Bug, was to form the German controlled *General-Gouvernement* under Governor-General Frank. The new West Prussia, with its centre at Danzig, became the territorial base of *Wehrkreis*

XX while a *Wehrkreis XXI* was formed in the Warthegau with its head-quarters at Posen.

According to von Manstein, disciplinary action was taken against members of the *Wehrmacht* charged with offences against the civilian population. List issued an army order on 18 September prohibiting looting, raping of women, burning of synagogues and shooting of Jews, and it is perhaps indicative of the state of discipline that he found it necessary to do so. But, under a Heydrich-Wagner protocol, the responsibility for law and order was soon removed from the German Army and put in the hands of the Gestapo and SS, responsible to Frank inside the *General-Gouvernement* and to Himmler in the recently annexed eastern territories of the Reich. General Petzel, the newly appointed commander of *Wehrkreis XXI* in Posen, complained about the murders of Jews taking place in the Warthegau, and von Küchler, the commander of 3 Army, reported the capricious and repressive measures taken by Koch, the *Gauleiter* in East Prussia, against the Polish inhabitants of the border regions.[11] Blaskowitz took the view that the German Army should have no part 'in supporting the activities of SS murder gangs' and was said to have sent a protest to Hitler when no disciplinary action was taken to punish SS crimes against the civilian population.* From that October onwards began the destruction of the Jewish population and the Polish ruling and middle classes, the Polish clergy and intelligentsia, culminating in the collective mass murders and the liquidation camps at Auschwitz, Lublin and Maidanek.† Frank's diary alone has told how the three and a half million Jews in the *General-Gouvernement* in 1941 had virtually disappeared by the beginning of 1944. It was in Poland that the generals and the officers and other ranks of the German Army were brought face to face with the stark reality of Hitler's racial policies, for the brutalities of the round-ups were there for all to see. By degrees all ranks became accustomed to them; and the generals, since they were no longer responsible for internal security in the occupied territories, came to believe that the atrocities were not their concern: after that winter they neither resigned their commands nor remonstrated in any other way.‡ Germany's path to national and moral degeneration and destruction began in Poland, and the time was not far off when the German Army itself was, on Hitler's order, to carry out the mass shootings of prisoners.

---

* Of the six *Heeresgruppen* commanders in July 1939, Blaskowitz was the only one not promoted to field-marshal in 1940.

† The OKH was fully aware of what was going on, but did not want to dirty its hands, for as early as 9 September a Heydrich remark had been reported to Halder: '*Die kleinen Leute wollen wir schonen, der Adel, die Popen und Juden müssen aber umgebracht werden.*' The officers in the field were not so well informed, however, but Hilberg considers that many of their protests were motivated not by compassion or justice but by concern for army discipline and by a desire to get even with the SS. (Hilberg, pp. 125–30; see also Messerschmidt, pp. 390–3 and K.-J. Müller, *Das Heer und Hitler*, p. 427)

‡ Blaskowitz's reports were circulated by Groscurth to the commanders in the west in January 1940, causing von Leeb and von Bock to protest to the OKH; von Brauchitsch well knew that Himmler was acting on Hitler's orders.

The German victory would not have been possible without the airplane and the tank, and the German military leaders were aware of this. For von Bock, the commander of Army Group North, told von Brauchitsch on 24 September that, remarkable though the victory was, it could not conceal the fact that the inner steadfastness and morale of the troops, and in particular of the infantry formations, could not be compared with that of the imperial army of 1914.[12] Von Leeb, the commander of Army Group West, held very much the same view, and he said that the category 3 infantry divisions were only fit for static war in quiet areas, while the category 4 formations would require further training to meet even that limited standard.* And the category 5 infantry divisions raised that September, made up of men from older age groups and provided with Czech equipment, were not expected to be any better.†

Von Brauchitsch and Halder were agreed that the German Army needed reforming and training. The field headquarters had all been rapidly improvised and needed reorganizing before they would be fit for further service; this applied, too, to the patchwork of army artillery and rearward services. Von Brauchitsch was certain that no more infantry divisions beyond those of category 5 were required for the moment, and that priority should be given to reorganizing and retraining the *Feldheer* so that two-thirds of it could play its full part in any future war of movement; obsolete material would need to be discarded and the older reservists replaced by younger trained conscripts. The conversion of *Grenztruppen* into regular field divisions was yet to be completed, and the panzer divisions required to be strengthened. The motorized divisions on the other hand needed to be streamlined down to two regiments, as the three-regiment organization had been found to be unwieldy; and time was required to convert the light divisions into panzer divisions as soon as the equipment should be available.

In the west the French had taken no offensive action and indeed nothing of importance had occurred there during the course of the short war in Poland. It was von Brauchitsch's intention to thin out his formations from the east, while reorganization and refitting took place. The initiative, thought von Brauchitsch, should be left to the French; the German Army would take no offensive action unless the French attacked and even then operations would be restricted.

Some weeks after the start of the Polish war the *Wehrmacht* commanders-in-chief still had no idea of Hitler's intentions about the west. Jodl, who was often the first to hear what was in the dictator's mind, did not know, and he refused even to hazard a guess to his staff. When the OKW army staff officer

---

* Von Bock, who had formerly been an officer in the imperial foot guards, was arrogant, aloof, cynical, vain and unbending: yet he was to become on good terms with Hitler, of whom he stood a little in awe. Von Leeb was of a very different type, a Bavarian, formerly of the artillery, catholic in his religion and most catholic in his tastes; almost alone amongst his fellows he was of a reflective cast of mind and was quick to recognize, and admit, his own, and German errors. He regarded any German offensive as madness and condemned Hitler's *Reichstag* speech as a lie. (*KTB des OKW*, Vol. 1, p. 55E)

† There were five of these in all, numbering from 93 to 97.

von Lossberg visited the OKH in Zossen during those days, Karl-Heinrich von Stülpnagel, Halder's immediate deputy, told him that von Brauchitsch 'had left Hitler in no doubt that the German Army was not ready for further war' and that the Führer had answered 'that it would not come to that as an agreement would be reached with Britain and France'. The army formations returning from the east, said von Stülpnagel, were being put on the defensive in accordance with von Brauchitsch's orders; and, in answer to a question from von Lossberg as to whether the Führer's permission had been obtained to do this, von Stülpnagel said that it had not – and 'nor indeed was it necessary'.[13]

When Keitel and Jodl returned to Berlin with the Führer, Jodl had at last been briefed as to the dictator's plans, and these showed how wide of the mark had been von Brauchitsch's assumptions. For Hitler had told Jodl of his determination to attack the western powers that year in what he described as 'the fateful struggle of the German people'. A decision could be obtained only by an attack – never by defence – and time was working in the enemy's favour. The most dangerous enemy was England.[14] Every month of waiting brought more British divisions to France and these were of a much higher fighting value than the French, this assessment being based, as usual, on the dictator's own prejudice rather than on any intelligence evaluation. There was no question, the dictator told Jodl, of attacking the Maginot line frontally, since this *must* be outflanked from the north by way of Belgium and Holland. The new *Y Tag* should be set for 15 October.[15] Warlimont, too, had been told by Keitel, as early as 20 September, of the Führer's determination to attack in the west as quickly as possible, should there be no possibility of an agreement with England. The most extraordinary aspect of these events, as Greiner has noted, was that the Führer could, even in 1939, come to these momentous decisions without consulting his commanders-in-chief or his ministers. But Hitler had always been motivated only by his own *Führerprinzip*, sharing his power and confidences with no one.

Von Brauchitsch was already in great disfavour with the dictator. Hitler still nurtured the strongest of dislike, almost hatred, for von Fritsch, and he continued to blame him for many of the army's omissions. When, on 22 September, von Fritsch was killed in front of Warsaw with the artillery regiment of which he was the honorary colonel, von Brauchitsch issued an order of the day in his predecessor's honour, and this called down Hitler's rage upon his luckless head.* And the Führer also learned with anger, presumably from Himmler through the SS and police formations, of what was said to be von Brauchitsch's intention of converting a number of field divisions to static frontier defensive divisions.[16] Beck had always considered that, in the event of war with France, Germany's salvation, in its present state of unreadiness, must rest on its ability *to defend* in the west; any idea of

---

* Hitler had earlier considered giving the command of an army to von Blomberg: but when Keitel had reminded him that if he did so, he could not in all fairness refuse to give an army to von Fritsch, that had decided the question. Under no circumstances would Hitler re-employ von Fritsch.

an immediate offensive war against France had never been seriously entertained, even by a general staff that had been nurtured since infancy on the primacy of the offensive. It was now apparent to Hitler that the rapid victory over the Poles had not altered von Brauchitsch's mind or that of his staff subordinates. Von Brauchitsch, in Hitler's view, could think of nothing but his difficulties, of the lack of training of his troops, of the absence of reserves and of the precarious situation with regard to munitions.

Karl-Heinrich von Stülpnagel had, on 24 September, completed a written study in which he had, in fact, actually examined the possibility of waging an immediate offensive war against France, and he gave the gist of its main conclusions to Warlimont. The German Army, said von Stülpnagel, would not be ready to come to grips (*ein entscheidender Wandel*) with the French until 1942, particularly since this would involve attacking the Maginot line frontally. Warlimont had just been told by Keitel of the Führer's intention to attack France at the very earliest opportunity and invade the Low Countries, but he was not yet at liberty to divulge what he had heard. Warlimont guardedly asked von Stülpnagel for his views on the possibility of attacking into Holland and Belgium in order to gain some protection for the Ruhr from air attack. Von Stülpnagel thought that German troops could undoubtedly reach the Jjssel–Maas line in Holland, but that the Belgian line of fortresses would be too strong for the German Army in its present state. The contents of the von Stülpnagel study would undoubtedly have become known to the Führer, thought Greiner, even before 27 September.[17]

On 27 September, the day that Warsaw fell, Hitler summoned the commanders and principal staffs of the *Wehrmacht* to the new Berlin chancellery to inform them of his plans. The time was opportune, he said, to make use of the unifying surge of German nationalism and to exploit the political and moral weaknesses of the French: another important factor was the superiority of the German Army and *Luftwaffe* over the Anglo–French forces, since these were still not ready for battle. And, without permitting his listeners the opportunity for any discussion, he went on to direct how the war was to be fought. As in the First World War, Belgium would be invaded – and this time the southern tip of Holland also – but the campaign would in no way be a repetition of the old Schlieffen plan since the German left flank in the south would be much stronger than it had been in 1914: and this would mean that the main theatre axis would be pivotted to run west-north-west to the Channel coast rather than in a wide envelopment to the north of Paris. The Führer justified the violation of Belgian neutrality (that he had only a month before pledged to guarantee), by hinting at Belgian collusion with the Anglo–French in an enemy plan to invade the Ruhr by way of the Low Countries: for all the Belgian defences, the dictator brazenly reasoned, faced eastwards and not westwards. All that the Führer required to know from his commanders-in-chief was how long it would take them to complete the transfer of forces to the west, so that he himself could decide on the date of the new war.[18] The commanders-in-chief left the chancellery, having

122

said nothing, and all, according to Warlimont, were in a despondent mood.

Von Brauchitsch raised no objections when he and Halder were summoned by Hitler on 10 October, to have a memorandum read to them – said to have been penned by the dictator himself. Should Britain not respond to peace overtures, it was Hitler's intention to go over to the offensive as soon as the *Luftwaffe* could be assured of a period of fine weather, and he wanted the army to use every single formation that had *any* offensive value in this new campaign, leaving only skeleton forces in the east. But Hitler did not for one moment intend, or foresee, a lightning war that would decisively defeat the French Army at a blow; he wanted only to clear the Dutch, Belgian and the North French coast, so as to be able to protect the Ruhr and provide a base for a sea and air war against Britain.[19] The formal written orders were then issued in an OKW directive signed by Hitler and dated 9 October 1939.

On 15 October Halder told Jodl of his reservations regarding an offensive in 1939, reservations with which Jodl certainly did not agree.* This conversation may have been reported to the dictator, for, the next day, Hitler emphasized to von Brauchitsch that he was determined on an immediate offensive and he set the date at 'between 15 and 20 November', this being the earliest time by which the panzer and motorized divisions could be made ready. By 22 October Hitler had decided that the offensive would start on 12 November, and he at first held rigidly to this date, in spite of the representations made by von Brauchitsch and Halder to both Keitel and Jodl that the army could not be ready by this time; finally, however, he ordered that the offensive *might* take place on 12 November, subject to a review of the position to be made on 5 November, one week before the planned date for the new offensive.

Von Bock, and the two army commanders von Kluge and von Reichenau, were also of the opinion that the army was not ready for a new war, and von Reichenau apparently urged the Führer to postpone it until the spring. Again Hitler would not agree, since he reasoned that time was running out for Germany, and any delay would be put to good use by the Anglo–French enemy. Because von Brauchitsch was afraid of the Führer and because he reasoned that he might achieve more by tact and diplomacy than by a direct confrontation, he had delayed taking any action, hoping even that the severe winter weather would make an offensive entirely impracticable. But as the time passed von Brauchitsch was finally forced to take his objections personally to the dictator and not relay them in a watered-down form by way of Keitel and Jodl. On 5 November, at the hour on which the Führer was due to confirm the opening day of the new campaign, von Brauchitsch went to the chancellery for a private interview with the dictator. He began to read from his own manuscript notes the description that he had gleaned from von Bock

---

* Jodl noted in his diary 'we will win this war [against the West] even though this should run counter to the doctrine of the general staff a hundred times, because we have better troops, better equipment, better nerves and a leadership that knows where it is going'. (Greiner, p. 64)

about the army's unpreparedness and about the cases of indiscipline similar to those that had happened in 1918. The 1939 army, said von Brauchitsch, could not be compared with the imperial army that had taken generations to build.[20]

This last remark proved the breaking point of the dictator's patience, and Hitler's sudden outburst of rage made any continuation impossible: he wanted to know which were these formations; he would himself visit them the next night. The luckless von Brauchitsch, inconceivable though this may appear, did not know *which* formations he was talking about. And this brought on a torrent of personal insults that sped von Brauchitsch on his way. What enraged the dictator above all else was that *his* National-Socialist German Army should have been compared unfavourably with that of the old empire.

Hitler's anger was such that he forgot that the time to issue the code word for the offensive was overdue, as he recounted to Keitel what had happened during von Brauchitsch's private interview. Eventually he had to be reminded by Warlimont, who was acting in Jodl's absence, and the date of the opening of the new war was immediately confirmed, not as a closely reasoned and logical decision, but in a fit of resentment and pique against von Brauchitsch and the German Army.* When the detailed information that von Brauchitsch had been unable to provide was eventually furnished by the OKH it was not of the slightest interest to Hitler, who went his own way, having all senior officers down to corps commanders, with their chiefs of staff, assembled in the chancellery to listen to an address that lasted many hours in which he reiterated all that he had said before, concluding that it was his unalterable resolve to attack before the French and British should first invade Belgium and Holland. On 23 November, in a secret speech to his generals, he threatened that 'he would ruthlessly destroy any defeatist (*Miesmacher*) and anyone who opposed *him* and *his* plans for the offensive'.

Guderian, never one to accept reproaches lightly, decided to protest. As von Rundstedt was unwilling to act for the officer corps and von Reichenau declined to get mixed up in it, Guderian asked for an audience. Guderian was still one of Hitler's firm favourites and the dictator, having heard him out, said, not entirely truthfully, that his criticism was not against the army but against von Brauchitsch. Hitler then went on to discuss with Guderian, who as a corps commander was a comparatively junior general, possible candidates to replace the commander-in-chief.[21]

One of the important consequences of von Brauchitsch's disastrous meeting on 5 November was that from that time onwards Hitler rarely gave him verbal orders but put these in writing.† This was to increase Jodl's import-

* When the order was issued to Heusinger in the OKH he refused to believe it, telling the OKW that 'von Brauchitsch was talking to the Führer, in order to ensure that there would be no offensive'.

† Another was that K-H. von Stülpnagel sounded the senior generals and found that only two were adamantly opposed to Hitler – von Leeb and von Witzleben.

ance enormously, since, as the drafter of these directives and memoranda to the OKH, he talked them over with the dictator, so that some of the OKH staff thought that Jodl had 'been hoisted into the saddle'. Von Brauchitsch's friendly conversations with Hitler, on which the general had laid great value, ceased from this time, and von Brauchitsch henceforth saw the dictator only when he was sent for, and usually in Keitel's or Jodl's presence.[22] The written instructions, that increased with every month of the war, covered a very wide field, from operations to tactics, from disciplinary staff and troop regulations to administrative measures, and were detailed and binding in their application.* One of the most significant of these early orders was Basic Order No. 1 dated 11 January 1940 that forbade any person to know more of any secret material than was required for the performance of his duties. For although this had been occasioned by the loss of two officers carrying secret papers, whose aircraft had strayed over Belgian territory, its long term effect was entirely in Hitler's favour, in that the army generals, even those at the centre, became ever more restricted in their knowledge of the overall war and military situation than they had been before.[23]

As it so transpired, von Brauchitsch and his generals were not forced into the new war during the autumn of 1939, for the bad weather that made troop movement difficult, and close air support virtually impossible, led to the frequent postponement of the opening of the campaign in the west until the following summer. It was, said von Lossberg, the greatest of fortune that Hitler did not begin the war in the winter of 1939: for it was the only occasion during the whole of the Second World War that the passing of time actually worked in Germany's favour.

The movement of troops from west to east had started before the end of September and had continued throughout October. Von Rundstedt's Army Group South was redesignated Army Group A and took up a central position in the west on the right of von Leeb's Army Group C.[24] Von Bock's Army Group North became Army Group B and formed the right wing to the north of von Rundstedt. Many of the army headquarters were redeployed in the west and several of them were given new numbers as a deception measure.† In all, eight army headquarters were deployed against the French and Belgian borders, to be increased to nine by the beginning of May. On the eastern front a new headquarters, the *Stab Oberost*, was raised to command the forces remaining there and this controlled the three border sectors, North, Centre and South.

At the beginning of 1940 the German Army consisted of twenty-seven field corps (*Generalkommandos*) and seven corps-equivalent headquarters (the old border *Kommandos*), in addition to the seventeen home based

---

* These were named variously, without anyone being entirely clear as to the difference, *Weisungen, Sonderweisungen, Kampf u. Dienstanweisungen, Richtlinien, Anordnungen, Erlasse* and *Denkschriften.*

† 3 Army became 16 Army, 8 Army became 2 Army, 10 became 6, 14 became 12 and 5 became 18 Army: the new numbering of the armies deployed in the west was therefore: 1, 2, 4, 6, 7, 12, 16 and 18; a new *AOK 9* came from the east in May.

corps *Wehrkreise* districts.* Between January and May 1940 another ten corps headquarters were formed, of which two were motorized and designed to control either panzer or motorized divisions.

When Hitler had decided on a November offensive against France, the last field formations to be raised had been the five (category 5) divisions in September, and these were not yet ready for battle. It was therefore ordered that nine divisions should remain with the *Oberost* facing east, and that the other ninety-six divisions should attack westwards. Meanwhile Hitler demanded that every use be made of existing resources and that further divisions should be hurriedly put together to swell the ranks of the Field Army in the coming war. In consequence, the forming of new infantry divisions was resumed in November and a further twenty-seven were actually raised during the winter.† Many of these new divisions could be provided, however, with only one artillery battalion of six light batteries, and the guns could only be found by removing them from the divisions remaining in the east and from the training units of the *Ersatzheer*.

Nor did Hitler intend that any field division capable of fighting the French should remain in a defensive and static role. In February 1940 four *Oberrhein-Divisionen* were formed from elderly *Landesschützen* with light scales of equipment and no heavy supporting arms, these relieving field divisions in what was to be a quiet frontier sector in the south-west.[25] Then there followed nine (category 9) *Landesschützen* infantry divisions that assembled from March onwards, these taking the place of eight (category 3) field divisions in Poland which were moved to the west.‡

The intention was to throw every available man into the battle in the west together with every tank and gun that could be mustered, in order to achieve a quick decision – not to put France out of the war but to clear the enemy from the Netherlands and the Channel coast. But it was, as Müller-Hillebrand has said, a hand to mouth improvisation. It was designed to get immediate results and could be successful only in the first few weeks of the campaign.

The Field and Replacement Armies had originally been planned by the army general staff on the Prussian pattern, so that each field division left behind a replacement regiment and each regiment in the field was linked to a replacement depot battalion, squadron or *Abteilung*. The *Ersatzheer* had subsequently been modified to maintain a wartime *Feldheer* of eighty-nine infantry divisions. But when, from October 1939 onwards, the OKH was pressed into raising many more new formations, it was no longer able to provide for a reinforcement and training regiment for each of these addi-

* In 1940 the old border *Kommandos* became corps headquarters (31 to 37) but were still without transport or corps troops.

† Four (category 6) divisions with Czech equipment mustered in November (and numbered from 81 to 88), followed by thirteen (category 7) divisions (161 to 198) – originally with two and then with three regiments. In February 1940 another ten (category 8) divisions (290 to 299) were raised from troops given up from the *Feldheer* and *Ersatzheer*.

‡ The *Oberrhein* divisions were numbered from 554 to 557; the category 9 from 351 to 399.

tional divisions; and so it was that all infantry divisions from category 5 onwards were obliged to rely for reinforcements on the original eighty-nine *Ersatzregimenter* and that the basic ratio of one reinforcement to three field units no longer held good. This ratio continued to decline further as more formations came into being during 1940 and 1941.

Another part of the general staff planned reinforcement system that was sacrificed to Hitler's demand for new formations was the *Feldersatzbataillon*, a battalion of reinforcements that took the field with all of the regular infantry divisions and was intended to cover the immediate replacement of casualties, so that there should be no delay waiting for the reinforcements to come up from the base.[26] These field replacement battalions also acted as divisional battle schools, to acclimatize newly arriving replacements both to battle and to local conditions. By December 1939 the divisional reinforcement battalions no longer existed, having been grouped together to form the third regiment of the category 7 divisions. The loss of this reinforcement organization was to be sorely felt, as it was a loss that could not be made good by the hurried raising of the eighty-eight reinforcement march battalions (one for each infantry division) immediately before the opening of the war in the west. For the march battalions were nothing more than a collection of soldiers, hardly out of the recruit stage, largely without officers and non-commissioned officers.

Another serious problem that beset the *Ersatzheer* during 1939–40 was that of winter accommodation, for many of the troops of the Replacement Army had to be moved from their permanent barracks in Western and Central Germany to the east and to Poland, to provide winter accommodation for the *Feldheer* massing on the western frontier. The same difficulty arose (in reverse) in early 1941 when the *Wehrkreise* in the east had to make way for the build-up against Russia.

By May 1940 the call-up classes for 1919 and 1920 (that is to say the twenty-one and twenty year old) were entering the *Ersatzheer* to begin training, while the earlier classes from 1915–18 were already with the Field Army. In September 1939 the *Feldheer* had stood at 2.76 million men, but the rapid increase in the number of newly raised infantry divisions brought the *Feldheer* total, by March 1940, to 3.3 million men.[27] Casualties had been negligible and, as the *Ersatzheer* had a training capacity of 550,000 men and it was reckoned that these could take their place in the *Feldheer* after only eight weeks' training, sufficient numbers of trained recruits were available for the moment, although these could not of course replace the experienced and trained non-commissioned officers. The position with regard to young officer junior leaders was satisfactory in that, by March 1940, between 1,500 and 2,000 *Offizieranwärter* a month completed their courses and went to troop duty. After a successful trial period these then became officers.

Contrary to the reasonably assured personnel position, the situation with regard to *matériel* was, however, very insecure. The lack of equipment governed the speed at which new formations could be raised, however much

Hitler tried to hasten the process. Optical and signal equipment, in particular, was in short supply. Shortages had resulted in a lack of uniformity in both equipment and organization tables (resulting in the category designation of divisions). An increase in production was out of the question as there was a lack of raw materials, and production was in any case ruled by other priorities. The manufacture of weapons since the beginning of the war had not kept pace with the order of battle increase of a further fifty divisions, nor could it replace the losses to be expected in battle.[28] There were few weapon reserves, so that only quick and decisive victories could prevent a break-down of weapon supply.*

Nor was the ammunition position very much better. During the Polish War there had been a very high expenditure of gunpowder and explosives, using up eighty per cent of the powder and 167 per cent of the explosive production figure for the month of November. The gun ammunition fired off in the month of September far exceeded the monthly production, in some cases threefold, and the initial stocks held were in any case very meagre. If the French had attacked across the Rhine in September 1939 then all the gun ammunition stocks would inevitably have been fired off within two months. This was one of the factors that was foremost in von Brauchitsch's mind when he had wanted to remain on the defensive in the west. By April 1940, however, there had been some improvement in ammunition production, and stocks had accumulated following the inactivity that winter on the western front.

The production of all armoured vehicles was less than 200 a month and, although a great effort was being made to increase this figure to a threefold target, the change to the production of the Mark III and IV tanks at the expense of the earlier lighter models had caused a substantial drop in the number of tanks in service – a total of 2,574 in May 1940 compared with 2,980 in September 1939; and of this May 1940 strength a significant proportion was made up of Czech 35 ton and 38 ton models.†

The position regarding motor transport was entirely unsatisfactory in that, although the army equipment tables totalled 120,000 motor vehicles, the

---

* The weapon state (not including captured weapons) was as follows:

	Sep. 39	Apr. 40
Rifles and carbines	2,770,000	3,137,000
MGs	126,000	147,000
Anti-tank guns	11,000	12,800
80 mm mortars	4,600	6,790
Inf. guns 75	2,900	3,300
Inf. guns 150	400	465
Lt fd hows 105	4,800	5,300
Hy fd hows 150	2,000	2,300

(Müller-Hillebrand, *Das Heer*, Vol. 2, p. 41 *et seq*).

† German panzer strength for May 1940 (the September 1939 figure in brackets):
Pz I (928) 523; Czech 35t (202) 106; Pz II (1,231) 955; Czech 38t (98) 228; Pz III (148) 349; Pz IV (213) 279; Comd tks (160) 135; Totals (2,980) 2,574. (Nehring, p. 124)

monthly production of new vehicles was only 1,000, this being insufficient even to replace normal wear and tear of such an establishment figure. And so the horse came to be regarded as the natural substitute for the motor engine and formation motor transport holdings remained much deficient of establishment.[29] The lack of rubber and steel had a serious impact on vehicle production and the severe rationing of MT fuels restricted vehicle use and training. Inevitably the *Wehrmacht* relied on the Reich railway system for much of its movement and supply, but even this was in a poor state, for the track was in indifferent condition, coaling stocks were low, and the locomotives and wagons were largely worn out. In January 1940 the *Reichsbahn* told the *Heerestransportchef* that it was unable to meet the army's demands that would be required in the event of an offensive against France, and the situation was resolved only after Hitler's personal intervention, when he diverted other resources from the office of the Four Years' Plan.

The occupation of Poland and Czecho-Slovakia and the 1939 mutual aid agreement with the Soviet Union had marginally improved the German war economy, but this and other treaty obligations had increased Germany's foreign commitments and the export of arms. The USSR required machinery, ships' equipment and weapons, in return for foodstuffs and raw materials; but since the technical equipment being delivered to the Russians was badly needed by the *Wehrmacht*, Hitler decided, in March 1940, to default on his agreement and restrict these exports. Some deliveries of war equipment were being made, too, to Italy, Yugo-Slavia and Finland, and Rumania required a significant proportion of the German production of anti-tank weapons (as well as Polish war booty) in exchange for oil. Yet Germany should have been able to meet these needs and rapidly improve its own armament position if proper action had been taken to plan and control resources and industrial production. But the whole economy lacked co-ordination and system, and was controlled by too many competing agencies. And the Führer himself issued frequent and contradictory directives with ever-changing priorities, the rapidly altering demands originating from the fact that there was in existence no strategic plan for the war. For the dictator's way was to meet each political, military or economic situation and difficulty as it arose, with no long-term plan and without projecting himself into the future. For Hitler, as Buchheit has said, there was no '*Nachher*', no follow-up or contingency plan.[30] And he shirked taking any measures that would cut the production of consumer goods in the Reich.

The shortages of equipment and raw materials remained a decisive weakness in Germany's war potential, and most of these shortages were never overcome: and the great qualitative start in armament compared with the other powers gave the German armed forces only a glittering façade. Germany was not equipped to win a long war against powers with superior economies, and this was set out quite clearly in the monthly OKW secret economic *Lageberichte* that were put before the dictator. But Hitler intended to avoid a protracted material-consuming many-front war and he expected to attain his aims without it; he wanted only to achieve a quick breadth of armament without depth, and he imposed this view on his military and party chiefs.[31]

CHAPTER SIX

The Emergence of the Feldherr

The Soviet Union had attacked Finland on 30 November 1939 and it was assumed in Berlin that Britain and France would send expeditionary forces to Finland's aid. Any such move would, thought Hitler, threaten the northern Norwegian port of Narvik which was the main link in the export of Swedish iron ore to Germany. Raeder's fears were even greater, for he told the dictator that if the British should seize the Norwegian coast then it would follow that they would close the Skagerrak and dominate the Baltic by Norwegian based bombers. On the other hand, continued Raeder, if Germany were to occupy Norway, not only would the northern flank of the Reich and the iron ore supply be made secure but the navy would be given an enormous advantage in that the newly acquired Norwegian air and U-boat bases would control the North Sea, giving easy access into the Atlantic.[1]

On 13 December Hitler instructed that Jodl's *Wehrmachtführungsamt* – not the OKH – should study and plan the military occupation of Norway and Denmark, and, on 27 January, a small all-arms staff was added to the OKW, outside of Warlimont's *Landesverteidigungabteilung*, to plan the new war that was to be known as *Weserübung*. Both Hitler and Raeder were entirely clear as to the risks involved and knew that failure could entail the loss of the German grand fleet.

Hitler's fears that the London government would use the Finnish war as a pretext for a full scale invasion of Norway were heightened by British naval activity off the Norwegian coast and the seizure, on 16 February, of the German support ship *Altmark* within Norwegian territorial waters. And so he determined to forestall the enemy *coup*.[2]

Hitler had already met a General von Falkenhorst during an army demonstration at the beginning of 1940 and had learned that von Falkenhorst had served in Finland in 1918. So, on 20 February, von Falkenhorst was called to Berlin, where, to his great surprise, he was told by Hitler that he was to 'invade Norway with a force of six divisions'; Jodl would provide him with the theatre background. Von Falkenhorst was told to prepare an invasion plan by 1700 hours that day, at which time he was to return to Hitler to brief him as to how it could be done. Von Falkenhorst bought an armful of Baedekers and set to work for several hours in a hotel room in the *Kaiserhof* hotel opposite the chancellery. The same evening von Falkenhorst's outline plan was agreed by the dictator, except that, following objections from Raeder and Göring, von Falkenhorst was not to be permitted to have the supporting naval and *Luftwaffe* forces under his own command.[3] Von Falkenhorst then continued the detail of his preparation together with Jodl's special all-services staff, the responsibility henceforth being assumed by von Falkenhorst and his 21 Corps headquarters. The invasion of Denmark, that was to be launched at the same time northwards up the Jutland peninsula, was to be carried out by a separate 31 Corps with two divisions and a motorized brigade. Of the nine divisions eventually allotted to the invasion of Scandinavia only three were of seasoned quality, the two mountain divisions and one category 2 infantry division. The remaining six divisions had only been raised in the winter of 1939/40.[4]

On 7 March 1940, when the OKW issued the directive for the new campaign, von Falkenhorst was put under the direct command of Adolf Hitler as the Supreme Commander-in-Chief, von Brauchitsch and the OKH being cut out of the chain of command, so it was said, in order that the OKH might devote all its energies to preparing for the invasion of France; and in this way the first of the OKW theatres was born. This planning and command innovation was entirely against Halder's wishes, and it began the complete split of the German Army between two separate high commands and was to be the harbinger of the dismissal of von Brauchitsch and the abolition of the post of army commander-in-chief.[5]

The German landings in Norway began on 9 April and an Anglo–French expeditionary force arrived there shortly afterwards. If the Royal Navy had been a little more fortunate and the British army command a little less hesitant, then Hitler's first foray as a *Feldherr* would have ended in a German disaster. For the threatening situation soon caused the dictator to have a crisis of nerves, and, on 18 April, he dictated a signal to Keitel for transmission to Dietl, in command of the mountain troops in Narvik, ordering him to withdraw his men to Sweden, there to be interned; at all costs Hitler wanted to avoid a surrender to the British. When von Lossberg was called to the chancellery to take charge of the transmitting of the signal, he found Keitel and Jodl together, both of them looking depressed. Having read the Hitler signal, von Lossberg volunteered the opinion that it should not be sent, comparing it with the unlucky crisis of nerves in the German high command in 1914 at the time of the Marne. The indecisive Keitel diplomatically left the room. Jodl told von Lossberg that he shared his doubts but the order 'could not be questioned as Hitler himself had dictated it'. Von Lossberg asked permission to delay the order until he had spoken to von Brauchitsch.[6]

Von Brauchitsch, busy though he was with the planning of the campaign into France, saw von Lossberg immediately at his own Berlin house. When he had learned von Lossberg's errand, he declined to get mixed up in it, saying that von Falkenhorst and Dietl were directly under the Führer and were not responsible to him, adding, with typical von Brauchitsch cynicism, that he 'certainly was not going to make the journey to that talking shop[the chancellery] on his own volition'.* Eventually von Lossberg and von Brauchitsch arrived at a compromise, whereby von Brauchitsch acted as if he were in ignorance of Hitler's intention, and sent to Dietl a personal signal from the OKH congratulating the Narvik commander on his recent promotion and trusting that he would defend 'to the last man'. As von Brauchitsch signed this signal he asked von Lossberg, caustically and rhetorically, how they were going to manage in the coming offensive in the west if the Führer was already losing his nerve and going to pieces in front of Narvik.

The Führer telegram to Dietl was never sent, for Jodl pocketed it saying that he would explain matters at the next briefing session: Jodl did not intend to divulge the whole truth and he reasoned that the dictator, when apprised of the congratulatory telegram, would not want it known, particularly to von Brauchitsch, that his nerves had failed; rather than lose face he would let matters stand.

The Führer was so worried that he could no longer sleep and he ordered von Lossberg and Schmundt to fly to Oslo and Trondheim on a fact finding mission, for 'his suspicious nature caused him to rely on messengers against the views of his own generals'. Von Lossberg found von Falkenhorst 'knowing well what he was about' and determined to use the poor signal communications between himself and the Führer to very best advantage in that he got on with the task in his own way. On von Lossberg's return to Berlin he was cross-examined by a tense and dejected Hitler in Keitel's presence. When told that about 5,000 British troops were moving on Trondheim, Hitler was horrified at the numbers, and von Lossberg's consolatory remark that Norway was in any case only a secondary theatre and that 'the more British troops there were there, then the less there would be in France', was regarded by the dictator as impertinent flippancy. Von Lossberg was subsequently marked down for removal.

Norway was the first strategical and tactical success against the western allies, and German army and air casualties had been trifling. At sea, however, the losses to the surface fleet, that in 1939 was hardly an eighth of the size of the Royal Navy, had been staggering, for they included one heavy and two light cruisers, ten destroyers, a gunnery ship, three minesweepers and eleven transports all sunk, and one battleship and three cruisers heavily damaged and out of commission. From the middle of June only one heavy cruiser, two light cruisers, four destroyers and nineteen torpedo-boats remained in service.[7]

Scandinavia remained a Hitler child until the end of the war and the dictator soon came to regard it as his own personal success and Churchill's personal failure, telling von Falkenhorst that if he (Hitler) had been Churchill he would have taken Narvik and the Swedish iron ore area 'even if

* *'In diese Schwatzbude fahre ich freiwillig nicht!'*

it were to cost a million men'. This early OKW success had the effect of binding Jodl closer to the dictator. For the Führer considered, for the moment at least, that Jodl's nerves and judgement had been superior to his own. Henceforth, when the dictator was with the *Hauptquartier*, Jodl could be found, at the express wish of the dictator, taking his dinner at the Führer's side.

Meanwhile the preparation for the attack on the western allies (*Fall Gelb*) had continued throughout the winter. But von Brauchitsch and the OKH had not been permitted to develop their own plans since they were subjected to continual interference in matters great and small. For the Supreme Commander of the *Wehrmacht* meddled more and more in army matters, concerning himself both with the grand design and with the detail, obstructing and directing, and, as his ideas took root, forcing through his demands against the judgement of his advisers and commanders. During this time the dictator developed his own personal style of command, different from anything that the German Army had ever known before, in which he arrogated to himself both von Brauchitsch's and Halder's functions; later he was to take responsibility from the commanders in the field.[8] This particular *Führungsstil* was characterized by a growing confidence in his own military ability – until it eventually became infallibility – and an ever increasing mistrust of, and contempt for, his military staffs and commanders.[*] Moreover, his purely military decisions came to be based on a curious and mischievous confusion of military, political and economic factors. The first winter of the war was marked by the transformation of the political leader, the dictator and the *Volksführer*, to the military dictator and 'the greatest war-lord of all time', so that, in the end, Hitler abandoned his true function of politician and statesman, preferring to wage war for war's sake.

Von Brauchitsch and Halder had originally based their preparations on Hitler's verbal instructions and his OKW directive of 29 October, so that their first battle plan was designed to destroy the enemy forces north of the Somme and bring the German Army on to the Channel, Hitler's long-term strategic aim being to secure a coastal base from which the *Luftwaffe* and German Navy would conduct their war against Britain. The main role was to be given to von Bock's Army Group B in the north, with four armies that would include nine panzer and four motorized divisions, between Venlo and Houffalize attacking on an axis that ran from Liège to Brussels and Ghent. Immediately to its south von Rundstedt's Army Group A of two armies would have the task of covering von Bock's left flank by moving westwards through the Ardennes on both sides of Bastogne to the Meuse. Von Leeb's Army Group C in the far south, also consisting of two armies, had merely a defensive role, that of covering the frontier from Mettlach to Basle. The general staff had considered that von Rundstedt's front facing the

---

[*] Behind their backs Hitler expressed contempt for nearly everyone. Whether he genuinely felt this contempt or whether it was voiced for effect, or merely to boost his own vanity, even Speer did not know.

wooded area of the Ardennes would be too difficult for armoured movement, particularly in winter, and for this reason had decided that the main
panzer and motorized thrust should be launched by von Bock to the north
and south of Liège, even though the OKH knew that this armoured axis was
not wholly suitable in that the Meuse and the Albert Canal would have to be
crossed, and a delay there of even a few days might be fatal to the whole plan.
At first Hitler agreed with this OKH plan, but then began to have doubts
about the river obstacles and the Belgian defences in the north. On 30
October 1939 he came up with a new idea – to make a subsidiary armoured
thrust through the Ardennes from Arlon to Sedan.[9] Halder at first resisted it,
but by 5 November the OKH was forced to agree that Guderian's 19
Motorized Corps of a panzer and a motorized division and the brigade *SS
Leibstandarte Adolf Hitler* should be assigned this new role.*

But then Hitler was no longer satisfied with this change, and he quickly
warmed to the idea of having two irons in the fire with the secondary
armoured thrust being made in the south. The more he looked at the Liège
panzer axis the less he liked it and the more attractive appeared the
Ardennes route to Sedan. How much of this was Hitler's original thinking
and how much of it was prompted by opinions given to him by *avant-garde*
and disgruntled generals in the field, cannot be established. It is known,
however, that the Führer was in touch with Guderian on 10 November, using
Keitel as his ears and mouthpiece. Schmundt was also carrying ideas gleaned
from von Rundstedt's chief of staff von Manstein – and indirectly from
Guderian – back to his master, and both von Manstein and Guderian had
some interest in securing for Army Group A a more significant role in the
coming battle. But whereas von Lossberg believed that Hitler shamelessly
adopted von Manstein's plans as his own, von Manstein doubted that Hitler
was fully aware of the Army Group A representations (that were being made
to, and rejected by, the OKH) in favour of a strong panzer breakthrough in
the Ardennes.[10]

Another factor that told heavily in favour of a main offensive in the
Ardennes was the very strong Anglo–French grouping in the north that von
Bock was likely to meet head-on. This was mentioned in the OKW Directive
No. 8 of 20 November, that spoke of the possibility that the *Schwerpunkt* of
the operations might have to be switched from Army Group B to Army
Group A, so that these strong enemy forces might be outflanked from the
south.

The plan was being continually changed and added to throughout that
winter, with the Führer, as usual, having the directing hand. It is said that the
changes were resisted by both von Brauchitsch and Halder and that these
were forced on them from above and below. Greiner on the other hand

---

* The official name for corps headquarters designed to command either panzer or motorized infantry
divisions was 'motorized'. By degrees, however, it became customary to call those corps that had panzer
divisions under command 'panzer corps', and during 1940 and early 1941 they might be called either
'motorized' or 'panzer'. By 1942, however, all motorized corps were officially redesignated as 'panzer corps'.

credits them with a more objective approach, saying that, as early as the first week of December, both had come to agree that a mass of the armour should be committed in the area of List's 12 Army in the Ardennes. Greiner's account does not tally, however, with the fact that war-games attended by the chief of the army general staff were being held as late as 7 and 14 February in Koblenz and Mayen to test the feasibility of a main armoured thrust in the Ardennes, these leading to sharp differences of opinion between Halder and Guderian. At the first of the war-games it was apparently concluded that Guderian's 19 Panzer Corps was not strong enough by itself to force the Meuse, and at the second, when two panzer corps had been allotted to the 12 Army sector, there was a divergence of views as to the action that the two panzer corps should take on reaching the Meuse in the event of the infantry divisions having been left far behind. Hitler was present at both of these war-games.[11]

The situation was finally brought to a head on the occasion of the posting of von Manstein. Von Manstein suspected that he was regarded as a difficult subordinate by the OKH, and, in early February, he had been relieved as von Rundstedt's chief of staff by von Sodenstern. At the time of changing his appointment he was interviewed by Hitler on 17 February and he himself assumed that this somewhat unusual interview had been arranged, at Hitler's bidding, through the Army Group A staff officer von Tresckow and his friend Schmundt. Hitler wanted to hear von Manstein's proposals at the strategic level for the invasion of France, at the level that properly belonged to von Brauchitsch and Halder, neither of whom was present at the interview. Von Manstein later said that he had no idea whether or not Hitler had already heard the full details of the Manstein plan from Schmundt, but certain it was that the dictator showed a quick and comprehensive grasp of the operations involved and appeared to be in full agreement with von Manstein's ideas, that the main armoured thrust should be made in the Ardennes.[12] New plans were then produced by the OKH, and these closely followed the proposals made by von Manstein. By 24 February, the outline plan with which the German Army attacked in the west was in being.

Hitler did not confine himself to what might happen in the Ardennes, newly chosen as the *Schwerpunkt* for the offensive, but he also busied himself with the action to be taken in the subsidiary axes and the defensive sectors. Nor was his attention necessarily restricted to the army, for the *Luftwaffe*, too, suffered from his inquisition.

It had been intended originally that only the south-east tip of Holland in the area of Venlo should be crossed; but then, in deference to Göring's request, the invasion had been extended northwards to take in the centre of Holland right through to the North Sea coast, Göring arguing that since the Royal Air Force would be unlikely to respect Dutch neutrality, on its way to bomb the Ruhr, it was essential to station *Luftwaffe* air bases and an early warning system as far forward as possible on Dutch soil. In accepting this, the

Führer extended von Bock's sector further to the north. But Hitler was particularly interested in how von Bock was going to overcome his movement problems through Belgium, irrespective of whether this axis through Liège was to form the main or the secondary sector of the offensive.[13]

The extensive Belgian defences from Namur to Liège and behind the Albert Canal and the Dyle position back to Antwerp, engrossed the dictator's attention. It was essential to break through these defences quickly before the Belgian Army and the western allies could come into action, so that von Bock might make uninterrupted progress westwards on his main axis from Liège to Ghent and Thuin. The OKH and the OKL were agreed that this might best be done by the landing of *Luftwaffe* parachute troops and army air-landed formations to take the defences in the rear.* Hitler, however, thought otherwise. He had taken it into his head that, as soon as the German Army made any breach into the defences, the Belgian Army would withdraw north-westwards into what had become known as 'the National Redoubt' north of the Lys between Antwerp and the mouth of the Schelde. The dictator was determined to get German troops into this deep hinterland before the Belgians could withdraw and so, at the end of October, he ordered that Student's 7 Parachute Division and 22 Air-Landed Division should occupy this Ghent bridgehead, nearly 120 miles from the borders of the Reich. The OKH regarded the plan as fantasy.

Göring told Hitler on 6 November that he disagreed with the plan. The area was too far removed from the battle and unnecessarily endangered his valuable parachute soldiers; Göring would have preferred to use them to capture the bridges between Liège and Antwerp.[14] He did not convince Hitler, however, who then had another idea. If the bridges over the Meuse and over the canals to the north of Liège should be demolished early by the enemy, so preventing von Reichenau's 6 Army making a rapid breakthrough, then the target of the airborne troops should be switched to the Meuse bridges between Namur and Dinant to keep them open for the armoured thrusts further to the south in von Kluge's 4 Army sector. And Hitler himself 'would decide on the morning of the invasion' whether the *Luftwaffe* and army airborne troops should land in the Ghent bridgehead or between Namur and Dinant. Jeschonnek, the chief of the air staff, and Student, the parachute divisional commander, protested against this plan on 29 December, pointing out that it was impossible to train for two such different roles and tasks, not knowing until the very last moment which was to be undertaken. In a further meeting, on 10 January, Jeschonnek said that he thought the area of the Meuse between Namur and Dinant was too difficult for the landing of parachutists anyway, and he suggested instead that they be used in Holland in the area of Amsterdam (presumably in a later phase) to assist von Küchler's 18 Army in the rapid occupation of '*Festung Holland*'. Hitler seized on this suggestion but required the airborne troops to land further to the south in the area of Rotterdam–Dordrecht, to take the

---

* Air-landed troops (*22. LL Division*) were not parachute troops and remained part of the army.

Moerdijk bridgehead over the Maas and the bridges over the Lek and Waal.*

The planning of the *coup de main* operations in front of von Reichenau's 6 Army had already been taken over by the dictator. It was of particular importance that von Reichenau should secure the rail and road bridges over the Maas at Maastricht, just inside the Dutch border, and the Albert Canal bridges immediately to the west and south-west of the town, and then reduce the strongly constructed Belgian Fort Eben-Emael three miles to the south. This task fascinated Hitler, who interested himself in the details of the planning, elbowing out the general staff of the army in favour of the *Luftwaffe* and SS. The fort was to be taken by surprise at dawn on the opening day of the war by specially trained troops that would land on the target in gliders; the Albert Canal bridges were to be taken by *Luftwaffe* parachutists while the Maastricht bridges were to be captured by a band of SS men provided with Dutch Army uniforms who were to be positioned in the town previous to the invasion.[15]

These incidents in the course of preparing the 1940 offensive are of minor importance in themselves, but they illustrate the difficulties that von Brauchitsch – and Göring – met with in preparing their plans, and the extent to which the dictator was immersing himself in army matters. For he was already the commander-in-chief of the German Army. It is true of course that he often introduced new, daring and irregular ideas, sometimes out of bravado or pique, and often out of a stubborn determination to alter von Brauchitsch's and Halder's orthodox way of thinking. But it sometimes took weeks to talk him out of his wilder extravagancies.

By May 1940 the strength of the German ground forces of the active army had grown to 156 divisions these including all infantry divisions up to category 8, the four static divisions and three SS divisions. Of this total, ten were panzer, six (including two SS) were motorized infantry, one was a motorized rifle brigade and the other a cavalry division. All the panzer and motorized divisions were allotted to the west. Of the infantry and mountain divisions, eight were in Scandinavia, three were to remain in the Reich and ten were on the eastern frontier against the Russian border, these ten being reduced to five as further divisions were moved westwards during the latter part of May, leaving 118 infantry divisions (rising to 123) for the war in the west. A total of 136 divisions stood ready on the western frontiers on 10 May 1940.[16]

Von Bock's Army Group B in the north had only two armies: von Küchler's 18 Army that was to invade Holland on a flank that was so far removed from the battle in Belgium and France that it was taken from von

---

* One of the reasons that caused Hitler to change some of his ideas was the 10 January internment in Belgium of two German staff officers (one of whom belonged to 7 Parachute Division), when their plane lost its way. Hitler immediately suspected treachery, had the officers' wives arrested and replaced Felmy (in *Luftflotte 2*) by Kesselring.

Bock in the second phase of the campaign and came directly under the OKH; and von Reichenau's 6 Army that was entrusted with the important, though secondary, task of striking on a narrow front due westwards from the area north of Aachen on to Maastricht and the area north of Liège. Von Bock had a total of twenty-nine divisions of which three were panzer and two motorized, the armoured and mobile troops coming under Rudolf Schmidt's 39 Panzer Corps in support of von Küchler, and Hoepner's 16 Panzer Corps in support of von Reichenau. Schmidt had only a single panzer division of 230 tanks while Hoepner had two divisions totalling 650 tanks.[17] Kesselring's *Luftflotte 2* was to support Army Group B.

Immediately to the south of von Bock, von Rundstedt's Army Group A stretched roughly from Aachen to Saarbrücken and had the main task, complementary to the Hoepner/Reichenau armoured thrust on its right, of making the wide sickle sweep in the south that was to envelop the enemy to the north of the Somme. Von Rundstedt had three armies, von Kluge's 4, List's 12 and Busch's 16 Armies, totalling thirty-five infantry divisions.

Von Rundstedt's armour was to form two distinct groupings. The first, Hoth's 15 Panzer Corps, was to be committed in von Kluge's 4 Army sector and, from 14–30 May, was actually to come under von Kluge's command; it consisted of two panzer and one motorized division, in all about 500 tanks. This grouping formed the pivot of von Kleist's encircling movement further south in the Ardennes and was to move westwards, south of Liège on Namur–Dinant, in concert with its immediate neighbour, von Reichenau's force to the north. The second grouping, the main armoured mass, entirely separate from Hoth's corps and directly under von Rundstedt, was concentrated on the Luxembourg frontier to the south of von Kluge, and formed Panzer Group von Kleist; it consisted of a further 1,270 tanks (out of the total strength of 2,600 tanks in the west). It was to be committed in the Ardennes in List's 12 Army area.

Panzer Group von Kleist had been formed on von Kleist's 22 Motorized Corps, and Zeitzler was its chief of staff. Von Kleist had three corps under his command, Guderian's 19 Panzer Corps firstly of two, then of three, panzer divisions, Reinhardt's 41 Panzer Corps of two panzer divisions and von Wietersheim's 14 Motorized Corps of two motorized infantry divisions.

List's and von Kleist's task was to invade neutral Luxembourg and cross the Ardennes in a wide envelopment movement, bridging the Meuse on a broad front between Namur and Sedan and then moving westwards and north-north-westwards down the upper Somme, so outflanking the Anglo–French forces in the north, whether these remained in French Flanders or whether they moved forward into Belgium. Busch's 16 Army was to protect List's open flank to the south. Von Rundstedt was to be supported by Sperrle's *Luftflotte 3*.

The subordinate and defensive role during the first phase fell, as before, to von Leeb's Army Group C in the south. Von Leeb had only two armies, von Witzleben's 1 and Dollmann's 7 Armies, disposing of forty-one infantry divisions, many of them of low quality, this early May strength dropping to twenty-four as formations were pulled out to reinforce Army Group A. Von Leeb had two motorized divisions that formed his mobile reserve, but no tanks had been allotted to his support.

On the opening day of the war von Weichs's 2 Army headquarters was held in reserve with no formations under command, and twenty-five of the army group divisions had been earmarked as 'in OKH reserve' in that they could not be committed to battle without OKH sanction. A new 9 Army was to come into being on the western front on 15 May under Blaskowitz, who had given up his *Oberost* command to *Freiherr* von Gienanth.

Too much significance cannot be placed on Hitler's confident predictions for he displayed the boldest of fronts right to the end of the war even when the Russian was on his doorstep and his own chancellery was falling about his ears. But at the end of November 1939 he had already told his staffs that the attack in the west would lead to 'the greatest victory in world history'.[18] And, when the offensive was finally ordered for 0535 hours on 10 May, he gave the impression that success was assured.*

The details of the six week campaign that overthrew the western allies, defeating an equal number of divisions and a superior number of tanks, so putting France out of the war, are out of place here. The attacker of course usually has the benefit of surprise. But the victory was due principally to the superiority of the *Luftwaffe* and then to the imaginative use of the new panzer arm: without these two advantages the initial momentum would have been lost, the German offensive would eventually have been brought to a halt, and the Second World War would, in all probability, have followed the course of the First. The defects in training and the equipment deficiencies in the German Army were undoubtedly as serious as von Brauchitsch, von Bock and von Leeb believed them to be, and the troops could not have been brought up to the high standard required by those generals until 1942 or 1943. But the fact remained that much of the German Army equipment in 1940 was newer and better than that held by the western forces, and that its discipline and training, inadequate though it might have been by the old Prussian standards, was still better than that to be found at that time in the French and British Armies. The motorized, mountain and category 1 infantry divisions that formed the main hitting power of the offensive, had put the winter training period to good use, and were of a very high standard, even though the performance of the other category divisions left much to be desired.[19] The rank and file everywhere were enthusiastic, and the majority had had some battle experience, however short, in Poland. The training of its officers was in the main satisfactory and the command in the field, particularly at the operative level, was infinitely better than that shown by the French and British senior commanders. The quality of the German tanks in armour and firepower was admittedly inferior to many of those in the

* According to Speer this confidence was entirely shared even by the laconic and critical Fromm.

Anglo–French armies, but this was more than compensated for by superior mobility, better optical, radio and fire control equipment and a high command that was determined to use armour *en masse* as an operative main arm. It was, in many respects, a victory of ideas, Lutz's, Guderian's – even Hitler's – but the tank alone, without supporting air power, could never, by itself, have brought victory. Without this quick six week victory Germany would have shot its bolt, and would have been plunged into a long war for which there were no equipment stocks or reserves.

In 1940 Hitler wrote to Mussolini giving his opinions, for what they were worth, of the fighting value of Germany's enemies, gleaned from reports that came from the battlefield in May and June. The Dutch Army had been taken by surprise and had not put up a concerted or strong resistance though it was tougher than had been expected. The Belgians had fought courageously and well. The French Army, on the other hand, was very uneven, with formations varying from the very good to the very bad. The British troops were what they had always been and were no different from those in the First World War, tough, obstinate and slow, with their officers showing a distinct lack of military professionalism.

The opening stages of the war exceeded Hitler's highest expectations. Admittedly many of the Meuse and canal bridges were destroyed by the defenders, but Fort Eben-Emael and some of the Maastricht bridges fell into German hands. But although the violence of von Bock's offensive did succeed in pinning a large part of the enemy forces, this was not where the war was to be won; the decisive breakthrough was made by von Kleist through the southern Ardennes to Sedan and beyond. The French high command had misread the situation in that it considered the Ardennes to be virtually impossible for tank formations and moved strong forces into Belgium on the line Namur–Antwerp to meet what it considered to be the German *Schwerpunkt* on the Liège–Brussels axis. The first phase of the war, *Fall Gelb*, the breakthrough to the Channel coast, was decided in the first five days.

Hitler, however, was not content to leave well alone, and the tensions between him and the OKH increased. On 17 May, in another fit of nerves, he became convinced that von Kleist, who was already fifty miles beyond the Meuse, and well ahead of List's infantry divisions toiling along in the rear, was in acute danger of being attacked in the flanks. The dictator wanted von Kleist halted immediately. Von Brauchitsch and Halder, neither of whom could be called in any way impetuous, did not agree. In the present disorganized state of the French Army, an immediate enemy counter-offensive, they thought, was unlikely; on the other hand, if von Kleist were to be halted then the enemy would, undoubtedly, soon collect his wits, regroup and counterattack. Although this interference did not halt the advance significantly since Guderian and List circumvented it, it caused continual difficulties and disputes, not only between the OKH and Hitler but between Guderian and von Kleist. Von Kleist intended to dismiss Guderian, who forestalled him by resigning: on von Rundstedt's authority List had to act as peacemaker.[20]

Three days later, on 20 May, only ten days after the opening of the war, von Kleist reached Abbeville at the mouth of the Somme on the Channel coast, and the strong Anglo–French and Belgian forces in the north were surrounded. Although the Germans did not yet know it, this decided the fate of France. Von Kleist then moved north-eastwards along the coast towards Calais and St Omer in order to compress the enemy bridgehead from the west; but, on 24 May, his advance was again halted by Hitler. Von Kleist's commanders urged that they be permitted to cut off the beleaguered enemy from the sea but the Supreme Commander would not hear of it. It is possible that the Führer may have wanted to keep his panzer forces intact for the second phase of the war in Central France, though these were not the reasons that he gave to von Brauchitsch at the time.

The situation was, however, more complicated than some of Hitler's critics can have known. Halder had proposed that von Bock should be the anvil while what was now von Rundstedt's left wing (von Kleist and List) should be the hammer. Von Brauchitsch however could see a confused situation arising, and was inclined to leave the final stages of the liquidation of the enemy cauldron to von Bock. Hitler then came to the wrongful conclusion that the Flanders terrain with its many canals and ditches would be difficult for von Kleist's tanks. He was, however, by no means certain of himself and, on the morning of 24 May, he turned to von Rundstedt for his opinion, telling the army group commander that he thought that the motorized formations should be rested. Von Rundstedt, as was his wont when dealing with Hitler, prevaricated, advising neither one thing nor the other; he thought Hitler 'right to spare the panzer divisions' but only if von Bock could close in rapidly and bar the way to the coast.[21] On 25 May von Rundstedt had cause to change his mind when it became obvious that the enemy was moving north to the Channel beaches.

Meanwhile on 24 May Hitler had returned to his own headquarters, at the *Felsennest* in the Eifel. At midday he received von Brauchitsch and Halder.[22] Both were by now certain that von Kleist must continue the offensive to prevent any enemy escape over the Channel. But, advised by Göring and supported by Keitel and Jodl, Hitler decided that the destruction of the enemy in front of Dunkirk should be left to the *Luftwaffe* and to von Bock, who was forcing the enemy westwards: the enemy was, however, according to Greiner, still putting up a most determined resistance and was giving ground only slowly. This Hitler halt-order allowed the withdrawal and escape of the British expeditionary force and a number of French formations.*

The second phase of the French campaign, known as *Rot*, began on the

---

* An idea of Hitler's views and the mentality of the staff nearest to him, Keitel and Jodl, may be gathered from Jodl's silencing of von Lossberg's protest: 'The war is won and all we have to do is to end it: it is not worth losing a single tank when the *Luftwaffe* can do the job better.' (Von Lossberg, p. 81)

morning of 5 June by von Bock's attack south-westwards across the Somme, with von Kluge's 4, von Reichenau's 6 and the newly arrived 9 Army (now under Strauss). The offensive was then taken up in the centre by von Rundstedt with von Weichs's 2 Army and List's 12 Army across the Aisne, and by von Leeb with von Witzleben's 1 Army from the area of Saarbrücken and Dollmann's 7 Army across the Upper Rhine. The panzer forces had been reformed into two groups, Group von Kleist with von Wietersheim and Hoepner under command and Group Guderian with the panzer corps Reinhardt and Schmidt. Since, however, Halder believed that strong enemy forces were massing near Paris, he wanted to move the centre further to the south-west so that the main forces, together with both panzer groups, should deal with this threat, it being left to von Leeb, with an additional third army (Busch), to clear the Maginot line and the French forces in the south-east.

The Halder plan was vetoed by Hitler on 6 June as being too risky.[23] Priority must be given, said Hitler, to the Maginot line and Alsace-Lorraine: the first plan must be adhered to. When von Bock reached the Marne, however, Hitler approved Halder's proposal that von Kleist should change direction westwards through Château Thierry to Troyes while Guderian should move on Bar le Duc. Paris was occupied as von Bock moved southwards to the Loire, while von Kleist took Dijon and Lyon, and Guderian moved through Besançon to the Swiss frontier. List then moved down through Grenoble to open the Alpine passes and meet the Italians, who had entered the war on 11 June.

French resistance had all but ceased. With the armistice, on 25 June, the fighting came to an end.

Hitler was already the fully fledged and only commander-in-chief of the ground forces and von Brauchitsch and Halder lacked the status, the prestige, even the determination to restrain him or, alternatively, to quit their posts.* When the dictator wanted to test ideas he turned to Jodl, to Göring, to von Manstein, to von Rundstedt and to Guderian or anyone else who suited his purpose. Speer has said that Hitler 'claimed the total credit for the success of the [French] campaign: the plan for it, he said, came from himself'; for, according to what Hitler told his circle, he had read de Gaulle on motorized warfare 'again and again' and had learned a great deal from it.† Keitel, Jodl, Schmundt and Scherff encouraged the dictator in his illusions and so he became 'the greatest *Feldherr* of all time'.

But the Führer was generous to his generals – even to von Brauchitsch and Halder. For during the *Reichstag* session on 19 July Hitler announced that

---

* Von Brauchitsch said to Faber on 10.8.40: 'I just cannot imagine how we are going to rewrite Field Service Regulations, for this war has shown how all our previously accepted principles and views have been worthless.' (Faber du Faur, p. 253)

† An increasingly uttered retort, used by the Führer to silence his military circle, was that *he* had *studied* Clausewitz, Schlieffen and all other authorities; Speer later doubted that Hitler really read, let alone reread or studied, any book on any subject; all he did was to borrow the drift or theme (that he sometimes got wrong and misquoted) to use it to support the course he had set himself. (cf. *Spandau – The Secret Diaries*, p. 118)

Generalfeldmarschall Göring had been appointed *Reichsmarschall*, and Colonels-General Keitel, von Brauchitsch, von Rundstedt, *Ritter* von Leeb, von Bock, List, von Kluge, von Witzleben, von Reichenau and Milch, together with *Generale der Flieger* Sperrle and Kesselring, had been promoted to field-marshal: Halder had become a colonel-general and Major-General Jodl a general of artillery. Some of the new field-marshals and at least one colonel-general were yet to be given *Dotationen*, gifts of money from his privy purse, property and grants of land, usually in occupied territory. And although some German generals have since defended the practice to the author on the grounds that money grants were not unknown, some thirty years earlier, both in the German empire – and indeed in Britain – the difference was that the honours bestowed by the Kaiser or the British King were made public and approved by the cabinet before being put to the vote in the *Reichstag* or parliament. They did not rest on the whim of a single individual, nor were the gifts so successfully kept from the public knowledge that some of the recipients denied, after the war, that the gifts had ever been made to them.

CHAPTER SEVEN

New Commitments 1941

The second phase of the war in France had not yet begun when Hitler discussed with von Brauchitsch the future organization of the peacetime German Army. Experiences in Poland and France had fully justified the raising of panzer and motorized divisions and, 'in view of the open terrain in the east and the fact that the Soviet Union was Germany's neighbour', Hitler wanted the number of panzer divisions doubled to a strength of twenty. And 'taking into account the German armament potential' he set the peacetime army at twenty panzer, ten motorized, and thirty to forty infantry and mountain divisions. No more divisions should be raised and Hitler instructed that the forming of the latest category 9 and 10 divisions should be halted. Then, on 15 June, the dictator ordered the immediate reduction of the army to an interim size of thirty motorized and ninety infantry divisions.* Industrial and equipment priority was to be given to the *Luftwaffe* and the navy.[1]

These new orders were received by von Brauchitsch with some misgiving and, on 13 July, he got Hitler's permission to disband only seventeen divisions and to send the personnel of the other eighteen on leave, provided that they took jobs in industry or agriculture, retaining permanent cadres so that the divisions could be speedily reformed. As some of the formations to be disbanded were low category divisions, static divisions and *Landwehr* and *Landesschützen* formations in Poland and East Prussia, von Brauchitsch had to replace them and provide a further reinforcement for the very thinly guarded eastern frontier; for in June the Soviet Union had annexed the Baltic States and was beginning to menace Rumania. In July von Küchler's 18 Army, together with six corps headquarters, fifteen infantry divisions and one cavalry division, was transferred from the west. The *Oberost* headquarters reverted to a static territorial responsibility within the *General-Gouvernement*, with three *Oberfeldkommandanturen* formed from the headquarters of three disbanded *Landesschützendivisionen* ready to plan the reception of more troops and installations as they arrived in the area.[2]

Meanwhile the German Army in the west had halted at the water's edge,

---

* These infantry divisions were all to be brought up to category 1 standard, according to the Führer's orders. This was not done, however.

from which, it had been understood, the *Luftwaffe* and the German Navy would, if necessary, reduce the United Kingdom to submission.

In the previous November 1939 Raeder had instructed his naval staff to carry out some preliminary planning on the possibility of invading the United Kingdom, but such an invasion had never been seriously considered by the army general staff, or, apparently, by Hitler; and it was Raeder who first broached the subject on 21 May, the day after von Kleist reached the Channel coast, and he brought the matter up again on 20 June.[3] Yet it was not until 13 July that Hitler told von Brauchitsch and Halder to begin planning and preparation for a landing in England (*Unternehmen Seelöwe*), and it was apparently for this reason that he permitted von Brauchitsch to vary the earlier order for the disbandment of thirty-five infantry divisions in that eighteen of these were to remain in being in cadre form. On 16 July the dictator signed his first directive in the form of outline orders for the invasion. Meanwhile the *Luftwaffe* had been ordered to begin its air war over Britain – the destruction of the Royal Air Force having the first priority – and Göring entrusted the task to Kesselring's 2 and Sperrle's 3 Air Fleets, based in North France, with 2,700 warplanes of which nearly a thousand were fighters.

Von Brauchitsch's outline army plan for the invasion of Britain envisaged Busch's 16 Army on the right, landing on the Kent coast, while Strauss's 9 Army secured the centre in Hampshire and Sussex, both of these armies being under von Rundstedt's Army Group A. Von Bock's Army Group B was to land von Reichenau's 6 Army in Dorset with the task of covering the left flank. The whole force was to comprise about thirty-six divisions. The first objections came from Raeder. His preparations could not be completed before 15 September nor could he meet the army's requirement for a broad front invasion covering almost the whole of the southern English coast, for this, said Raeder, would be suicide. The army plan was therefore altered, at Hitler's direction, putting von Reichenau's army in reserve and restricting the assault frontage to east of Southampton Water. But then Raeder said that he could not fulfil the army's requirements in sea transport capacity and timings, and he became increasingly apprehensive about his ability to protect even a narrow sea passage. Meanwhile Göring's air war was resulting in high losses and a realization that the *Luftwaffe* was going to have difficulty in achieving its primary aim, the defeat and destruction of the enemy air force.[4] So it was that Raeder soon found himself opposed to any landings during 1940, and Göring, too, began to have doubts. Von Brauchitsch and Halder on the other hand showed an optimism and an enthusiasm for *Seelöwe* that was markedly different from their previous attitudes to most of Hitler's plans.[5]

The issue, however, was summarized and the outcome much influenced by a Jodl paper drawn up on 13 August, in which he set out for Hitler the opposing views and requirements of the army, navy and *Luftwaffe*. The most important factor was that the navy still could not satisfy the army's needs as to frontage of assault and build-up of forces; moreover, unless the Royal Navy could be eliminated by air attack, the landings could not take place at all. The *Luftwaffe* could still not guarantee acceptable air cover and support nor could it yet meet the army's demands for the landing of parachute and air landed troops. The diplomatic Jodl said that he considered that the *Luftwaffe* would in due course be victorious and complete its task: in the meantime, however, it was becoming increasingly plain that the navy, in any event, would not be in a position to meet the army's minimum demands, 'with which he was fully in agreement'. This being the case, said Jodl, an attempted landing in England was an act of desperation (*Verzweiflungstat*) and failure could have political consequences that would completely overshadow any loss of military prestige. In any event, concluded Jodl, there were other ways of putting England out of the war, by an air offensive against the British economy, by a U-boat war launched from French naval bases, by an occupation of Egypt by the Italians – if necessary with German help – and the seizure of Gibraltar in conjunction with Italy and Spain. These alternative proposals, as set out by Jodl, were to become the guidelines along which Hitler was to conduct his war against Britain for the next three years.[6]

On the afternoon of 13 August Raeder had an audience with Hitler in Berlin in which the admiral gave as his opinion that the invasion should take place only as a last resort and only if the war could not be brought to an end in any other way. Hitler fully agreed with everything that Raeder said.[7] Preparations should continue, however, in case the situation should change in Germany's favour, the target date for readiness being the first week in September. September came and went, with Hitler continually postponing the date on which the final decision should be given. Göring was already convinced that an invasion would not be possible that year and Raeder told the Führer on 26 September that if the invasion were not launched before 15 October it would be best to postpone it until the following year or abandon it entirely.

In the end it was the requirements of the army as directed by Hitler's plans in the east that decided the issue. In a paper to Jodl's *Wehrmachtführungsstab* dated 30 September, Halder pointed out that the troops on the Channel coast could not be kept waiting indefinitely in a state of readiness, concentrated at the points of embarkation: for the repeated English air raids were resulting in personnel and equipment losses.* Even more important was the fact that Halder and the OKH had been given new and heavy commitments in the east that were to involve a far-reaching reorganization of the German Army. Eventually most divisions, including those standing poised in the west, would be required to give up at least a third of their strength to form new formations, the gaps in the ranks being filled by recruits. Moreover the invasion divisions had been temporarily allocated numbers of support and technical units that had been removed from other formations, including

* The *Wehrmachtführungsamt* became the *Wehrmachtführungsstab* on 8 August.

147

many of the divisions in the east; these detachments could not continue as the troops were required by their parent organizations, and their absence from their own stations was holding up the reorganization ordered by the Führer. A final decision was therefore of the utmost urgency.

Hitler could delay no longer and on 12 October *Unternehmen Seelöwe* was postponed, in reality until the Greek Kalends. For Hitler now had a far more ambitious project in mind, in which no seas had to be crossed and in which Raeder would play no part.

On Sunday 30 June, only a few days after the French had laid down their arms, Halder noted in his diary Hitler's views, passed on to him by von Weizsäcker of the foreign office; among the cryptic headings were jottings 'eyes must be fixed on the east' and 'the surrender of England will leave our backs free for the east'.[8] In consequence, when, three weeks later, von Brauchitsch was instructed to study the problems of a campaign against the Soviet Union, both he and his chief of staff had already given the problem some preliminary thought.

Hitler was in a quandary. The risks involved in the invasion of Britain had led to an indefinite postponement, but the longer the operation was deferred the less the likelihood that it would ever be undertaken, for Hitler rightly reckoned that time was on the side of the British, and the British would, he knew, look for fresh allies; the United States was already in the Churchill camp. Hitler had no immediate reason to fear America and he intended in any case to encourage Japan to divert the attention of the United States to the Pacific. On the other hand, any suspicion of collaboration between the United Kingdom and the USSR was of immediate and close concern to him; merely a hint of British–Russian accord, though entirely unfounded, served as an irritant and fed the Führer's suspicious mind.

Hitler, no less than the Soviet Union, was convinced of the incompatibility of the capitalist and communist states, and he had never for one moment altered his political beliefs that saw Germany's future prosperity linked with expansion in the east. Hitler believed that if Germany were to become heavily engaged in a war elsewhere, the USSR would, if it could safely do so, extend its hold in Central Europe, the Baltic and the Balkans. At such a time it might cut off the delivery of supplies without which Germany could not wage war. If Germany were ever near collapse the Red Army would occupy the whole of South-East and Central Europe and take what it could of German soil. Not without reason did he regard the USSR as a threat. Yet it is certain that, come what may, and whatever the attitude of the Soviet Union, he intended to destroy it, firstly because he coveted its territories and secondly because it was communist. Hitler therefore exaggerated and dramatized the danger from the Soviet Union – it was in fact no immediate danger provided that Germany was strong. But for Hitler, the simplifier, the issues were clear cut. In the east the enemy could be speedily cut down by the might of the German Army, the finest that the world had ever seen and then at the peak of its efficiency. In the west, as he told Keitel, this fine army availed him nothing and would go stale watching the beaches.[9]

The first estimate of the forces needed in the east put the figure at from eighty to one hundred divisions – though this was much increased later – and it was considered that about four to six weeks would be needed to concentrate such a force on the frontier. In laying down his design for the war, Hitler saw the future campaign as a repetition of that which had been so successful in the west, an even vaster blitzkrieg, which, due to the severity of the Russian winter and the difficulty of movement between November and April, would have to be concluded in the short summer season. After the glorious victory in France comparatively few of his senior generals appeared to have had doubts, according to the contemporary evidence – whatever they may have said subsequent to the war – that such a rapid campaign was militarily possible, and, for the first and the last time, Hitler was in general agreement with his army high command. Such was the spirit of Hitler's buoyant optimism that consideration was even given to the possibility of mounting a lightning and decisive war in the autumn of 1940. From August 1940 the plans and preparation for the new war went forward without check, and administrative installations and training areas were set up in East Prussia and the *General-Gouvernement* of Poland.

One of the few army generals who was not convinced was Halder. He began to consider that the German measures were half-hearted, for, if war with the Soviet Union was inevitable then he thought that it must be total, with a far greater strengthening of the German Army in men and materials than that envisaged by Hitler. And Halder told von Brauchitsch that he really could not see the necessity to go to war at all with the Soviet Union, for such a war would not help Germany in any way with its fight against England and could only lead to a worsening of the German economy.[10] Halder said that he certainly did not underestimate the danger in the west (from Britain) and he regarded Italy's entry into the war with misgiving, since, if matters went wrong, Germany could get bogged down in the Mediterranean trying to extricate its Axis partner.* Raeder, too, was already convinced that the proposed war would not bring Germany a step nearer its immediate and true aim of defeating Great Britain and its Commonwealth and Empire, and he spoke out constantly and steadfastly against it. A war against the Soviet Union, the admiral said, would involve too great an expenditure in German strength and it was impossible to tell where it would end; as an immediate alternative Raeder would have preferred to seize Gibraltar, Egypt and Palestine, and Göring and von Brauchitsch added their support in favour of this proposal. Even the foreign office disapproved of the venture on the ground of logic and economics, for Germany's stocks of strategic war

---

* Von Bock was another senior army general who questioned Hitler's political and strategic aims. Von Bock did not know that the die was cast until 3 December 1940 when Hitler visited him in hospital. His reaction, that 'Russia was an enormous country whose military strength was unknown', and that 'such a war might be difficult even for the *Wehrmacht*', offended Hitler.

materials, in particular rubber, oil, copper, platinum, zinc, asbestos, jute and tungsten, were so low that even the interruption of Soviet supplies might cause serious difficulties. If, said von Weizsäcker, every destroyed Russian town were as important to Germany as every sunk British warship, then he would be in favour of the new war.[11] But as it was, he saw a future of military victories but economic losses.

By 31 July Hitler's plans had already taken shape in his own head, and he was losing interest in the invasion of Britain for which he had ordered the plans only fourteen days before. Hitler was now firmly set on preparations for war against the Soviet Union and, in a complete reversal of what he had decided before, he ordered the army field strength to be raised to 180 divisions. The planning to invade Britain was to continue, however, and the dictator had also accepted that German troops might have to be earmarked for campaigns in Spain and North Africa. Directive 17, issued on 1 August, showed that Hitler had returned to his earlier idea that Britain was to be reduced by the air and naval war, and that a landing would be 'dependent on the success of such an offensive'. If the land invasion did not take place then the offensive would be extended to the Mediterranean.

During the early autumn, as the possibilities of an invasion receded, the Mediterranean came to the fore. On 12 August Hitler ordered that a panzer brigade be made ready in case it should be wanted to support the Italians in a projected invasion of Egypt, for the Italian General Pariani had told Keitel at their Innsbruck meeting on 4 and 5 April that the Italian Army needed several years of peace before it would be fit for offensive operations.[12]

Raeder seems to have had some influence over the Führer, at least until 1941, in that his strategic ideas were attractive. The prompting to occupy Norway had come from Raeder; Raeder had somewhat impetuously raised the question of invading the British Isles and then, almost immediately, advised against the idea as being impracticable; but Hitler does not appear to have been put off by this sudden change of opinion, for he continued to agree with the admiral on most matters. And when Raeder came up with alternative proposals rather than that of invading Britain – the seizure of the exits to the Mediterranean at Gibraltar and Suez, the dictator was once more captivated by these novelties.

The original idea of an occupation of Gibraltar and the North African coast had apparently been put to the dictator as early as June 1940 by Guderian, who had asked that the armistice with the French be delayed, so that he (Guderian), with two panzer divisions, might cross Spain and the Straits of Gibraltar and occupy French North Africa. Jodl, in his paper of 13 August (and presumably taking his ideas from the OKM), had suggested, as an alternative to the invasion of Britain, the seizure of Gibraltar and Suez. And the German war planners and members of the armistice commission were soon to be made aware of the difficulties in enforcing their demands when these concerned French-occupied territories overseas; French North and West Africa, in particular, were to prove areas of contention.

Raeder pressed upon the Führer the necessity of occupying Gibraltar and controlling the Straits; Raeder thought that the British would probably occupy the Azores and the Canary Islands, particularly if they thought Gibraltar to be threatened. If the United States were to become involved in the war, Raeder could even see French North Africa and Dakar being taken by unfriendly forces. Hitler shared Raeder's fears and wanted the OKM to begin planning for landings in the Azores and the Canaries so that these might become *Luftwaffe* bases. The OKM, Jodl, and Heusinger of the OKH were set to work to produce draft schemes, known under the collective name of *Unternehmen Felix*, and the conception was extended to examining the possibility of the occupation of the Cape Verde Islands off the coast of West Africa, as far distant from Gibraltar as Gibraltar is from Berlin.[13]

Meanwhile Göring was busying himself with his own strategic proposals that envisaged the use of three main groups of ground forces; the first to move through Spain and take Gibraltar; the second to land in Morocco and occupy French Africa; and the third to cross the Balkans and Turkey and move on the Suez Canal through Palestine.

Admiral Canaris of the OKW *Abwehr* had been sent to Spain in late July, together with a small staff, in order to get information on the Gibraltar defences, and on his return, at the beginning of August, the OKW *Landesverteidigung Abteilung* produced draft mission paragraphs for the attack on the fortress; these saw the attack being made under German, and not Spanish, command, by army and *Luftwaffe* forces that would first be concentrated near Bordeaux. The paragraphs were approved by Hitler on 14 August, and it took only ten days to produce the first draft and get Hitler to agree to it. But a few days later the dictator instructed that further plans be drawn up to include the stationing of German garrisons on the Azores and the Canaries. And the Atlantic theatre took on even greater significance to Hitler, when, on 23 September, a strong British naval force with Free-French (Gaullist) forces on board appeared off Dakar on the Senegal coast demanding the surrender of the port and the French warships there. By 12 November the German military plans had already taken shape.

The reduction of the Gibraltar rock was to be entrusted to the Garmisch *Gebirgsjäger-Regiment Nr. 98* and the motorized infantry regiment *Grossdeutschland* that had been formed from the ceremonial guard troops in Berlin. This small infantry force was to be supported by a very heavy weight of artillery, the ground force being under the command of Kübler, the commander of 49 Corps.[14]

The attack on the fortress was planned under Hitler's personal supervision, and the date was set provisionally for 10 January. No air attack should be made, the dictator said, until the German troops were in front of the rock, and, to make sure that there would be no hitch in the deployment, Hitler ordered that the special formation of the *Amt Ausland/Abwehr*, the regiment *Brandenburg* that had been trained for *coup de main* and covert missions, should enter Spain in advance of the main body and, together with the Spanish division outside Gibraltar, secure and prepare the area over which the assault was to be made. The first days of air attack, said the Führer, might not be too successful in view of the strength of the enemy anti-aircraft artillery, but he proposed to neutralize and destroy this and the Gibraltar ground defences by the heaviest possible artillery '*Trommelfeuer*' and the demolition of casemates; for, said the dictator, he was going to use materials to save German blood. The infantry assault would be supported by the fire of the heaviest tanks available, and the flat plain to the north of the rock would be ploughed by shells to destroy the minefields there. And he closely examined General Brand, who presented the inspectorate of artillery's plan for the preparatory bombardment and covering fire programme; this involved the allotment of '9,360 shells to the preparatory phase and 10,800 shells for the covering fire' together with an additional plan for eighteen batteries 'to fire off 6,000 shells on targets to the north of the rock so blowing six assault lanes each twenty-five metres wide' through the minefields and wire. The individual British batteries, casemates and bunkers had all been marked on Hitler's map and he required to know the anticipated expenditure of gun and heavy mortar ammunition on each; even the details of the ammunition supply of 8,500 tons drew his attention and he wanted to know why it could not be shipped direct to Málaga from Italy. All the minutiae of the assault on the few acres of rock had to be decided by the Führer.[15]

By 1940 this was the way in which operations were conducted. What was, however, remarkable was the speed at which the OKW and OKH drew up their plans; and also, at least as far as the proposed campaigns into Spain and the Balkans were concerned, that no planning detail or material preparation was to be neglected. But the Germans had the decided advantage that this was carried out covertly in pro-Axis, though supposedly neutral, states over a period of several months. When the blow finally fell, the *coup de main* could only be crowned with success.

By 14 November, Raeder had changed his mind again, and he told Hitler that it would be impossible to hold on to the Azores and Cape Verde Islands, and Madeira was of no use to the Reich; but the admiral still wanted the Canaries. At first the Führer was not satisfied with this change of front and he sent German officers in civilian clothes to the islands to make a close study of the problem; and in one of his more romantic flights of fancy he said that he wanted the Azores anyway, to turn it into a *Luftwaffe* base for aircraft with a 4,000 mile range.[16] Eventually Hitler settled for the Canaries only, and proposed to station four heavy artillery batteries there.

The final plan that was ready by the beginning of December saw a group under the command of von Reichenau, consisting of Kübler's Gibraltar force, together with a panzer and a motorized division that were to cross to Morocco, a further panzer and two motorized divisions being earmarked for the occupation of Portugal; a number of 240 mm and 150 mm naval coastal batteries were held ready for movement to Ceuta. The *Luftwaffe* element, under von Richthofen, was made up of ten *Gruppen*, of which eight were dive-bombers, some reconnaissance squadrons and six flak battalions, supported by a supply fleet of 3,000 lorries. Göring resisted with vigour the OKH request to Hitler that von Richthofen be put under von Reichenau's command. The Spanish role was to be solely that of providing and safeguarding communications.

On 5 December von Brauchitsch told Hitler that a decision on *Felix* must be given by mid December, as the attack on Gibraltar could not take place until 25–38 days after the crossing of the Franco–Spanish frontier and 'the campaign itself would take a month'. By mid May at the latest many of these German troops in Spain and Morocco would have to be withdrawn to the east.[17]

This forced Hitler to attempt to pin Franco to an agreement and, two days later, on 7 December, the *Caudillo* declined to allow the new campaign, basing his refusal on Spain's dependence on the USA and Britain for the means to live. Then followed the final cancellation of *Felix* the next day, although plans were immediately put in hand for the military occupation of unoccupied France (*Attila*), should this be necessary, the project having been occasioned by a stiffening of the Vichy attitude and the fear that French North Africa might throw in its hand with the British.

Hitler wanted Mussolini to attack Suez and not Greece, and it had been decided, as early as 10 August 1940, that, if the invasion of Britain were not undertaken that year, then a panzer corps should be offered to the Italians in Libya. Planning began for the preparation and movement of these troops. Immediately afterwards, however, Hitler reduced the offer to a brigade 'since he did not want to hurt the Italians' feelings', but by 26 August he favoured once more the despatch of a corps.[18] Von Rintelen, the military attaché in Rome, who, from 20 September, had become the OKW representative to the *Comando Supremo*, then reported that the Italians were more interested in the support of German dive-bombers than armour; but this was contradicted by Mussolini, who told Hitler on 4 October that he wanted tanks, and the figure of a panzer regiment of 100 tanks seems to have been agreed between the two. But then, after *Ritter* von Thoma, the commander of 3 Panzer Division that was finding some of the troops, returned from Libya, his report was so discouraging that Hitler decided that the force should continue its preparation, but should not be despatched.[19] Meanwhile the Italian invasion of Egypt, that had begun on 12 September, had come to a halt about sixty miles from the frontier.

It was obvious to von Rintelen and to the OKW that the Italians were about to invade Greece from Albania, although the Italian generals denied it. And, as Greiner has said, it gives an indication of Hitler's relationship with his military staff in that Jodl should have assumed, and told his own OKW subordinates, that Hitler 'must have been consulted and have given approval for the [Italian] invasion [of Greece]'; but for some reason the dictator was believed to have concealed it from his staff.[20] Hitler in fact did not know, and he was only informed of the 28 October invasion immediately before it took place. From then onwards, he said, he 'would no longer co-operate with the Italians'.

Circumstances, however, forced him to do so. The Supreme Commander-in-Chief was shortly to move an air transport group to Albania and 10 Air Corps to Sicily, this latter formation having the task of neutralizing Malta as a sea and air base and so protecting the Italian sea communications to North Africa. For the Italian battle fleet in Taranto had suffered serious loss by air torpedo attack, and the Italian Libyan Army was in danger of disintegration following the British counter-offensive from Egypt that had begun on 9 December. On 19 December von Rintelen was requesting the immediate despatch of a panzer division to Tripoli (and war material to equip ten Italian divisions) while, on 28 December, General Marras, who was von Rintelen's Italian counter-part in the OKW, told Keitel that, although Cyrenaica could not be held, the arrival of 'even a small German formation might save the situation in Tripolitania in that it would force caution not only on the British but also on the French in North Africa'.[21]

On 9 January Hitler decided on the despatch not of a panzer formation but of what he called a *Sperrverband*, 'a blocking formation', particularly strong in defensive weapons. And so the first Libyan force was an *ad hoc* 5 Light Division made up of elements of panzer and army troops: it consisted of *Regt Stab 200*, a reconnaissance battalion, two anti-tank and two machine-gun battalions, an artillery and army flak battalion and a *Luftwaffe* reconnaissance squadron and flak battalion.[22] The grouping was strong in armoured cars, anti-tank guns and flak and medium machine-guns and consisted of 8,000 men and 1,300 vehicles. Its commander, *Freiherr* von Funk, was sent to Libya immediately.

The Italian situation continued to deteriorate rapidly and it was described when von Funk returned and made his report to the Führer on 1 February, in the presence of Keitel, Jodl, von Brauchitsch and Halder. Von Funk thought that at least a further panzer division should be added to the force if catastrophe was to be averted, and although this pessimistic opinion was supported by both von Brauchitsch and von Rintelen it cost von Funk his command, for he was replaced, presumably at Hitler's bidding, by Streich.[23] It was decided, however, to add 5 Panzer Regiment to 5 Light Division, and 15 Panzer Division, under von Prittwitz und Gaffron, was to be included in the force that had by then grown to 29,000 men and 6,300 vehicles. This new *Afrika Korps* was put under Rommel, an infantry officer who had been speedily advanced from the command of the Führer guard in 1939 to a panzer division in France in 1940. By early March the force was already landing in Africa, and Rommel's energetic intervention soon transformed the scene, so that the British, involved in Greece, withdrew almost without a fight. By May, after Rommel had reached Tobruk, his rapid advance came to a stop. The resistance there was so tough that German casualties mounted fast; and the Italians, and his own commander Streich, disapproved of the obstinacy of the corps commander's attacks, for they believed that he was merely dissipating German strength.

The battle was, however, directed not only by Rommel, but also by the overseer in distant Berlin. For Paulus, the *O Qu 1* and Halder's deputy, was sent to Rommel's headquarters on a fact finding mission. Paulus, like the Italians, thought that the battle should be broken off for regrouping and rest during the hottest months of the year.[24] But this was not Rommel's way and he proposed to stay in front of Tobruk and continue his offensive probes elsewhere. Rommel, disapproved of by Halder and regarded as an adventurer and *parvenu* by some of the more senior members of the *Generalität*, found favour in Hitler's eyes, and his present plans were agreed.

Meanwhile, however, the general political situation was becoming increasingly unsettled in the east from the Balkans to the North Cape. Russia, in addition to annexing the Baltic States, had occupied Bessarabia and part of Bukovina, and continued to menace Rumania, presumably seeking to control Rumanian oil and the Danube waterway. Hungary had threatened to go to war with Rumania over the return of Transylvanian territories lost after the First World War, and it appeared possible that the Red Army might intervene there. Moscow was also laying claim to the Petsamo nickel mines in North Finland.

The first requirement was to bolster the lightly defended eastern frontiers. A German mountain corps was sent to Kirkenes, the far northern border of Norway close to Petsamo. Then, on 6 September 1940, von Bock's Army Group B was ordered from Normandy to the east together with von Kluge's 4 Army and List's 12 Army, so that, fourteen days later, von Bock had under his command on the eastern frontier, three armies, 18, 4 and 12 (from north to south), together with an additional four corps (of one panzer and nine infantry divisions) from France and another corps and two panzer and two infantry divisions from the Reich. In order to find room for these new formations the Replacement Army units in *Wehrkreis I* (East Prussia) and *Wehrkreis VIII* (Upper Silesia) were sent to Bohemia-Moravia and Alsace.[25]

A separate operation was planned to safeguard the Rumanian oil so essential for the German war economy. As a first step two panzer divisions were removed to Vienna, and Halder began to prepare for the quick occupation of the Rumanian oilfields should this become necessary, earmarking 16 Motorized Corps and 40 Corps for the task, these having under command four panzer and three motorized infantry divisions.*

* 2, 5, 6, 9 Pz Divs; 2, 13 Mot Inf Divs and 60 Inf Div (about to be motorized) and 11 Rifle Bde.

The danger to Rumania was somewhat relieved by German mediation and the enforced settlement of the Hungarian claim by the August 1940 Vienna Award, and, the following month, by General Antonescu's assumption of power, for the new Rumanian dictator began to work closely with the Germans, asking for war equipment and for German troops to be stationed in his country to train the Rumanian Army. On 10 October 13 Motorized Infantry Division crossed Hungary and entered Rumania (where it was reorganized as 13 Panzer Division) and 16 Panzer Division joined it in December. *Luftwaffe* and naval missions and forces followed, having as their task not only the training of the Rumanian armed forces but also the defence of the Ploesti oil and the Danube waterway. All the OKW forces in Rumania came under the head of the army mission.

Mussolini's adventure into Greece was, however, causing the German dictator further concern, and he feared British intervention in the Greek peninsula that would provide his enemy with mainland air bases for attacking the Rumanian oilfields. Hitler wanted above all to bring in Bulgaria as a German ally and hold Turkey in check. *Weisung 18* on 18 November ordered a new major offensive (*Marita*) to be prepared by the OKH for a force of ten (later raised to twelve) divisions to move into Bulgaria and then across the Greek frontier, so occupying Greece, including the Peloponnese, in order to forestall the British.[26] The careful and detailed planning and vast preparatory work that followed, spread over many months, enabled the German Army to occupy in the following April not only Greece but also Yugo-Slavia in a short whirlwind campaign, so rescuing their Italian ally. From that November the *Luftwaffe* had already established inside Bulgaria a 1,000 man strong air early warning organization, its members wearing civilian clothes.

The *Marita* plan, produced by Halder and accepted by Hitler on 5 December, provided for a spring offensive to be made by an army (originally this was von Kluge's 4 Army but was later changed to List's 12 Army) consisting of von Kleist's Panzer Group 1 and a force of five corps, four panzer, two motorized, two mountain and ten infantry divisions, supported by von Richthofen's 8 Air Corps. Further provision was made to increase List's force to twenty-four divisions should this be necessary. Hitler busied himself with many of the details, requiring a study as to whether the Greek islands could not be occupied by glider-borne troops, and directing that at least six divisions be held on the southern flank 'ready to attack Turkey should it interfere'. 12 Army was to enter Rumania and hold itself at twelve hours notice, from 25 January, to cross into Bulgaria, and German military engineers were to collect men and material ready to throw a bridge over the Danube as soon as the order was given. Zeitzler, von Kleist's chief of staff, and a number of army reconnaissance groups in civilian clothes were to go to Bulgaria straightaway, and work was begun on improving Bulgarian roads and bridges.[27] On 9 January Hitler approved von Brauchitsch's proposal that the first wave of troops, consisting of armour, the army troops and four infantry divisions, should cross the frozen Danube at the beginning of February without waiting for the pioneers' bridge to be built. Two panzer divisions, in accordance with Bulgarian wishes, were already in the Dobrudja south of the Danube. The building of the German bridge over the Danube began on 28 February and, at dawn on 2 March, 12 Army moved into Bulgaria, all Bulgarian communications and frontiers having been sealed from the outside world.[28]

The bulk of List's force was therefore poised and ready long before the spring of 1941 and this explains, in large part, the brilliant success of the Balkan campaign in the following April.

At the meeting on 9 January 1941, at which von Brauchitsch had been present, Hitler had clarified his intentions as to priorities for the coming year. The invasion of the Soviet Union (*Barbarossa*) was the decisive task; and Hitler explained that the aim in the Balkans was the safeguarding of German interests and the protection of the flank, and, together with the expedition into North Africa, to prevent Italy from breaking up. This was certainly reflected in the great swing of the preponderance of the German formations from the west to the centre during the winter months and by the rapid expansion in the number of infantry divisions. By 7 October 1940 the German Army had a total strength of 155 divisions of which only sixty-four stood in France: fifty were in the Reich, either being raised or reformed. There were ten divisions in Scandinavia but, as yet, only thirty divisions were deployed against the eastern frontiers. Most of the motorized formations had already been withdrawn from the west. By 21 December the deployment ratio was very much the same, for, although the German Army strength had been increased to 184 divisions, sixty-two stood in the west, with nine in Scandinavia, and still only thirty on the eastern frontier (with a further two panzer divisions in Rumania).[29] The newly formed divisions were held back in the Reich, for the total there had risen from fifty to eighty-one.

There were other changes in the field command that gave some indication of the swing from west to east. On 30 October von Brauchitsch moved his OKH headquarters from Fontainebleau back to Zossen. Only five days before that, von Leeb's Army Group C together with von Weichs's 2 Army were recalled from France to Germany to take command of a new 11 Army and the recently raised divisions from the *Ersatzheer*. Von Rundstedt became Commander-in-Chief West (*OB West*) together with his own Army Group A and a newly raised Army Group D, it being the intention that von Rundstedt's army group headquarters should eventually be moved eastwards to take a major role in the invasion of Russia, the command in the west being transferred to von Witzleben's Army Group D. Three of the most experienced of the five armies still standing in the west, von Reichenau's 6, Strauss's 9 and Busch's 16 Armies, were yet to be transferred to the east in the coming months of the new year.

The greatest change, however, was that in the divisional pattern. On 31 July when Hitler had ordered an increase in the army strength to 180 divisions, a further sixty divisions were needed because of the earlier disbandments following the dictator's directions that the army should be run down. This latest intended increase demanded, in addition, the raising of further higher headquarters and the strengthening of Fromm's *Ersatzheer*.

The first step in the expansion was to raise the required number of panzer and motorized divisions. The ten panzer divisions were to be doubled in number but each was to be halved in its tank strength – from its earlier divisional organization of two panzer regiments with a total establishment of about 280 tanks, to a single tank regiment of about 140 tanks, and the panzer brigade headquarters within the division was to be done away with. But, whereas most of the early 1940 panzer divisions had had only one rifle regiment of two battalions, all new panzer divisions were to be increased to two *Schützenregimenter*, each of two battalions of five companies, most of these being lorry-borne infantry.[30] Guderian attacked this change most bitterly inasmuch as the actual tank strength of the panzer division had been halved and the overall German Army order of battle had not been improved by a single tank. Hitler liked the change in that he had a more imposing divisional battle list, and he well knew that German industry was as yet unable to increase the overall tank holdings. Nehring, who was Guderian's loyal and admiring subordinate, took a different view, however, from that of his former chief, for he had regarded the 280 tank panzer division as being too large and unwieldy for one divisional commander to handle.[31]

From the autumn of 1940 all the panzer divisions were reduced to one panzer regiment of two battalions (*Abteilungen*) although a number of the divisions did in fact keep three battalions (so that their tank establishment remained at three quarters of the June 1940 figure). Five of the divisions were still equipped with Czech tanks mounting 37 mm guns.* The panzer regiments that were given up were taken in to the new panzer divisions that numbered from 11 to 20. The framework of these ten divisions was not based, however, on the old panzer arm but, instead, on the existing motorized infantry and infantry divisions that were transformed into new panzer divisions merely by the addition of the panzer regiment to their two existing motorized infantry regiments, or, where infantry divisions had been selected for conversion, two infantry regiments converted to a lorry-borne role.†

In early 1940 there had been only four motorized divisions in the German Army (2, 13, 20 and 29) and these had been reduced to two regiments each

* 7, 8, 12, 19 and 20 Pz Divs.

† 11 Pz Div was formed on *Mot. Schütz. Bde 11*; 12 Pz Div on *2 ID (mot)*; 13 Pz Div on *13 ID (mot)*; 14 Pz Div on *4 ID*; 15 Pz Div on *33 ID*; 16 Pz Div on *16 ID*; 17 Pz Div on *27 ID*; 19 Pz Div from *19 ID*; and 18 and 20 Pz Divs from surplus regiments.

(as opposed to the motorized divisions of the *Waffen SS* that still retained three). The conversion of 2 and 13 Motorized Infantry to panzer divisions left only two motorized divisions remaining, and these had to be increased to ten by converting a further eight divisions from infantry, bringing the total of panzer/motorized divisions up to thirty.*

The conversion of infantry to *Schnelle Truppe* formations left further gaps in the infantry formation order of battle. The rapid increase from 120 to 180 field divisions was achieved in the time-honoured fashion of divide and split and then reform, and this certainly ensured that all new formations had a proportion of experienced personnel. On the other hand it meant that seventy-three infantry divisions had at least one third of their troops removed from them, to be replaced by inexperienced half-trained men. Nor did this involve merely the removal of regiments or separate battalions, but it cut through the whole of the divisional organization. The first phase of this reorganization started in mid November, twenty-one of the affected infantry divisions being in the west and twenty-three in the east, so that, as Müller-Hillebrand has said, an invasion of Britain would in any event have been impossible after this date. At the end of November a further twenty-two divisions in the west were torn apart as phase two of the expansion. For a few months the efficiency of the field army had suffered a serious reduction; this left Germany vulnerable to attack, that at that time could only have come from the east, from Soviet Russia. In the circumstances however it was the only solution in the time available.

The category system of raising new divisions that had been used in 1938 was continued. Thirty category 1 (and some category 4) divisions that formed the kernel of the field force each gave up one regimental head-quarters and all regiments gave up their third battalion, so that these immediately formed ten new (category 11) divisions. Another ten divisions (of category 12) were afterwards formed in exactly the same fashion and from the same source, six of the new divisions being infantry and four of them light divisions, these having five company battalions similar to those of mountain troops, since they were intended for use in desert or roadless terrain. It was then the turn of the category 2, 7 and 8 infantry divisions to give up a third of their strength to form nine (category 13) static (*bodenstän-dige*) divisions to hold the French beaches, each having three regiments on reduced scales of equipment and lacking the regimental 13 and 14 com-panies. These were followed by the embodiment of a further eight category 14 divisions. The fifteen category 15 divisions were two-regiment occu-pation divisions that had no medium mortars or medium machine-gun companies, or anti-tank and infantry-gun support, while the final (category 16) divisions were formed by breaking up three infantry divisions to make nine security divisions without any support weapons, designed mainly for the rearward areas in the east.[32] The reorganization applied not only to infantry

---

* The infantry divisions that became motorized were: 3, 10, 14, 18, 25, 36 and 60, together with a newly formed *16 ID (mot)* from elements of *16 ID* (the rest formed 16 Pz Div).

but to all the divisional supporting arms and services, all of which were broken up and reformed.*

As a result of this vast reorganization that took place during the winter of 1940–41, a total of eighty-four new divisions of all type had been formed at the cost of the conversion or the breaking up of seventeen of the 1939 motorized infantry or infantry divisions, so that by June 1941 the German Army order of battle had been increased to 205 divisions. Yet it is doubtful whether this vast army was in reality any more powerful than the 140 divisions that had poured into France in May 1940. The tank and artillery strength had not increased, although there had been some improvement in the pattern of equipment. Much Czech material was still in use. The actual increase in the number of divisions was in part a façade, for it had sometimes been achieved by a drastic reduction in divisional bayonet strength, and sometimes by forming numbers of divisions that were 'men with rifles', lacking mortar, medium machine-gun, artillery and anti-tank support. Nearly all of these formations had a very reduced fighting value.

The planning, logistical maintenance and the operational and tactical capabilities of the infantry divisions continued to be bedevilled by the category system, for everything depended on the category–strength, organization, equipment, mobility and fighting potential. So it came about that the enemy, like the Zossen general staff, soon began to group the German army divisions by these categories (since these could often be deduced from the numbering), and from the category the enemy evaluated their likely fighting value. Many of the standard divisions remaining in the west in 1941 and 1942 came to be so drained of personnel and equipment that they were officially designated 'not to be used in the east' (*nicht ostfähig*), while the newly raised occupation and security divisions that were deployed in the east and the Balkans were intended not for warfare but for policing and anti-partisan duties.

By June 1941 the troops in western Europe had been reduced to thirty-eight skeleton infantry divisions of which seven were category 15 static divisions. Not a single panzer or motorized division remained, and the few tanks that von Witzleben had as his only armoured reserve were captured tanks grouped into two panzer brigades.†

---

* The category 11 divisions were numbered from 121 to 137, category 12 from 97 to 113, category 13 from 302 to 327, category 14 from 332 to 342, and category 15 from 702 to 719 Infantry Divisions.

† The divisional order of battle on 21 June 1941 was as follows: France 38; Norway 12; Balkans 7; Libya 2; Denmark 1; East 145: total 205 divisions. Five of these were *Waffen SS*. (*Schematische Kriegsgliederung 27.6.41 Gen St d H Op Abt III Pruf. Nr 16272*)

CHAPTER EIGHT

Barbarossa

During the period between August 1939 and June 1941 the status of the German Army within the high command and government had continued to deteriorate. On 30 August 1939 the Führer had instructed that a ministerial defence council be set up under the chairmanship of Göring; but this council consisted of the chiefs of the Reich chancellery and the party chancellery, and the two General-Commissioners (*Generalbevollmächtigte*) for the Economy and for Administration; Keitel was the only military member and the army was not otherwise represented.[1]

In March 1940, a civilian ministry for armaments and munitions had been introduced to relieve the military of the responsibility for ensuring the adequate manufacture of equipment; but this also began to have the effect of divorcing the army from its production sources and resulted in the army's requirements as to design and development being neglected. Then again, the movement of von Brauchitsch and the OKH to Zossen and Wunsdorf, while Hitler and the OKW remained over twenty miles away in the chancellery and the Bendlerstrasse in the centre of Berlin, with Göring in Potsdam, was to lead to serious difficulties and was contrary to the command needs in war. A large part of the headquarters of the *Ersatzheer*, too, was in Berlin. The political and military leadership and the waging of war by land and air could not be separated in this way. Already, by 10 September 1939, von Brauchitsch had told Halder how difficult he found it to work now that the army high command had been hived off from political development and direction, with the leadership of the armed forces being split between OKW and OKH.[2]

Consequently, the army planning was often at odds with what was being arranged in the OKW, and this state of affairs was made worse by Hitler's character, for the dictator rarely told any one of his long-term plans. Instead, he gave voice to incomplete ideas as they entered his head; sometimes his views were prompted by contrariness or caprice, and, not unnaturally, these spread confusion in his own circle and throughout the government. Any attempt by the OKH and army general staff to think for itself and plan ahead, so that it might be in a better position to accommodate itself to sudden changes in policy or to new political and military developments, split

161

it even further from the suspicious dictator, who would not tolerate any independent judgement of the situation being made by von Brauchitsch or his staff. Directives might be issued by Hitler through Jodl or Keitel, in which case it was likely that all interested services and ministers would be kept informed. But many of Hitler's orders were given out in the course of private conversations with Göring and Raeder, occasionally even with von Brauchitsch; whether or not the other armed services and the foreign office were kept informed depended, as often as not, on the efforts of painstaking staff officers who had to translate these orders into action. Halder sometimes submitted to the OKW draft orders for signature and return to the OKH, with copies to other ministries, these orders being based on verbal instructions already given to von Brauchitsch by the dictator.[3]

Much of the weakness in the high command organization lay in the fact that it had not been designed for war – at least not for a long war; it was merely an improvised system that would have seen Germany through two or three lightning campaigns.

The OKH organization of 1939 continued throughout 1940 and early 1941 without any major change. The *ObdH* (von Brauchitsch) was advised and served by his trinity of senior staff officers, Halder, the chief of the army general staff, the younger Keitel as chief of the *Personalamt*, and Fromm as the commander of the Replacement Army. The field element of the general staff in Zossen could not operate efficiently for any length of time without the rump that had been left in Berlin at the outbreak of war, and the greater part was eventually removed from Berlin to join von Brauchitsch. It was found too that the main arms were no longer properly represented within the OKH and that von Brauchitsch had no one in his immediate circle on whom he could call for arms advice, since the arms inspectors were overloaded with organization and administrative work within the *Ersatzheer*. New and additional posts of arms generals (*Waffengenerale*) were therefore created within the OKH, and these general officers formed part of von Brauchitsch's close staff.

Other changes that had been made were relatively minor. Fromm, originally approved by Hitler on 1 September 1939 as *Chef der Heeresrüstung u. Befehlshaber des Ersatzheeres*, was both the commander of the Replacement Army while also continuing in his former appointment as the *Chef* of the *Allgemeines Heeresamt*; one of his direct responsibilities was removed from him when, on 15 February 1940, Olbricht was appointed as *Chef des AHA*.[4]

Later that year a *General z.b.V* (Eugen Müller) was added to von Brauchitsch's own personal staff, in what was to become an independent *Gruppe III (Rechtswesen)*, 'to define and safeguard the legal position of the troops and to take care of army public relations'.*

---

* *General zu besonderer Verfügung*, i.e., a supernumerary general for special duties that appear to have included propaganda among German troops to prepare and fortify them against the action of the *SD Einsatzgruppen* murder *Kommandos*. (cf. Hilberg, p. 197 note 45)

The main deterioration in the standing of the German Army in the high command had been caused, however, by the worsening of von Brauchitsch's personal relationship with Hitler. For von Brauchitsch, although most competent professionally, was in reality a weak man who lost composure when in Hitler's presence and was completely dominated by him. The Bavarian Halder, his chief of staff, was a much more stubborn character than von Brauchitsch and in the early days was apparently impervious to the oppressive atmosphere of the Führer's presence; the extent of his activities was very wide, he was a meticulous master of detail, and had earned the professional respect of his fellows. Yet, until late in 1941, his diary showed him as a loyal, hardworking executive and, if he disapproved of many of the Führer's views, he rarely recorded it. It was only when operations started to go wrong in Russia that the bitter animosity grew between the two.

The first recorded military aim of the proposed war against the Soviet Union, as expressed by the Führer, was written into Halder's diary as early as 22 July 1940; the dictator's intention was imprecise and contained no fewer than three aims, each capable of conflicting with the other, for it read:

To defeat the Russian Army or at least [oder wenigstens] to occupy as much Russian soil as is necessary to protect Berlin from air attack. It is desired to establish our own positions so far to the east that our own air force can destroy the most important areas of Russia.[5]

This vague mission was to be carried forward in various forms in directives and orders, and to it, at Hitler's instigation, were to be added other political and economic aims. Less than three months after Germany had launched itself eastwards in the greatest war of its existence, operations were to be brought to a standstill because of fierce disputes as to the true purpose of the war.

Yet the method by which Halder set to work is perhaps of note in that he did not in the first place depute the responsibility for the project to Paulus and Heusinger, but instead attached Marcks, von Küchler's chief of staff, to the OKH for this purpose, the same Marcks who had once been von Schleicher's press officer. Marcks produced, on 5 August, an outline plan for the invasion that was in itself a remarkable document, in that it introduced in its aims material that was to prove both controversial and dangerous to the subsequent operations – the political and economic importance of Moscow, the Ukraine, the Donets basin and the Leningrad industrial centre – since all these were soon seized on by Hitler as the politico-economic objectives of the war, objectives that he altered in priority according to his whim.[6] Weighty aims, the destruction of Soviet military power and the occupation of strategic areas immediately relevant to this power formed no part of Marcks's main mission. There were other inconsistencies which appeared for the first time in the Marcks plan that were carried into the final directives, such as the erroneous belief that the Soviet Union would hold on to the

Baltic States and that the forces there constituted a threat to the flank of a main thrust on Moscow.

The whole of this early general staff planning, even before Hitler took a hand in it, was a remarkable exercise that displayed little acuity of general staff vision and much confusion of thought. But Kinzel's *Fremde Heere Ost* within the OKH was hardly well informed on conditions in the Soviet Union or indeed on the Red Army beyond the immediate border areas.[7] And, this being the case, the OKH was at a great disadvantage in having to jump into the unknown and make its plans as if in a vacuum.

Hitler, however, did not intend to comment on and alter the Halder plan without first having someone else outside the OKH produce an alternative for the dictator's own information and use. Whereas Norway and then France (from 1941) were held to be OKW theatres, there was no doubt that the east was the responsibility of the OKH alone; that, however, did not prevent Hitler from instructing Jodl to prepare a separate plan for the invasion of the USSR, this being kept confidential and unknown to Halder and the OKH. Jodl in his turn set von Lossberg to work preparing an OKW campaign plan that eventually found its way to Hitler's desk, so that the ideas there could be used to test and to refute those put forward by von Brauchitsch and Halder.[8] This von Lossberg plan was virtually the plan on which Germany went to war.[9] One of the main factors that governed the whole design of the Lossberg plan was that the continuation of the offensive on Moscow beyond the Orsha landbridge–Smolensk area should be dependent on the progress made on the flanks. So Hitler came to believe that as soon as Smolensk had been reached then the advance might have to be halted and forces diverted from the centre to the Baltic and the Ukraine.

On 29 October Paulus, Halder's *O Qu I*, completed his own immediate invasion proposals and these appear to have been accepted by Halder.[10] Two army groups (von Leeb and von Bock) were to be used to the north of the Pripet marshes, one moving towards Leningrad and the other on Moscow; a third army group (von Rundstedt) was to enter the Ukraine in the south. This first phase plan attached only minor importance to the Soviet forces in the Baltic States and laid more stress on the German Army's immediate interest in gaining military victory by destroying the enemy than on accruing economic advantages. Between 28 November and 3 December a series of war-games were played under Paulus's direction, and the three army group chiefs of staff were set to work, independently of each other, to examine the strategic (operative) problems involved. All of them became impressed by the apparent difficulties of space and manpower, and they pointed out that the funnel shape of the Russian hinterland was such that the deeper one penetrated the wider became the frontage; what was initially a front of 1,300 miles rapidly extended to 2,500 miles.

This led to the ventilation of other problems, including the difficulties in maintaining a force of three and a half million men and half a million horses in a vast country in which there were few roads and where the railways could not be used for through running, since the Soviet rail track was wider than that used in Germany and Central Europe. Fromm had already emphasized that the Replacement Army holding of reinforcements, less than half a million, was only enough to replace the wastage of a summer campaign. There was an acute shortage of motor vehicles and the vehicle fuel position was very tight indeed, there being no more than three months' reserves of petrol and one month's reserve of diesel. Rubber, too, was a problem and tank production was never more than 250 vehicles a month.[11]

By then von Brauchitsch's new and Halder's old doubts as to the direction of the Führer's strategy came to the fore. If war against the USSR were really necessary, they were convinced that the destruction of the Red Army was the overriding aim and that economic considerations should not take priority. The main thrust must be made all the way to Moscow. An advance on the capital would, they thought, draw on it the main enemy forces; the seizing of the Moscow area would not only inflict on the USSR a loss of control and communications but would leave a great hole in any form of continuous Red Army front.*

At the fateful meeting on 5 December von Brauchitsch was bold enough to tell the Führer that he doubted whether the *Luftwaffe* had sufficient forces to support the army in the east and at the same time carry on the fight against England; but he fell silent when Hitler told him tartly that it was certainly strong enough to wage war on two fronts 'provided that the army did not drag out the new campaign'. Halder, however, continued to press for a powerful centre thrust, to be made by von Bock, direct on Moscow. Hitler would have none of it, and he retorted with contrary ideas, some probably his own but others attributable to Göring, Jodl, and von Lossberg – the need to protect the Reich from air attack, and the importance of the Baltic and Ukrainian flanks, and economic objectives; 'Moscow after all was not so very important'. At this point von Brauchitsch came to the support of Halder, stressing the importance in the Russian mind of the old Smolensk-Moscow road, only to be crushed by insults and abuse. So it was left that the initial planning should take Army Group Centre as far as Smolensk, some 200 miles short of Moscow; thereafter the Führer did not want to commit himself as to further operations but would decide the issue at Smolensk when the time came.[12] In this lacuna lay one of the causes of German failure in 1941.

On 18 December 1940 Hitler signed Directive 21, *Fall Barbarossa*, a directive that was long, rambling and indecisive in its aims, its language and its form. The aim given was to crush Russia in a rapid campaign; under its general intention heading, however, it was stated that the final mission was to form a barrier against Asiatic Russia on the general line

---

* It is now known from study of Soviet sources, since made public, that von Brauchitsch and Halder were entirely correct in this operative reasoning. (cf. Stalin, *Kratkaia Biografiia*, p. 197)

Archangel–Volga.[13] The significance of this arbitrary line is difficult to determine. If the USSR were already defeated there was no reason why German power should not have extended to the Pacific to link with the Japanese. Moreover Hitler had said that he would destroy bolshevik power and this aim would not have been achieved by the continued existence of a Soviet Empire east of the Volga.* In the body of the directive could be traced the hand of Hitler, wearing in turn his many hats, that of industrialist and economist, of commander-in-chief of all the armed services, of commander of army formations down to corps (he discussed the use of divisions in the Rovaniemi area) and even of Hitler the airman as he instructed the *Luftwaffe* how to deal with river bridges. The directive thus contained a large number of disconnected objectives with priority given to none. Hitler was about to send the German Army into the Soviet Union, on a four year will-o'-the-wisp chase after seaports, cities, oil, corn, coal, nickel, manganese and iron ore.

The preparations made by the German Army to fit itself for this venture, due to start in May, had not been very extensive.[14] Halder had wanted to increase the number of field formations beyond that ordered by Hitler, but the dictator had refused to allow more to be raised; and the *Ersatzheer* training capacity and replacement holdings were no larger than they had been in September 1939. There was in fact not a great deal that von Brauchitsch and Halder could have done to transform the German Army and fit it for its new, and very different, tasks in the east, since they were severely restricted by manpower and equipment limitations. And while much of this planning was going on, they were also burdened with the preparations of projected campaigns that might have developed into lengthy wars, in Spain and Africa, the Balkans and in Finland. The commitments in fact were already far outstripping the resources.

The problems associated with great frontages and depth had certainly been given much attention, insufficient though this might have been. Additional signal troops were raised and provided with long-range radio equipment, and 15,000 Polish pattern *Panjewagen* horse-drawn carts were acquired for the infantry divisions, to give them some extra mobility. The army railway troops were strengthened so that they might rapidly convert the Russian rail track (by closing the rail gauge by about five inches) to Central European pattern and, as an interim measure, 170 small motor locomotives of Russian gauge were made ready. The third line army motor transport lift (*Grosstransportraum*) was increased from 20,000 to 45,000 tons, and Wagner introduced a field supply organization that would set up

---

* Von Bock had disquieting doubts as to the clarity of the intention. On 2 February he asked Hitler what action would be taken if, when they arrived on this line, the Soviet government should still be in being. The Führer gave an evasive answer as if he had not yet considered such a situation, and he assured von Bock that by then 'the communists would have asked for terms'. If not, then he, Hitler, would advance to the Urals. Hitler, added that he was determined to fight and refused to consider any form of settlement with the USSR. (Von Bock, *Tagebuch*, 3.2.41)

great supply dumps in army group areas.[15] Measures were also taken, woefully inadequate though these were to prove, to develop and provide winter equipment and winter clothing, the requirement apparently having been based on 'a static occupation force of sixty divisions' mainly distributed under cover in garrisons.[16] This was in line with OKH planning to eliminate the Soviet Union in a short summer campaign.

From the operative and the tactical points of view there were to be no major changes in ideas, organization or equipment to transform the German Army. Partisan activity was expected and a few special formations had been raised to combat it. It was certain that more tanks and more motorization would be needed but the additional equipment necessary was not to be had. And, since the Red Army was known to have large armoured forces, it was decided to develop the use of panzer groups on the pattern of Group Kleist that had been so successful in the Ardennes. With this end in view, all motorized forces were concentrated into four panzer groups, each of two or three panzer and motorized corps. The panzer groups, like armies, would be capable of independent long-range tasks, driving wedge-like blows that would tear open the enemy's front and help the infantry armies forward to their operative objectives. Panzer groups were to be without territorial or supply responsibilities and it would be the task of the army in the sector in which they operated to maintain them in the field.[17]

This swing in the emphasis on the use of the tank in independent operative mass meant that other formations would be deprived of tank support in the infantry battle; and to compensate for this it had been decided to expand the development and use of the *Sturmgeschütz* assault gun that had owed its origin to von Manstein's early sponsorship in 1935. This was a turretless track-mounted fully armoured tank chassis, mounting a limited-traverse gun in the hull; the earlier models had no armoured top. This vehicle had a low silhouette, was lighter than a tank and could be produced more economically in money, labour and material. These fighting vehicles could move on to objectives together with the assaulting infantry, quickly engaging pin-point targets, infantry, gun-crews or tanks; they could thus provide immediate covering and defensive fire and anti-tank protection, and, if need be, increase the density of the field artillery's indirect fire in depth. They were manned by the artillery and not by the panzer arm.

The assault gun was produced in very large numbers later in the war and it is important to note that it was in no way a self-propelled gun, which was an artillery piece endowed with particular mobility in that it was provided with a self-propelled (and sometimes tracked and partially armoured) firing platform. The assault gun was a heavily armoured fighting vehicle designed to be used in the forefront of the battle. Its very heavily armoured front and main armament enabled it to fight it out with enemy tanks, something that a self-propelled gun could not do. Later, as the assault gun came to be provided with a heavier high-velocity gun, it proved to be an ideal tank-killer, and was later to be introduced as part of some panzer regiments. For the *Sturmgeschütz* was in reality a tank and not a gun; for its weight it could mount a more powerful gun than the comparable tank with the rotating turret and its only disadvantage lay in that the vehicle could not readily engage targets on the flank.*

The other preparation made for 1941 brought the German Army for the first time into the field of the political and the race war and was not entirely welcome to officers of the high command.

Hitler had a good understanding of communism and of the aims and working of the bolshevik government, and he was not ignorant of the political and ethnic complexity of the peoples that formed the population of the Soviet Union. He rightly reasoned that, because of the diversity of the races and the deep schisms within the Soviet peoples, the USSR lacked solidity, and this gave rise to his belief that 'one good kick would bring the tottering and rotten structure down'. His argument had validity and weight. But not to have enlisted the support of all the multi-racial Soviet peoples, including the Great Russians, was a grave political and military error. Hitler did even worse: his brain was teeming with insane doctrinaire and ideological obsessions so that, far from calling in the Soviet peoples to his aid, he determined that this Slav vermin, as once he had called them, should be kept in their proper station at the disposal of the master race. For this reason he ordered the economic despoliation of the conquered territories, the liquidation of the Jews and the communist intelligentsia and the virtual enslavement of the population. The Great Russians, as Halder noted in his diary, 'were to be subjected to the most brutal force'.[18]

On 30 March, at a meeting in the chancellery, the Führer addressed senior commanders in a long diatribe on the waging of a race war without pity, an address that, according to the later testimony of the audience, occasioned resentment and dissent; this was not voiced to Hitler, however, but to Halder and von Brauchitsch, who took no action.[19] Thereafter came orders that indemnified the armed forces against the legal consequences of any action against the Soviet population. Then followed the notorious order by which the Red Army commissars were to be denied the treatment normally accorded to prisoners of war, the draft orders for which, following the Führer order, appear to have actually been initiated in the OKH and sent to the OKW for concurrence.[20] The order was rejected by von Leeb and brought an angry protest from von Bock; later an attempt was made to withdraw all copies, it being understood that the responsibility for the shooting of the commissars would be that of the *Sicherheitsdienst* (*SD*) and not of the army. The responsibility for the control of the occupied territories was to be handed to the SS who were to maintain order by 'terror methods', mass murder, torture, deportations and confiscations, irrespective of age or sex.[21]

* In 1937 von Fritsch had intended that an assault gun battalion should be organic to all regular infantry divisions. Von Brauchitsch retained them, however, as army troops.

And the German Army, in common with most German citizens, knew that this was going on.*

Meanwhile, however, before the main invasion could be launched against the Soviet Union, it was necessary to clear up once and for all the uncertain, even menacing, position on the far northern and southern flanks.

In the Balkans the situation still hung fire, the German staff planning for *Marita* having been complicated by the fact that many of the commanding generals and some of the headquarters and troops had also been earmarked for *Felix*, the movement into Spain and Morocco; it was for this reason that the cancellation of the attack on Gibraltar eventually came to be regarded in Zossen as good fortune.

Hungary had already joined the Three Power Pact with Germany and Italy, but, as Yugo-Slavia was reluctant to do so, no use could be made of its road or railways system to get German troops to Greece. List's 12 Army was to be obliged therefore to attack from Bulgaria. But there were too many uncertainties, political and military, that were to complicate the plans and, in particular, the timings; Bulgaria's attitude was still in the balance, and King Boris was afraid of both the Soviet Union and Turkey; nor was it known in Berlin how Turkey would react to German troops being in Bulgaria.[22] The poor rail communications in the Balkans meant that reliance would have to be placed on road transport, particularly motor-trucks; distances were long and the road system was very primitive. Yet, under no circumstances could the German field divisions afford to become bogged down in South-East Europe since most of them were wanted by May for the invasion of the Soviet Union; and so the planning had to be based on lightning and successful campaigns – not wars. No other state and no other armed forces at that time could, or would, have simultaneously undertaken such enormous tasks over terrain that stretched for many thousands of miles from north to south and from east to west. And a special staff study had actually been completed, covering an attack on the Turkish formations in Thrace, to drive them out of Europe and secure the Bosphorus. To Hitler, and this appears to have applied also in some measure to von Brauchitsch and to Halder at this time, there was no task too difficult for the German soldier.

List's 12 Army, of four panzer, two motorized and twelve infantry divisions, had already been concentrated in Rumania in January and

---

* The senior commanders protested but did not resign, and their objections were principally that they wished to spare German troops the task. Yet Heydrich and *Generalquartiermeister* Wagner jointly drafted an order in May 1941 whereby mobile killer groups (the *Einsatzgruppen* made up of *SD*, *Waffen SS* and police) were to carry out the mass murders of Jews, commissars, hostages and suspected partisans in army areas in the east, with the support (except in the round-ups and killings) of the German Army. The only army troops that were to forbid such German *Sonderkommando* activity in their areas were the Hungarians. Nor was the *Wehrmacht* averse to reprisals for Otto von Stülpnagel, the *Militärbefehlshaber* in France, on 5 December 1941 asked permission to shoot 100 hostages and deport 1,000 Jews because a *Luftwaffe* officer had been wounded by an assassin. (Hilberg, pp. 183–200 and 404). Not for nothing did Hitler repeatedly say: 'Gentlemen, if we are to lose this war, you would do well to provide yourselves with a rope!' (Speer, *Spandau – The Secret Diaries*, p. 19)

February and, on 2 March, it had entered Bulgaria. Shortly afterwards, British troops landed in Greece. On 17 March Hitler ended the political and military uncertainty when he ordered the OKW to make ready to occupy Greece so that the British threat could be eliminated and German air control established over the East Mediterranean.[23] On this same day the Führer ordered that Rommel (whose troops were still unloading at the Tripolitanian ports) should go over to the offensive, and the dictator began to think on the lines of the earlier Göring proposal, that German troops should attack Suez not only through Egypt but also through Turkey and Syria.

It was obvious to the Zossen planners that List's 12 Army headquarters could not plan and make itself ready to invade the Soviet Union in May if it was to subdue the Balkans in April. *Ritter* von Schobert's 11 Army was therefore moved from the Reich to the Bessarabian border to take over the planning of what would have been List's mission, that of attacking into the Ukraine from Rumania.

When, on 27 March, the Yugo-Slav government was overthrown in favour of one that rebutted German efforts to draw it into an alliance, Hitler ordered the invasion and occupation of Yugo-Slavia in addition to the occupation of Greece.[24] Since Yugo-Slavia had a common frontier with Austria, Hungary and Italy there was to be no problem in selecting invasion axes, and both Italy and Hungary found some formations for the invasion force. The main task fell, however, to the German Army and, since List's troops were already fully extended, another army (von Weichs's 2 Army) had to undertake the invasion of Yugo-Slavia from the north, together with five corps headquarters, five panzer divisions, two motorized infantry and seven infantry divisions and a *Luftwaffe* brigade (of flak troops and one infantry battalion).[25] Of these fifteen formations, five came from France, eight from the Reich and one from the east. The force used for the occupation of the Balkans (List's and von Weichs's armies) totalled thirty-three divisions of which four were held back in Bulgaria as the army reserve.[26]

The offensive was launched on 6 April with a surprise *Luftwaffe* terror raid on Belgrade. Hitler and his OKW staff took the field once more in his special train, moving to the area of Wiener Neustadt where von Brauchitsch and Göring had already sited their command headquarters. German troops moved into action without waiting for their reserves to close up.

The invasion of the Balkans was the last of the glorious blitzkrieg campaigns of the German Army, for the initial occupation was over in three weeks. The Yugo-Slav and Greek armed forces had been overcome and the British expeditionary corps had been expelled with a heavy loss of equipment and a substantial loss in casualties. Once again the German success was largely due to the use of air power and armoured forces, but the campaign showed that all staffs and troops had been trained to a high standard. Casualties were very low, but the wear and tear on motorized vehicles had been considerable and the panzer and motorized divisions required a rest period of three weeks for technical maintenance. It was this delay that forced the postponement of the attack on the Soviet Union.

According to Jodl's earlier appreciation Crete was the cornerstone of the defence of the Balkans against attack from the British in the Middle East, and its occupation would further allow Germany to control the whole of the Eastern Mediterranean. On 20 May the OKL launched its invasion of the island by parachutists of Student's 7. *Flieger (Fallschirm) Division*, together with 5 and elements of 6 Mountain Divisions, the whole force being under von Richthofen's 8 Air Corps. The British and Greek losses in ground troops were very heavy as they were unable to withdraw from the island, and British air and naval losses were considerable. Yet Student's casualties in dead and wounded totalled about 8,000 men and German aircraft losses were not light.[27] So it was decided, by Hitler, that the days of the big airborne operations were over and this was to mean that no further action was taken in planning an air operation against Malta.

Fortress Crete was given a *Luftwaffe* commander, but its strategic value was to depend largely on the German ability to keep it out of the hands of the enemy, for it was not, thereafter, used for any offensive measures against the British.

Field-Marshal List's 12 Army remained in Salonica where it became *Wehrmachtbefehlshaber Südost (AOK 12)* having under its command three German territorial districts, for Serbia, for North and for South Greece based on Belgrade, Salonica and Athens. List was also the commander-in-chief over all *Luftwaffe* and naval forces in the area that had not been earmarked for special operational offensives to be conducted by the OKL and OKM. This was an unusual arrangement in that Hitler rarely appointed a single commander over all the armed services. List had the additional task of liaising with, and sometimes co-ordinating, the Italian and Bulgarian troops holding Yugo-Slav and Greek territories in occupation. Only one infantry and two mountain divisions were to remain in Greece and Crete, together with four weak (category 15) occupation divisions. The South-East Command of the Balkans became an OKW theatre.

The trackless mountains were to form the refuge for wild turbulent peoples who had not yet recovered from the sudden shock of the invasion. The war in the Balkans had in fact not yet begun.

Meanwhile it was necessary to make secure the other flank on the eastern front, Norway and Finland.

The principal role of von Falkenhorst's 21 Corps Group, that had become, from the beginning of 1941, an army (*AOK Norwegen*), was to protect the coastline against British landings. A large part of his command was made up of coastal artillery since, following on the March 1941 Lofoten raid, Hitler had ordered the army coastal batteries to be increased in number from thirteen to 160, these being provided for the main part by captured enemy equipment. Von Falkenhorst's Norway Army was increased to two corps, with two infantry divisions on the west coast and four in the south. A further two divisions were sent to Norway in June 1941.[28]

In addition to von Falkenhorst's command, a separate mountain corps grouping of two divisions was being built up in the Arctic circle near Kirkenes, so that the force might, if necessary, cross into the coastal Petsamo area of North Finland.

During 1940 there had been a number of talks with the Finnish high command, and in September 1940 permission was given for the German troops in North Norway to be supplied overland through Finland from the Baltic. General staff talks took place in January and again in May and, on 13 June, a general officer (Erfurth) was detached as a liaison officer to the Finns. Then a German 70 Corps (additional to the mountain corps) consisting of an infantry division and an SS brigade was made ready for despatch to North Finland in order to secure the mountain corps communications with the south.[29]

The Finns were insistent that they did not want German troops in their country except in the deserted far north, as they were confident, should it come to war again, that they could hold their own frontiers. Nor did they even want to be linked to Germany as allies, preferring to call themselves 'brothers-in-arms'. They did, however, require of Germany imports of food and armament, particularly small arms, with which to re-equip their forces.

The German Army strength in May 1941 stood at 1,200,000 men in the Replacement Army and 3,800,000 in the Field Army, of which 3,300,000 stood ready for the war in the east. The *Luftwaffe* numbered 1,700,000 men (these including flak artillery and parachute troops), while the *Kriegsmarine* stood at 400,000. The *Waffen SS* had increased threefold from its 1940 strength of 50,000 to 150,000 men.[30]

The increase in the *Feldheer* to 180 infantry divisions had made it necessary to transfer the classes 19 and 20 (the twenty-one and twenty-two year old) from the *Ersatzheer*, and, to replace these, the class 21 was called to the colours on 1 March with class 22 following two months later. At the end of May 80,000 men were formed into reinforcement march battalions ready for the new war, leaving about 350,000 men, mainly of class 21, still in the Replacement Army, as the only immediate source of reinforcements. These had undergone only three months' training. Since, however, it was commonly assumed that the war with the Soviet Union would be a short one, and the total army losses from the beginning of the hostilities in Europe had totalled only 160,000 dead and missing, it was reckoned that these would be sufficient for the foreseeable future. And the Reich itself would have no difficulty in finding manpower for the forces or for industry.

Since the summer of 1940 there had been an intensive drive to improve the standard of junior leaders, both officers and non-commissioned officers, and to train replacements, and this had been particularly successful. The recruiting, training and replacement of general staff officers (as opposed to officers who were performing staff duties) were, however, by no means as satisfactory; there was a severe shortage of general staff officers to fill general staff vacancies, particularly as the officers promoted to general rank to fill command appointments were usually selected from those who belonged to the general staff. It was moreover a deliberate, and possibly mistaken, policy severely to restrict the admission of aspirants to the general staff corps so that even the very reduced establishment figure (1,053 in June 1941) could not be filled. This meant that the general staff was overworked, overloaded and, in the final outcome, overwhelmed. As an interim measure about a hundred former staff officers of the First World War were re-employed and four ten-week courses were put in hand, from January 1940, to produce another 250 officers capable of filling these vacant appointments; meanwhile regimental officers were trained for specialist duties with *1b* and *1c*.[31]

The equipment situation with regard to both replacement stocks and reserves never was satisfactory but, on the other hand, some re-equipping of field formations had taken place during the winter, so that armament and equipment had become more uniform, and the variety of types had been reduced. The infantry in particular had been given a good supply of indirect fire weapons, mortars and infantry guns. New weapons had come into service, the 20 mm *Vierling* flak, a 50 mm anti-tank gun in addition to the 37 mm, a 150 mm *Sechsling Nebelwerfer* mortar, with a range of nearly 7,000 yards, and multiple 280 mm and 320 mm ground to ground rockets.

The panzer arm too was being improved in that the Czech *35t* and the Mks I and II were being withdrawn from the east as obsolescent and were being steadily exchanged for the Mk III on which the 37 mm gun had been replaced by the 50 mm as the main armament. About 370 *Sturmgeschütze* assault guns had been manufactured of which 250 stood ready in the east. In numbers, however, the tank production was anything but satisfactory. The OKW monthly target set in early 1940 had been for 600 tanks and assault guns by 1943; the 1940 average, however, was less than 200. In January 1941 the OKH *Waffenamt*, taking note of the possible requirements for the new war, had required from the ministry of armament and munitions a monthly production of 1,250 armoured track vehicles, it being known that any change in production would take a year to realize. But since the minister considered this demand to be excessive, Keitel reduced it to 600. Meanwhile less than 700 tanks of all types were produced in the first quarter of 1941, and even by the last quarter of the year the figure had risen to only 1,100. These figures were, of course, entirely inadequate, and the war in Russia was to bring out the tank deficiencies, not only in numbers but also in perform-ance, armour, armament and tactical mobility.[32]

The lack of tank production was naturally reflected in the actual strength of the panzer divisions. In 1939 the average strength was about 300 tanks out of an establishment of 324 and this dropped by wear and tear, by casualties and by reorganization losses to an average of 258 in 1940.[33] By

1941, after the reduction in the establishment, the average tank strength stood at 196 (between 147 and 299 – depending on whether the division had two or three tank battalions).

The manufacture of ammunition had been severely cut back since June 1940, but the stocks were generally considered to be satisfactory since there had been no consumption. Yet, in terms of rounds per gun, they were the same as those held at the beginning of the war in France – only in the heavier calibres was it exceeded. And anti-tank ammunition was generally in short supply because of a shortage in raw materials.[34] Bridging and radio equipment were also much deficient.

There was a great lack of motor vehicles – a difficulty that could never be overcome – and the holdings of eighty-eight infantry and three motorized divisions were made up, said Müller-Hillebrand, 'of a frightful number of patterns and types', largely war booty and the output of French factories. These were entirely unsuited to conditions in the east and presented an enormous difficulty in technical maintenance and repair. And because of the shortage of towing vehicles, the army heavy artillery in June 1941 was proportionally lower than that in June 1940.

The expansion in the number of field divisions and the occupation of enemy territory had made necessary a corresponding increase in the number of army troops required to support the force and ensure the security of communications and coastline of the occupied mainland of Europe. This included 113 heavy artillery batteries with guns of calibre from 150–210 mm, twenty railway batteries with armament from 150–280 mm, 233 coastal batteries, of which 160 were in Norway, and fifty-four pioneer battalions.[35] Much of the heavy artillery equipment was war booty.

The security of rearward communications in Russia was to prove a problem, though some of these difficulties had been foreseen. Hitler's OKW order of 13 March had directed that the administration and government of rearward areas was to be handed over by the army to *Reichskommissare* as quickly as possible, these being responsible directly to Hitler and receiving their orders through the minister for occupied territories. Military administration and government were to be confined to a very narrow strip of territory behind the front in the army and army group areas. But even there the order restricted the army's responsibility, in that 'the organs of the *Reichsführer SS*' were permitted to operate independently of the army in these areas 'in their special assignments *zur Vorbereitung der politischen Verwaltung*', this activity covering political or race liquidations and deportations.

For anti-partisan activities the army group and army commanders relied on rear organizations of a headquarters controlling *Feld* or *Orts-kommandanturen*, a system of garrisons and town majors, supported by security divisions or by *Wach* or *Landesschützen* battalions.[36]

The concentration in the east was deferred as long as possible, most of it taking place from the beginning of April. It was intended to deploy 152 army and SS divisions against the Soviet Union (including those in Finland), while only fifty-six divisions remained in other theatres. In reality the strength of the German Army committed in the east was much higher than the seventy-five per cent of its field formations appear to indicate, for the divisions in France and in the Balkans had been reduced to skeletons and were in no way battleworthy. Moreover the figures are misleading also in that they do not reveal that nearly all the army troops, artillery, engineers and signals that represent a substantial but hidden proportion of the order of battle, had been allocated to the east. Only von Witzleben's Army Group D remained in France, together with Blaskowitz's 1, Dollmann's 7 and *Freiherr* von Vietinghoff's 15 Army (newly formed on 15 January). In the east there stood three army groups and eight armies (not including the troops in the Arctic and List's 12 Army) and four panzer groups.

The invasion of the Soviet Union was to be made by the three army groups each supported by an air fleet. Von Leeb's Army Group North (formerly C) consisted of two armies (Busch and von Küchler) and one panzer group (Hoepner) with twenty-six divisions, of which three were panzer and three motorized. Von Leeb was to attack from East Prussia through the Baltic States on to Leningrad. The largest force, von Bock's Army Group Centre (formerly B) consisted of two armies (von Kluge and Strauss) and two panzer groups (Hoth and Guderian), in all fifty divisions of which nine were panzer and six motorized. Von Bock was to attack north of the Pripet marshes due east on Smolensk. Von Rundstedt's Army Group South (formerly A) was to attack in two separate wings, one from Poland and one from Rumania. In Poland von Reichenau's 6 Army, with von Kleist's panzer group, was to strike towards Kiev, its right flank being covered by a newly formed 17 Army under K-H von Stülpnagel; the forces from Rumania consisted of von Schobert's 11 Army together with the Rumanians. Von Rundstedt's force totalled forty-one German divisions, of which five were panzer and three motorized, and the equivalent of fourteen Rumanian divisions. All the remaining German divisions and von Weichs's 2 Army were in OKH reserve.[37]

Opposing these powerful armies on the western frontiers of the Soviet Union stood 150 Red Army divisions.[38]

CHAPTER NINE

The First Disasters

Just after three o'clock, at dawn on the fine Sunday morning of 22 June, German troops crossed the frontier from the Baltic coast in the north, to the Carpathians near the Hungarian frontier in the south. Although the Russian high command was not unaware of the danger that threatened it, the German troops gained tactical surprise everywhere.

Von Leeb's Army Group North advanced steadily through the Baltic States on its way towards Leningrad, the enemy falling back in confusion. Nowhere was there any evidence that the Red Army intended to make a stand in the Baltic States, and only towards the end of July, when von Leeb was already nearing Leningrad, did the resistance stiffen.[1] Soviet losses in equipment were heavy, but few Red Army prisoners were taken.

In the centre, the 1939 Russian frontier projected westwards in the huge Bialystok salient and von Bock intended to pinch out this bulge in a double envelopment by Strauss's 9 and von Kluge's 4 Armies while Hoth's 3 and Guderian's 2 Panzer Groups made a deeper double envelopment as far as Smolensk, nearly 400 miles to the east. During the planning stages Hitler had, however, opposed this objective as being too deep since the motorized formations would leave the marching infantry far behind, but no clear and binding decision had been given either by the Führer or by von Brauchitsch. So it came about that, after the first forty-eight hours, von Bock, Hoth and Guderian were uncertain as to whether the panzer thrusts should close on Minsk or on Smolensk.[2] Serious frictions developed with each censuring the next senior in the chain of command, while Hitler laid the blame on his staffs and on his commanders.

Von Bock, stiff and unbending, was regarded by the OKH as being difficult and unco-operative; and there was some antipathy between him and von Brauchitsch.[3] Von Bock's intolerance was further aggravated by von Brauchitsch's apparent indecision, for von Bock did not realize the extent to which von Brauchitsch was already overshadowed by Hitler; and von Bock became increasingly impatient with what he regarded as interference and excessively close control by the OKH. Von Bock was not, however, inhibited from severely restricting the initiative of his own army commanders: his relationship with the level-headed Hoth was reasonably satisfactory and with the *Luftflotte* commander Kesselring it was very good; but tensions arose between himself and von Kluge and Strauss; and he had little time for the impetuous and indisciplined Guderian. Between von Kluge and Guderian there was bitter animosity.

Only three days after the start of the war, the Führer, in a fit of nerves, bypassed von Brauchitsch and suggested to von Bock that the motorized encirclement on Minsk should be abandoned in favour of a much shorter one, and this von Bock resisted with all the arguments at his command. By 29 June, when Hoth's and Guderian's panzer spearheads met near Minsk, 300,000 prisoners had been taken and, so it was claimed, 2,500 enemy tanks were put out of action. On this day Halder recorded in his diary that the war, which he called a campaign (*Feldzug*), 'had been virtually won within fourteen days'.[4] Hitler, against von Bock's wishes, then removed 2 and 3 Panzer Groups from von Bock's direct command and put them under von Kluge, who temporarily relinquished the command of his infantry corps, ready for the resumption of the march on Smolensk.*

By 25 July, when Smolensk had been passed, the tank troops were already too extended and the marching infantry too far behind to seal off the cauldron. Hitler was on the telephone to von Bock, excited and angry, and von Bock told him 'as much as it was good for him to know'. Keitel arrived the next day to emphasize his master's displeasure, and Guderian, censured by von Bock, was demanding to be removed from his appointment.[5] By 5 August, however, all resistance inside the new pocket had ceased and a further 300,000 prisoners and 3,000 tanks, intact or knocked out, were in German hands. Since 16 July, Guderian and Hoth had been standing at Smolensk, 400 miles from their start-line and only 200 miles from Moscow.

In the second half of July the Führer considered that the war was over. It only remained, he said, for Hoth's panzer group to move 400 miles to the north to help von Leeb on to Leningrad, while Guderian's panzer group should go 400 miles to the south to clear up the enemy flank forces near Korosten and Kiev. Hoepner's panzer group (with von Leeb) could afterwards be withdrawn to the Reich.[6]

At this point the violent argument arose again within the high command, as to whether or not Moscow should be taken before Leningrad and the Ukraine, with Hitler on the one side and Halder, von Bock, von Rundstedt, Guderian and Hoth on the other. Even Jodl had changed his mind and considered that Moscow must be the next objective. Von Brauchitsch, who was tired and dispirited, was being reproached by the Führer for weakness, 'being too much influenced by the army group commanders'. Meanwhile Army Group Centre stood still at Smolensk from 16 July and was not to resume the advance on Moscow until the beginning of October.

Guderian had expressed his views so violently that he was deputed by von Bock, and at Halder's invitation, to put the case to the Führer at his East

---

* Von Kluge's command was called, temporarily and unofficially and for want of a better name, 4 Panzer Army. It was used only for the advance to Smolensk.

Prussian headquarters; but when Guderian arrived at Rastenburg he had much of the ground cut from under his feet when von Brauchitsch told him that the Führer had already decided 'and that it was no use bleating against it'. In any event, according to Halder and contrary to what he, himself, said in his memoirs, Guderian made a very feeble attempt to change the dictator's mind. Indeed, he came away convinced of the correctness of the Führer's views, so earning for himself von Bock's and Halder's disgust.[7] Guderian further angered both von Brauchitsch and Halder when, on returning to his headquarters and regretting his too ready acquiescence, he bombarded the OKH with a deluge of demands for reinforcements and fresh formations to enable him to carry out his drive south into the Ukraine.

Hoth was then ordered north into von Leeb's theatre where he achieved little, except that Leningrad was isolated from the Soviet Union. Guderian moved south to the area east of Kiev to get behind the enemy grouping that was attempting to make a stand on the Dnieper in front of von Rundstedt's steady advance through the Ukraine. Guderian's southward thrust, in conjunction with the northward move of von Kleist's 1 Panzer Group resulted in the destruction of the whole of the enemy South-West Front (Army Group) by 24 September, with the taking of 665,000 prisoners and an enormous collection of booty. This great victory was noted with enthusiasm by the *Generalquartiermeister* Wagner in his diary, as 'being solely Hitler's idea, an undertaking against which he had been warned by nearly all his advisers'.[8]

Hitler had, as early as 5 September, already decided on the next stage of the war, the return of Hoth's and Guderian's panzer groups to the centre, and the building up of von Bock's force to eighty divisions, of which fourteen would be panzer and eight motorized infantry, ready for an immediate advance on Moscow and beyond to the demarcation line Archangel–Astrakhan.

Von Leeb was to join up with the Finns on the Svir and von Rundstedt was to move into the Caucasus. This new general offensive was to begin at the beginning of October, at which time the Russian winter was due. As the offensive was about to start, Hitler issued an order of the day promising his troops that 'in this last decisive battle of the year the enemy would be destroyed' and, on 3 October, he announced to the German people that 'the foe was already broken and would never rise again'.

The resumption of the offensive was to become a race against time, to arrive at such far-flung objectives as Yaroslavl, Gorki and Ryazan, in a line nearly 200 miles east of Moscow, and then find winter quarters. No winter equipment or winter clothing had as yet reached the troops, and that which had been despatched was to be lost in the railway system as soon as the first bitter winter weather brought this to a halt. Even before this great offensive was mounted the troops had been feeling the effects of over-exertion and poor supply.

The tank battle casualties, Hoth had told Schmundt, 'were no greater, comparatively, than they had been in the French campaign; but the wear and tear caused by distances and operating conditions had been far worse than had been expected'.[9] The transport and supply organization had been over-burdened and, at the end of August, tank formations had been reduced to fifty per cent of establishment and there was great difficulty in obtaining vehicle assemblies and parts. If Guderian is to be believed, Munzel's 6 Panzer Regiment had, on 14 September, been reduced to a fighting strength of ten tanks. Motorized rifle companies were sometimes down to fifty men each, and there was a lack of combat training and toughness among the few replacements; there was an acute shortage of boots, socks and shirts.[10]

The marching infantry fared immeasurably worse. The war diarist of 98 Infantry Division, one of those on the long 400 mile march from Kiev northwards to the area west of Moscow, recorded that the division was 3,800 men under strength on 27 September, and that when the first few reinforcements began to arrive they were 'but a drop in the ocean'. The modern general service carts with their rubber tyres and ball-bearing mounted wheels had long since broken up under the stress of the appalling tracks, and had been replaced by Russian farm carts. Good quality German horses foundered daily through exhaustion and poor food, but the scrubby Russian ponies, although in reality too light for the heavy draught work they were doing, lived on, eating birch twigs and the thatched roofs of cottages. Equipment, including many tons of the divisional reserve of ammunition, had to be abandoned at the roadside for lack of transport to carry it. Gradually the most simple necessities of life disappeared, razor-blades, soap, toothpaste, shoe repairing materials, needles and thread. Even in September, and before the onset of winter, there was incessant rain and a cold north-east wind, so that every night brought with it the scramble for shelter, squalid and bug-ridden though this usually was. When this could not be found the troops plumbed the very depths of wretchedness. The rain, cold and lack of rest increased sickness that, in normal circumstances, would have warranted admission to hospital; but the sick had to march with the column over distances of up to twenty-five miles a day, since there was no transport to carry them and they could not be left behind in the wild bandit-infested forests. The regulation boots, the *Kommissstiefel*, were falling to pieces. All ranks were filthy and bearded, with dirty, rotting and verminous under-clothing; typhus was shortly to follow.[11]

By 26 September the German losses had risen to 534,000 men, considerably more than the *Ersatzheer* could replace, particularly since the greater porportion of this figure was infantry.[12]

The German offensive started well, however, with a double envelopment by Hoepner's panzer group (removed from von Leeb) in the north, and by Hoth's panzer group in the south launched from the area of Smolensk on to Vyazma, this destroying forty-five Soviet divisions and taking 650,000 prisoners by the second week in October. Then came a break in the weather with heavy rains and wet snow that turned all roads and tracks into quagmires, and the German advance came to a halt and could not begin again until 15 November, when the arrival of the bitterly cold weather hardened the ground, so making a resumption of movement possible. This second stage of the offensive, after 15 November, became known as 'the flight forward (*Flucht nach vorn*)', a desperate attempt to get to Moscow and find shelter.

The strain was taking its toll, too, of the generals. Von Brauchitsch was ill, apparently with a heart attack, and von Weichs was sick; most of the others were already very apprehensive.* Halder, or so it would appear from the reading of his diary, varied from the grimly determined, as he urged von Bock on, to the confused and pessimistic, when he warned the dictator of the parlous state of the troops and the impossible supply situation. Von Bock censured Hitler (in the privacy of his diary) for turning away from Moscow in the previous August, for, said von Bock, 'stuck in the mud as he now was, the capital might as well be 600 kilometres away'.[13] Hoepner spoke out, as early as 26 October, against any resumption of the offensive and was in favour of an immediate withdrawal 150 miles to the rear.

Thomas of the OKW *Wi Rü Amt*, too, had had reason to change his earlier opinion, for, in a report dated 2 October, he said that even if the German Army got to Gorki and Baku, the Soviet Union still would not break up. Fromm, whose appointment gave him an excellent insight into the army's losses and needs, thought that Germany had already had enough, and he suggested to von Brauchitsch, though tentatively and timidly, that the time had come to make peace proposals to Moscow.[14]

Hitler betrayed no doubts in the future success of the offensive, and in order to ensure the co-operation of the half-hearted, he expressly forbade the preparation of any rearward defensive positions for use in case of failure. The unfortunate von Brauchitsch, who had left his sickbed, had become infected with the impatience of the Führer and began to goad the field commanders forward. Halder, and even von Bock, appear to have been temporarily convinced that success was a matter of will-power and the throwing in of the last reserves.

By the first few days in December, von Bock's offensive had finally come to a halt a few miles outside the city of Moscow. The tension within the OKH and Army Group Centre at the time was so great that the senior command itself appeared to be in danger of collapse. Strong Soviet counter-attacks were developing into heavy counter-offensives, not only in the centre near Moscow but also on the far flanks from the Sea of Azov to Lake Ladoga. Von Leeb had told the Führer that he must withdraw from Tikhvin to avoid being encircled and, on 28 November, von Rundstedt had ordered a general retirement to the west of Rostov, a decision that the OKH approved. When the Führer heard of it, however, he became angered and forbade any withdrawal.[15]

* In these conditions age was a limiting factor in the efficiency of the senior German generals, for many were in their sixties. The equivalent Red Army commanders, on the other hand, were mostly in their forties.

Halder was to bemoan in his diary that 'they', meaning Hitler, had no idea of the condition of the troops and indulged in flights of fancy in a vacuum. At one o'clock in the afternoon of 28 November von Brauchitsch was sent for by the Führer, and he returned very shaken from what Halder described as a one-sided and thoroughly unpleasant meeting, during which the dictator, giving vent to his wrath, had issued impossible orders and heaped insults on von Brauchitsch's head. Von Brauchitsch then sent out, over his own signature, the Führer's standstill order; but when von Rundstedt's answer was received asking either that the order be rescinded or that he be relieved of his command, von Brauchitsch could do nothing but send the teleprints direct to Hitler. For, as Halder was to note, von Brauchitsch had become little more than the Führer's messenger. At four o'clock in the morning of 1 December the dictator himself removed von Rundstedt from his command, replacing him by von Reichenau, and ordered that von Kleist's forces stop their withdrawal and attack on Voroshilovgrad.

On that morning of 1 December Halder discussed the situation on the telephone with von Sodenstern, the chief of staff of Army Group South; von Reichenau, calculating and unscrupulous, butted in on the conversation to say that the Führer was quite right and that he (von Reichenau) would take the necessary responsibility even though von Kleist thought he would be defeated if he stayed. That afternoon, Halder, frightened at the situation in the south, took the unusual step of bringing in Jodl, asking him to reason with Hitler.[16] Then he entreated von Brauchitsch to go and see the dictator once more, and while the army commander-in-chief was actually talking to the dictator, von Reichenau telephoned Hitler direct to say that the Russians had broken through the *SS Leibstandarte*; he begged to be allowed to fall back to the Mius, the rearward position that von Rundstedt had intended to occupy. And the permission was then given.

The Führer, in company with Schmundt, flew to Mariupol on his own fact finding mission to see Sepp Dietrich, a party crony well known to the dictator since, in earlier days, he had often acted as Hitler's driver and bodyguard. Dietrich was now the divisional commander of the *Leibstandarte*. Hitler had apparently hoped to hear a condemnation of the army field leadership, but in this he was disappointed because the SS were convinced that if they had not been withdrawn they would not have survived. Hitler returned to Rastenburg with his mind inflamed, not against von Rundstedt, but against von Reichenau, for the new army group commander, by censuring von Rundstedt and von Brauchitsch, had indirectly criticized the Führer himself.[17]

On 30 November, the same day as the von Rundstedt crisis, von Bock had a long telephone conversation with von Brauchitsch, during which he reported his position as dangerous – even critical. Von Brauchitsch, however, was not an attentive listener that day, and pathetically sought crumbs of comfort. 'But was not Guderian over the Oka?', and 'we have heard that von Kluge has already broken the defences west of Moscow'. Von Brauchitsch made it clear that in no circumstances was he prepared to take von Bock's tale of misery to the Führer; the Führer was convinced, said von Brauchitsch, that the Russian was at the end of his tether; and the army commander-in-chief took the attitude that von Bock had received his orders and had better carry them out, and that he, von Brauchitsch, had no intention of becoming involved as a go-between.

Von Bock, taken aback, became both worried and irritated, but with the exercise of much control, he explained the position. Guderian to the south of Moscow had spent his strength and could not hold; von Kluge's behaviour, said von Bock, was a mystery, for although pressed (by von Bock) time and time again to begin his thrust from the west of the capital, he had been reluctant to move and had done nothing. From this von Bock went on to the subject of winter equipment, and he reminded von Brauchitsch that no winter clothing had yet been received. At this point, unbelievable though it may seem, von Brauchitsch contradicted von Bock, telling him that winter clothing and equipment *had* been delivered to the troops. When von Bock demanded bluntly that the Führer should be informed of the true position, von Brauchitsch was struck with deafness and countered with the reply that he wished only to inform the Führer of the anticipated date when von Bock would take Moscow. Any further words by von Bock were answered by the same demand, repeated almost parrot-fashion.[18] To such straits had the army command been reduced.*

The Soviet counter-offensive in the centre was to throw Army Group Centre back nearly 200 miles. Among the casualties was von Brauchitsch, dismissed by Hitler on 19 December. The Führer closeted himself with Schmundt for several hours that day discussing the question of a successor; the views of the two Keitels or Jodl were not asked for, and certainly not that of Halder. For Hitler eventually decided that he himself would take over the operational control of the army on the eastern front, and he and Schmundt spent much of their time drafting an order of the day announcing the Führer's taking over of command, a situation that had in reality existed since the beginning of the war. Von Bock gave up at his own request, invalided sick with an ulcer, his place being taken by von Kluge. Von Kluge was certainly not the man to shelter his subordinates from the Führer's wrath – indeed he was more likely to bring their failings, or indiscipline (for that was what the use of initiative had become), to the attention of the dictator. Guderian was soon at odds with the new army group commander and was reported to Rastenburg; he was dismissed to the reserve and replaced by Rudolf Schmidt.† Hoepner was on bad terms with von Kluge since he had earlier told the 4 Army commander to his face what he thought of him 'for letting the panzer group down' in front of Moscow; Hoepner was similarly

---

* Meanwhile Hitler was calling von Brauchitsch 'strawhead', a 'nincompoop', and 'a vain cowardly wretch'. (*Goebbels' Diary* 20.3.42, p. 92).

† Von Kluge added a weak little note to his war diary that 'although he was basically in agreement with Guderian, Guderian must obey orders' (*Heeresgruppe Mitte KTB*, p. 1075). Rudolf Schmidt wrote a private letter dated 27.1.42 describing the 'tragedy of leadership that he would not have believed possible'.

reported to the Führer by von Kluge for withdrawing without orders and was replaced by Ruoff; Strauss asked to go and was relieved by Model.*

In the south von Reichenau had a stroke shortly after taking command, and died; K-H. von Stülpnagel had gone and von Schobert had been killed. In the north von Leeb asked to be relieved of his duties early in the new year since Hitler would not agree to any further withdrawals; he was replaced by von Küchler. In the eight months since the beginning of the war nearly all of the senior commanders had been replaced because they displeased Hitler, usually because they did not agree with him. They were to be followed by a host of subordinate general officers who became casualties to strain, or because they would not or could not conform to the demands of the new army commander-in-chief.

By the beginning of the war against the Soviet Union the German fronts had already become known as either OKW or OKH theatres, the eastern front remaining as the sole OKH theatre. This split applied however only to the German Army and not to the other two armed services, for the *Luftwaffe* and navy in the so-called OKW theatres continued to come directly under their OKL and OKM commands and not under Hitler and his personal OKW staff. Similarly the army designation of Commander-in-Chief West (*OB West*) was by no means an exact one, since von Witzleben had no command powers over the *Luftwaffe* or navy, and comparatively few over the *Waffen SS* or the static military occupation organization.

The division of the army command into OKW and OKH theatres raised a very real complication in that Hitler and Jodl's *Wehrmachtführungsstab* had no direct responsibility for the training, organization, intelligence, equipping, personnel or supply of the army field formations, and their efficiency remained the responsibility of the OKH for all theatres, whether OKH or OKW.

The division of the theatres into different OKW and OKH command chains had originally been intended, so Hitler said, to lighten the OKH load in the preparation of the war in the east. When it had become obvious that the war there was not going to be won in a short summer campaign it was then necessary, in the interest of unity of command, to restore the OKW theatres to the OKH, or alternatively, to have devised a new system of command. This was not done, however, due to the winter crisis in the east and due to Hitler's growing mistrust of, and his disillusionment with, the army generals and the army general staff.

Although Hitler had publicly assumed von Brauchitsch's post as army commander-in-chief in addition to holding that of the *de facto* Supreme Commander-in-Chief over all the armed services, he was not, in reality, the

---

* Between 5 October 1941 and 1 January 1942 the four panzer groups in the east were redesignated as panzer armies. Thereafter they were no longer entirely motorized but took infantry corps under their command and were given territorial and supply responsibilities. They were henceforth indistinguishable from field armies.

Oberbefehlshaber des Heeres, and nor did he propose to be. He intended only to take upon himself the command in the field, the operative leadership of the army groups in the east – he had already taken it over in the OKW theatres. And to do this, he proposed to retain Halder and the operational *Abteilungen* of the OKH as his own command organ for the east, while Jodl's *Wehrmachtführungsstab* would perform the same function for Finland, Norway, the Balkans, the West and the Mediterranean. Hitler had little interest in the remainder of von Brauchitsch's widespread and onerous responsibilities – organization, personnel, equipping, supply and the *Ersatzheer* – and he intended to transfer most of them to Keitel. The German Army had indeed been orphaned, for, unlike the *Luftwaffe* and German Navy, it no longer had a senior officer solely responsible for its command, development, training, discipline, and, above all, its welfare.[19] Henceforth it became virtually defenceless against interference, and dismemberment, by outside forces – Hitler, Himmler, Göring and even Keitel and Jodl.

The winter crisis and the dismissal of von Brauchitsch brought a further decline in the status of the commanding generals. Unlucky, incompetent or displeasing generals can always be reproved or retired, even in the armies of the democracies, and a head of state and a cabinet often influence the decision to do so. But in Germany Hitler had for some time been the only authority who decided on all military appointments that came under his notice. From this time onwards the dictator was to order arrest, dismissal, or, through his henchmen, imprisonment or death. Hoepner's removal had been occasioned by an 'unauthorized withdrawal', but, if Guderian is to be believed, Hoepner had at the time given free expression of his views as to the direction of 'the civilian military leadership'; and von Kluge's reports had certainly exacerbated the situation.[20] Hitler ordered, without any form of trial, that Hoepner be cashiered and deprived of all rights and pension, and it was only due to the efforts of Schmundt that this illegal sentence was revoked.[21] *Graf* Sponeck, a corps commander in the Crimea, relieved of his duties by von Manstein (von Schobert's successor in 11 Army) for another unauthorized withdrawal, was arrested at Hitler's order, tried and sentenced to death by a military court that had Göring for its president.[22] Justice, decency, law and order, unknown in the German streets and countryside from the early days of 1933, were now fast disappearing from the close and intimate circle of the *Generalität*. The time was shortly to come when many generals, even field-marshals, were at Hitler's or Himmler's orders to be murdered or else done to death by specially arranged courts.

Keitel's guardianship of the army's interests was without substance for, like Jodl, he was the dictator's man; and he possessed neither the army's trust nor its respect. The removal of the *General z.b.V.* and the *Heereswesenabteilung* from the OKH to Keitel meant that the army was left without even the semblance of legal protection; and whereas von Brauchitsch had at least thought fit to protest against the SS atrocities in

Poland and the shooting of prisoners of war in the west, Keitel refused even to hear complaints against the SS or the party régime.

The *Personalamt*, responsible for officer appointments, formerly von Brauchitsch's cherished preserve and still under Bodewin Keitel, had been transferred to the OKW; and the younger brother was, henceforth, supposed to be responsible to the elder, Wilhelm. But this did not satisfy Hitler since the dictator intended to be free to exercise the closest control over the generals and the officer corps. In the autumn of 1942 the *Personalamt* was therefore taken over by Schmundt from the younger Keitel, and it came directly under Hitler's orders. Schmundt, the ardent Hitler admirer, by then raised to general's rank, continued to hold the appointment as chief adjutant that he had, as a major, taken over in 1938. Schmundt was rapidly becoming one of the most influential in Hitler's immediate circle, in all military matters – not merely in the matter of appointments – in that his ceaseless and fulsome praise reinforced in the dictator's mind his own military genius and infallibility. Careerists and adventurers, common to all society, were not typical of the German officer corps. Yet, in the closing years of the Third Reich, opportunism, *Kameraderie*, nepotism, injustice and corruption became the order of the day at the top, in the OKW and in the OKH.[23] These deep-rooted changes, the first of which had been marked by the dismissal of von Fritsch, gathered momentum with the coming defeats and were to tear the upper structure of the German Army apart.

Halder, possibly because he thought he had a duty to the troops in the field, or for other reasons of his own, chose to remain at his post, although the dictator apparently gave him the option of following von Brauchitsch to the reserve.* His function was henceforth merely that of Hitler's operational executive and he no longer had even the co-ordinating responsibility for the *Ersatzheer* and the other *Ämter* of the OKH, since these were to come under Keitel. The nature of Halder's duties made it essential that he should co-operate with them and keep them informed, and so great was Halder's authority among his fellows that both Fromm and the younger Keitel assured Halder at the time of the break-up of the OKH that they would continue to work with him as closely as before.[24] It was in all a grotesque situation, for the OKH no longer existed.

The Red Army losses in the first campaign of the war had been enormous, for the contemporary records of Army Group Centre showed a tally of 1,912,376 Soviet prisoners of war by 31 December 1941. By 20 March 1942 the total of Soviet prisoners on all the fronts stood at 3,461,338. There seems little doubt that, if the Soviet Union, like France, had had a territorial depth no greater than 600 miles and had been enclosed by the ocean, it would have perished in a summer campaign. But space, terrain and climate had presented an entirely different situation so that, in spite of its appalling losses

---

* At this time Hitler made the remark that 'this little affair of operational command [of army groups] was something that anybody could do'. (Halder, *Hitler as Warlord*, p. 51)

in men and *matériel*, it was apparent by the new year that the Red Army was fighting with more determination and greater skill than it had shown in the previous summer. For Stalin, fired by his reading of Russian history of 1812, was intent on smashing the invading armies and finishing off Germany in 1942.[25] The winter war proved a most sobering experience for German officers and men. The sense of crisis at the front, in December of that year, had been such that Japan's attack on the British and American dependencies in the Pacific and Hitler's declaration of war against the United States went almost unnoticed.

German losses in the first eight weeks of the war were 100,000 in dead alone. By 20 November three quarters of a million had become casualties, of which 230,000 were dead, and Fromm's reserve of 400,000 had long been used up; the *Ostheer* remained 340,000 below establishment, the greater part of these deficiencies being in the infantry. The OKH was already recommending that twenty divisions in the east should be disbanded to provide reinforcements.

In October 1941 came the first of many 'comb-outs' of all army units in the Reich and in the west, to provide a quarter of a million fit men in the younger age group to replace the older men at the front. In September 1941 began the movement of the first infantry division from west to east, to be followed by individual battalions, re-equipped and refitted to make them *ostfähig*; then a further five divisions were removed from France in November and December. The troops in the east had, meanwhile, recruited Russian prisoners of war and civilians as cooks, drivers and labour, the volunteer *Hilfswillige* or *Hiwis*, in order to thin out men for combat duty.

All these measures, the best that could be taken in the circumstances, were, however, very limited in their effect and brought little change to the crisis situation in Army Group Centre where Hitler's standstill order threatened to have calamitous consequences. For already military reason had given way to dramatic poses that originated with the dictator; for, on 3 January, Hitler, in another angry scene, had said that he no longer had any faith in the ability of the generals to take hard and unpopular decisions. The generals at the top were, however, steadily being conditioned to the Führer attitude and some were beginning to ape his methods. On 5 January Heinrici of 43 Corps told Kübler, the commander of 4 Army, that the present position was intolerable and that first-rate regimental commanders were almost desperate for lack of any plan or control. 'Was he to instruct his commanders to fight as the enemy did during the last year, for the Russian, never capable of learning, had simply stood his ground until he was surrounded?' Kübler heard Heinrici out and then referred the question, exactly as the corps commander had put it, to von Kluge. The conversation that followed between Kübler and his army group commander is illuminating. Von Kluge struck an attitude. Such a mentality (presumably Heinrici's), he said, must be suppressed and nerves held in check; a withdrawal would be difficult to justify 'to those up above'. Kübler was not so easily mollified and he told von Kluge that in the not too far distant future 4 Army would have no men left at all. To which von Kluge replied, somewhat inconsequentially, '*that* of course is the problem'.

On 6 January, following this conversation, 4 Army received a telephone call direct from Paulus, the *O Qu 1*, who, although he had been chief of staff to von Reichenau's 6 Army in 1940, had commanded nothing larger than a motor transport battalion. Paulus had heard something of Schmundt's briefing to Hitler on returning from 4 Army. And, speaking from the warm comfort of his OKH office in East Prussia, he asked 'whether there was not an air of pessimism within 4 Army'. Even today the written record of the conversation still conveys something of a sneer.[26] Kübler asked to be removed and Heinrici took his place.

The *Ersatzheer* had, however, hurriedly raised thirteen more divisions. The first four of these were raised in fourteen days, having only six battalions and having originally been intended as part of an internal security emergency plan, known as *Walküre*, in case of unrest in the Reich or in the occupied territories. The divisions were ordered to join 4 Army, that had already been pushed back to Tomino; they made the 500 mile march from Suwalki to Lukow on foot. They were followed by five divisions made up of *Rheingold* regiments and then, finally, by four new divisions that were eventually sent to South Russia.* During the spring there continued to be a further move of divisions from the west, these being exchanged for burned-out divisional cadres that were sent to France for rest and reforming.[27]

On 14 July 1941 Hitler had signed a memorandum containing guidelines for cutting back the manufacture of all army equipment except for tanks, and these guidelines were not reversed until January 1942.† And the 1941 summer and autumn campaigns, because they were victorious and because they involved more movement than fighting, had resulted in a comparatively light expenditure of ammunition and little loss of equipment. Only the panzer groups had suffered appreciable casualties in tanks and this had been caused principally by the wear and tear of great mileages, dust, heat and the rugged terrain; by the beginning of September, for example, Guderian's Panzer Group 2 had been reduced to a tank fighting strength of twenty-five per cent of its establishment, and, overall, the four groups averaged under fifty per cent of the equipment table figure. But by repair and replacement the situation had been improved a month later to an average of over seventy-five per cent. Assault gun vehicles, because they did not cover the great distances imposed on the tanks, had negligible casualties.

The winter campaign and the German withdrawal, however, caused a very steep rise in both personnel and material losses. The 376,000 battle casualties (of which 108,000 were dead and missing) suffered during the winter

---

* The *Walküre I* divisions were category 17 (328 to 331), the *Rheingold* were category 18 (383–389) and those for South Russia category 19 (370–377).

† This was to result in a dangerous drop in ammunition holdings by May 1942, in some types of artillery to one-third of that held in June 1941. In January 1942 the Führer gave serious consideration as to whether the newly invented hollow-charge projectiles had not made all tanks obsolete.

months from 27 November to 31 March, were not excessive given the scale of the fighting; but the sickness casualty rate mainly due to exposure, poor food and typhus, increased this total to 900,000, and this was heavier than the German formations could afford.* By the beginning of April the overall deficiency in the east stood at 625,000 men. At this time material losses were possibly easier to bear than personnel casualties, but, even so, the equipment lost during the withdrawal was considerable. A quarter of a million horses, half of those that had entered Russia, had died; and a total of 2,300 armoured vehicles had been written off, of which 1,600 were Mk III or IV tanks or assault guns.[28] The artillery and panzer arms were left at the end of the winter with 2,000 guns and 7,000 anti-tank guns lacking from their establishments.

Hitler, in his guideline memorandum of 14 July 1941, had ordered the preparation of equipment for four 'tropical panzer divisions' and this figure was raised in the spring of 1942 to a total of eight. At the same time he had begun to plan an increase of panzer divisions from twenty to thirty-six, and of motorized infantry from ten to eighteen.[29] These targets were in fact unattainable since the equipment production did not allow it.

At the beginning of January 1942 Hitler was demanding that a new offensive be launched into Russia that year, and the OKW and OKH general staff began to examine the possibility of making a main thrust from the Ukraine in the south while the other two army groups stood on the defensive. But when Buhle, the new 'chief of the OKW army staff', instructed Halder that the offensive would have to be made on a limited front with the materials and personnel to hand, and that the means would be lacking to sustain an 'extensive (weitreichende) offensive', Halder noted in his diary that 'they are going to begin an attack that they cannot finish'. And so it proved.

On 28 March 1942 Hitler approved a general plan for the new offensive that had been prepared by Halder, but it became immediately obvious that the men were not to be had. Hitler refused to disband the twenty divisions that von Brauchitsch had earmarked in the previous November to provide reinforcements for the rest of the eastern front. The dictator said that such disbandments would have a bad effect on the morale of German troops, would disquieten allies and hearten enemies.[30] And he was not to be moved from this conviction during the whole war. Instead, he required a further eleven divisions to be raised to reinforce Army Group South, together with another six divisions to be removed from France.

The most obvious weakness in the dictator's determination to keep these understrength infantry divisions in being, was that, since the heaviest casualties were borne by the infantry, the arm structure soon became out of balance, with supporting arms, staffs and services almost intact, but with a lack of bayonets in the line. Run down divisions became entirely unfitted for

* There were 228,000 frostbite cases alone.

offensive tasks because of this reduced fighting strength, and so they were tied to ground; eventually, if their infantry strength fell below the critical level, they were without defensive capability. The loss of infantry, as well as the loss of transport, both motorized and horse-drawn, meant that the army could no longer fight its way forward, or even move itself and its fighting equipment. Whereas the victories of 1939 and 1940 had been won, sometimes against an enemy superior in numbers, by air power, by the vigour of the initial assault and, particularly, by the superior mobility of the motorized and infantry formations, from December 1941 this situation no longer existed in Army Group North or Army Group Centre, for these two formations, holding up to sixty per cent of the total frontage in the east, were first to be dominated, then dislodged, and in the final outcome of the war overwhelmed by their Russian foe.* The two army group commanders were constantly begging Hitler to allot them fresh, up to strength and fully equipped, formations, in order that they might use them to gain some freedom of manoeuvre, and the dictator used this, in argument against the chief of the army general staff, as a justification for the raising of more formations.

About 270,000 men of the 22 class had joined the *Feldheer* by April 1942 and the 23 class that had just entered the *Ersatzheer* would not become available until late September. The OKW reckoned, over-optimistically, that 30,000 of the sick and wounded would be returning to duty each month; but the total of these assets, whether recruits or returned veterans, was not enough to cover the casualty rate.[31] Keitel's OKW promises were rarely realized. Over five million young and fit men remained in reserved civilian occupations, and the OKH asked in vain that 100,000 of these be given up to the army each month. The OKH protested, too, against the many fit young men held in idleness by the *Luftwaffe* and *Kriegsmarine*, asking that these be transferred to the army against an exchange of unfit or elderly soldiers. The volunteers from the 25 class, who entered the forces on their own volition two years ahead of call-up, were much sought after by all services as leader material; but nearly a half of these were allocated by Keitel to the *Luftwaffe* and the navy. It remained to the army to do what it could for itself by repeated 'comb-outs' of army installations and rear areas and by improvisation and self-help; and the organization of women auxiliaries, the *Stabshelferinnen*, introduced in January 1942, released more troops for active duty. But the measures were too limited to make any real difference to the situation.

Then, after April, the OKH eastern front was to meet, for the first time, competition in the allocation of army resources, the resistance coming from the OKW theatres, in the first instance from Army Group D in France. For

---

* The *Luftwaffe* could no longer keep up its tempo of attack in the east. Many air formations had been permanently withdrawn for the defence of the Reich, or for refitting, and Kesselring's 2 Air Fleet had gone to Italy. In December a puzzled Stalin reckoned that 1,200 *Luftwaffe* warplanes had disappeared and asked the visiting Eden 'where they had all gone'.

Hitler came to the conclusion that he had cut the defending forces there to below the danger point and that they would no longer be effective in the event of an enemy landing. Three panzer and five infantry divisions were sent from Russia to France; and eleven of the 13 and 14 category and seven of the 15 category infantry divisions already in France that formed the kernel of the defence were improved by additions of personnel and equipment to bring them up to east front standard. In addition thirty-three new army coastal batteries were formed for the west. In the summer of 1942 there was a hurried raising of more formations, this time for France, three *Walküre II* divisions and five *bodenständige* divisions, these last static formations being made up of 'combed-out' personnel.* New divisions usually had six battalions only, with either two or three regiments, and this was in line with the changes in Russia where casualties had forced the reorganization of many divisions on the six battalion basis. In consequence the west grew at the expense of the east, so that casualties in, and removals from, the east, from April onwards were twice the rate of the reinforcements. This led, too, to another phenomenum that was to hold good until the Anglo-American invasion of France in mid 1944, in that the divisions in the west, from July 1942 onwards, were generally up to strength while those in the east were steadily burned-out. Even in July 1942 the *Ostfront* had grown, in comparison to its June 1941 figures, by twenty-nine divisions while its strength had sunk by 359,000 men: whereas in the OKW theatres the divisional strength had dropped by six, but the manpower had risen by 377,000. By that time there was an overall deficiency against the establishment of 650,000 all ranks, and all of them were in the east.

In the autumn of 1942 there was an extensive reshaping of Fromm's *Ersatzheer*, partly to bring the reinforcement organization closer to the troops and partly to provide for improved security inside the countries overrun by the *Wehrmacht*. Instead of carrying out all their training in the *Wehrkreise*, the recruits were, in future, inducted, documented and clothed by *Wehrkreis* reception units and then despatched to *Reservedivisionen* in Poland, occupied Soviet territory or in occupied France and Croatia. A total of seven reserve divisions were formed in the east, ten in the west and one in Croatia, these being grouped under newly formed reserve corps head-quarters that remained under the command of Fromm's *Ersatzheer*. In the east the final stages of training were carried out in one of five field training divisions, these coming not under the Replacement Army but directly under the army groups.[32] These *Feldausbildungs* and *Reservedivisionen* were shortly to be used not merely for the training of recruits and internal security duties, but for operational commitments such as the occupation of Vichy France; by 1944 they were to be drawn into the fighting side by side with the veteran field divisions, so that the whole training organization was destroyed.

---

* The *Walküre II* were category 20 (38, 39 and 65) and the static divisions (343–348) had no category.

The Führer's 1942 offensive from the Ukraine was linked to a grander strategy, for Hitler had once more conjured up a picture, which he described to Mussolini in a letter dated 22 June 1942, of German armies crossing the Caucasus and, together with the Axis forces in Egypt (which at that time were hardly a hundred miles from Alexandria) occupying the Soviet oil producing area and the whole of the British Middle East.* Directive 41, which the Führer had himself drafted, was an untidy disarray of disconnected thoughts containing many asides and irrelevancies, a hotchpotch of strategy and tactics.[33]

Von Küchler's Army Group North and von Kluge's Army Group Centre were to remain on the defensive and sixty-nine of their seventy-five infantry divisions had been run down to two regiments.† There had been some reinforcement but no re-equipping and von Küchler's and von Kluge's ten panzer and seven motorized divisions were very much below strength. Army Group South on the other hand had been raised to sixty-eight divisions by the addition of twenty divisions (of which eleven, category 18 and 19, came from the Reich and six from the west) and these included two newly raised panzer divisions (23 and 24). In addition, Army Group South was to control the equivalent of fifty divisions of Germany's allies, grouped into two Rumanian, one Italian and one Hungarian armies.[34] Nearly all the German divisions had been brought up to near war establishment. The nine panzer divisions had been increased (by removals from the other army groups), from two to three *Abteilungen*, each of two light and one medium tank companies, some of the Mk IV tanks having the long barrelled 75 mm gun. The average panzer divisional strength was about 140 tanks; and one rifle company in each of the motor-cycle battalions and two companies in one of the rifle battalions were mounted in armoured half-tracks, and these were the first of the *Panzergrenadiere*. Army Group South had also six motorized infantry divisions and some of these had their own armoured assault gun support. A number of 20 mm army flak companies and 88 mm army flak batteries were added as part of the panzer and motorized divisional establishment. Whereas the reinforced and refitted infantry divisions in the south were reckoned to have the same fighting value as the June 1941 infantry division, the motorized divisions of the 1942 pattern were believed to be better than those of a year before.

Von Bock, recovered from his stomach ulcer, had returned to duty and had assumed the vacant command of Army Group South, while Paulus had been appointed to the command of 6 Army, one of the strongest on the eastern front. Von Bock had been entrusted with the opening stages of the 1942 offensive that was to involve the completion of the occupation of the Crimea by von Manstein's 11 Army, and the punching out of the great

---

* A special corps headquarters was even to be formed (from *Sonderstab F* (Felmy)) for service in Iraq.

† These had six, or sometimes seven, battalions. From 15 October most infantry regiments were renamed as *Grenadier-Regimenter* except for those that had some traditional link to *Füsilier-* or *Schützen-Regimenter*. The difference was only one of name and they all remained infantry line regiments as before.

Soviet Izyum salient near Kharkov by Paulus's 6 Army and von Kleist's 1 Panzer Army. This was achieved in fine style in May and June, with a heavy toll in Red Army prisoners. Von Bock's next task was to drive due eastwards on Voronezh with von Weichs's 2 Army and Hoth's 4 Panzer Army, and then to move south-eastwards down the right bank of the Don to the Don-Volga landbridge; while Paulus took the landbridge in the centre, Ruoff's 17 Army and von Kleist's 1 Panzer Army were to follow the Sea of Azov coast to Rostov and then enter the Caucasus. For the final stage of the campaign Army Group South would split into an Army Group B in the north, under von Bock, and a new Army Group A in the Caucasus under List, a recent arrival to the theatre from the Balkans.

The first stage of the main thrust eastwards, in spite of the brilliant preliminaries, failed, in that von Bock became involved in heavy fighting near Voronezh and was delayed in the follow-up to the south-east – at least this is what Hitler said, for the dictator subsequently blamed von Bock for the outcome of the whole campaign. The intention to destroy the Soviet forces west of the Don was never fulfilled. The dictator had vacillated and his orders were anything but clear as to whether Voronezh (a few miles east of the Don) should or should not be taken by Army Group South.* When Hitler visited von Bock he was all sweet reasonableness, but no sooner had he returned to his own headquarters than his suspicions and criticisms began to mount again. Endless telephoning went on between the Führer, von Bock, von Sodenstern, Keitel and Halder, the worst part of it, according to Halder, being the pointless chit-chat with Keitel.[35] On 11 July von Bock criticized an OKH directive; to criticize the OKH was now to criticize the Führer. On 13 July Keitel phoned von Bock to say that his command was to be given to von Weichs and that he (Keitel) strongly advised von Bock to ask to be relieved of his duties because of sickness. Von Salmuth took over 2 Army from von Weichs and von Bock went into retirement, worrying and fretting about his ill-usage. He was not re-employed.

Nor was List more fortunate. His Army Group A was soon deep in the Caucasus and had reached part of the oil producing area; von Kleist was on the Terek, near the Caspian shore. Hitler then instructed List to move troops down the Black Sea littoral to Batum and the Turkish border. List, who was obviously out of touch and had little understanding of the Führer régime in the east, declined to do so since this would have split his strung-out forces even further and put the Caucasus mountain ranges between them. On 31 August he was called to Vinnitsa, where the Führer headquarters was now established, and he was heard out with apparent friendliness and under-standing. But no sooner had he taken to the air on his return trip to Stalino than Hitler began to rage once more against him.[36] On 6 September List told the OKH that he would not be answerable for any further advance and the next day he convinced the visiting Jodl that he was right.†

---

* On 12 April Hitler wanted Voronezh taken; by 3 July, he left it to von Bock to take it or not as he pleased.
† List was, apparently, one of the few senior officers who had declined a Führer offered *Dotation*.

192

On his return to Vinnitsa that same night Jodl had reported to Hitler his own agreement with List's appreciation, and this enraged the dictator and caused a breach between the two men. Jodl was, thereafter, no longer to sit at meals in privilege at the side of the Führer, who, in his pettiness, henceforth refused to shake hands with either Jodl or Keitel. From this time onwards Hitler took his solitary meals in his dim depressing quarters; at the daily briefings discussion was to be forbidden and the formal atmosphere was not improved by the presence of two duty stenographers who recorded every word that was spoken.* List was removed from his appointment on 9 September and the Führer put himself in command of Army Group A until the third week in November, when the threat of calamities near Stalingrad and in North Africa forced him to hand over command to von Kleist. The List incident brought out into the open Hitler's disgust with all his generals, and the situation now called for a clean sweep. Keitel shared Jodl's disgrace and it was rumoured that he was to be replaced by Kesselring. Jodl, it was believed, would give way to Paulus after Stalingrad had been taken. And it was at this time that the *Personalamt* was removed from the Keitels and put under Schmundt, and the *Zentralabteilung* of the general staff, that had been responsible since 1935 for the appointments on the general staff, was transferred back to the *Personalamt*. Schmundt no longer regarded himself as part of the army general staff and sent a deputy to represent him there. Halder was to go.[37]

Halder's position had deteriorated since the removal of von Brauchitsch, for he was now subordinate to Keitel as well as to the Führer. Sometimes Hitler used Jodl for tasks that were Halder's. Jodl tended, in so far as the dictator would permit it, to meddle and give gratuitous advice concerning the *Ostfront* and he had got his desserts for letting himself get involved in List's problems. And Jodl was the driving force in the competition against Halder for troops and resources for the OKW theatres. There was little doubt that Halder was losing ground. Gloomy and tired, he voiced his displeasure and fears to the dictator. Hitler wanted neither professional competence nor advice, but an unquestioning obedience to his own person. His choice fell on Zeitzler.

Zeitzler, a newly promoted major-general with a reputation as a live wire, had formerly been a subordinate of Jodl's in the OKW. A great friend of Schmundt, and known personally to the Führer, Zeitzler, as chief of staff to Army Group D, had gained some credit for the repulse of the British-Canadian raid on Dieppe in August 1942.† Towards his subordinates he was hot-tempered and brutal, and Faber du Faur thought him an adventurer.‡ But Hitler wanted a man who was optimistic and ready for anything, the

---

* Speer thought that this was done so that history might be written according to the Hitler version; the army general staff, however, believed that it was originally a counter to Halder, who himself noted what was said in his own *Gabelsberger* shorthand.

† Army Group D was commanded from 15 March 1942 by von Rundstedt who had been reappointed to active duty from the Führer's reserve.

‡ 'Zeitzler tried, with the mask of an adventurer, for a lucky gambler's *coup*.' (Faber du Faur, p. 165)

antithesis of Halder the pessimist and the prophet of doom, always infecting the army groups with his wailing. Zeitzler was promoted to general, jumping the rank of lieutenant-general as Jodl had before him, and, on 24 September, Halder went out in the wilderness, firstly to retirement and then, after the attempt on Hitler's life, to arrest, prison and a concentration camp.

In the eyes of the army group commanders, the new chief of army staff had none of the advantages of seniority, experience or authority. He did not even control his own general staff appointments. But, nothing daunted, Zeitzler made it clear to his staff that loyalty and confidence in the Führer were the order of the day; one of the first casualties was Müller-Hillebrand, heading the organization *Abteilung* of the general staff. For the *Luftwaffe* had at last been ordered to make men available for the army, but Göring had insisted instead that he form his own *Luftwaffe* infantry (field) divisions; and Müller-Hillebrand spoke out against Zeitzler's acceptance of the order.[38] But outside the OKH the sun shone brightly on Zeitzler. The rest of the Führer's court followed suit, and even Jodl sought to profit by the popularity of his former subordinate. Jodl hoped that Zeitzler would acquiesce to the OKW assuming overall control over the eastern front. Zeitzler, however, promptly disassociated himself from the OKW, and, profiting from the weakness of Jodl's personal position, adroitly did away with the overlapping of some of the dual command responsibilities, and even won back some of the ground lost by Halder in the preceding nine months; as far as possible Zeitler excluded Jodl from all business concerning the eastern front. Within six months his relationship with Jodl was anything but cordial.

Zeitzler failed as chief of army general staff, although it is certain that no other man could have succeeded under such a commander-in-chief. In his first year of office Zeitzler enjoyed Hitler's confidence because he did what he was told, and was little more than a mouthpiece and telephonic link between the Führer and the army groups; but as soon as he permitted himself to doubt the dictator's direction, then, like Halder, he was marked out for removal. Some contemporary evidence at the time of 6 Army's capitulation does not support the robust line that Zeitzler said he took when in Hitler's presence.[39] Yet Speer thought him straight-forward, insensitive, a man of backbone and candour though not given to independent thinking, and Heusinger has said that there were occasions on which Zeitzler rounded on Hitler with vigour and heat.[40]

Zeitzler had been replaced as chief of staff to von Rundstedt by Blumentritt, who gave up his appointment as *O Qu 1* to Heusinger, a former head of the operations *Abteilung*.

In the south-east the German tragedy continued to unfold. Hitler became obsessed with the taking of the city of Stalingrad on the Volga, although this objective had formed no part of the mission he had set in the summer. He wanted the city, he said, to close the Volga river supply route (although this could in fact have been cut anywhere in the surrounding steppe and the river

194

was due to freeze anyway); and he wanted to seize or destroy the Stalingrad industrial complex. In reality, knowing that Stalin had based his military fame on his pretended defence of the city in the civil war, Hitler wanted to take the city to bolster his own propaganda image. Stalin appeared to be determined to hold Stalingrad for much the same reason. And so both poured troops into the area in a very costly and deadly battle that raged for months. Paulus's 6 Army that was originally to hold the northern flank, so protecting the Caucasus, was drawn by the fighting eastwards into the city where it was fast burning itself out, and the protection of the 400 mile northern flank along the Don was entrusted to the four Rumanian, Italian and Hungarian armies, none of which had any high fighting value. The first Soviet winter counter-offensive, launched from the north in a deep enveloping move, broke open the Rumanians, and in four days Paulus's army of twenty German and two Rumanian divisions was surrounded.

Paulus could have broken out if he had been so instructed, or if he had wanted to do so. But, although he was undoubtedly an able man, Paulus was indecisive and unsure of himself – a good subordinate to carry out orders. At the time of the Izyum battle he believed that the dictator's judgement was better than his own. His character being what it was, it was unthinkable that he would be the man to defy any Führer standstill order, although he was pressingly urged by one of his subordinate corps commanders, von Seydlitz-Kurzbach, to do so.[41] If he had decided to break out in defiance of orders, his corps commanders would have supported him.*

On 20 November Rastenburg was in disarray. Hitler was nervous and irresolute. Zeitzler and the OKH came up with no clear proposals, and the only logical suggestion, that put forward by Jodl that the whole battle should be left to von Weichs, was overruled.[42] Von Weichs and Paulus fully recognized the dangers. Von Weichs warned the OKH on 23 November that the *Luftwaffe* could not air supply a tenth of 6 Army's requirements and he wanted Paulus to have permission to break out immediately. That day Hitler agreed 'in principle' that a break-out should be made, and Zeitzler subsequently blamed Keitel and Jodl for supporting, or acquiescing to, Hitler's afterthoughts, that Paulus should remain where he was on the Volga.[43] That Keitel gave such support is probable; that Jodl acquiesced is possible, since he was much chastened since the List affair. Yet the dictator had in public speeches twice committed himself in the most bombastic terms to remain in Stalingrad, and anything that Paulus, von Weichs or Zeitzler said was unlikely to have had the slightest effect on him.[44] When Göring appeared and, against the advice given to him by von Richthofen, assured the Führer that the *Luftwaffe* could keep 6 Army supplied, Hitler had found either his salvation or his scapegoat.[45] Paulus's 6 Army was doomed.

* Von Seydlitz-Kurzbach's 70/71 correspondence to the author. Paulus's chief of staff, General Arthur Schmidt, in a manuscript critique to the author dated 24.4.73, takes a very different view, maintaining that 6 Army would have broken out 'even against orders', if it had been strong enough to do so. This view, in the opinion of the author, is not corroborated by available contemporary evidence.

The battle was taken out of von Weichs's hands and an attempt was made to throw together a relieving force. Von Manstein, a field-marshal since his victory at Sevastopol, was brought from Vitebsk to Novocherkassk, and his 11 Army headquarters was redesignated with the weighty and sonorous title of Army Group Don, even though it had no troops; a panzer division was railed from France to the Don, and formations and detachments were raked together from elsewhere on the front. The force, except for 6 Panzer Division that came from the west, was very much understrength and had not the offensive power of an army. The weather and the Russian were firmly against him and von Manstein made only slow progress; his command over Paulus, shortly to be promoted to field-marshal's rank, was illusory, for Paulus was controlled directly from Rastenburg; and von Manstein himself, notwithstanding his air of the *grand seigneur* and the somewhat condescending tones in which he spoke of the dictator after the war, was, at the time, like his fellows, overshadowed by, and completely subordinate to, Hitler.* An officer on von Manstein's staff, whose duty it was to listen in to all radio telephone conversations, including those with Hitler, has described to the author how von Manstein asked for the withdrawal of von Kleist's Army Group A from the Caucasus, in order that it might be used offensively against the enemy Volga grouping; and how Hitler replied that such a withdrawal would mean the loss of Baku oil and the loss of the war. And the same officer told the author that, having listened in to the last radio conversations between von Manstein and Paulus, he was a witness 'to the frightful failure of both of the field-marshals – for neither of them had the strength of character or the greatness of mind to take independent action in defiance of Hitler's madness'.[46] And so over 200,000 men were lost in dead or prisoners.† And successive Russian hammer blows on Rumanians, Italians and Hungarians, in ever-widening arcs, in great enveloping movements each deeper into the German rear, were to clear the Caucasus and the Ukraine so that the great German 1942 summer offensive was thrown back to its starting point.

The Mediterranean and North Africa remained for the moment a secondary OKW theatre and, as far as the German Army was concerned, a war area of no great importance, however much Hitler and Goebbels tried to make propaganda capital out of Rommel's exploits. Kesselring's *Luftflotte 2* arrived in Italy in December 1941 and was put under the *Comando Supremo,* with the mission of keeping open the air and sea routes between Italy and North Africa. Rommel's small Africa corps was theoretically under Italian tactical control; German command channels back to the OKW were,

* Or as Guderian expressed it: 'Manstein, as often when face to face with Hitler, was not at his best ...' (*Panzer Leader,* pp. 306–7)

† Paulus, though married into the Rumanian nobility, came from the lower German middle-class: his major defect was not that he lacked command experience – for the same could be said of the elder von Moltke – but that his character, pleasing to Hitler, lacked decisiveness and sturdy independence. Among the army general staff he was known as *Cunctator.*

however, confused, since Rommel's orders sometimes came direct from Rastenburg and sometimes through von Rintelen with the *Comando Supremo*. Kesselring, although designated as *Oberbefehlshaber Süd*, still controlled only *Luftwaffe* forces, but he did take a hand with the *Comando Supremo* in all strategic planning.

In November, a British offensive (*Crusader*), with about 700 tanks, threw the German-Italian forces out of Cyrenaica. But then, in the last week in January 1942, the Italo-German force launched its own counter-offensive that rapidly cleared the lost area, took Tobruk and threatened Egypt.

Rommel's command technique was not uncommon in the German Army at that time among the younger generals disparaged by their seniors as the *arrivistes* and *parvenus*; it was used, in particular, by generals of the panzer arm, by Guderian and later by Model. Rommel's methods of leading from the front were effective, though they had their weaknesses. Rommel himself was somewhat indisciplined, for although he was only the commander of a corps (redesignated as a panzer army from 30 January 1942) of no more than three divisions, and was not a commander-in-chief, he did very much as he pleased and he decided all policy that affected his command, this bringing him into conflict with Kesselring and the Italians and, later, with the Führer. On the battlefield he interested himself in points of detail, closely controlling and frequently interfering with his staff and subordinates.

In the late summer of 1942 the African panzer army was further reinforced by a new 164 Light Division made up of regiments from 22 Infantry Division airtransported from Crete, a parachute training (*Fallschirm-Lehr*) brigade and a Brigade 999 made up of political and criminal German prisoners.

At the end of October came the Axis defeat near El Alamein, and four German and eight Italian divisions ceased to exist as an effective fighting force. The remainder, disregarding the Führer's order to hold to the last, streamed away westwards, not to fight again until it reached Mareth and Tunisia 1,600 miles away.

Germany's fate was already in the balance when it invaded the USSR; it was finally sealed in December 1941 when Hitler declared war on the United States. Yet the effect of the American participation was not to become apparent until after November 1942. In the air and at sea the Anglo-American war effort had admittedly been powerful and had tied down substantial air and some land forces in Western Europe, but, as far as the land fighting was concerned, only the British had taken a very minor part. On 7 November, a few days after El Alamein, came news of the Anglo-American landings in Algeria and Morocco. Up to this time the ability of the British or the Americans to fight a war by land had not been taken very seriously in Rastenburg and for this reason the defeat and landing came as unpleasant tidings to the OKW and as a surprise to the German public, where the significance of Rommel and his force had been much exaggerated. Hitler's reaction was, however, immediate. He ordered the overrunning of unoccupied Vichy France (*Attila*) by von Rundstedt's troops, an operation in which the reserve divisions of the *Ersatzheer* took part together with 4 Italian Army from the south. German troops were to be moved to Tunisia.

A few days later Stalingrad was enveloped and besieged. There were no OKH reserves available and there never had been since the beginning of the Russian war. The new Tunisian force, given the weighty designation of 5 Panzer Army, was based on 90 Corps headquarters; it was originally a scratch force thrown together from what could be collected in France: 10 Panzer Division, in process of re-equipping; 334 Infantry Division, a formation of limited fighting value, made up of *Ersatzheer* detachments; part of the *Hermann Göring* brigade and part of three infantry divisions in the west; a few army panzer battalions. Both 5 Panzer Army and the remnants of the African Panzer Army were formed into a German-Italian army group, firstly under Rommel and then under von Arnim, this coming under Kesselring as Commander-in-Chief South.

When Nehring, the first commander of the German force, reported that he doubted the wisdom of holding Tunisia, he was, on 9 November, removed from his command.[47] But this became Rommel's view, too, and the commander whose aggressiveness had once recommended him to the Führer, was soon to be dubbed by the dictator as a pessimist, a fair-weather soldier lacking stamina in adversity. When the end finally came in the second week in May 1943, the new army group was entirely destroyed in front of Bizerta and Tunis with an Axis loss of a quarter of a million men, a half of which were German. About 94,000 German troops went into captivity, the same number that had been taken in Stalingrad.

CHAPTER TEN

The Loss of Strategic Initiative

After the heavy defeats in North Africa and Stalingrad the differences between Jodl and Zeitzler became more acute; these differences always centred on the allocation of formations, reinforcements and equipment. Germany needed an OKW combined services planning and advisory staff of authority and experience to co-ordinate a world-wide strategy for all the armed forces and for the civil economy, a staff that would be capable of regulating conflicting interests and demands. But Germany, unlike its western enemies, had no such body authorized or able to fill this function. The only person, other than the Führer himself, who aspired to such an office was Jodl. In reality, however, Jodl was unfitted and unequipped for the task by reason of his mentality, his lack of political and military education, and a complete dearth of staff and resources. Jodl lacked the perspective and acuity of vision and would have been unable to have put himself on a higher plane from which he could have surveyed the world situation with an eye and mind attuned to warfare in all its aspects. Jodl was, in many respects, the child of his German age and a product of the general staff system; for he was a military technician, narrow-minded and blinkered, who venerated the Führer's genius as much as did Schmundt, and who would have thought it presumptuous even to consider the strategy and higher conduct of war, for that was the Führer's business. Jodl accepted the planning by *Führerprinzip* and he wanted only military orders.

Nor did the composition of Jodl's planning staffs and cells permit them to undertake such work. Jodl regarded his subordinates as executives rather than as advisers or promoters of new strategic thought, and just as Jodl accepted his direction and orders from Hitler, so were Jodl's officers expected to carry out orders from above and not formulate policy from below. Although some of his staff spoke well of him, others found him secretive, cold, aloof, disdainful and arrogant; they mistrusted his ambition. Nor did he get on well with all his fellow generals in the OKH or with the party officials and ministries – Goebbels and Göring, for reasons of their own, appear to have disliked him, and the OKL and OKM ignored any efforts that he might have made to co-ordinate air and sea planning. But Jodl soon gave up any pretensions in that direction and restricted himself to the fighting of the land battle, his activity rarely transcending the operative level.

And since he had no formal responsibility for the eastern front he concentrated his attention, and what resources he could lay his hands on, on the OKW theatres in Western Europe from the North Cape to Crete. This is exactly what Hitler required him to do. Jodl's activity in no way covered the responsibilities that should have been required from a properly organized *Wehrmachtführungsstab*.

So it came about that Jodl and Zeitzler were rival army chiefs of staff to Hitler. Hitler, by now tiring visibly and showing symptoms of a nervous disease or disorder that seems to have been aggravated by the severe strain to which he was subjected, was becoming a casualty to his own irregular method of government and military command. For the Führer was the only source of authority and knowledge; and as the dictator had ordered that he should be consulted and give decisions on any matters of importance, his working hours were filled with interviews, conferences, telephone calls, reports and memoranda. All government centralized in one man was beginning to falter and fail; conflicting interests and demands, even within the army high command, were placing an intolerable stress on the dictator, for the army group commanders in the east, bickering between themselves over frontages and resources, and knowing that these differences could not be settled by Zeitzler, did not hesitate to telephone the Führer and state their case. And, as soon as he had decided in favour of the one, the other was sure to ring the dictator back and complain. As he grew increasingly tired, he tended to put off objections by empty promises or to give in to the last caller – provided of course that the project under discussion was not one that the Führer had himself ordered. And these arguments usually centred on what must now seem relatively trivial matters, although they did not appear so at the time to the hard-pressed commanders. Even Jodl and Zeitzler would quarrel over the allocation of a single division, carrying their tales to the Führer so that the dictator ruled that he would not hear the objections of the one without the other being present.

Questions were therefore decided, often without prior warning, consultation and deliberation, as they were raised; these covered the most diverse subjects and might have global application, involving foreign policy, the higher conduct of war, the war economy, industrial resources, manpower, equipment and personnel, the order of battle, strategy and tactics; the matters might be very trivial, or of prime importance to the survival of the Reich. And Hitler either decided them on the spot, by an impromptu ruling, or, increasingly often as the war progressed and as he became exhausted, by postponing a decision, sometimes indefinitely. His military decisions given to his two chiefs of staff were issued in the same way, being based on intuition or snap judgement, for expert opinion or impartial advice were seldom sought. And meanwhile Schmundt stood at the dictator's side, the third in the trinity of military executives. A fourth dimension was yet to be added.

During 1942 Hitler had taken a directing role in the development of German armour, particularly in tank construction. He wanted the Mk VI

Tiger tank improved, both in design and in the numbers produced, and he was an enthusiastic joint planner of the production of a new tank, the Panther Mk V weighing about 40 tons, smaller than the Tiger but more powerful than the Mk IV. During the many meetings on tank manufacture with Speer and Saur of the ministry of armaments and war production, the dictator scrutinized closely, and did not hesitate to have altered, the technical specifications for armament, armour, weight and mobility.

According to what Guderian has said, and the information was gleaned partly by hearsay and partly from Saur's notes, the OKH had requested that the manufacture of all tanks except the Mks V and VI should cease, an impossible request in the short term since by now the Mk IV was the army's work horse, just as the Mk III had been during 1942. To cut off the supply of the Mk IV would have meant an immediate and serious reduction in the number of tanks produced.

On 17 February 1943, Guderian, to his very great surprise, was recalled from the reserve and ordered to report to the Führer at Vinnitsa, and one assumes that this was Schmundt's work.[1] The idea was, so Schmundt told Guderian, to lift the panzer arm out of its doldrums and centralize it under Guderian as the single co-ordinating authority. If Guderian is to be believed, it was he who insisted to Schmundt on his own terms of re-employment. He was to be called not the inspector, but the Inspector-General; and, unlike the previous inspector within the OKH who had been personally subordinate to von Brauchitsch but had had his inspectorate responsible in its day to day dealings to Fromm, the new Inspector-General for Panzer Troops was to have his own independent *Kommando*, subordinate not to Zeitzler or to the rump of the OKH, or to the Replacement Army, but only to Hitler. Guderian wanted to 'be in a position to influence the development of armoured equipment both with the army ordnance office and with the armaments ministry ... and finally must be able to exert the same influence over the organization and training of the tank units of the *Waffen SS* and the *Luftwaffe*'. Guderian put all this in a paper that preceded him to Vinnitsa, where he was due to be interviewed by the Führer on 9 March 1943.

Guderian, in spite of his impetuous and hot-tempered nature, was knowledgeable and experienced in the intrigues of the high command and was usually astute enough to get his own way in the face of outside opposition. But this time he had, he said, made the mistake of sending to Schmundt's office a résumé of what he intended to say, and this had, presumably, been circulated to all concerned. So, instead of having the desired *tête-à-tête* with Hitler, he was alarmed to see 'the whole OKW, Zeitzler and a number of his department heads, the inspectors of artillery and infantry and, finally, Schmundt' come trooping in, all intent on defending their own interests. Most of the artillerymen present, in addition to the inspector of artillery, successfully opposed Guderian's proposal that the artillery assault gun arm be transferred to the panzer troops, but this was the extent of their victory, since what appears to have been Guderian's paper was otherwise approved by Hitler in its entirety.[2]

But Guderian's memoirs do not accurately portray what these changes were to mean, for in reality they altered the structure, not only of the army high command, but of much of the German Army. Guderian was set up in what was to develop as a command outside of a command, not responsible to the OKW or the OKH but having the status of an independent army (*AOK*) directly under the Führer. Guderian's duties were to centre on the organization, training and technical development of the panzer arm in all its aspects, and the *Panzertruppen* that replaced the *Schnelle Truppen* were to include tank troops, the heavy motorized *Panzerjäger* tank-killers (but not the lighter *Sturmgeschütze* manned by the artillery), the panzer and motorized reconnaissance battalions, dismounted anti-tank gunners and the armoured railway troops. All of these arms were to wear the pink (*rosa*) piping once worn by the *Reichsheer Kraftfahrtruppen*. Moreover motorized infantry were to go to Guderian: these included infantry of the panzer divisions, all of whom, since April 1942, had been redesignated as panzer grenadier (irrespective of whether or not they went into battle in armoured carriers or motor trucks) and grenadier infantry of the motorized infantry divisions. All of these were grouped with the *Panzertruppen*. *

Guderian had in fact his own private army, equivalent to the *Waffen SS* owned by Himmler and the *Luftwaffe* field divisions in Göring's empire. Unlike the other arms generals he had no responsibilities to the chief of the army general staff and had only 'to keep him informed'. The panzer *Waffengeneral* was replaced by Guderian's liaison officer. In the field of equipment design, development and industrial output, Guderian was responsible to no military authority (beyond of course Hitler). And the command of all *Panzertruppen* formations, units, schools and installations in the Reich, and those abroad that still came under the *Ersatzheer,* was separated from the Replacement Army and put directly under Guderian. This applied, too, to the *Inspekteur der Panzertruppe* with Fromm's headquarters, and the newly appointed *Kommandeure der Panzertruppe* with each of the *Wehrkreise.* Yet the allocation of new recruits to the panzer arm still remained Fromm's responsibility; not unnaturally the whole arrangement gave rise to much friction between Guderian's *Kommando* and the *Ersatzheer.* Guderian's appointment was backdated to February 1943, and Thomale was appointed as his deputy. One of Guderian's main tasks was to increase production from 600 to 1,450 tanks a month.[3]

Exactly why Hitler should have made this decision to separate the motorized troops from the rest of the army is difficult to determine. The reasons may have been those that he gave Schmundt when he sent him to visit

---

* Panzer grenadiers wore green piping and the motorized grenadiers the white piping of line infantry. Horsed and motor cycle cavalry continued to wear gold piping but henceforth were administered by infantry: 24 Panzer (formerly 1 Cavalry) Division continued to wear gold but was absorbed by Guderian's *Panzertruppen*.

Guderian. The dictator may have wished to be rid of the immediate burden of resolving another set of conflicting demands; and he probably wished to restore the armoured arm to its earlier effectiveness and glory. On the other hand the demand for complete separation of the panzer arm from the rest of the army may have come from Guderian – as he said it did – for the whole idea is in keeping with Guderian's character. After the 20 July 1944 military uprising, Hitler crowed at the plotters' discomfiture in that they had little armour at their call, and he said, rightly or wrongly, that he had carried out this surgery with this end in view.

Guderian had been elevated to a position that was of hardly less importance than that of Jodl and Zeitzler, with whom he should have worked in co-operation. In fact, each of the three disliked the others, and the new appointment and the split organization were to lead to difficulties. For not only were these three required to work with each other but they were also expected to maintain close, if not cordial, links with the *Waffen SS*, which, by 1 July 1943, totalled nearly twelve field divisions of which eight were motorized, and with a *Luftwaffe* that maintained at this time two parachute light divisions, one panzer division and no fewer than twenty-one *Luftwaffe-Infanterie* field divisions, in addition to 2,000 heavy and 1,400 medium and light flak batteries. No other nation could have offered so diverse a command organization for ground troops.

The strength of divisions in France had been allowed to drop during the winter of 1940/41 to eighteen, and these of very limited fighting value, but by June of 1942 the numbers were being restored to twenty-five, with a further increase by September to thirty-three. During the next winter a further fourteen divisions were raised in France, of which three were *Luftwaffe* and two SS, and four divisions were brought from the east for refitting. But the same number of divisions were sent back to the east, leaving the *OB West* strength at thirty-two divisions. In the summer of 1943 a further twenty-three divisions were to be raised in France, and six motorized divisions were brought in from the east, but the overall total was reduced by the exchange of twenty-three divisions already in France that were sent to other theatres – nine to the east, twelve to Italy and two to the Balkans. By late summer of 1943 von Rundstedt had thirty-eight divisions. By 1 July 1943 the actual strength of the *Feldheer* in the east without the *Waffen SS* and *Luftwaffe* field divisions was to rise temporarily to 3,100,000 while the OKW theatre *Feldheer* was to drop to 1,300,000 men.[4]

The rapidly increasing strength of the Soviet and the Anglo-American powers indicated that, unless Germany's enemies fell out amongst themselves, the Axis would not survive. Japan had shot its bolt and had suffered telling defeats in the Pacific; Mussolini wanted to end the war against the USSR and the Italian people wanted peace with east and west at almost any price; Finland was considering means by which it could safely extricate itself; the Rumanian dictator Antonescu wanted peace with the west but a continuation of war against the Soviet Union; all of Germany's allies, including the Japanese, saw that Germany faced defeat by land, air and sea. This spurred on Hitler to a new excess in an effort to prove himself.

Hitler, his OKW and OKH staffs, and Guderian, reasoned that as an invasion of Europe by the Anglo-Americans was imminent, there was no longer any hope of knocking the USSR out of the war in 1943. Jodl was in favour of going on to the defensive in the east and removing formations there for France and the Mediterranean; Guderian agreed with him in that he was against any offensive that would prevent him from building up his armoured reserves ready to engage the Second Front. The OKH, on the other hand, had no responsibility and little interest in any theatre outside of Russia, and would not willingly accept the removal of formations from the east unless frontages and commitments could be correspondingly reduced. This Hitler refused to do, both for reasons of prestige and because he maintained, quite erroneously, that the war economy could not sustain the loss of territory and resources. In this way the tug-of-war between east and west and between OKW and OKH staffs was accentuated, with Guderian, intent on building a new panzer arm, plotting his own course.

Hitler was of the opinion, and in this he was encouraged by Zeitzler, that the best means of defence in Russia was a short powerful offensive with limited objectives to be made immediately after the thaw had dried out the ground and before the Americans and British could mount their attack in Europe. In this belief he harked back to the highly successful battle of the Izyum bulge made in the late spring of 1942; he also found some encouragement in the limited success of von Manstein's recent Kharkov battle. He wanted to attack the Soviet enemy before the Germans were themselves attacked, in order to eliminate, if only temporarily and partially, the offensive capability of the Red Army. The need was to capture men and equipment, and, at the same time, restore the reputation of German arms and the faith of his Axis allies, by gaining a quick but spectacular victory.[5] This, in his own words, would shine out to the world like a beacon.[6]

The sector chosen for the new offensive was the enemy salient at Kursk, very similar to, and not far distant from, the earlier bulge at Izyum. The Kursk bulge was dangerously exposed and invited attack, particularly since the Russians were known to be reinforcing it, presumably as a jumping off place for the next winter's offensive. The Kursk salient extended westwards between what were in effect two German salients jutting eastwards, the northern including the town of Orel while that in the south centred round the city of Kharkov. Hitler's and Zeitzler's plan intended that Model's 9 Army of von Kluge's Army Group Centre should attack southwards on Kursk, while Hoth's 4 Panzer Army and Group Kempf of von Manstein's Army Group South should attack northwards from the Kharkov salient to meet Model in a double envelopment. The surrounded Soviet enemy in the salient would then be destroyed.* It was, in fact, a repetition of the Izyum battle of 1942.

The offensive was frequently postponed because Model, on whose opinion Hitler attached great importance, doubted the adequacy of his forces and repeatedly asked for more formations. On 4 May, Hitler held a meeting in Munich at which Guderian vehemently opposed any offensive being made at all, his attitude and remarks exciting the anger of his old enemy von Kluge who, according to Guderian, 'afterwards gave way to hysteria' and challenged him to a duel, inviting Hitler to be his second.[7] Zeitzler was all in favour of the offensive. Von Manstein and von Kluge also agreed with it although they did not want any further postponement. Model, who presented his views in a letter, still had some reservations.[8] The decision had to be the Führer's and he came down in favour of the operation. When the dictator addressed his senior commanders on 1 July, he said that he knew the offensive (*Citadel*) would be a gamble but he was convinced it would come off.[9]

The number of German forces in the Kursk battle, in a sector that was hardly a hundred miles square, was enormous, far greater than those in the whole of Western Europe. Von Manstein in the south had twenty-two divisions and of these six were panzer and five panzer grenadier. Four of the panzer grenadier were SS and the fifth, the army motorized division *Grossdeutschland*, was, by Hitler's orders, brought up to the SS establishment; all these panzer grenadier divisions were in fact far stronger than the army panzer divisions, each having over a hundred tanks and thirty assault guns, for the army panzer divisions were now down to an actual strength of no more than seventy tanks. Von Manstein's force totalled over 1,300 tanks and *Sturmgeschütze*. In the north, Model had twenty-one divisions of which six were panzer and one panzer grenadier, in all between 700 and 800 tanks. So it came about that, out of a total German Army and SS holding of 3,100 tanks and 1,400 assault guns, 2,200 tanks and 1,000 assault guns were on the *Ostfront*, nearly seventy per cent of these being concentrated near Kursk.[10]

The offensive began on 4 July and raged for the next three weeks. Then, on 10 July, the Anglo-Americans began landing in Sicily and it became obvious that the Italians were going to fight no longer. Hitler, fearing that the loss of Italy and the Italian-held Balkans might open up his southern flank, required the OKW to overhaul the emergency military plans already prepared for such a contingency and he warned von Kluge and von Manstein on 13 July that SS formations might have to be moved from the Kursk battle to the west. But von Manstein has given a very misleading account when he said that success was snatched from his grasp by Hitler's 'decision to break off the *Citadel* offensive', for the contemporary record makes it clear that the offensive was not broken off and no final decision was taken to remove the *Waffen SS* until 25 July, when it was certain that *Citadel* had failed

---

* Speer and Dietrich said that Hitler had first intended that Soviet prisoners taken at Kursk should be shot in retaliation for the murder of German prisoners. (*Inside the Third Reich*, p. 369)

completely.[11] By then the Soviet counter-offensives launched in the rear of the German attacks in the areas of Orel and Kharkov had transformed the situation, and it was apparent that Model and Army Group South were threatened with encirclement.

Citadel failed because the plan was badly conceived. Frequent postponements led to a loss of surprise. Moreover, the concept of attacking a strong Soviet enemy in well prepared positions, a situation in which the Russian excelled, was of doubtful wisdom. Hitler and the OKH underestimated the strength of the Red Army forces concentrated in and near the Kursk salient, nor did they know that these forces were in reality being made ready not for a winter but a summer offensive, the first Soviet summer offensive of the war, and that the Soviet high command was on the point of launching this if *Citadel* had been further delayed beyond 4 July.[12] The offensive power of the Red Air Force, too, had come as an unpleasant surprise: *Luftflotten 4* and *6* had made extravagant claims in the first few days of the fighting but by the third week in the month air superiority over the battlefield had been lost in the face of 'much increased Red Air Force activity and bad weather'. In truth the German high command and the German Army had been out-generalled and outfought. The loss of air superiority brought final failure.

Hitler and Göring had never been close to the realities of the fighting on the eastern front and even Zeitzler had had comparatively little experience of war there. It was noticeable that the more distant the opinion from the fighting line, the more sanguine it became. Whereas von Kluge was inclined to scepticism, Model had little confidence in the outcome of the attack; the same tendency was apparent in Army Group South where Hoth resisted von Manstein's pressure to burn out his exhausted troops.

The breaking off of *Citadel* opened up the sluice gates of a mighty Russian summer offensive that was to throw the Germans out of the Ukraine. With the German decline came a corresponding improvement in the Soviet command and the performance of the Red Army field formations: the Soviet forces were now strong enough to be used offensively in summer.

The German losses at Kursk have never been accurately computed but the losses over the whole of the eastern front between 1 July and 1 October totalled a million men of which only a half could be replaced: this was reflected in the overall decrease in army strength (excluding the SS and *Luftwaffe* divisions) on the eastern front from 3,100,000 on 1 July to 2,564,000 on 1 October.[13]

Up to 1943 the Germans usually succeeded tactically but failed strategically. At Kursk they failed strategically because they were unsuccessful tactically. The whole concept of the *Citadel* offensive reflected the bankruptcy of the German high command. After *Citadel* the Axis lost all initiative on the eastern front and was never to regain it.

Following the destruction of the six German divisions in Tunisia, three new divisions were immediately raised from the rear parties left in Italy, and to these could be added the *Luftwaffe Panzer-Division Hermann Göring* less the regimental group lost in Africa. This scratch force formed the only German troops readily available to bolster the Italian defence in Sicily. The German divisions came under the tactical command of Guzzoni's 6 Italian Army, a German liaison officer, von Senger und Etterlin, being attached to Guzzoni, partly as an adviser and partly to look after the German interest. Following the allied landings in Sicily and the failure of the Italian Army to provide an adequate defence, a further five divisions moved into the Italian mainland from France on 24 July; of these two were panzer, two panzer grenadier, and one a parachute light division.

Even before the fall of Tunis, the OKW staffs had been directed to produce contingency plans to safeguard against Italy's collapse, for Hitler intended to keep the Italians in the war by force. Mussolini, notwithstanding his apparently cordial relationship with Hitler, held Germans in no great favour; nor did he have their confidence. Ambrosio, the chief of the armed forces staff (*Comando Supremo*), and Roatta, the chief of the army general staff, were much mistrusted in Rastenburg.

The German plans that had begun as early as that May provided for a total occupation of Italy (codename *Alarich*) and the Balkans (*Konstantin*), the military action against the Italian armed forces having the codename *Achse*.[14] Von Rundstedt, the *OB West*, was to be ready to intern 4 Italian Army on the French riviera and to secure the French-Italian Alpine passes for German use. Löhr, List's successor as the Commander-in-Chief South-East in the Balkans, had been ordered to plan the disarming, firstly of 11 Italian Army in Greece and then the other Italian troops in the Balkans that came under the Italian Army Group East in Albania. An army staff, based on von Weichs's Army Group B headquarters (withdrawn from the Ukraine) was set up in Munich under Rommel, to plan the movement of German troops into Italy. For the time being Kesselring, who got on well with the Italians and who was for the moment fully occupied with the battle in the south, was kept in the dark as to the intention. Then, following the meeting with Mussolini at Feltre on 19 July when Hitler learned how unpopular Rommel was with the Italians, the dictator decided that the field-marshal should not be employed in Italy and he sent him to the Balkans as the new *OB Südost*. A few days later, after Mussolini had been arrested and the Badoglio government had taken office, Hitler changed his mind again and Rommel was told to return from Salonica to his former post in Munich; Löhr reassumed his old appointment until von Weichs should arrive in Salonica.[15]

The next ten days was a period of hectic German activity in South Germany, South France, the Balkans and Italy, so that the battle situation in Sicily, as seen from Rastenburg, was of relatively minor importance. Kesselring, who was still in ignorance of Rommel's activities and proposed role in Italy, continued to believe that Badoglio intended to stay in the war. Hitler, however, and rightly this time, knew better, and decided that a further eight divisions, of which one was panzer and one a parachute light division, should be moved 'or filtered' into North Italy. Meanwhile Hube's 14 Panzer Corps headquarters was to take the German troops in Sicily under command. On 26 July Kesselring was informed (by a personal liaison officer sent by the Führer) of the OKW plan (*Schwarz*) whereby the *Luftwaffe* general Student, in the event of *Achse* being ordered, was to seize Rome, arrest the Badoglio government and release the Duce, using 2 Parachute Division and 3 Panzer Grenadier Division that were stationed in the area. Kesselring, normally an optimist, was appalled at this plan, for he thought the Führer's fears were groundless; he had little hope that *Schwarz* would succeed, and he told the OKW on 5 August that 'if 5 Italian Army [with five divisions near Rome] should put up even the slightest resistance . . . six German divisions in Italy would be put in jeopardy'.[16] The relationship between the German Army and the Italian troops and civil population was worsening, and incidents, sometimes violent, were becoming commonplace. Each side suspected what the other was about, with the Germans filtering divisions into North Italy in the face of every Italian obstruction, while the Italians, for their part, were moving troops up to the Alpine passes.

On 14 August when Kesselring learned of the part that was likely to be played by Rommel, who was to be put in overall command and above Kesselring, he asked to resign. Although his resignation was refused by Hitler, the incident caused the dictator to revise his plans and, in due course, to substitute Kesselring for Rommel as the designate Commander-in-Chief South-West. By September a new German army headquarters (von Vietinghoff's *AOK 10*) and two panzer corps and one parachute corps headquarters were already in Italy.

Badoglio's withdrawal from the war and the Anglo-American Salerno landings took place during the night of 8–9 September and *Achse* was ordered from Rastenburg. The task began of rounding up and disarming, not only the numerous Italian troops in the homeland but also the equivalent of about thirty Italian divisions in the Balkans and South France.[17] This was carried out successfully within a matter of days with very little resistance. In the Balkans, however, the defection of Italy was to transform the whole theatre, not merely because the Italian troops had to be replaced by German occupation forces, but principally because very large quantities of Italian arms and equipment were given to, or seized by, Tito's partisans. Within three weeks, as von Weichs, the new *OB Südost*, reported to the OKW, Tito's guerrillas took on the aspect of regular forces with fully equipped corps and divisions, many of them capable of holding vast areas and engaging the German occupation troops in pitched battles.*

Hitler drew up his own code of rules for disarming the Italians. Although,

* Löhr's 12 Army headquarters had been redesignated as Army Group E from the beginning of 1943 and Löhr, a *Luftwaffe* general originally from the Austrian air force, was also *OB Südost* from 1 January to 12 August. Then a new Army Group F (von Weichs) at Belgrade took over the command in the Balkans: headquarters 2 Panzer Army (Rendulic) came from Orel to Kragujevac to take over command in the north while Löhr at Salonica remained responsible for the south, his headquarters functioning as an *AOK*.

during preliminary negotiations, German commanders could and did promise the Italian formations that they could disband themselves and return to their homes after being disarmed, they were in fact to be treated as prisoners of war and transported to Germany. Where formations either resisted a German ultimatum, or had allowed their weapons to fall into the hands of partisans, the Italian officers were to be shot on the spot and the men sent to Russia.[18] And the German Army – for the *Waffen SS* and the *Sicherheitsdienst* had no part in it – appears to have been ready to carry out these orders, just as it was to shoot hostages in Yugo-Slavia.

General Gandin, commanding the Italian *Acqui* infantry division on the Greek island of Cephalonia, with a detached regiment on Corfu, had been ordered by the Badoglio government to resist any attempt by the Germans to disarm his troops. In consequence, when fighting broke out on Corfu he told the local representative of the German Army that a landing on Cephalonia would be met by force. German Army troops landed, notwithstanding, and fighting went on for nearly a week. That the Germans were justified in disarming the Italians by force there can be no doubt, just as the Italians were entirely right in defending themselves. But Hitler ordered that all Italians of the *Acqui* division on Cephalonia, soldiers as well as officers, who had taken part in the action against the German troops should be shot after capture. The shooting of Italian officers, all of whom owed their loyalty to the King of Italy, was afterwards carried out by troops of the German Army. Such was the mentality at that time, that the German commanders regarded the Italian defence as 'treachery' and the shooting of Italian prisoners to be in accordance with military law and usage (*standrechtlich*).*

Hitler had always been sure that Britain intended to land in the Balkans in order to free the Dardanelles-Bosphorus sea route to Russia and to deny Germany the Balkan mineral sources, an opinion shared by Jodl. This was one of the main reasons that Hitler determined to hold Italy, however much it cost him. Yet German strength in the Balkans, fifteen divisions (as well as eight Bulgarian and Croatian divisions) in October 1943, was never sufficient to do more than keep open the main communications.[19] The planned German contingency operation for occupying Turkish Thrace and securing the Black Sea straits was abandoned that autumn for lack of troops.

Back on the Italian mainland the six divisions of von Vietinghoff's 10 Army were no longer withdrawing, except under the heaviest of pressure, for Hitler was threatening the direst of penalties against any officer who failed to maintain his position or fell short of his duties; 10 Army was

---

* '*Standrechtlich*' was the word used to the author by the German formation commander in justification of such action. The official Italian general staff history published in Rome in 1975 says that the other ranks were shot in addition to the officers (*Ministero della Difesa, Stato Maggiore dell' Esercito-Ufficio Storico, Le Operazioni delle Unità Italiane, nel Settembre-Ottobre 1943*, p. 490) but in spite of many months of reserch the author has been unable to arrive at any definite conclusion as to whether or not Hitler's orders were carried out to the letter. The Freiburg Militärarchiv has been unable to unearth firm documentary evidence and Professor Hubatsch, who was a OKW KTB diarist in 1943, was incredulous when the author first gave him the Italian account.

Kesselring's only command with the parachute *Fliegerkorps XI* his only reserve. In the north, and entirely separate from Kesselring, Rommel sat at Canossa with Army Group B, having under command no armies, but four corps and nine divisions, none of which were in battle: he was responsible only for the security of what was now called the North Italian Republic and for the safety of the Alpine passes and the land communications to the Balkans. Finally, on 6 November, Hitler regularized this top heavy organization by withdrawing Rommel's Army Group B, replacing it by a new 14 Army under von Mackensen (from 1 Panzer Army in Russia). Kesselring took over the whole of the Italian command as *OB Südwest* and Commander of Army Group C.

From 22 January 1944, following the Anglo-American landings at Anzio-Nettuno just south of Rome, von Mackensen's army was drawn into the battle in the south and had to be further reinforced by a division from the Balkans and another from France and detachments from the Reich, including the staff and students from training schools, all that could be spared at that time. For not only was the tension beginning to mount in France, where the invasion was, according to the German forecasts, already overdue, but the German *Ostheer*, reeling under the Red Army summer and winter offensives, was suffering fearful losses and had been thrown back everywhere from a hundred to 600 miles.

Von Manstein's Army Group South had been left after Kursk with its right shoulder dangerously exposed. A substantial weight of German armour was sent to help hold this southern flank, but the move was disastrous, for the Red Army then attacked the northern flank, the strength of each successive enemy offensive surprising both the Führer and von Manstein. Von Manstein, seeking in vain for freedom to make his own decisions, asked that he be given more troops or be allowed to abandon the exposed right shoulder in the Donets basin. Hitler would not hear of giving up this industrial area, but promised von Manstein some of von Kluge's troops. But later von Kluge himself came under the heaviest of attack, and he hastened to Hitler in East Prussia to resist any transfer of troops to Army Group South.[20] And so von Manstein got nothing. Then he came under renewed attack near Taganrog, and the new 6 Army nearly went the way of the old; it was saved only by further withdrawals.

In early September von Manstein and von Kluge went to Rastenburg to beg the Führer to restore to the chief of the army general staff his responsibility for all theatres – in other words to cut Jodl's function from the high command.[21] Hitler, who regarded von Manstein as over-ambitious, would have none of it.* An earlier letter of von Manstein's to Zeitzler, suggesting

---

* This is von Manstein's version that may, or may not, be true. When the conspirators of *die Berliner Fronde* approached him in the summer of 1943, however, he told Gersdorff that he was *persona non grata* with Hitler, and suggested that they ask von Rundstedt or von Kluge to represent to Hitler that he should give up the military command.

that the risk should be accepted of denuding France in order to send troops to Russia, had caused an outburst of rage when shown to the dictator.* Von Manstein wanted to fall back behind the Dnieper, but the Führer still refused to allow the evacuation of the Donets basin.

Hitler was eventually obliged to agree to withdrawals although he often withheld permission until after the troops had been broken and the equipment lost. The German troops were soon moving westwards, forced back from feature to feature, mainly on foot and in conditions of great hardship. Ordered demolition programmes could not be carried out for lack of manpower, time and resources. Infantry casualties mounted steadily and the few replacements lacked training and were often elderly or otherwise unsuitable for front line duties, so that Fretter-Pico, one of the corps commanders, was to note sourly that when the navy, the *Luftwaffe*, the SS and the supporting and technical arms had taken their pick, what remained went to the infantry. Meanwhile the small groups trudged on, orienting themselves, often without maps and compasses, as best they might. Every man knew that his safety depended on the group and he took good care not to become separated from his own mob (*Haufen*).[22] Propaganda pamphlets were showered on them from the air and the Soviet loudspeakers were rarely silent. All, however, feared Soviet captivity more than death.

There was a repetition of the previous year's events at Kharkov, with panic and disorder in the rear areas during the enforced withdrawals in the south; this applied particularly to supply troops and officials of the base installations and the civil administration. At Dnepropetrovsk the equipment being evacuated did not apparently extend beyond that required for the comfort of the German officials, for these disposed of fleets of lorries full of beds, furniture and food, while the fighting formations had had to leave behind bridging equipment that they could not move for lack of transport.

After the failure of *Citadel* Zeitzler had wanted to prepare and fortify a shortened defensive front that was to be known as the East Wall or Panther line, running from the Narva near the Baltic down to the Dnieper and then to the Sea of Azov, covering the whole of the eastern front. But his plan had remained a line on the map, because the Führer refused permission for any defensive work to begin. The dictator was opposed in principle to rearward defences since, according to him, they encouraged the field commanders to withdraw when the enemy pressure got inconvenient; in any event, he said, all fortification materials were needed for the Atlantic defences in France. That Jodl discussed Zeitzler's proposals with the Führer and presumably sided with his master, there appears to be no doubt, for he recorded in the OKW diary the probable effects of such a withdrawal, the usual political and

* In the autumn of 1943, Hitler, in a fit of anger, cried out that if von Manstein did not mend his ways 'it would be an easy matter to have him disappear from the face of the earth by an accident or some such'. When this was reported back to von Manstein by the 20 July conspirators, von Manstein said he did not believe it, but his staff noted that he took energetic and immediate measures to improve his own personal security.

economic arguments so dear to the dictator's heart: Finland and Sweden, Germany's use of the Baltic for sea-borne supplies and U-boat training, the giving up of thirty-two developed airfields and the loss of the industry and ores of the Donets basin and Krivoi Rog.[23] Not until 12 August were the three army groups permitted to begin work on fortifying the Panther line, but they were expressly forbidden to fall back on the line until ordered to do so.

The line was in any event valueless, although during its short life its name was kept in the public eye for propaganda purposes. Fortifications could not be developed in a few weeks with the use of civilian labour, rearward troops and supervisors who had little idea of tactical lay-out. They consisted mainly of earthworks, without wire or concrete, and Fretter-Pico said they were so poorly sited as to be useless. The Dnieper itself was a water obstacle of tactical use only if it could be covered by observation and fire, and then only until it froze. The fighting strength of German formations had sunk so low that they bore little relationship to their designation, and the bayonet strength of many infantry divisions was no more than 1,000 men. Since Army Group South had thirty-seven such infantry divisions to defend 450 miles of front, the divisions, that were in reality much understrength regiments, were each required to cover about twelve miles of front and this allowed for no deployment in depth and no reserves. Seventeen panzer and panzer grenadier divisions remained to von Manstein, but these lacked fire and shock power, the panzer divisions often being reduced to forty or fifty tanks while the panzer grenadier divisions were deficient in both assault guns and infantry. On 7 September von Manstein's tank strength, as recorded in the OKW diary, was down to 257 tanks and 220 assault guns.[24]

Hitler still harboured the most extravagant ideas and ambitions regarding the Ukraine, the Black Sea and the Caucasus. The iron and manganese ores of Krivoi Rog and Nikopol were indispensable; and so was the Crimea, since it opened on to the Taman bridgehead that von Kleist was holding awaiting a change in Germany's fortunes, and this bridgehead, said Hitler, would enable German troops to reoccupy the Caucasus in the summer of 1944. In any case, reasoned Hitler, the holding of the Crimea was essential for the *Luftwaffe* control of the Black Sea; if it were given up it would endanger the Ploesti oil supply and would have a decisive effect on the attitudes of Turkey, Rumania and Bulgaria to the war. And von Manstein must, at all costs, keep his right shoulder forward, in order to safeguard von Kleist's land communications into the Crimea. To assist von Manstein in doing this, von Kleist's Army Group A had been ordered to give 100,000 troops as reinforcement to Army Group South, but even so fourteen German and seven Rumanian divisions remained locked up in the Goth's Head bridgehead in Taman.[25] Taman was eventually given up under Red Army pressure that autumn but the dictator was still determined to hold the Crimea.

Long before the onset of winter Kiev had been taken and the Panther line had been breached, but still the German divisions hung on, praying for a break in the fine weather and for the rain and mud that would bring the Soviet offensives to a halt. The German divisions relied on self-help for survival, for no help could be expected from above or from one's neighbours, all of whom were in equally desperate straits. Divisions were finding their own mobile reserves by mounting one battalion in lorries, often seized from the civil administration. Many of the anti-tank guns, particularly the heavy 75 mm or 88 mm *Pak*, had been lost in earlier encirclements and hasty withdrawals, for they were heavy and difficult to manoeuvre, and, because of the shortage of tractors, horses and men, had been abandoned. One field gun was therefore removed from each of the artillery batteries and given to the infantry to site in the forward areas as an anti-tank gun. Neither tank nor air support was to be had, and it was a desperate time for German leaders of all ranks: the divisional commanders themselves were to be seen daily in the battalion areas, many of them saving the defence in moments of crisis by their presence.[26] By November the Crimea had been cut off, with Soviet troops investing it from the east and the north.

Requests for private interviews by Zeitzler or by his senior commanders in the east were already an anathema to Hitler and, whenever he could, he refused them, because he associated them with unpleasant tidings or views that he would rather not hear. In the first week in January von Manstein again, according to his own account, tried to persuade the dictator to restore the chief of army general staff to his rightful position and, so he has said, to appoint a field commander for the whole of the eastern front.

Nor was von Manstein the only commander desperately seeking a way out of the impasse. At his headquarters in Orsha von Kluge was beset by difficulties hardly less grievous than those in the Ukraine. Von Kluge noted how the Soviet high command and Red Army troops had become much more confident and aggressive since their victory at Kursk; he, himself, however, worried at his rapidly sinking fighting strength, had become reluctant to make any move that might involve him in casualties. For this reason he had forbidden the mounting of counter-attacks, other than those of a very localized nature, without his personal authority. And this in its turn had added to the Red Army's confidence and daring. Reinhardt of 3 Panzer Army complained to von Kluge that his troops were stretched beyond their limit and that his only reserves had been diverted to anti-partisan operations in the rear. The strength of the panzer army (now panzer only in name) had dropped to 290,000 men in May 1943 and by September it was further reduced to 230,000. He doubted the dependability of his 20,000 non-German *Osttruppen* as they were already deserting in numbers, and, in company with all other army commanders, Reinhardt attached little value to the *Luftwaffe* field divisions, because of their inadequate leadership and training.

Army Group Centre was paralysed not only by von Kluge's veto on any tactical initiative on the part of his subordinates, but also because he had to refer all matters, some of them seemingly trivial, to Hitler. He himself had much less confidence – he said 'in the OKH' but he presumably meant Hitler – and he told his staff that he thought that Zeitzler's days were numbered, for he was very tired and had no further influence with the Führer.[27]

On 14 October von Kluge had written a long personal letter to Hitler (with expressions of personal loyalty that were now a *sine qua non* in any report to the Führer), pointing out that 'although the morale of the fighting men remained good', they were beset by a feeling of isolation and neglect, facing as they did the massed numbers of Red Army infantry. Army Group Centre was 200,000 men deficient of establishment and the recent losses had been so great that the drop in fighting strength of the formations that had borne the brunt of the attacks was frightening. The standard of such replacements that had been received, said von Kluge, left much to be desired, many of them lacking training and inner soldierly qualities. Von Kluge stressed that the danger of the trend had to be faced, and he ended the letter by saying that although it was commonly assumed that the Russian had the same losses and the same problems, this was in reality not the case, because the Red Army could always obtain numerical superiority by concentrating its forces at the point of attack.[28] No answer was received to this letter and, on 27 October, von Kluge was invalided from his post as a result of a motor vehicle accident. He was replaced by Busch, the former commander of 16 Army.

The Soviet offensive was renewed in the second week in November and Reinhardt was in danger of losing two of his corps. But when he asked Busch for permission to withdraw, Busch merely transmitted his request to the Führer who ordered the formations to remain where they were. The Germans had managed to stabilize the position by Christmas and hang on to Vitebsk, but, for the first time during the war, a perceptible lowering in German morale was noted; there was some desertion, hitherto almost unknown, and some cases of detachments taking to panic-stricken flight.

In the north the situation was very much the same. Von Küchler, knowing that a big Soviet offensive was about to break on him, wanted to withdraw to the shorter Panther line in his rear.[29] Hitler refused. When the storm came in January, Novgorod was encircled and it looked as if Lindemann's 18 Army might disintegrate. The Red Air Force bombed and machine-gunned every movement, formations became mixed and confused, and stragglers, leave and baggage men were used to plug gaps. All suffered from the wet and lack of sleep and food, and unless supply column commanders took most energetic action to maintain contact, replenishment failed. In the infantry divisions most of the regimental and battalion commanders had been killed or wounded; divisional infantry strengths fell to 500 men, scaremonger rumours ran up and down the front and there were some cases of panic and flight. The *Luftwaffe* field divisions fell apart.[30]

On 28 January von Küchler, on his own responsibility, ordered 18 Army to withdraw to the Luga, although he could offer Hitler no assurance that he could hold there. Hitler, ignoring the fact that 18 Army was in danger of encirclement and disintegration, blamed von Küchler for withdrawing in the first place, and he remarked bitterly to Zeitzler at the midday conference that the experience of the last three years, if it had shown anything, had proved that when one retired from one position to shorten the front or build a new defence line, the new position could never be held.[31] Von Küchler was retired and replaced by Model, who was in Hitler's favour having gained a reputation as a lion of the defence; Model knew this and, although he would never willingly give ground, he was prepared to use his own initiative to get the Führer-desired results. So Model stopped the withdrawal of 18 Army by simply reinforcing it from 16 Army; but no sooner had he done so than a new offensive broke on 16 Army, and the whole of the army group appeared to be in danger of encirclement from the south. Hitler was then forced to agree to withdraw out of Russia on to the Panther line.

The situation in the Ukraine and the Crimea had meanwhile steadily worsened, whole corps being encircled and scattered while the enforced retreat continued; tanks, workshops, vehicle and equipment parks were abandoned to the enemy for lack of time and means to move them. Von Vormann, a corps commander with Wöhler's 8 German Army in the south, has told of the temperatures of minus twenty degrees centigrade, where any change in the battle position on the infantryman's part, even of only a few hundred yards, meant that he had to find himself a new fire trench and fresh shelter from artillery fire and from the cold, often an impossible task in the iron-hard ground. Many of the troops were already a prey to fear as to the future and the outcome of the war. Letters from home told of the devastating bombing and of the increasingly heavy police controls. Few could understand the seemingly useless orders that came from above, apparently from the highest. Most knew that there could be no hope of terms with the Soviets or with the Anglo-Americans. To the soldier in the field Hitler was the Supreme Commander and the army commander-in-chief, and there was no general of sufficient stature who could replace him. The Führer remained their only salvation.[32]

Although the Führer maintained a semblance of good relations with von Manstein, he was in fact very hostile to him, and von Manstein's proposals to move his own headquarters from Vinnitsa to Lvov were discussed by the Führer with Zeitzler and Jodl and subjected to mockery and bitter sarcasm.[33] Von Manstein was indeed very ambitious, a man of operative genius whose great abilities were clouded by a pose of arrogance and conceit; he wanted the powers of a von Hindenburg and the fame of the elder von Moltke, with a unified *Oberkommando* with himself at its head. Yet, in truth, he was uncertain of himself; he had little understanding of human nature and his attitude to his subordinates could be very unpleasant. Von Tresckow saw him as an opportunist. For von Manstein was aware of the general staff conspiracy against Hitler that was developing in von Kluge's Army Group Centre; indeed, he was even in touch with it through his personal staff, and yet he did not want to commit himself until he could be certain of his future,

215

and probably of his own safety. How close von Manstein was to the troops must remain a matter of doubt, for he had become stale, a man of habit and routine, absorbed with the evening ritual of bridge that was forced on to his immediate circle.[34]

Before the end of March 1944 von Manstein's front had begun to disintegrate and Hube's 1 Panzer Army, a force of four corps and about eighteen divisions numbering between 200,000 and 300,000 men, was encircled near the Rumanian border; and this was von Manstein's death knell. The Führer made it clear to von Manstein where he thought the responsibility lay and blamed the German Army for running away without a fight. The Führer had Müller-Hillebrand flown out of the pocket and brought to Rastenburg, to be cross-examined by him, and this officer has told the author that the dictator seemed collected and rational, and, on that day, showed no signs of the nervous disorder that was said to be afflicting him.[35] Hube's army was ordered to break out westwards to meet a SS panzer corps that had been brought into Galicia from the west, in an effort to extricate the surrounded troops. 1 Panzer Army succeeded in freeing itself at the cost of the loss of most of its equipment.

On 30 March von Manstein and von Kleist were removed from their commands, being replaced by Model and Schörner. The Führer hinted to von Manstein that he might be wanted to take over command in the west, and so he retired to his home near Liegnitz trying to keep the plotters at arm's length and himself abreast of military developments while he awaited the call.[36] He was never re-employed.*

The final German defeat of the year came in the Crimea and it was probably the greatest. Hitler had refused to withdraw the beleaguered 17 Army from the peninsula, and Schörner, the new commander of Army Group A, at first assured the dictator that it could hold out. Shortly afterwards, however, Schörner revised his opinion and agreed with the army commander, Jaenecke, that 17 Army was in great danger of being overrun. Nothing, however, that Schörner or Jaenecke said could make Hitler reverse his decision and Jaenecke was removed from his command for speaking too freely. When the Red Army offensive finally came, in May of 1944, 17 Army was virtually destroyed; 29,000 German and 7,000 Rumanian troops went into captivity just outside of Sevastopol. The total Axis loss was very much higher; nearly 80,000 men and most of the equipment had been lost.[37]

The underlying theme of the Führer's strategy, 'to stand firm and keep one's nerve', remained unaltered by any disaster and the dictator was likely

* Among von Manstein's successes were his contribution to the French campaign in 1940, the overrunning of the Crimea and the containing of part of the spring 1943 Soviet offensive in the Ukraine. He achieved little else. Yet, by the late summer of 1944, his opinion of his own and the German Army's capabilities had become bizarre, so that he thought that, with himself as C-in-C, he could outfight both east and west and force his enemies to the conference table. The allied and Russian military leadership, according to von Manstein, was 'wretched (*miserabel*)', and he said this at a time when German armies, even army groups, were being completely destroyed, both in the east and in the west.

to vent his anger on commanders whom he suspected of giving ground too easily.

The defeat in Tunisia had cost about six divisions, and that in Stalingrad another twenty, with a further six divisions that had been virtually destroyed on the Don, making a total of about thirty-two divisions in all. But between *Citadel* and May 1944 a further forty-one divisions had been burned out in the east, eight in Army Group A, sixteen in Army Group South, thirteen in Army Group Centre and four in Army Group North.[38] What was left of twenty-seven of these divisions was converted into divisional groups – often barely having the strength of a weak regiment – and these were incorporated either into other infantry divisions or into one of six new corps groups (*Korpsabteilungen*) each of which was approximate to a weak division. But these divisional groups continued to bear their original divisional number and designation, partly because it was hoped, at a later date, to reform them as standard divisions, and partly as a deceptive measure to keep up the numbered order of battle. The surplus supporting arms and administrative troops were used to form new formations. The *Korpsabteilungen* were only used on the eastern front and, since they did not prove very satisfactory, they were disbanded in the early summer of 1944. Of the other formations making up the forty-one divisions, four infantry and one panzer and one panzer grenadier divisions were disbanded entirely; the remaining eight were *Luftwaffe* field divisions.

According to a report by Reinhardt's 3 Panzer Army of 15 October 1943 on the effectiveness of these troops, one particular *Luftwaffe* field division had lost only 700 men in the recent fighting: its weapon losses at the same time, however, amounted to 2,600 rifles, 1,100 pistols, 550 machine-guns, thirty mortars, twenty-six anti-tank guns and forty flak guns. This 'shameful loss' could not be attributed to lack of transport, said the report, but to a complete failure on the part of commanders and troops.[39] On 21 October Hitler ordered that the *Luftwaffe* divisions in the east should be progressively disbanded and their personnel transferred to the army.

The disappearance of these infantry divisions and the difficulty in maintaining the 170 divisions already in the field in the east did not of course affect the process of continually raising further divisons. Of the thirteen infantry divisions lost in Stalingrad seven new ones of the same numbering were immediately raised in France, a further six coming into existence the following summer, firstly as *Kampfgruppen* and then as divisions. Some of those lost in Africa and in the Don bend were similarly reincarnated. Then from June to September 1943 another seven (*bodenständige*) divisions were raised for France, these having three regiments each of three battalions with supporting arms and strong anti-tank support: they had no category rating and took their designations in the numbered block from 242 to 266 Infantry Divisions. The strength of these seven static divisions was such that some of their battalions were removed to the east and replaced by *Ostbataillone*, battalions of newly recruited prisoners of war. For by 1943 there was a shortage of manpower that could not be met by German nationals. A call-up in the new German territories, Alsace-Lorraine, Luxembourg and Eupen-Malmédy and of the 78,000 *Volksdeutsch* of *Liste III* in the east had only brought in another 122,000 men, or three per cent of the strength of the *Feldheer*.[40] The SS was already recruiting very widely, not only in occupied Western Europe but also among the Slav peoples in the east, and the German Army had formed a Turkestan infantry division and an Indian infantry regiment from prisoners of war.

From 1943 onwards the system used in raising fresh divisions made an already complicated organization even more complex, for although the category system continued to be used it had less real significance than it had before. The 'new type (*n.A.*)' divisions raised from this time onwards were usually of three regiments, each of two battalions with a full complement of infantry supporting weapons, although this was by no means always the case; for there were occasionally two-regiment divisions of six battalions, or even three-regiment divisions of nine battalions. In November ten new category 21 divisions (*n.A.*) were raised from headquarters and supporting arms removed from Army Group Centre, filled with recruits and sent to the west, while the six category 22 divisions (*n.A.*) for the west and south took into their organizations some ready-formed basic training battalions of the *Ersatzheer* reserve divisions in the west. Then five category 23 divisions in the east were formed on the field training (*Feldausbildung*) divisions already there. On 23 November, three reserve divisons in the west (that had already lost some of their battalions to category 22) were converted to regular three regiment (*bodenständige*) infantry divisions, while the reserve division in the Balkans became a *Jäger* division. This scraping of the barrel in an effort to put more divisions in the field spelt the end of the *Ersatzheer* training organization in the west.

In 1944 there arose a new conception of reinforcing the field army. The raising of full divisions with supporting arms and services was obviously wasteful in that the main reinforcement requirement was for infantry. Moreover it was found by experience that the raising of fresh divisions without affiliation or tradition was not satisfactory. So another somewhat half-hearted attempt was made to revert to the earlier system of linking certain reinforcement formations to formations in the field. This led to the introduction of shadow divisions (*Schatten-Divisionen*), without rearward services, to serve as replacements for stricken divisions in the east.[41] The first four of these were formed on four of the remaining reserve divisions, these being given territorial names instead of numbers. But this did not affect the continual process of forming new divisions from anything to hand. For the *Ersatzheer* organization was being further milked to produce the nuclei for six two-regiment divisions of category 25, these having reduced artillery support. In May 1944, there came the raising of another four shadow divisions of category 26 meant to support the formations in Italy and South

France, but then category 27 went back to the earlier system of stamping a further five *bodenständige* divisions (*n.A.44*) out of the ground for France and Italy, these being neither shadow nor linked to shadow divisions.*

Rarely can any modern army have been raised by such a complicated process. But in its insistence on new formations and a swollen divisional order of battle it bore the imprint of the hand of the dictator, for he was obsessed not only by considerations of prestige but also by the determination to have as many divisions as possible in the field before the threatened Anglo-American landing. How these could be kept in being thereafter without a proper reinforcement and support system was only of minor concern to him, because he had come to the conclusion that if the enemy could be thrown off the beaches and back into the sea, then he would have one, maybe two, years respite from the western enemy, during which he would come to grips once more with Russia.

Meanwhile the Führer intended to bind all commanders and troops more closely to himself and the party, and, since he considered that the Red Army derived much of its strength from its political commissar system, he ordered, on 22 December 1943, that a roughly similar organization be introduced into the German armed forces. This system of 'political leaders' (NSFO and *NS-Führungsstab*) provided for political representatives and staffs at all headquarters from the OKW down to the level of divisions, these representatives being specially selected combatant officers who underwent a course on Nazi political doctrine and propaganda.† Although these political leaders had no command or veto functions comparable with those of Red Army commissars, their task, like that of the commissars, was to promote political awareness and allegiance to the dictator and the party and, as the party representatives within the army, provide the party with an additional information network as to the activities of commanders down to divisions. These political officers were later appointed down to battalions, although at the lower levels they normally carried out some additional military function.[42]

---

* Category 21 divisions were numbered from 349–367 ID; category 22 from 271–278; category 23 divisions never took the field as new formations; category 24 were known as *Mielau*, *Milowitz*, *Demba* and *Wahn*; category 25 divisions were numbered from 77–92; category 26 took the names *Wildflecken*, *Mielau* (2), *Neuhammer*, *Milowitz* (2); category 27 were numbered 59 and 64 and from 226–237 ID.

† Schörner had been appointed in February 1944 to head the *NS-Führungsstab* within the OKH because of his very strong Nazi sympathies. Originally commissioned from the ranks in November 1914 as a lieutenant of the reserve, he was awarded the *Pour le Mérite* in 1917. According to von Mellenthin, who gives a favourable, even friendly, account of his subject, Schörner was 'energetic, brave, ruthless, harsh, boorish and coarse, with a robust and loud-mouthed manner'. Schörner declined to answer the author's questions put to him in 1970.

CHAPTER ELEVEN

The Twentieth of July

It had been Hitler's intention to base the defence of Western Europe on static coastal fortifications, and these, beginning as early as March 1942, had been built up steadily during 1943 and 1944. The early scattered defences were then developed into a series of fortresses, strong points and resistance centres many of which had coastal artillery and heavily concreted emplacements, while the shores and part of the tidal beaches were mined and covered with landing-craft obstacles. Although the preparations in the fortresses were impressive, they covered only the major ports that might be of use to the enemy, the intervening areas between these fortresses being only lightly fortified, or sometimes not defended at all. There was a serious shortage of labour and of materials, particularly cement and wire.[1]

Von Rundstedt, the *OB West*, informed the OKW in October 1943 that the Atlantic Wall could not be defended, but only *covered* by the troops at his disposal; nor could he guarantee even to cover the Atlantic coastline south of the Loire, since he could 'only keep it under observation'. The permanent fortifications, von Rundstedt conceded, were 'indispensable and valuable for battle as well as for propaganda', but he went on to qualify their value in that 'as a rigid German defence was impossible there for any length of time, the outcome of the battle must depend on the use of a mobile and armoured reserve'. This of course was the crux of the matter. Although von Rundstedt did not express the view so bluntly, it meant that a determined and powerful enemy with the support of massive air and sea fleets could make a landing, and stay ashore, and, if he could support himself in the early stages without the use of a major port, he could bypass the coastal fortresses. Such an enemy could hardly be dislodged from the bridgeheads without strong armoured and motorized forces and – although von Rundstedt did not dwell on this – a decisive air superiority.

Hitler, however, regarded the situation somewhat differently in that he foresaw the coastal fortresses and strongpoints holding out almost indefinitely, and he was, at about this time, ordering that the strongpoints should be stocked with eight months' ammunition and supplies. This conception of the battle was, in its way, a copy of Hitler's defence blueprint for the east, the conversion of all main centres of communication into fortresses and the sacrificing of their garrisons (that often had a strength of two or more divisions) in an effort to bring the Red flood to a halt.

The failure of the German Army to hold France in 1944, like the winter defeat in Russia in 1941, might be attributed in part to the poverty of German military intelligence both in the OKW *Abwehr* and the intelligence departments of the OKH. But this lack of intelligence was in fact of only subsidiary importance, because appreciations of the enemy's strength and intentions that mattered originated not in the OKH but with the Führer, who succeeded in imposing *his* opinions on the military chain of command. The general tenor of the Führer's thoughts appear to have permeated downwards, into the *Fremde Heere Abteilungen*. This was the pattern, too, elsewhere in the general staff, where even the operations departments no longer tested plans by repeated war-games as they had done earlier in the war. The direction came from above and the dictator would not listen to views that did not coincide with his own.

According to Hitler's summing-up of the likely enemy strategy, the Anglo-Americans would first make widely separated landings from Normandy to Norway – merely as diversionary operations prior to the main landing in the Pas de Calais. For the Pas de Calais, said Hitler, had the tactical benefit of a short air and sea haul, and a weighty strategic advantage in that it opened directly into Belgium and the Reich. This prediction of a main blow across the Straits of Dover became a not to be questioned Hitler premise, fully accepted by the field-marshals in the west, and was to result in large German forces being kept idle in the Pas de Calais long after the invasion had taken place.[2]

At the end of August 1943 the strength in France stood at thirty-eight divisions. The staff of the OKW and Army Group D were fast becoming aware of the rapidly growing threat of an invasion and what this might mean; the OKW diariest recorded that the fighting in Italy was in many respects tougher and more bitter than that experienced on the Russian front, and he concluded that the fighting in France would be the same. Blumentritt, von Rundstedt's chief of staff, had drawn Jodl's attention to the fact that German divisions were unfitted for a war of movement and were in no way comparable with the Anglo-American formations, since these were the finest-equipped that the world had ever seen; and he included in his letter a list of the forty-seven German divisions that had been removed from *OB West* during the last year.[3]

Blumentritt's letter resulted in what was said to be an absolute priority being given to the west over all other theatres, including the eastern front; and this enabled von Rundstedt's forces to be built up steadily throughout the winter and spring until they reached their peak strength in June 1944. Even so, von Rundstedt had from time to time been ordered to send divisions to the east for a variety of tasks: he had for example to assist in extricating Hube's 1 Panzer Army, and in occupying Hungary to prevent

that unhappy country from going out of the war. And the removed formations did not always return. So it was that von Rundstedt's reinforcement of
twenty-one newly raised divisions and thirteen that came in from other
theatres had to be reduced by seventeen divisions, ten that went to the east,
five sent to Italy and two to the Balkans. For although Hitler, in an expansive
moment, had once said that he intended to create a mobile armoured reserve
of twenty-five divisions for use either in the east or the west, he was never in a
position to boast of any reserve at all. The best that he could do was to move
a few divisions, or perhaps a SS corps, from west to east to south and back
again, as the emergencies arose; these formations were in no way an uncommitted reserve since, except for the periods of rail movement, they were
nearly always in the line. The last uncommitted OKH reserve was that held
on 22 June 1941. The situation in 1944 was such that, although the German
strength stood at about 285 nominal divisions, Jodl and Zeitzler quarrelled
over single divisions since this was all they had to form either an OKW or an
OKH reserve.

In 1944 von Rundstedt was sixty-eight years of age. He had been commissioned in 1893 in the *Infanterie-Regiment von Wittich (3. Kurhess.) Nr. 83*;
promotion had come slowly to him so that in 1914, after twenty-one years
service, he was a captain; at the end of the war he had only advanced to
major. In 1920 he joined the *Reichsheer* as a lieutenant-colonel and rose
rapidly in rank thereafter, commanding 2 Cavalry Division in 1928, *Wehrkreis III* in 1932 and then, at the end of that year, *Gruppenkommando I* in
Berlin. The reason for his rapid advancement in the *Reichsheer* after so
undistinguished a career in the Prussian Army cannot be explained. Like
many of his fellows he was, later in life, apt to try to present to the outside
world an exterior, a shell, to hide the man within; and so he strove for
imperturbability, dignity, poise and harmony of mind, without, in the end,
achieving any of them.[4] For in reality he was a conservative, without strong
views on anything, a middle of the road man, who, unsure of himself, when
faced with difficult situations kept his own counsel. There was something
about him that conjured up a picture of von Seeckt, an august dignified
presence that was a cover from the outside world. Of the two, von Seeckt was
the stronger character. Like von Manstein, von Rundstedt spoke after the
war patronizingly of Hitler; during the war he was his loyal, obedient and
often admiring, subordinate; and he himself was esteemed by Hitler because
he deferred to him in everything.*

Von Rundstedt's command presented a very untidy picture. As *OB West*,
he had no command over Krancke, the admiral commanding Group West,
even though Krancke controlled the naval-manned coastal artillery and the

---

* Such post-war condescension was common among German generals, an extreme example being that of
Göring – of whom Speer said 'he belittled [the dead] Hitler, but no one kow-towed to Hitler as much as he
did'. (*Spandau – The Secret Diaries*, p. 60)

large shore-based installations in France, numbering in all 100,000 men; these became a bone of contention between the army and the navy staff, since the navy resisted what it considered to be army dictation on the matter of coastal defence, and was reluctant to find naval ratings to take part in the ground battle under the local army command. The flying component of the *Luftwaffe* came under Sperrle's 3 Air Fleet, whose headquarters, like Krancke's, was at Paris. Sperrle was responsible only to Göring. Air defence artillery, equipped for the most part with 88 mm dual purpose guns particularly suitable in an anti-tank role, were also under Sperrle. The *Luftwaffe* strength was nearly 340,000 men of a *Wehrmacht* total in France of 1,400,000, but of this number about 100,000 were flak troops and 30,000 belonged to the ground force parachute divisions.[5]

Von Rundstedt was not in fact master in his own house even over the ground force troops. Parachute, flak and SS divisions could be allocated to him or taken away again by Göring or Himmler, although they could not normally do this without OKW (and that meant Hitler's) consent; these troops on tactical loan were disciplined, trained, equipped and administered by the *Luftwaffe* and the SS. The army panzer and anti-tank and motorized infantry formations, although under von Rundstedt's command, had been allocated from Guderian's domain, and both army and SS motorized formations were often removed from von Rundstedt's control in that they were frozen as part of Hitler's OKW reserve and could be committed only to tasks designed or approved by the Führer, with Guderian at his side. The reserve divisions that remained in the west were available to von Rundstedt for tactical tasks, but remained under Fromm's command, unless they were panzer training units when they came under Guderian. Moreover the responsibility for the internal security of the rearward areas in the west was largely out of von Rundstedt's hands in that it was delegated to the military governors, Karl-Heinrich von Stülpnagel for the larger part of France, and von Falkenhausen for Belgium and the French departments near the Belgian frontier; both were subordinate to the OKW, with special responsibilities to Himmler and von Ribbentrop. The civil administration throughout France was controlled, at the German dictation, by the Vichy régime, except that the coastal twenty mile-wide belt could, at von Rundstedt's discretion, be put under military control.

Von Rundstedt's operational command consisted of the *Luftwaffe* general Christiansen's Armed Forces Netherlands, administered directly by the OKW, von Salmuth's 15 Army covering the Channel coast from Belgium to central Normandy, Dollmann's 7 Army in west Normandy and Brittany, von der Chevallerie's 1 Army covering the Atlantic coast south of Brittany, while von Sodenstern's 19 Army defended the Mediterranean littoral from Spain to Italy. A central panzer reserve, Geyr von Schweppenburg's Panzer Group West, had its headquarters near Paris.[6] By the end of May von Rundstedt's overall command stood at fifty-nine divisions of which

223

eight were panzer and two panzer grenadier, twenty-three were static divisions and six were reserve training formations.*

The centre of gravity or defensive *Schwerpunkt* of the German forces was in the north against the English Channel, the largest number of divisions having been allocated to 15 Army covering Flanders, Artois, Picardy and the mouth of the Seine. This army frontage, including the area of the Pas de Calais, was of particular importance to Hitler since not only was it believed to be the place in which the Anglo-Americans would make their main lodgement, but it was also required as the launching base for Hitler's secret reprisal weapons.

German rocket development had owed its origin to a small group of private enthusiasts who began their research in Breslau in 1927. In 1930 the German Army had become interested and the group was joined by a Captain Walter Dornberger of the artillery who arranged for the society to receive some aid from army funds through Becker of *Wa Prüf 1*. Two years later von Braun was hired by von Vollard-Bockelberg's *Waffenamt* and assigned to Dornberger, and together they continued experiments on liquid propellant rockets at the rocket centre at Kummersdorf. In 1934 two A-2 rockets were launched from the North Sea island of Borkum, and, although these reached an altitude of only 8,000 feet, they were reckoned to be successful according to the standards of the time; two years later the artilleryman von Fritsch witnessed a static firing of an A-3 at Kummersdorf and was sufficiently impressed to support the enlargement of the missile programme.

Göring, however, also wanted to be associated with the programme, and in 1936 Kesselring and Becker together worked out their joint and separate responsibilities. A combined army-air development centre was then set up on the northern tip of Usedom island at Peenemünde, of which Dornberger's section, now part of Becker's new *Wa Prüf 11*, formed the army organization. The *Luftwaffe* began developing rocket and jet aircraft while the army concentrated on the missile rocketry.

The A-4 experimental rocket missile, designated by Hitler as the Reprisal Weapon 2 (V-2) was successfully launched by the Dornberger-von Braun team on 3 October 1942. By then Dornberger was a major-general. The series development of the A-4 for operational use was seriously delayed, however, by allied air attacks beginning with the RAF 600 bomber raid on Peenemünde on 17–18 August 1943, so that in December of that year the mass production of the A-4 was transferred to a subterranean plant near Nordhausen in Lower Saxony. Himmler wanted to control the army rocket organization and, at one time, in an effort to discredit the OKH, had had von Braun arrested as a security suspect.[7]

The A-4 (V-2) liquid oxygen and alcohol propelled projectile was the

---

* The SS complement totalled two panzer and two panzer grenadier divisions; the *Luftwaffe* element was three parachute and three field divisions; the SS and *Luftwaffe* totalled 90,000 of a *Feldheer* in the west of 890,000.

most successful weapon produced at that time, for it had a range of about 200 miles and an altitude of sixty miles, delivering a high-explosive war-head of about a ton at an impact velocity of 1,750 miles an hour. It was a ballistic missile, without guidance after its initial programmed turn in the direction of the target; except that its war-head was subject to premature explosion, it eventually proved to be a reliable weapon for area destruction. Its arrival before impact was at twice the speed of sound and there was virtually no possibility of the enemy getting any warning in the target area, and since the flight took only a matter of four to five minutes and the strike could not be forecast with any degree of accuracy, the British could have no defence against it.

The first launching sites were prepared at Watten near Calais, these being in the form of heavy concrete bunkers, but they were abandoned in August 1943 due to the heavy bombing raids on the sites. The change was then made to mobile launchings by artillery missile units from improvised earth or road launching pads, the batteries being able to quit the firing area with all their ancillary equipment within a space of thirty minutes after launching. Both the V-2 batteries and the *Luftwaffe* pilotless jet aircraft (V-1) needed, however, to operate in or near the Pas de Calais in order to make the best use of their range. The V-1 was first used in June and the V-2 in September 1944.

The V-2 batteries were grouped under a new 65 Corps designed for the control of army reprisal weapons, and they were staffed largely by rocketry specialist officers trained at Peenemünde.[8] Except of course that the V-2 could penetrate the enemy air defence, its efficiency was inferior to that of a manned bomber because of inaccuracy and limited pay-load.

On 5 November 1943 von Rundstedt was subjected to further interference when the Führer appointed Rommel to make an inspection of coastal defences, firstly in Jutland and then in Army Group D. Rommel was to be directly under the Führer's orders and was to take his inspection report personally to the dictator. When Rommel had completed his inspection the Führer decided that he and his Army Group B headquarters should be assigned to France and come under von Rundstedt as the *OB West*.

Hitler ordered that Rommel should take command of the two armies (7 and 15) on the Channel coast in the area most threatened by the enemy. Although it was not unknown for one army group to be under the command of another, the most unusual feature of this reorganization was that, according to Hitler's order of 15 January, Rommel was to have only *tactical* control over the two armies, his command being limited to the coastal belt that stretched from 400 yards below high water level to six miles behind the shore. Any measures that involved *operative* movement, particularly the movement of motorized divisions, could only be done through von Rundstedt. Hitler said that von Rundstedt was to remain responsible for the organization, training, equipping and supply of Rommel's two armies, while

225

Rommel 'was to keep close contact with Krancke and Sperrle, referring any difficulties to von Rundstedt'. In the same order, all motorized divisions in the theatre were put under the direct command of Geyr von Schweppenburg's Panzer Group West, whose command had the same standing as that of a panzer army and came directly under von Rundstedt. That such an extraordinary order should ever have been issued is a reflection of the degeneration of the German high command. But the arrangement suited the Führer in that he had injected new ideas and now had a second opinion that could be used as a check against von Rundstedt; he had, moreover, effected yet another split in the military command.[9]

That either of these two field-marshals should have accepted such an unorthodox and unworkable command arrangement in the first place is remarkable. Shortly afterwards, however, von Rundstedt began to complain that his authority was being restricted by Rommel's presence, while Rommel was not slow in bringing his own dissatisfaction directly to the Führer's notice. The two field-marshals could hardly have been more dissimilar: von Rundstedt, elderly, tired, almost indolent, content to exercise control in the fashion of earlier days through his chief of staff, delegating and decentralizing his responsibilities, content to view the grand picture – and always from his headquarters that he rarely left; Rommel, on the other hand, still in the prime of life, energetic, continually on the move to see things for himself, interfering with detail that was not always his concern, always ready to fight the battle from the front.

Rommel disagreed with von Rundstedt's concept of the coming battle, for von Rundstedt, harking back to the halcyon days of 1940, intended to destroy the enemy after he reached open country by the fast moving encircling operations of his panzer reserve. Rommel was convinced that the enemy air strength would be such that the German motorized formations would be pinned to the ground by day and would have little or no freedom of movement in the short summer nights; in consequence, said Rommel, the Anglo–Americans must be destroyed on the beaches; for if the enemy could not be held at the Atlantic Wall, then 'not only the campaign but the whole war would be lost'.[10] For this reason Rommel wanted the panzer formations to be allotted to his control and sited right forward near the coast where they could come into action within hours of the first enemy soldier coming ashore. In fact both of these field-marshals were in the wrong; von Rundstedt had no conception of the fury of the coming allied air offensive that would indeed pin and scatter his panzer and motorized reserves before they could be brought into battle; and the weakness of Rommel's argument was twofold. Firstly, his two armies were covering a frontage from the Loire to the Schelde, many hundreds of miles in length, and Rommel's three or four panzer divisions would have been entirely lost in such sectors unless Rommel knew exactly where the enemy landings were to be made; and Rommel's surmise, like Hitler's, was very wide of the mark. Secondly, Rommel had no idea of the overwhelming effects of the naval gunfire that was to control not only the beaches but also the hinterland nearly fifteen miles away to the rear.

However this may be, on 20 March Rommel took his complaints to Klessheim and to Hitler; the dictator was temporarily won over to many of his views and he concluded that Rommel must be allotted part of von Rundstedt's armour; but Hitler added a surprising postcript, that Rommel should also be given some responsibility for 1 and 19 Armies (on the Atlantic and Mediterranean coasts) in matters of coastal defence.[11] This postcript, together with the bad compromise over the armour, completely undermined von Rundstedt's position, and still was not enough for Rommel, who continued to press for the whole of the armoured reserve to be sited under him and in the forward areas.

This brought remonstrations from von Rundstedt once more, and the Führer then went back on his previous ruling, deciding this time in favour of *OB West*, in that the *Panzer Gruppe* and *AOK 1* and *AOK 19* were not to be put under Rommel, although it was understood that Rommel 'should have an inspector's brief there'. But worse was yet to come when Hitler decided that 'Rommel should take overall command where the enemy landed', so that should the enemy land in the south from the Mediterranean or from the Bay of Biscay, then 1 and 19 Armies would immediately become Rommel's command, leaving von Rundstedt to command in the north. The OKW diarist added what appears to be more than an understatement, that 'some confusion and duplication in command appears unavoidable because of this arrangement, but this has been taken into account'. It was, in all, a most extraordinary sequence of orders that reflect discredit not merely on him who gave them but also on the close military staffs who framed and issued them.

All this was little to von Rundstedt's liking, and he countered by suggesting a new headquarters for the south to exercise operative control over the two armies there, and *Armee Gruppe Blaskowitz* came into being.* For the moment, however, this did not alter the very confusing high command arrangements for the west.[12]

Meanwhile Rommel was instructed to show himself publicly in the south of France, and numerous formation billeting parties were directed into 1 and 19 Army areas to earmark accommodation for troop movement that was not intended and for formations that did not exist. The object, once again, was to hide the lack of troops in the south and frighten off the enemy.

The Anglo-American landings made in Normandy from 6 June gained ground steadily in spite of the dogged – at times desperate – defence of the German ground formations. By the end of the month the Americans had broken out of the beachhead and taken Cherbourg. Hitler alone was in control of the German tactical battle.

* An *Armee Gruppe* is not a *Heeresgruppe* (army group) but is a headquarters intermediate between an army and an army group.

On 1 July von Rundstedt presented the unvarnished truth to the dictator, even though he did this by sending the written views of Dollmann and Geyr von Schweppenburg, together with his concurrence.[13] The Caen troops must be drawn back, they said, 'in order to get them out of the range of the ships' guns and prevent the panzer formations from collapsing'. Geyr von Schweppenburg had added that 'the choice was either patchwork cobbling (*Flickarbeit*) that meant defending every foot of ground and leaving the initiative to the enemy, or elastic and fluid operations that, at the best, might allow some German initiative for part of the time'. In this judgement the army commanders condemned Rommel's concept of winning the battle by close coastal defence and now wanted to go back to von Rundstedt's idea. On this document, dated 1 July, Jodl wrote, for the information of the Führer, that this was 'a final acceptance that the enemy landing would never be defeated'. The situation, continued Jodl, really called for the evacuation of France and withdrawal to the shortest line of defence behind the West Wall on the frontiers of the Reich.

On 2 July von Rundstedt was relieved by von Kluge, still convalescing from his motor injury; Geyr von Schweppenburg gave way to Eberbach; Dollmann was replaced by SS General Hausser. The next day Hitler ordered all formations to remain exactly where they were.

Von Kluge had spent a fortnight with Hitler and Jodl and had been briefed on what they called 'the spirit of defeatism of the commanders in the west'; and so von Kluge arrived in Paris optimistic and determined to put some backbone into his new command, this leading to a violent altercation between himself and the disillusioned Rommel.* The realities of command and a tour of the forward areas, however, soon changed von Kluge's views, and by 10 July he, too, was asking for permission to withdraw – requests that were generally ignored in the OKW.[14] Fourteen days later von Kluge reported the German losses as over 2,000 tanks and 340 aircraft (nearly all that were available) together with 113,000 battle casualties against the arrival of only 10,000 reinforcements.[15] And he was the first senior German commander to doubt that the Allies would make a second landing in the Pas de Calais or elsewhere.

On 9 June the Russians had begun another onslaught in Finland and this time the offensive was so heavy that the Finns were in danger of breaking. The Finnish opinion of the fighting value of German troops in the marshy northern forests was not very high, but they were obliged to ask Berlin for six German divisions to take over the quiet sectors of the front, so relieving Finnish troops that could be moved to the main fighting sectors.[16] Hitler had none to spare, but he did send one infantry division, though he was shortly to ask that it be returned to him. Then, from 22 June, came a series of massive

---

* That von Kluge, who was already a conspirator, could censure Rommel for his lack of faith in the Führer, has been commented on by Buchheit. Von Kluge lacked strength of character and when removed from the influence of von Tresckow, von Schlabrendorff and von Gersdorff, his loyalty to Hitler was restored.

Russian offensives, the first being made against Busch's Army Group Centre in Belorussia. Within a week Busch's army group had fallen apart and the greater part of twenty-eight divisions (nearly 300,000 men) simply disappeared.[17] Model replaced Busch at the beginning of July, commanding not only Army Group Centre but also his own Army Group North Ukraine immediately to the south.

Model toured his two army groups keeping up a display of fanatical energy as he conducted his whirlwind visits, livening up his divisions and leaving a trail of disorder behind him, losing some of the respect and confidence of his subordinate commanders by a wanton interference in details that were none of his concern. For no German general, unless it were Schörner, was more attuned to the demands of the Führer and the party, even to the extent of being an enthusiastic supporter of the system of Nazi military commissars; and he required that one of his personal *aides* should be from the SS, with the object, so said his detractors, of ingratiating himself with the party. Model was extraordinarily active, both mentally and physically and he wanted to see everything – and do everything – for himself; he was erratic and inconsistent, an excellent improviser, with few social graces, inclined to curry favour with the rank and file at the expense of the officers. How much Model really believed in the Führer or in Nazism, or whether he was motivated only by self-interest, can only be a matter of conjecture, for he told Boldt during this month that 'the war was lost'.* He continued to enjoy the dictator's highest regard, particularly for the way in which he had 'brought the enemy Belorussian offensive to a halt'. But the price of Model's temporary success in Army Group Centre was about to be paid for in Army Group North Ukraine, for Model had been moving divisions from Army Group North Ukraine to plug the gaping hole in Belorussia.

On 14 July the third in the series of Soviet offensives, falling like hammer blows in sequence from north to south, was launched against Army Group North Ukraine, the army group that Model had just left. Hauffe's 13 Corps of 40,000 men was virtually destroyed and another great hole was blown in the front, through which Red Army forces streamed across South Poland to a depth of 130 miles, reaching the Carpathians and the Czecho-Slovak border.[18] Worse was later to come in Rumania; but, even on 20 July, it looked as if the whole eastern front was about to collapse.

On the breaking up of Army Group Centre, the Führer sent his *Wolfschanze* guard troops from Rastenburg into Belorussia, and a state of emergency was ordered, *Walküre IV* for the *Ersatzheer* in the Reich, and *Brunhilde* for the *General-Gouvernement*, based on a Hitler plan to raise more divisions to meet such a calamitous situation.† As reinforcements were no longer available, the dictator approved the idea of raising twenty

* Boldt, p. 29. Of Model, his staff officer von Mellenthin said 'it remains an open question whether Model supported Hitler out of conviction or to further his ambitions'. (*German Generals of WW II*, p. 148)

† Speer has said that he suggested some such emergency plan to the dictator 'in case the British should land in North Germany', an idea that met with Jodl's disapproval but was eagerly taken up by Hitler. (*Inside the Third Reich*, p. 508)

divisions on the spot by requisitioning all leave men that were in the Reich. Unlike the Russian, the British and, to a large extent, the American Armies, where the soldier who went campaigning took leave of his family for years, the German soldier had always enjoyed regular and generous home leave, however strained the battle situation and however distant his theatre of war. At least 10,000 soldiers a day passed each way through the leave centres, each man carrying his rifle or other personal weapon. These, according to Hitler, offered the potential for at least twenty new divisions. The first step was to draft these men into the framework of five new static divisions and four cadres of what had been burned-out infantry divisions, and after that to form another fifty-six furlough battalions, ready either to replace other stricken battalions or form new divisions. All these battalions were thrown together at the border leave collecting centres from the men returning from leave and on their way back to their units.[19]

The effect of this measure can easily be imagined. The men were of all ranks and all arms and carried only rifles. From these, battalions were formed without supporting arms, equipment, transport, signals or a command organization, with no man knowing his officer or neighbour. All the men were mistrustful, many of them were indignant and were apparently not slow to voice their protests. Some of them deserted and many of them took leave of absence and set off, as best they might, in search of their own units, usually many hundreds of miles away. The morale and efficiency of those that remained were not high. Many of these so-called battalions were not destined to form or join formations, since the disaster in Belorussia required that they should be moved eastwards and committed to battle just as they were. The effect on the formations, particularly those in battle, that had their returning leave men, many of whom were key personnel, taken from them, was no less dire, for a man sent on leave could be a man lost, a casualty that would not be replaced.

To counter the alarm occasioned by these measures, Hitler called, on 13 July, the commanders and National Socialist Guidance Officers (NSFOs) from all fronts to Obersalzberg, to give them a lecture on the need to economize and go without.

From this time onwards, military names and designations were to take on a different significance, being intended to bolster German morale and, at the same time, unnerve the enemy. Whereas before 1944 a brigade was usually a grouping of two regiments of the same arm, from July onwards it was applied to an infantry regiment grouping, that is to say an infantry regiment with supporting artillery and engineers. Alternatively it might mean merely a reinforced assault gun *Abteilung*. Henceforth numerous panzer brigades were to be raised although these were in effect merely panzer *Abteilungen* of fifty to sixty tanks together with a battalion of armoured infantry. Another misleading name was that of 'artillery corps' since these rarely consisted of more than a regiment.

New infantry divisions were to be raised differing from the 1944 new model (*n.A. 44*) division in organization, in that they were *Sperr-Divisionen* (blocking divisions) later known as *Grenadier-Divisionen* of two regiments each of three battalions.

Some of the requisitioned leave men were used to complete the earlier category 27 divisions (*n.A. 44*) and the others began to fill out newly raised divisions.[20] The category 28 were four more shadow divisions (*Jütland*, *Schlesien*, *Grafenwöhr* and *Munsingen*), but these almost immediately gave up their strength to the fifteen category 29 grenadier divisions that started forming on 18 July and were on their way to the front only twelve days later.*

Because of the loss of a large number of leave battalions to the fighting in Belorussia and because of the need to find reinforcements for other divisions, Hitler never got his twenty division central reserve. Instead, the leave men were diverted from their own formations to others newly forming.

The original general staff conspiracy against Hitler that would appear to have died for lack of support at the time of Munich in 1938, had meanwhile been revived, not only by the disgruntled and the disillusioned, but also by others of good faith and perspicacity who had always been troubled by Germany's plight. As Germany's fortunes waned so did the conspiracy gather further support.†

Although it had some civilian members, the main body of the conspirators came from the German Army and, in particular, from the general staff. And it says much for the camaraderie and closeness of this organization that the secret shared by so many army men was so well kept, not only from the SS and Gestapo but also from the other armed services and from those senior army officers who would not have hesitated to denounce the plotters.

The conspiracy had originally found much support from the general staff officers in von Bock's (later von Kluge's) Army Group Centre, but it soon had its cells or representatives in von Manstein's army group, in the OKH itself, in the *Ersatzheer*, in the military government in Paris and in Army Group B in the west. Many retired officers were in the plot. Halder, as the presumed originator, had some knowledge of it; von Witzleben, Beck and Hoepner were among the prime movers. In the OKH Fellgiebel, Wagner and Stieff were all deeply committed, although the executive action was to centre on Olbricht and von Stauffenberg of the *Ersatzheer* who were planning their own version of the *Walküre* operation (for they used the same codeword as that for the state of emergency), but *their* plan was aimed at seizing power within the Reich. Rommel knew of, and presumably fully supported, the conspiracy, as certainly did Karl-Heinrich von Stülpnagel in Paris. Zeitzler, so Heusinger told the author, 'must have known'; Hitler apparently thought so, too, for Zeitzler was dismissed hours after the bomb

* These at first took the numbers from 541 to 562, although later some assumed the identities of divisions earlier destroyed in the east.

† A German general said that 'the attitude of the resistance must be judged by how it received the [earlier German] victories ... Canaris, Witzleben, Rommel, Hoepner, Halder, Kluge and many others were enthusiastic [at the time] ... it was the latter-day defeats they did not like.' (Faber du Faur, p. 178)

explosion without the right to wear uniform, and his military aide was executed.

Fromm was waiting developments from the side-line and was primarily interested in safeguarding his own position. Von Rundstedt probably knew that a military cabal was in existence that boded no good for Hitler, for he had been approached earlier by dissidents; but he had apparently been kept, or had taken care to keep himself, in ignorance of its activities. Guderian, too, came in this category.[21] Von Bock had been a little more closely involved, though he had kept himself clear of entanglements and suspicion. Von Kluge was privy to the plot but could not make up his mind whether to join it. For von Kluge, another careful opportunist who had taken a grant of money from Hitler, was determined never to put a foot wrong; and so he wavered and havered.* Von Manstein's position was the same as von Kluge's, for, according to good evidence, he well knew that an attempt was about to be made on the dictator's life.[22] Like von Kluge he was not prepared to risk himself in the consequence of failure. His wife, too, may have had some influence on him, for Frau von Manstein was apparently one of the many millions of German women who trusted Hitler to the very end.

The 20 July bomb assassination attempt made in the conference hut at Rastenburg failed and Hitler remained unhurt. There were four who died, among them Korten, the *Luftwaffe* chief of staff, and Schmundt. Schmundt had, unwittingly, done enormous damage to the German Army. Yet he was, according to those who knew him, like Jodl 'a decent enough man', and when Burgdorf took over the *Personalamt*, the passing of Schmundt came to be regretted. The oafish Burgdorf (Guderian's words), was Hitler's accomplice in the death of Rommel: and he died, as he himself said, despised by commanders and staffs alike.[23]

Although the army *coup*, such as it was, was in fact put down by the German Army and not by the SS, the army was damned in Hitler's view and he began hunting down army officers suspected of any disloyalty to his person and régime, and the terror was to continue until his death. An anonymous complaint, sent in by an other rank with a grievance, could be sufficient to imprison, remove or reduce an officer to the ranks. The German high command and military organization were in this way destroyed from within at the time of the greatest crisis in the war. The NSFO organization showed itself in its true colours, redoubling its efforts in spying on and denouncing commanders. On 23 July the military salute was replaced by *der deutsche Gruss* (the '*Heil Hitler!*' and fascist salute) and the next day it was ruled that, before any general could fill any appointment, a rigorous enquiry should be made as to the candidate's and his wife's political reliability and religious views. Then, on 1 August, came the introduction of *Sippenhaft*, whereby the relatives of the troops became responsible for the actions of the

---

* When, on the evening of 20 July, after it had been learned that Hitler had escaped assassination, von Kluge was asked by the conspirators to make up his mind whether or not he was with them, he replied, with a shrug of the shoulders, '*Ja, wenn das Schwein* [Hitler] *tot wäre!*' (cit., Buchheit, *Hitler der Feldherr*, p. 431)

individual – a criminal practice that had long been common in communist Russia; families were imprisoned or executed for the disloyalty, even the failure that was often no more than suspected, of their menfolk.[24]

From 20 July Himmler was appointed the commander of the *Ersatzheer* in place of the arrested Fromm and henceforth he was to be responsible for the raising of all new army formations – mainly infantry divisions, these to be known as *Volksgrenadier*. The manning, discipline and administration of these divisions was to be controlled entirely by the SS, a special *Abteilung 10* being set up in the *Heerespersonalamt* to provide 'SS approved' officer replacements for these divisions: thereafter the officers could not be posted elsewhere without SS permission. The *Volksgrenadier* divisions remained responsible to Himmler, as were the SS divisions, even when they took to the field. The word *Volk* added to the divisional titles was intended to emphasize the link between these later groupings and the people, and to give expression to the 'National-Socialist spirit' of these new troops, in contradistinction to the old style that was tainted by the reactionary officer corps.[25]

On 26 August all army formations that recruited foreigners were transferred to the SS and, since the SS was now raising its own SS army headquarters (*SS Armeeoberkommandos*) and additional corps headquarters, army general staff officers were transferred to the SS against their will to occupy technical appointments that the SS were not qualified to fill. By January 1945 candidates for army commissions could be compulsorily directed into the SS. Himmler had no wish to absorb the German Army into the *Waffen SS*, but he wanted to use army personnel, when absolutely necessary, to fill out the SS; for he jealously safeguarded the *Waffen SS* identity and exclusiveness. His intention was to have the German Army subordinated to, and controlled in its entirety by, the *Waffen SS* with himself at its head. The V-2 development and production programme and the control of firings and operational units was taken over by the SS immediately after 20 July.

That Himmler had *Feldherr* pretensions there can be no doubt; in September he became the commander at the front of all troops in the Upper Rhine, taking under his command 19 Army, *Wehrkreis V* and 14 and 18 SS Corps. At the turn of the year he was to take over Army Group Vistula on the eastern front. According to Goebbels, the question had been mooted, and presumably put to Hitler in late 1944, as to whether Himmler should not also be appointed as the German Army Commander-in-Chief.[26]

In order that accused officers might not be tried by other officers, as was indeed their legal right, Hitler ordered that they should first be tried by military courts of honour whose duty it was to discharge the accused from the army so that they might then be delivered up to the vengeance of 'the people's courts' presided over by Freisler, who later became known as the Nazi Vishinsky. Suitable general candidates for this unpleasant task were selected by Hitler to sit on these courts of honour, and they included von Rundstedt, Keitel and Guderian. The military victims of the bomb plot, either by suicide or by execution, included Rommel, von Witzleben, Beck, Wagner, Fellgiebel, Hoepner, Fromm, Olbricht, Karl-Heinrich von Stülp-nagel, Canaris, Stieff and many others, and the time was shortly to come when the Führer would appoint 'flying courts martial' to visit the fronts to try and condemn the disloyal, the recalcitrant or the unlucky; their sentences could be death and these were often executed shortly after pronounce-ment.[27]

Politically, the bomb attack confirmed to Germany's remaining allies what they already knew, that Germany's defeat was certain and not far away. The assassination attempt and the purge that followed shook the German Army to its foundations, and the party propaganda machine saw to it that its remaining hierarchy lost the respect and confidence of the German public and of the formations in the field. The 20 July was convenient to explain away the sudden and terrible losses in Belorussia as treason; for, said the party, the example was there for all to see and to hear, with the Officer Freedom Committee in Moscow lending its support to Soviet propaganda.[28] The purge, itself, was carried out with a vindictiveness intended to crush not only any vestige of resistance but also any remaining independence and initiative of military commanders, so that from the highest to the lowest, they would, mindful of the retribution that attended failure, do exactly what the Führer ordered. Even this was not necessarily enough to save them.

The regimental officers, the rank and file, and the German public at large, had had no opportunity to observe their Führer at close quarters and they knew very little about him. And they remained entirely loyal because they believed that national unity and the solidarity of the Nazi régime were the only hope against the great flood of Red terror, barbarity and bestiality that threatened to submerge the eastern territories of the Reich.

Like many others von Kluge awaited the expected telephone call from Keitel recalling him to Germany 'for consultation or reposting', the last journey that some of these generals made. Meanwhile his front was disintegrating. When Rommel had been wounded on 17 July, von Kluge had taken over his vacant command, henceforth commanding both Army Groups D and B, and he spent much of his time in the forward area. The Americans had broken out at Avranches and were moving on the Loire. Hausser's 7 Army had been crushed and a double envelopment was threatening near Falaise. The great counter-stroke, planned by the Führer, came to nothing and von Kluge got the blame, the Führer inferring that 'von Kluge's disobedience' had cost the dictator what might have been victory in the west.[29] On 15 August von Kluge was out of radio touch inside the Falaise pocket, and Hitler, knowing that von Kluge was well aware that he was wanted by the Gestapo, decided that the field-marshal had gone over to the enemy.[30] Model was ordered on 16 August to replace von Kluge in command of both army groups in the west. Von Kluge, ordered to return to Germany, committed suicide.

Model could do nothing but save what was left. A Franco–American force had landed in South France and Blaskowitz's *Armee Gruppe G* with the two armies in the south was ordered north; Paris fell and the complete evacuation of France had begun, with only two weakened armies, 15 and 19, still retaining cohesion and discipline; the remainder, 7 Army, 5 Panzer Army (formerly Panzer Group West) and 1 Army had been routed. The disservice that Model did for the Führer and for Germany that September was to talk buoyantly and nonsensically about launching a powerful counter-offensive into the allied flank from the area of the Ardennes.*

On the eastern front on the day of 20 July much of Army Group Centre had disappeared, and Army Group North Ukraine, at that time still under Model, appeared to be in danger of collapse. Army Group North, firstly under Lindemann and then under Friessner, had been encircled against the Baltic coast by the collapse of Army Group Centre, and the safety of Rendulic's 20 Army in Finland was about to be threatened since fighting was shortly to break out between German and Finn.[31] Zeitzler had gone and his principal deputies, Heusinger and Stieff, had been removed, so that no one remained responsible for the eastern front.

Hitler had meanwhile ordered Guderian 'to assume the duties of the former chief of army general staff' in addition to filling his existing appointment as the Inspector-General of Panzer Troops. The picture that Guderian has given of himself is not necessarily accepted in Germany.† And when Guderian made his first address to the officers of the general staff, as their new chief, they were required to leave their pistols outside.

Guderian was a man of no breadth of vision, a tactician rather than a strategist, and was hardly more fitted for the task than Zeitzler had been, except that Hitler had eroded the status and responsibilities of the post to that of an executive and transmitter of the dictator's orders to the army groups in the east. There remained to Guderian not a vestige of authority or initiative.[32] Guderian had, however, always been Hitler's man, and no doubts appear to have troubled him at that time.

When Guderian arrived in Rastenburg he found the general staff offices of the OKH almost deserted, for many of the staff had been sent back to the main headquarters at Zossen and many of the departmental heads had been taken away by the Gestapo. Guderian, undaunted, set to work in a flurry of energy, exactly as Zeitzler had before him, in spite of the fact that the Führer had categorically and forcefully refused to allow him to issue any orders on

* This was a senior officer attitude aped from the Führer; when a front was collapsing, or when the officer thought himself to be suspected of disloyalty or faintheartedness, he began talking in this fashion. Those guilty of such poses included Model, Schörner, Busch, Guderian and Himmler.

† Professor Müller has said: 'There was that type of one-sided military technician ... whose new-school initiative against long accepted doctrine and tradition went hand in hand with a lack of ballast and a willing readiness to be led astray, provided that the ambition of a modern and highly technical army could be achieved. In the most extreme cases this type ... did not question overmuch who offered him this opportunity or the political strings attached ... men like Lutz, Hoepner and Geyr von Schweppenburg were no less panzer-obsessed than Guderian and yet they kept Nazism at a cool distance ...' (*Das Heer und Hitler*, p. 47)

his own authority. For the Führer had done away with the commander-in-chief of the army, and, in reality, with the OKH, and he saw no reason to retain the designation and function of chief of army general staff.[33] To him even the general staff was an anachronism. However that may be, Guderian appears to have carried out his master's orders faithfully in his early days of office, for he was soon at loggerheads with Friessner who wanted to break out of encirclement.* This led to Hitler replacing Friessner by Schörner, the firm supporter of the Nazi régime, while Friessner was sent to Army Group South Ukraine in Rumania. Schörner, however, had no more fortune than his predecessors in Army Group North and shortly he, too, was pressing Hitler to allow him to pull back from Estonia.

The Führer was to carry out a further exchange of senior commanders in what was increasingly becoming a game of musical chairs, in that, if the general did not commit suicide, get murdered or imprisoned in the interim, he might eventually find himself back in command, or even in the same command from which he had just been dismissed a few months before. On 16 August Model had gone to the west to replace von Kluge, his place in Army Group Centre being taken by Reinhardt. Harpe took Model's other vacant appointment in Army Group North Ukraine. By the end of August von Rundstedt had been recalled to take back Army Group D and the appointment of *OB West*, while Model retained only the command of Army Group B in France.

Guderian proposed to the Führer that the reserves, mainly motorized divisions, held by Friessner in Rumania, be withdrawn to Army Group Centre and this was agreed. The decision proved disastrous for Army Group South Ukraine.

The German military command in Rumania was of a complicated pattern. As elsewhere, the *Luftwaffe* air and ground troops, including the two flak divisions at Ploesti, came under Göring and the OKL. All German troops inside Rumania, mainly training missions and base installations, came under the OKW. Friessner's two German armies on the frontier came under the OKH, with his two Rumanian armies responsible to the Rumanian command in Bucharest. The Rumanian commanders were by now hostile, not only to the Germans, but also to Antonescu, and secret negotiations had been going on with the Russians about which Antonescu knew nothing.[34] The armies, and in particular Fretter-Pico's 6 German Army, were very badly deployed. Friessner feared for the security of his communications, although Hitler would permit no adjustments or movement, having Keitel tell Friessner to concern himself with his battle front and not with his rear.[35] The removal to the north of the motorized divisions weakened the defence even further.

All these political and military deficiencies, with Hitler, Göring and Jodl

---

* When Friessner's chief of staff Kinzel warned Guderian on 21 July that 'holding' would mean destruction, Guderian's condemnation became violent, with threats of arrest and shooting. (*Hr Gr Nord Protokoll*, cit., Messerschmidt, p. 434 note 1439)

interference, contributed to the complete destruction of the reconstituted and ill-fated 6 German Army at the height of mid summer in barely seven days fighting, during that final week in August. The greater part of twenty divisions, in all between 180,000 and 200,000 men, disappeared entirely.[36] And the fact had to be faced that the lost German divisions were actually up to strength, having been heavily reinforced in the previous two months, although the standard of reinforcement obviously left much to be desired. German infantry without adequate air and armoured support were now unable to hold ground for even the shortest of periods.*

The Rumanians left the war on 23 August and a reprisal air raid on Bucharest, ordered by Hitler, gave them the justification for declaring war on Germany. Friessner fell back with the few German divisions of Wöhler's 8 Army and with 6 Army headquarters (the only element that had escaped encirclement) into Hungary. In Italy Rome had long since fallen and Florence was given up by Kesselring's retreating troops on 4 August. The Soviet occupation of Rumania now threatened the rear of von Weichs's Army Group F in the Balkans and he was ordered to withdraw by stages to the north.

The heavy losses between June and August did not fall off significantly with the German withdrawals, because these were made under heavy pressure and usually took the form of running battles or disorganized retreats. And the real losses were not necessarily reflected in the divisions destroyed or disbanded, for those divisions that remained in being were continually losing large numbers of men that were being replaced, if only in part, by reinforcements. As these were often inexperienced recruits, the standard of efficiency, already low, sank further. Many divisions were being used in roles for which they were not intended, the security divisions as line formations, and the static divisions in a mobile role, usually on their feet in the direction of withdrawal. The security divisions had no supporting weapons and the static divisions no transport. Equipment was abandoned in the haste to escape envelopment. Tank forces were hampered by lack of fuel, and the railways could no longer be used.

The losses in the west both in men, equipment and divisions tended to be lower than those in the east, not because the defeat was any less complete, but, in the view of one informed German general, because the Anglo-American enemy, in spite of his enormous superiority in equipment, tended to be slow, cumbersome and deliberate; for this reason many German formations that should have been destroyed, succeeded in escaping to fight another day.[37] Then again, the German troops in the east tended to be more distant and scattered with poorer road routes, and, having to cover longer distances in their withdrawals, they were often outpaced by Soviet

---

* In January 1944 Hitler had remarked to Zeitzler that German infantry could no longer stand its ground unless it had armoured support (Heiber, pp. 545–7). The importance of air power was disregarded, not only by Hitler, but also by Guderian, who had no experience of field command in conditions of air inferiority.

motorized troops that had struck deep into the German communication zones without regard to their flanks or rear.

However that may be, the staggering losses continued in the west as well as in the east. About twenty-nine divisions were lost in the west, mostly in August and September, either during the withdrawal or left behind in the so-called coastal fortress pockets. Three divisions had to be disbanded in the Balkans, two in Italy and a further ten in the east, making a total of forty-four in all. From June to September, both months inclusive, there were 55,000 dead and 340,000 missing in the west, and 215,000 dead and 627,000 missing in the east. The wounded could generally be computed at three times the figure of the dead.[38] The total loss of 1.2 million (in addition to three quarters of a million wounded) in those summer and autumn months was roughly the same as that suffered by the whole German Army from the beginning of the war until February 1943, including the Stalingrad casualties. In the whole of 1944 106 divisions were destroyed or had to be disbanded, more divisions than the German Army had in September 1939. To have attempted a major offensive from this time onwards could have only been an act of madness.

Before 1943 the Soviet armament industry was turning out many more guns, tanks and aircraft than were being produced in Germany, and qualitatively the standard of the Soviet gun and tank was equal and sometimes superior to that of its German equivalent. From 1943 onwards, however, the German armament production began rapidly to overtake that of the USSR.

The German economy and industry had suffered from a complexity of organization, an overlapping of directional responsibilities and a lack of skilled scientific control and research. The economic minister was Funk, but his main responsibilities had been assumed by Göring as head of the Four Years' Plan. Göring in his turn was to lose ground to the able Todt, the head of the large paramilitary organization, who, in 1940, had become minister for armaments and munitions. Todt and Göring, and to a much lesser extent Funk, all had some responsibility for Germany's war production, yet some of the planning was delegated to Milch of the OKL and, to a limited degree, to Thomas, the head of the *Wi Rü Amt* of the OKW. The OKM, too, had a decisive voice in naval production matters. In 1942, ninety per cent of the armament industry was still working on a single shift basis, and, due to the party's emphasis on the maintenance of relatively high German standards of living, much of industry and the industrial labour force was employed on the production of consumer goods. On 10 January 1942 a great increase was ordered in the manufacture of heavy equipment, and this may have reflected an abandoning by the Führer and Todt of the shallow blitzkrieg armament policy that had governed Germany's course up to then, in favour of preparation for a war of attrition and armament in depth.[39] However this may be, Todt died a month later in an aircraft crash, and he was succeeded as armaments minister by Speer. Speer had already acquired a reputation as a fixer, a man who could overcome seemingly impossible difficulties. The Führer had never made a happier choice.

The energetic Speer, one of the very few men who, at that time, had direct access to Hitler, soon used his position and gifts to reorganize and rationalize German industry. Funk was not really a rival. Göring was edged aside. In May 1942, Thomas and the *Wi Rü Amt* were removed from Keitel's control and incorporated into Speer's organization. Milch and Saur, Speer's deputy, formed a single executive body to concentrate on fighter production, and the German Navy, since the beginning of 1943 under Dönitz instead of Raeder, was no longer able to go its own way independent of everybody except Hitler. The labour force under Sauckel remained, however, outside Speer's influence.

Motivated by total war, although in fact many of the measures were much less than total, German war production began to show an immediate and most remarkable improvement. In 1943 the annual military aircraft production rose from 14,700 to 25,200 and in 1944 it rose again to 37,000, more than were being produced in the Soviet Union, although the German increase reflected the fact that fighters were being produced at the expense of bombers. The graph of tank production showed a similar rise: 2,875 medium tanks and assault guns were being produced in 1941 in addition to 2,200 lightly armoured vehicles of all types. In 1942, 4,300 medium assault guns and tanks and 1,200 self-propelled artillery pieces on tank chassis were turned out. In 1943 there was some difficulty in increasing the total, because the Mk III tank went out of production and the Mk V and Mk VI were being introduced, but even so, the medium tank and assault gun total for the year was 6,700, together with 2,500 heavy tanks and 2,600 self-propelled (SP) guns on tank chassis. In 1944 the production approached that of the Soviet Union, and was made up of 11,000 medium tanks and assault guns, 1,600 tank destroyers and 5,200 heavy tanks, in all 17,800 medium and heavy tanks and assault guns. To this total was added 1,250 SP guns on tank chassis and 10,000 lightly armoured vehicles of all types.[40] Even more significant was the improvement in the design of German armour that had done much to redress the inferiority of 1942 and 1943, since the Tiger and King Tiger were superior to all Soviet tanks, while the improved Mk V and IV and assault guns were to prove a match for the T34. In 1942 German gun production (75 mm and above) stood at 12,000 artillery and 2,400 tank guns, and by 1944 these figures had risen to 40,600 artillery and 15,300 tank guns a year.* Speer's great achievements, however, were made at the cost of using up stocks of raw materials, and before the end of 1944 the production figures must necessarily have declined sharply even though war factories were not overrun or destroyed from the air.

Hitler and his advisers, through ignorance and wilfulness, had until too

* Western production for 1944 was: Britain – 26,000 aircraft and 5,000 tanks: USA – 96,300 aircraft and 17,500 tanks (29,500 tanks in 1943). Soviet production for 1944 – 32,000 aircraft, 29,000 tanks and 56,000 anti-tank and field guns (according to the Soviet official history).

late failed to face the seriousness of Germany's position and three years that might have been used better to equip the German forces had been largely wasted. The key problem, of course, was that of raw materials, shortages that had always existed and that should have deterred Germany from ever entering into an offensive war. About forty-seven per cent of the iron ore requirement had had to be imported, mainly from Sweden and France, together with a hundred per cent of its needs of manganese and bauxite, mainly from Russia and the Balkans, forty-five per cent of its copper from Sweden, seventy-five per cent of its wolfram from Portugal and all its chrome from Turkey.[41] Only thirty per cent of Germany's oil had come from Rumania, the import being restricted by transportation difficulties; the remainder was found by home and synthetic oil production. The lack of oil remained the most immediate threat in the war economy in the last year of the war.

German manpower difficulties during 1943 and 1944 had been serious everywhere, but they were most crippling in the German Army where the losses among the junior leaders and soldiers of experience had been so high.

Hitler, in his order of 5 December 1943, had ordered that a further million men should be made available to the *Wehrmacht* and this had resulted in a rise in the numbers that had been inducted into the *Ersatzheer*, from 1,960,000 during 1943 to 2,556,000 in 1944. Then, on 25 July 1944, the Führer had issued a directive 'for total war' wherein Göring, as chairman of the council of ministers for defence, was charged with overhauling all war measures.[42] Goebbels was appointed as the commissioner or plenipotentiary (*Bevollmächtigter*) for total war, in order to clamp down on all waste. An additional million men were wanted for the *Wehrmacht* and this was again in due course to be reflected in the number of men that passed through the *Ersatzheer*, for this rose in the first quarter of 1945 to 1,626,000, three times that for the comparable period in 1944. They were, however, for the most part men with rifles, some of them seventeen years of age, inadequately trained and indifferently led, for the old army was nearly dead.

The *Volksgrenadier-Divisionen* had three infantry regiments each of two battalions each of three grenadier companies, these being particularly well equipped with machine-pistols, and a support company of medium machine-guns and medium mortars. The infantry-gun company had only four infantry-guns but it had in addition eight heavy mortars. Anti-tank guns had largely disappeared and the *Panzerjäger* (now called the *Panzerzerstörer*) company was equipped with short-range (*Panzerschreck*) hollow-charge weapons. The divisional headquarters had a fusilier company for reconnaissance and reserve and one battalion in each division was mounted on bicycles. The artillery was reduced to about sixty per cent of that in the earlier infantry divisions. Whereas the old type infantry division had an establishment of 17,000 and the (*n.A. 44*) division a strength of 12,000, the *Volksgrenadier* division had a full entitlement of 10,000 men.[43] In the field, however, they were often down to no more than 6,000. Rifles were not yet in short supply and the equipment position, thanks to the 1944 boom in output, was for the time being surprisingly good considering the disorganized state of the Reich.

The first (category 30) *Volksgrenadier* divisions were raised in August, four of them being based on remnants from the east and two being new. That same month five shadow divisions were converted into category 31 field formations. The category 32 divisions numbered twenty-five in all, some of these being formed in the east almost entirely from the *Volksdeutsch Liste III*, mainly men of German extraction born outside the Reich; other divisions were converted security and reserve divisions; some of the *Volksgrenadier* divisions were originally given names famous in Prussian history, *Dennewitz*, *Nieder-Görsdorf*, *Katzbach*, *Grossgörschen* and *Mockern*, before receiving new numbers or the numbers of the divisions that they replaced in the field.* Of the seventy-five line infantry divisions lost in 1944 (and this loss figure does not include motorized, mountain or other *Jäger* divisions destroyed), sixty-six were replaced by new or converted formations during the autumn of 1944; the replacements could hardly be compared, in fighting value, even with the tired and understrength formations, now lost, whose places they took.

On 10 December 1944 all infantry divisions of the *Feldheer*, except those in Norway, were put on to a restructured organization replacing the 1944 model (*n.A. 44*), and this became known simply as the infantry division 45 organization. It was designed to save manpower and was very close to that of the category 32 *Volksgrenadier* pattern, except that it had a divisional fusilier battalion on bicycles and that its *Panzerjäger Abteilung* had assault guns in addition to anti-tank guns. Its field artillery had fifty-four guns as opposed to thirty-two in the *Volksgrenadier* division.

The army panzer division had meanwhile not altered significantly in its general organization since 1943. Its single regiment had two *Abteilungen* each of four companies that in 1943 were supposed to have twenty-two tanks each, one *Abteilung* having Mk IV tanks and the other Mk V Panthers – about 170 tanks in all. But in fact, unlike the SS divisions or the army *Grossdeutschland* division, they rarely had half this number of tanks. The August 44 divisional establishment reduced the tank company yet again, to seventeen tanks.

The army panzer corps, like the panzer army, was in fact synonymous with a rifle formation in that it often commanded only infantry divisions. The numbered panzer divisions, all of which were growing steadily smaller in size and offensive power, had long since been divorced from operative tasks carried out by massed armoured forces, for they were used now to plug gaps, support infantry and put in counter-attacks with limited objectives. SS

* The 30 category divisions were numbered 12, 16, 19, 36, 560 and 563 VGD; the 31 category shadow divisions *Breslau*, *Döllersheim*, *Mähren*, *Röhn* and *Gross-Born* became 357, 564–570 VGD; the category 32 divisions became 571–582 and 584–588, while the reserve and security divisions kept their original numbers.

formations, on the other hand, tried to assume the earlier role performed by the 1941 and 1942 panzer groups, in that they were usually up to strength and were being continually upgraded, from line to motorized, and then from panzer grenadier to panzer divisions. A SS panzer corps was normally made up of up to strength SS panzer divisions.

In the autumn of 1944 an attempt was made to restore offensive power and mobility to four army panzer corps (in addition to the *Herman Göring Fallschirm-Panzer Korps*) by incorporating two 'reduced' panzer divisions in each, the support and administrative services being amalgamated under the corps headquarters in the interest of economy.* But in fact all they produced was one strong panzer division. And, as Nehring has said, it was already too late and too little, for when the enemy renewed his offensives these forma-tions or part formations were used singly or in detachments for fire support or to bolster the infantry defence.[44]

Neither Hitler nor Guderian was capable of understanding that the large *operative* tank formations could not even survive on the modern battlefield without tactical air superiority. Even if the OKH had been able to reassem-ble panzer groups of the 1940 and 1941 pattern, these panzer groups must inevitably have been halted and then destroyed in the fury of the enemy air attack, both in the east and in the west.†

* The formations were *PzK Grossdeutschland*, made up of the panzer grenadier divisions *Grossdeutsch-land* and *Brandenburg*; *PzK Feldherrnhalle*, with two panzer divisions of the same name (1) and (2); *24 PzK* with 16 and 17 Panzer Divisions; *40 PzK* was also designated for the same reorganization with 19 and 25 Panzer Divisions.

† Soviet ground successes, like those of the Anglo-Americans, multiplied with the growth of their air forces. The Red Air Force, weak and faltering in 1941, completely dominated the skies in 1944 over all the main eastern theatres, the Baltic, Belorussia, Galicia and Rumania.

CHAPTER TWELVE

The Collapse

During the withdrawal in France, firstly Model, and then the Führer, had dreamed of launching an armoured offensive from the south that would catch the advancing allies a shattering blow in the flank. Orders for such an operation were actually given out to 5 Panzer Army at the beginning of September, to a formation that had been recently crushed and had neither men nor equipment.[1] Even Jodl advised against it. The offensive was postponed. Then Hitler ordered that the old general staff appreciations and orders covering the 1940 Ardennes operation should be unearthed from the archives at Liegnitz, so that they might be restudied and used again. All planning, preparation and orders remained, as the OKW diarist noted, closely under the hand of the Führer, for he was even making the daily decisions as to the supply of vehicles and horses to the individual divisions making up the attacking force.[2]

Between 1 September and 15 October the German Army in the west had received an addition of 152,000 men either as new formations or reinforcements, but the casualties in this six week period had totalled 150,000. In addition von Rundstedt had to give up 86,000 men for transfer elsewhere. On 2 December, a fortnight before the great Ardennes offensive, the field-marshal reported that his command was 3,500 officers and 115,000 men short of establishment, while the efficiency of the reinforcements was poor.[3] Von Rundstedt certainly had little confidence in the likelihood of the success of the proposed offensive, and Model tended to send any protesters from below direct to the Führer above, as though he wanted to wash his hands of it.* On the evening of 15 December, the night before the attack began, Model confirmed that the Führer's orders had been passed on to Dietrich's 6 Panzer Army 'word for word', and there, implied Model, his responsibility ended.[4]

The two panzer armies, Dietrich's 6 Panzer and von Manteuffel's 5 Panzer, numbered sixteen divisions, half of them panzer only in name, and the two supporting armies on the flanks totalled another fifteen divisions, of which about a third came into action.[5] Complete surprise was achieved both in the timing and in the place of the attack, and the poor visibility compensated, in

* Speer said the same of Dietrich at this time. (*Spandau – The Secret Diaries*, p. 15)

part, for the German air inferiority. But by Christmas Day, only ten days later, it was obvious that the whole offensive had already failed. The Ardennes operation inflicted 75,000 casualties on the enemy, nearly all of them American. On the other hand the *Wehrmacht* losses had totalled 100,000 men, 800 tanks and 1,000 aircraft. The American losses would be easily made up; the German losses were irreplaceable. And so Hitler had lost what might have been his last strategic reserve for east or west, and its loss led to the breaking of the backbone of the defence on the Rhine.*

Hitler had lived too long in his shadowy world and, convinced of his own genius, he was pathologically suspicious of his subordinates, who, he was sure, wrecked his plans by failing to obey his orders in the minutest detail. The responsibility for losing the war was theirs. Commanders and staffs, including von Bonin, Guderian's chief of the operations department, continued to be arrested by the Gestapo. At the end of November Hitler had issued an order that was to be made known to every soldier, in which it was actually decreed that the commander of any fortress, garrison or post should, before retiring or breaking out from his defences, offer his command to anyone willing to take it. Any officer or soldier who thought that he could continue the defence, should then be given the full command, regardless of his rank and the battle should go on.[6]

The enemy's capabilities or likely intentions rarely had any place in the Führer's appreciations. Although, by stopping up his eyes and ears, he had usually refused to take any account of the Soviet threat during 1944, this resulting in the repeated disastrous defeats for Germany during that year, Hitler had learned nothing, for he again took the view that any further Soviet offensive in strength was most improbable. The only area in the east in which he considered himself at all concerned was in the defence of Budapest and the Hungarian oilfields.

Between the 12 and 15 January, another mighty Russian offensive broke loose between the Carpathians and East Prussia, and this led to numerous breakthroughs into the hinterland. No German armoured or motorized reserves were there to stop them. On 16 January Hitler returned from the west to Berlin (the Rastenburg *Wolfschanze* headquarters had been evacuated the previous November when the Russians overran the borders of East Prussia). Undeterred by the ruin of Harpe's Army Group A (formerly North Ukraine) and the plight of Army Group Centre, with the frightening consequences for millions of Germans as the Soviet spearheads neared the Oder, the dictator ordered Dietrich's 6 SS Panzer Army from the area of the Ardennes to Hungary.† Harpe lost his command to Schörner, who was replaced in Army Group North by Rendulic, another of the Führer's favourites. Army Group North, surrounded against the coast, became Army

---

* Yet Hitler still 'talked about a run of bad luck that meant nothing as far as ultimate victory was concerned; he was planning new offensives that would change the fortunes of war; the generals present [at Bad Nauheim] remained icily silent'. (Speer, Ibid., p. 238)

† 6 Panzer Army was redesignated as 6 SS Panzer Army.

244

Group Kurland. East Prussia was also cut off in a separate pocket, and Army Group Centre was encircled and under attack. Hitler marked places on the map and called them fortresses for which the commanders were to answer with their lives. Then, on 19 January, he issued an order that forbade any formation down to that of division from taking any action without first obtaining his permission, whether this should involve withdrawal, the giving up of any position, or even an attack that might draw the enemy's attention.[7] Having thus effectively paralysed his own troops, he determined to fight every move from his map boards in and under his chancellery; and it was owing to the excellence of the German signal system that he was able to do this until the very end. Meanwhile scores of civilians, usually members of the party, were appearing in military headquarters and even in forward battle positions, demanding, in their search for treachery, to check and control the actions of the officers.

Raus, the Austrian commander of 3 Panzer Army, told Himmler on 13 February, in the presence of Kinzel, Himmler's army chief of staff, that 'the high command has lost all sense (*Mass*) of time, space and relative strengths, and has so shackled the field commanders that they go into battle with their hands tied behind their backs and a halter around their necks, for they have to carry out the orders [given from above] under pain of death; and when the carrying out of these orders ends in failure they are thrown out in disgrace and condemned as traitors'.[8]

Jodl had little interest in the war in the east and much of his time would appear to have been spent in trying to thwart any attempt by Guderian to persuade the Führer to transfer troops from the west. The dictator, who had never diguised his contempt for Keitel, now thought Jodl, so he told Goebbels, 'a worn-out fuddy-duddy'.[9] Jodl's adversary Guderian, shorn of authority, was no less blinkered than Jodl. Taking his cue from the Führer, whose 'patch of bad luck' theme had changed to 'nothing ever went right now', Guderian was to blame his lack of success on the fact 'that Germany no longer had the commanders and troops of the 1940 quality'; and he was apparently incapable of taking this reasoning to its next logical progression and posing the question, as to how this state of affairs had come about, and who was primarily responsible.[10] Meanwhile Guderian busied himself in collecting a handful of tanks, for which fuel was in any case now in short supply, in his efforts to recapture the operative initiative. Never a man to have his feet firmly on the ground, he had entered the unreal world of Hitler and Himmler in his belief that these projected attacks would change the whole course of the fighting in the east. These attacks, if and when they were made, passed almost unnoticed by the Russians.

After the war Guderian blamed the Führer's military direction. Hitler at the time, however, was telling his political cronies that Guderian himself was responsible for Germany's defeats. It was, as the cynical Goebbels noted in his diary, so typically German that the officers should try to blame the party while the political leaders should lay the blame on the *Wehrmacht*.[11]

By February 1945 the enemy in the east had already occupied much of Silesia and had closed up to the Oder preparatory to making a last offensive into Saxony, Mecklenburg, Brandenburg and on to Berlin. In the west the Anglo–Americans were preparing to cross the Rhine. On the Baltic over twenty divisions of Group Kurland under Rendulic stood pinned against the sea, idle and isolated from the war; although sea communications were still open, the dictator refused to withdraw a man. In East Prussia, what had been Army Group Centre was now Army Group North, firstly under Rendulic and then under Weiss: this too was a detached and separate theatre, surrounded by the Russians. On the Lower Oder, covering what was left of Pomerania and protecting Mecklenburg and Brandenburg, was Army Group Vistula under Himmler. Schörner's Army Group Centre was in front of Saxony and Czecho-Slovakia while Wöhler's Army Group South was falling back from Hungary to Austria. In the west a new Army Group H under Student covered North-West Germany and Holland, while Army Group B was in the Ruhr and the middle Rhine. Hausser's Army Group G was responsible for the upper Rhine (since Himmler's organization there had been disbanded), while von Rundstedt remained in overall command as *OB West*. Kesselring's Army Group C continued to hold the Po valley in Italy while von Weichs's Army Group F occupied only the northern area of Yugo-Slavia.

During the last few months of 1944 thirteen panzer brigades had been raised, with numbers from 101 to 113, and of these the first nine had had a single panzer grenadier battalion as part of its establishment and the last three had panzer grenadier regiments. Nine of these brigades were then converted to single *Abteilung* panzer divisions taking their numbers from those that had been lost or disbanded.[12] In March 1945, came a far-reaching change, when the new establishment was produced for the *Panzer Division 45*; for this was to be the standard replacement for both the panzer and the panzer grenadier division.[13] The armoured infantry battalions – one to each of the panzer grenadier regiments – were transferred to the (sixty-four tank strong) panzer *Abteilung* to form with it a 'mixed' panzer regiment, together with artillery and pioneers. The remaining panzer grenadier regiments that had given up their *gepanzerte Grenadiere* were to lose their vehicles and become line infantry, as there was no more fuel or transport to lift them. This reorganization was a move in the right direction in that it could have provided a number of closely-knit all arms groups; as it was, however, it was born of necessity and was a counsel of despair. It was only partly implemented by the time the war ended.

At the beginning of 1945 a further ten infantry divisions had been embodied, mainly by refurbishing and resurrecting, and these were the category 33 formations. Then another nine divisions were raised to replace those lost during the January Vistula battle; but the system was becoming so irregular that they had neither category nor number. At the 25 January situation conference Hitler made the snap decision that henceforth all infantry divisions should be known by their numbers only, the use of functional designations such as *Reserve*, *Ausbildungs* and *Ersatz* being dropped.[14] Since these divisions often had the same numbers as field divisions, this resulted in a hasty renumbering of most of the replacement and training formations.

In the last few months of the war the German order of battle became increasingly confused, partly because Hitler, to deceive the enemy, was giving divisional numbers and designations to bodies of troops that were not divisions, and partly due to disruption and defeat; formations began to be thrown together in the fashion of the old *Freikorps* at the end of the First World War. *Osttruppen* and ships' crews in the Netherlands were listed as four infantry divisions, with the object of delaying the Canadian attacks.[15] Then, in February 1945, came the named divisions (without category), *Döberitz*, *Berlin*, *Hamburg*, *Jütland* and *Seeland*, these being called variously *Alarm*, *Reserve* or *Schatten* according to taste, although these names had no connection with the earlier designations. Meanwhile, as if to add to the disorder, the inspector for officer training (*Führernachwuchs*) was raising regiments independently of the *Wehrkreise*, the first ten regiments being based on *Fahnenjunker* cadets, although these were much outnumbered by recruits and *Volkssturm* taken in to make up the numbers. The other six regiments had included officers and reserve officers, up to 180 in each regiment, many of whom were serving in the ranks. Most of these regiments were used on the Oder.[16]

In February 1945 three new shadow divisions were thrown together, taking the names *Hannover*, *Dresden* and *Donau*, although these had only four battalions each; then, on 29 March, the final divisions of the war came hurriedly into being, many of them being incorporated into the so-called 12 Army (*Armee Wenck*) put together under the chief of the operations group of the general staff. This army was used by the dictator, firstly in vain attempts to extricate the surrounded forces in the Harz, and then to relieve Berlin from the west. Of these, the final category 35 divisions, three were recruited from the *Reichsarbeitsdienst* and the other four collected their intake from schools and *Ersatzheer* recruits.*

Independently of these measures the *Ersatzheer*, too, had its own role to play in withstanding invasion. In September 1944 the old *Walküre* code names were replaced, the Replacement Army alarm call being *Gneisenau*, while that for the *Feldheer* in the Reich was *Blücher*. On the issue of these code words all schools, administrative staffs, and recruits with four weeks' service, had to stand by, ready for immediate movement. *Gneisenau* was actually ordered on 17 September for *Wehrkreis VI* at the time of the Arnhem landings, and 176 Reserve Division, 406 and 526 Divisions had been committed with *Gneisenau* alarm units.

* The labour service formed the *Schlageter*, *Jahn* and the *Körner*; the other divisions were *Potsdam*, *Scharnhorst*, *Ulrich von Hütten* and *Ferdinand von Schill*.

On 26 March 1945 came *Aktion Leuthen*, the last alarm movement of the Replacement Army. The transfer was made to both the eastern and the western fronts, this being known as the march – mainly on foot – of the East and the West Goths, about 70,000 going to the Oder while 45,000 made their way to the Rhine. Most of these were Replacement Army training divisions of cadre strength (bearing numbers from 402 to 490), but they also included a number of named formations, some of which joined *Armee Wenck*, together with the skeleton panzer divisions *Jüterbog*, *Clausewitz* and *Müncheberg*, and panzer training formations.* With this movement of the Goths to the battle fronts the Replacement Army had come to an end.

On 28 March Guderian, together with Busse, the commander of 9 Army on the Oder, had appeared in the chancellery at Hitler's summons, where Busse was subjected to a torrent of abuse.† Guderian, at the end of his nervous resources, spoke out in defence of Busse and he was shortly afterwards dismissed from his posts, his staff being surprised and thankful that he had not joined his deputy von Bonin in a concentration camp.[17] Guderian was replaced by Krebs, a friend and drinking companion of Burgdorf.

Due to his failure in Pomerania Himmler had given way to Heinrici; after the withdrawal of Army Group South from Hungary into Austria, Wöhler was replaced by Rendulic. Von Rundstedt was retired and Kesselring took his place as *OB West*, von Vietinghoff thereafter commanding in Italy, where he, and his SS representative Wolff, had been for some time in secret touch with the allies. Von Weichs had given way to Löhr. Model, after his Army Group B in the Ruhr had been encircled and destroyed by the Americans, shot himself.

The 20 April was the Führer's birthday and many of his subordinates appeared in the chancellery to congratulate him, including Göring, Himmler, Speer, and the heads of the armed services. They then left Berlin.[18] Hitler himself seemed to be undecided whether to leave or not, but he did order the implementation of the previously agreed plan whereby, should Germany be cut through by the enemy from east and west, then Dönitz should take over command in the north, while it was assumed, though not confirmed, that Kesselring would command in the south.

On 22 April the last war conference was held in the chancellery. When it was reported that the Russians were already advancing deep into Mecklenburg to the north of Berlin, Hitler wanted to know the progress of the grandiose German counter-offensive that he had ordered the day before, an offensive that was to use formations that no longer existed. When he learned

---

* These included the training cadres *Grossdeutschland*, *Böhmen*, *Ostsee*, *Westfalen*, *Franken*, *Thüringen*, *Krampnitz*, *Bayern*, and the assault gun Schule Burg training school (*Ferdinand von Schill*).

† Such a scene was repeated two days later without Guderian being present, when Heinrici, Himmler's replacement in Army Group Vistula, met Hitler for the first time. Heinrici, to his surprise and consternation, was cut short when making his report by a violent outburst of threats. As one bystander said, 'none of the military present were prepared to take Heinrici's part'. (Boldt, p. 102)

that the ordered attacks had not taken place, he began to rant and rave, screaming about disloyalty, cowardice, treachery and insubordination, and he blamed both the army and the SS. He would, he said, stay in the capital.* Then sinking back in his chair, he started to sob, saying, 'It is all over. The war is lost. I shall shoot myself'.[19] According to Keitel, Hitler's face was yellow, his twitching was accentuated, he was extremely nervous and his mind kept wandering.

Goebbels had said, in praise of the retiring von Rundstedt, that he was 'a highly respectable officer who has done us [the party] great service, particularly in the liquidation [of the army officer conspirators] of 20 July'.[20] Meanwhile the hangings, the shooting and the imprisonment of officers continued on all fronts, not merely for what was said to be conspiracy, but for failure and for indiscipline, that is to say the expression of views contrary to those issued from the bunker under the chancellery garden. For, said the approving Goebbels, the Führer was rooting out the increasing indiscipline among the generals in the west by instituting itinerant courts martial, and having recalcitrant generals condemned and shot within two hours. One general who, according to Goebbels, refused to permit a NSFO to do his job 'was to be brought to trial and probably condemned to death'. On 10 March – even before the arrival of the Führer-commissioned General Hubner travelling court martial – a General von Bothmer shot himself, having just been sentenced to five years' imprisonment and the loss of all rank 'for failing to hold Bonn'.[21] Nor could officers opt out by finding an excuse for release from the army, for on 7 February Burgdorf's *Heerespersonalamt* had issued an order that officers were no longer permitted to leave the service, but would, if necessary, be employed in a junior rank vacancy – and, in cases where they had incurred official displeasure (*Verschulden*), they would be re-employed as non-commissioned officers.[22] And general staff and other officers were actually being hanged on lamp-posts and trees, by the main routes in the south and south-east, as an example to others.

The Führer's final spite was to order the arrest of Göring by the SS – both Göring and his wife were so arrested and remained in great fear for their lives, for the SS had begun to shoot prisoners in large numbers, with or without orders from the centre.[23] Meanwhile Hitler turned on the SS. The first victim was Fegelein, Himmler's SS liaison officer with the Führer (and Eva Braun's brother-in-law) whom Hitler had had shot outside the bunker. Himmler, safely out of the Führer's reach, was disowned, and Bormann, on 30 April, sent a radio signal to Dönitz ordering, in the Führer's name, 'instant and ruthless action' against the *Reichsführer SS*; Greim, Göring's successor as the commander-in-chief of the *Luftwaffe*, was ordered to fly out of Berlin to ensure that Himmler was in fact arrested.[24]

The reign of terror that had begun in 1933 had now reached its climax and

---

* Hitler had already demanded that Himmler remove the arm-bands from the *Leibstandarte* in Hungary, who had disgraced him by failure, and he had told Göring, in front of junior officers, that his *Luftwaffe* was rotten to the core.

finale. General officers, even field-marshals, trembled for their lives, for the whole world had gone mad around them. Kesselring, when he heard that von Vietinghoff was treating with the enemy, fearful, and in an effort to demonstrate his own loyalty to the Führer, ordered von Vietinghoff into arrest and sent Schulz to relieve him. Schulz was, however, himself arrested by von Vietinghoff, and both von Vietinghoff and Wolff made Army Group C in North Italy ready, not to continue to resist the Anglo-Americans, but to fight Löhr's Army (Group) E withdrawing from the Balkans, should Löhr attempt to intervene in the Führer's name.[25] Dönitz, shortly to be named by the dictator as his successor and head of state, was providing himself with strong naval guards in case Himmler should try to eliminate him. Dornberger, von Braun and the army V-2 scientific and experimental staff, suspecting that their SS supervisors intended to murder them all so that their secrets should not fall into enemy hands, gave the SS guards the slip and fled for the safety of the western prison camps.[26] Field-Marshal Busch, commanding an *ad hoc* grouping covering Hamburg and the north-west, after making a public to-do about the offensive he was going to launch 'in the Hitler spirit', set about surrendering his command to the British, but first required that they should envelop him from the east and so protect him from possible SS revenge.[27]

The suicide of Hitler (followed by that of Burgdorf and Krebs) brought with it not only the end of the Third German Reich but the end of the German Army. Keitel and Jodl, who had escaped from the capital, were used by the victorious allies as a figure head and an executive (little more than the pawns that they had always been to the dictator), merely to disarm and disband the *Wehrmacht* before they themselves stood trial for their lives.

Whereas in the First World War only sixty-three German generals had been killed or died on active service, with a further 103 dying from other causes, between 1939 and 1945 twenty-two general officers were condemned to death by German courts, 110 committed suicide, and 963 died (including those executed or dying in allied custody) or simply disappeared.[28] 'No word was used by their class more frequently than "loyalty", not only by the Keitels and the Kesselrings, but also by the Blombergs, the Mansteins and the Kluges; all used it to kill their doubts.'[29] While he who, like Machiavelli's Prince, 'knew how to cheat men's brains by trickery, in the end overcame those who had founded themselves on this loyalty'.

250

The Maps

MAP 1
German Military Districts (Wehrkreise)
1933

North
Sea

Baltic Sea

Memel

Flensburg

Danzig
Königsberg

Hamburg

II

Stettin

I

BELGIUM
HOLLAND

VI
Hanover

Munster

Berlin

Warsaw

POLAND

Demilitarized Zone
of Germany

LUX

IV

Kassel

Dresden

V

III

Breslau

FRANCE

Prague

CZECHO-

VII

Stuttgart

Munich

SLOVAKIA

Miles
0   50   100

AUSTRIA

0 50 100 150
Kilometres

SWITZERLAND

ITALY

MAP 2
German Conquest of Poland
1939

Baltic Sea

LITHUANIA

Memel

Königsberg

Danzig

EAST
PRUSSIA

POMERANIA

AGp North

19C (mot)

4A

3A

Bydgoszcz
(Bromberg)

Berlin

BRANDENBURG

P O L A N D

Warsaw

Brest
Litovsk

8A

Lodz

SILESIA

10A

15C (mot)

16C (mot)

14C (mot)

SUDETENLAND

Prague

BOHEMIA

Cracow

Lvov

14A

22C (mot)

AGp South

MORAVIA

SLOVAKIA

Vienna

Miles
0   50   100

0   50 100 150 200
Kilometres

Budapest

252

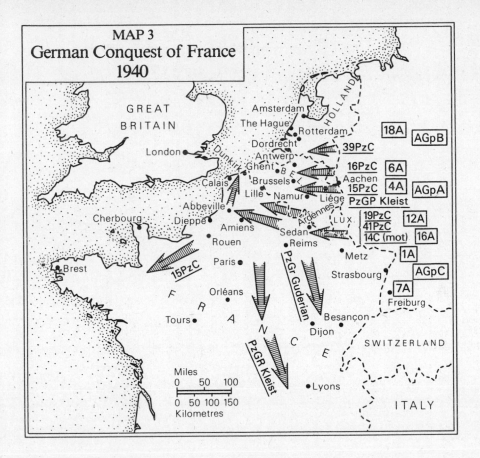

MAP 3
German Conquest of France
1940

GREAT BRITAIN

London

Amsterdam
The Hague
Rotterdam
Dordrecht
Antwerp
Ghent
Brussels
Lille
Namur
Dunkirk
Calais
Abbeville
Dieppe
Cherbourg
Amiens
Rouen
Brest
Paris
Orléans
Tours
F R A N C E
Sedan
Reims
Ardennes
Liège
LUX.
Metz
Strasbourg
Freiburg
Besançon
Dijon
Lyons
Aachen
BEL

HOLLAND

18A | AGpB

39PzC

16PzC | 6A

15PzC | 4A | AGpA

PzGP Kleist

19PzC | 12A
41PzC
14C (mot) | 16A

1A

AGpC

7A

15PzC

PzGr Guderian

PzGR Kleist

SWITZERLAND

ITALY

Miles
0   50   100

0   50 100 150
Kilometres

MAP 4
German Military Districts (Wehrkreise)
June 1941

North Sea

Baltic Sea

U. S. S. R.

Flensburg

HOLLAND

BELGIUM

Hamburg

X

II

Stettin

Danzig

Königsberg

I

XX

• Bialystok

FRANCE

Munster

VI

Hanover

XI

Berlin

III

Posen

XXI

• Brest Litovsk

• Warsaw

Kassel

IX

IV

Lodz

• Radom

Dresden

Breslau

VIII

• Lublin

XII

Wiesbaden

GENERAL
GOUVERNEMENT
OF
POLAND

• Lvov

UKRAINE
(U.S.S.R.)

Nuremberg

XIII

BOHEMIA

Prague

Cracow

Stuttgart

V

MORAVIA

SLOVAKIA

SWITZERLAND

Munich

VII

XVII

Vienna

HUNGARY

XVIII

Salzburg

Miles
0   100 200

0   150
Kilometres

ITALY

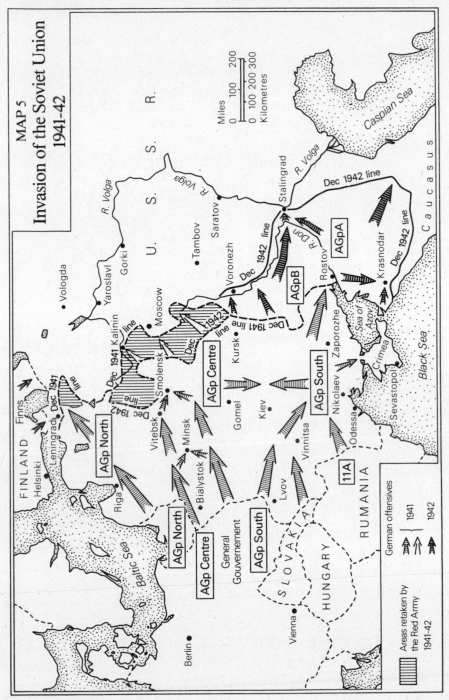

MAP 5

Invasion of the Soviet Union 1941-42

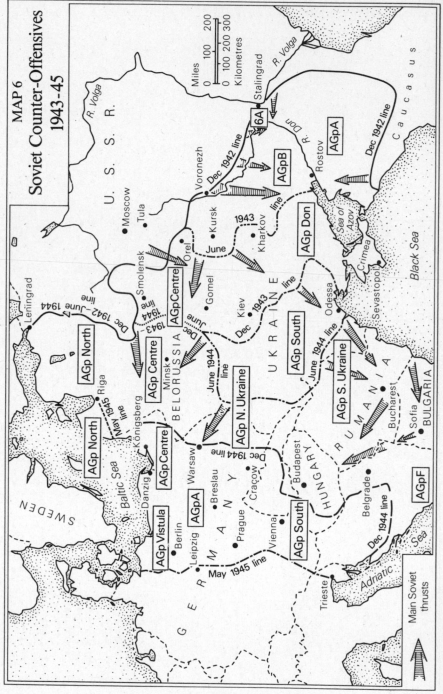

MAP 6

Soviet Counter-Offensives
1943-45

MAP 7
Anglo-American Invasions of Europe
1943–45

ARMY GROUPS IN THE WEST AND SOUTH
Showing Changes of Designation and Commanders

France and Germany

1939 Sep.					**C**
Nov.	**B** *(from East)*	**A** *(from East)*			Leeb
	Bock	Rundstedt			
1940 Aug.	*to East*				
Nov.			**D** *(new) (OB West)*	*to East*	
1941 Mar.		*to East*			
			Witzleben		
1942 Mar.			Rundstedt		
1943 Jun.					
Aug.					
Sep.					
Nov.					
1944 Jan.		**B**			
		Rommel			
Jul.		Kluge	Kluge		
Aug.		Model	Model		
		Model	Rundstedt		
Sep.					
	H	Student			
1945 Jan.					
Mar.			Kesselring		
Apr.	**NW**	*destroyed*			
May	Busch				

Italy   Balkans
_____ _____   _____

                                                          E
                                                          ‾‾‾
                                                          Löhr
                                                          (OB SE)

                              OB South
                              ‾‾‾‾‾‾‾‾‾‾‾
                              Kesselring   **F** *(OB SE)*
                                            ‾
            B   Weichs
            ‾
            Rommel

                              C *(OB SW)*
                              ‾
                              Kesselring

G
‾

Blaskowitz

Balck

Hausser   *disbanded*

                              Vietinghoff   *(OB SE)*

Schulz

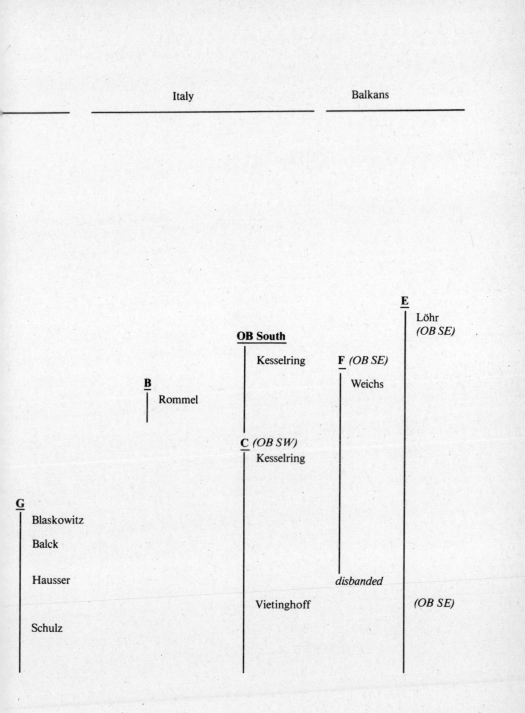

ARMY GROUPS IN THE EAST
Showing Changes of Designation and Commanders

1939 Sep.		**North** | Bock *to West (B)*	**South** | Rundstedt *to West (A)*		
1941 Jun.	**North (C)** | Leeb	**Centre (B)** | Bock	**South (A)** | Rundstedt		
Dec.		Kluge	Reichenau		
1942 Jan.	Küchler		Bock		
			B		**A** *(new)*
Jul.			| Weichs		| List
Sep.					Hitler
				Don *(new)*	Kleist
Nov.				| Manstein	
			to Reich		
1943 Feb.			**South**		
Oct.		Busch			
1944 Jan.	Model			**North Ukraine**	**South Ukraine**
Mar.	Lindemann			| Model	| Schörner
Jun.		Model			
Jul.	Friessner Schörner				Friessner
Aug.		Reinhardt		**A**	**South**
Sep.				| Harpe	
Dec.					Wöhler
1945 Jan.	Rendulic				
	Kurland	**North**	**Vistula** *(new)*	**Centre**	
	| Vietinghoff	| Rendulic	| Himmler	| Schörner	
Mar.	Rendulic	Weiss	Heinrici		
Apr.	Hilpert	*disbanded*			Rendulic
			Student		
May					**Ostmark** |

260

Notes on the Main German Arms

INFANTRY

In 1933 the infantry was regarded as the main and most important arm of the ground forces, all other arms existing to support it.

The senior German infantry officer responsible for infantry training, organization and equipment development, was the inspector of infantry. He was part of the ministry of defence until 1935, then part of the OKH and, after 1939, in the Replacement Army, with a representative (*Waffengeneral*) in the OKH.

The 1933 infantry division was commanded by a lieutenant-general having two deputies, either major-generals or colonels, one being the commander for infantry and the other the commander for artillery; if necessary, however, these could command all arms groups in the field, just as the brigade commanders had done in the old imperial army. The division was made up of three infantry regiments, an artillery group, a pioneer (engineer) battalion that was always grouped with the infantry, a horse-transport battalion that was always under the artillery, a signals and a MT battalion, and services. In peacetime the division numbered only 425 officers, 11,000 men, and thirty-six field guns or howitzers, 108 heavy machine-guns and 200 light machine-guns. Except for the MT battalion, its transport and guns were horse-drawn.

The 1933 infantry regiment was commanded by a colonel and had three battalions, usually commanded by majors, with a regimental mortar company and a training (depot) battalion. Each field battalion had three infantry companies of 160 men commanded by a captain, each of three platoons being commanded by a lieutenant or senior non-commissioned officer (*Feldwebel* or *Fähnrich*). The infantry platoon formed two light machine-gun groups, the remaining personnel forming the rifle groups being armed with rifle and bayonet. The machine-gun company, also commanded by a captain, had twelve medium machine-guns.

The training battalion took in recruits from civilian life twice a year, and clothed, equipped and trained them. After six months basic training they were ready to join the field battalions.

The rifle was the *Gewehr 98*, a bolt-action *Mauser* taking five 7.92 mm rimless cartridges; it had been first produced in 1898 and was used by all the services for nearly fifty years up to 1945. The rifle was sighted up to 2,000 metres but was rarely used beyond 600 metres. It could be used as a grenade thrower and was also manufactured in a shortened carbine pattern. It had a short sword bayonet about sixteen inches long.

The light machine-gun was the air-cooled *08/18* on bipod legs, with an easily replaced barrel to avoid overheating; it fired belted ammunition. The medium machine-gun was the tripod mounted *08/15* water-cooled weapon. The first had an effective range of about 1,000 metres, the second about 2,000 metres.

The mortar is a high trajectory smooth barrelled muzzle-loader and fires a heavy fin-stabilized bomb. In 1933 the old 81 mm *L15* was in use with a range of about 3,000 metres.

No infantry-guns or anti-tank guns were provided on the 1933 equipment tables but they were usually regarded as an invisible asset on field exercises, and their tactical siting and use were practised.

With the German rearmament came an expansion in the types of infantry since these later included mountain infantry and motorized infantry (after 1938 developed as a semi-dependent arm).

The basic organization of the infantry regiment did not alter materially from the 1933 pattern except that new equipment was taken into use and infantry-gun and anti-tank companies were introduced into each of the infantry regiments, these coming directly under the regimental commander. Since all the companies were numbered consecutively from 1 to 12 throughout the regiment (4, 8 and 12 being the machine-gun companies) these new companies invariably took the numbers 13 and 14.

The training (depot) battalions disappeared after 1934, being replaced by one, sometimes two, reinforcement battalions (*Ergänzungsbataillone*). These were, however, often diverted from the originally intended function of training recruits for the regiment.

Contrary to what has often been assumed outside of Germany, the infantry of the Third Reich had no direct connection or traditional ties to the infantry of the imperial army, except insofar as von Seeckt had fabricated artificial links within the battalions and companies of the *Reichsheer*.

From October 1935 machine-gun battalions were formed from infantry and the *Landespolizei*, and these were fully motorized. It had been intended that each infantry division should have its own machine-gun battalion but only eight had been raised by the outbreak of the war.

In 1938 the *Dreyse LMG 13* and the water-cooled *08/15* were still in use, but were being replaced by the dual purpose *MG 34* an air-cooled bipod or tripod mounted machine-gun fed by metal belt or by drum. It had a rapid rate of fire with an effective range, on a tripod, of up to 3,000 metres. The heavy water-cooled 250 round belt-fed *MG 08* remained in use where range and sustained fire were needed.

The anti-tank gun was a split-trail 37 mm *Pak*, firing a 1½ lb solid shot or shell, with a muzzle velocity of 2,600 feet per second that could penetrate nearly two inches of homogeneous armour at 30 degrees from normal at ranges within 400 metres. A new and much lighter 81 mm (*34*) mortar was also coming into service, this firing an eight pound bomb to ranges of up to 2,000 metres. The anti-tank rifle and the light mortar were soon discarded.

The infantry-guns provided the infantry regimental commander's own artillery fire power and were of two patterns: the light snub-nosed 75 mm *IG 18* that fired a 12 lb shell to a range of about 3,800 metres; the 150 mm infantry-gun fired an 80 lb shell to a range of about 5,000 metres. Both of these guns could be used in the upper or lower register (as howitzers or guns) and they and the 37 mm anti-tank gun remained in service throughout the war. When provided with the stick-bomb and the hollow-charge projectile later in the war they proved to be effective anti-tank guns.

These were the weapons that stood the infantry in good stead throughout the war years and the changes made were not particularly significant. Among the wartime small arms of note, however, were the 9 mm machine-pistol (*MP 40*), a weapon that operated on the blowback reloading principle of the automatic pistol; this had an effective range of up to 200 metres and was originally provided for parachute troops. Its introduction had long been opposed by Hitler until eventually the success of the Red Army *PP sh* forced him to change his views. Other machine-pistols and self-loading rifles were developed to take the 7.92 rimless round, but they were not widely used. A replacement for the *MG 34* known as the *MG 42* provided a machine-gun with a higher cyclic rate of fire.

The close quarter protection of infantry against tanks was greatly improved during the war by the development of hollow-charge rocket propelled projectiles and recoilless dischargers, since these provided the soldier with a light and personal close-range weapon that could penetrate a great thickness of armour.

The infantry division with which the German Army went to war was basically of the same organization as that of the 1933 *Reichsheer* enlarged by a reconnaissance battalion and an anti-tank battalion and by the regimental companies 13 and 14, but it had been raised to its war strength of 17,000 men. There were, however, differences in the old type organization and equipment scales according to category rating, the earlier and lower numbered categories being the best equipped and most powerful of the divisions. During 1942 and 1943 many divisions on the eastern front had lost a regiment through casualties, so that they became seven battalion divisions, the seventh battalion (sometimes called the fusilier battalion) being the divisional reserve. From 1942 onwards divisional strengths, particularly infantry, sank drastically, sometimes to half of their establishment. The infantry division 1944 new type (*n.A*) was a three regiment six battalion division with a divisional fusilier battalion instead of a reconnaissance battalion, and had a divisional establishment of 12,300.

The *Volksgrenadier* division formed after July 1944 was similar to the 1944 infantry division except that it had a fusilier company instead of a battalion and had one battalion mounted on bicycles; its infantry regiment anti-tank companies had rocket grenade weapons and not anti-tank guns, and the division had a significantly lighter scale of supporting artillery. *Volksgrenadier* division, although army formations, were controlled by the *Waffen SS*.

Army infantry, motorized infantry or panzer divisions, unlike the SS, did not usually carry an honorific title. The main exceptions were the *Grossdeutschland*, the *Brandenburg*, and the *Feldherrnhalle* (the latter so named because it once had a nucleus of members of the SA).

MOTORIZED INFANTRY

Motorized infantry were originally infantry divisions, numbered in the normal sequence, trained and equipped as infantry of the line and wearing the traditional white piping of the infantry arm. The only difference to the line was that they were lorry-borne. In 1939 they numbered four (2, 13, 20 and 29) divisions under 14 Motorized Corps; in early 1940 they were each reduced from three to two regiments, and the motorized *Grossdeutschland* regiment was developed from the ceremonial *Wachregiment Berlin*.

Immediately before the war with the Soviet Union 2 and 13 Motorized Infantry Divisions were converted to panzer divisions and 3, 10, 14, 16, 18, 25, 36, and 60 (*Feldherrnhalle*) Infantry Divisions were converted to two regiment motorized infantry divisions, making ten in all. In October 1942 the regiments were renamed as motorized grenadier regiments; then in June 1943, after they had been transferred to the panzer troop arm, the divisions were known as panzer grenadier divisions. That year 14 and 36 Motorized Infantry Divisions reverted to infantry, and 15, 20, 29 and 90 Infantry Divisions became panzer grenadier, making eleven in all. Then in May 1944, 16 Panzer Grenadier Division remnants were reformed as 116 Panzer Division. In December 1944 the *Grenadier-Regimenter (Motorisiert)* were renamed as panzer grenadier regiments.

The army panzer grenadier divisions (unlike *Grossdeutschland*, the *Feldherrnhalle* and the *Waffen SS* panzer grenadier divisions) had two regiments of three battalions and no tank or assault guns as part of the divisional establishment until late 1943, when a single panzer *Abteilung* of three assault gun or tank companies totalling 42 assault guns (or tanks) were added. The divisional reconnaissance battalion had a number of armoured half-track vehicles.

The infantry component of panzer divisions (as opposed to those infantry that made up the motorized divisions) had been taken from the cavalry and the line infantry, and these formed the single or, occasionally, the double rifle regiments (*Schützenregimenter*), each of two battalions, within the panzer divisions. In the early days all *Schützenregimenter* were lorry-borne and their role was to provide close support for the tanks in battle. In some cases they retained the yellow cavalry arm piping (particularly in the 1938 cavalry light divisions), but usually they wore the light infantry green piping that distinguished them from motorized infantry or line infantry. At the end of 1939 the light divisions became panzer divisions and most rifle regiments were increased to three or four battalions.

With the doubling of the number of panzer divisions in the autumn of 1940 all panzer divisions had their tank establishments cut by almost fifty per cent but their infantry content increased marginally in that all divisions had thereafter two *Schützenregimenter*, each regiment having two battalions of five companies. In April 1942 these regiments were redesignated as panzer grenadier regiments.

In 1943 the first rifle battalion in each of the panzer divisions was equipped with armoured carriers and became known as *gepanzerte* (armoured infantry), so that they could actually motor across country with the tanks and, if necessary, fight mounted. They had a special establishment of heavy weapons that included infantry-guns on self-propelled mounts and pioneers equipped with flame throwers. The remaining three battalions in the panzer division were lorry-borne and had to fight dismounted.

In March 1945 the *gepanzerte* battalion was removed from the regiment and integrated with the tank battalion. The remaining panzer grenadier regiments within the panzer division then lost their trucks, due to the shortage of vehicles and fuel.

PANZER TROOPS

It has been widely, and somewhat misleadingly, bruited that the literary works of de Gaulle and Liddell Hart were of prime importance to the founders of the new panzer arm, and this error was compounded by Churchill who told the Commons in 1942 that the idea 'of armoured forces as they are now being used was largely French, as General de Gaulle's book shows'. Liddell Hart took Churchill to task in a letter to *The Times* (9 July 1942), telling its readers that German methods had been 'expounded from the early twenties onwards – by Colonel Fuller and others'.

That de Gaulle, Liddell Hart and Fuller were read in Germany there can, of course, be no doubt. On the other hand, the T3 department of the *Truppenamt* had been engaged for years in collecting a vast quantity of the world's literature on armoured and motorized warfare, in which numerous theories were ventilated, including many of those dear to de Gaulle and Liddell Hart. And Guderian, writing not for the benefit of a 1946 western readership but in 1943 for the information of the German public in the Third Reich, admits simply that the new panzer arm was founded on the official British *Provisional Regulations (Part II)* of 1927, since these were comprehensive and sufficiently flexible to allow for variation and adaptation, and were in no way as rigid as those of the French. Then, by trial and error, by experiment and use, a German school of thought was developed.

Attention was paid to any foreign writer on army motorization, but in this respect de Gaulle and Liddell Hart were acknowledged by Guderian only in company with others who included Fuller, Martel and Swinton. Nehring, Guderian's deputy, in his post-war writings has said the same, adding that de Gaulle's 1934 *Vers l'Armée de Métier* had little influence on German thought as the panzer doctrine was already in being by then.

Even so there were wide differences of opinion that gave rise to two German schools of thought as to the use of tanks as a main arm *en masse*, or as a supporting arm to infantry. In truth of course tank formations must be able to perform both tasks, for it is unrealistic to deny infantry armoured support, when necessary, because of the unyielding dogma of the tank specialist. But Guderian, right on many matters, was wrong on this, for he was a rigid theorist obsessed by the operative capabilities of the tank arm; and, like Hitler, he thought that the *Blitzfeldzug* was the alpha and omega of waging war. Like Hitler, he clung to these illusions to the very end, unable to grasp that the operative panzer arm could not even survive on the modern battlefield without tactical air superiority.

The tank arm had originally been based on the seven motor trucking battalions (*Kraftfahrtruppen*) of the *Reichsheer*, although these were heavily reinforced during 1935 by units and reinforcements from cavalry and infantry. All panzer troops, together with those of the anti-tank arm, wore the pink (*rosa*) piping originally worn by the *Reichsheer Kraftfahrtruppen*.

The first three panzer divisions were formed in October 1935, each consisting of a panzer brigade of two tank regiments, and a rifle brigade, usually of a single rifle regiment. By 1938 a further four panzer brigades had been raised, of which two were incorporated into the newly forming 4 and 5 Panzer Divisions, while the other two, for the time being, remained independent. At the end of 1938 seventeen tank regiments had been formed.

Among the officers who developed or belonged to the tank or motorized troops at this time were Lutz, Guderian, Hoth, Hoepner, von Kleist, Rudolf Schmidt, Reinhardt, von Vietinghoff, Geyr von Schweppenburg, Harpe, von Weichs, Paulus and von Thoma. Others who were promoted into the *Panzertruppe*, but who were not yet active in the corps, were von Manstein, Rommel, Model, von Arnim, Heinrici, von Mackensen, Hube and Raus.

In 1938, at Hitler's bidding, all panzer infantry, panzer troops, cavalry, anti-tank and reconnaissance units were grouped into mobile troops (*Schnelle Truppen*) and made the responsibility of Guderian, the new inspector of panzer troops. This untidy grouping fell apart at the beginning of the war, to be revived again in April 1943, this time at Guderian's urging, to form, the *Panzertruppe*, embracing tank troops, panzer grenadiers, motorized infantry, reconnaissance troops, anti-tank units and armoured trains.

On mobilization in 1939 the German Army had five panzer divisions and four (cavalry) light divisions (these latter being made up of two regiments of lorry-borne riflemen together with a single panzer *Abteilung*). By the spring of 1940 the light divisions had become 6 – 9 Panzer Divisions and a new 10 Panzer Division had been raised from an independent panzer brigade; these panzer divisions usually had a single *Schützenregiment* of three or four battalions. Then, in the autumn of 1940, most panzer divisions were reduced from two to one panzer regiments and the panzer brigade headquarters was done away with; all surplus regiments were incorporated into motorized infantry divisions to form new panzer formations numbered from 11–20 Panzer Divisions. The rifle strength within the panzer division was marginally increased to two *Schützenregimenter* each of two battalions. Like infantry and motorized divisions, the panzer division had reconnaissance, signal, engineer, and anti-tank battalions; in the panzer divisions these were fully motorized and had a proportion of armoured and tracked vehicles; a flak battalion was often added.

In 1941, 21 Panzer Division was formed in Africa and in 1942 a further six panzer divisions came into being, 22 and 23 in France, 24 in East Prussia (from 1 Cavalry Division), 25 in Norway, 26 in France and 27 Panzer Division in South Russia. Three divisions (14, 16 and 24) were lost in Stalingrad, while 22 and 27 Panzer Divisions disintegrated in the Don bend; one light and a further three panzer divisions (10, 15 and 21) were lost in Tunisia.

When Guderian was recalled to duty as Inspector-General of Panzer Troops, the newly designated panzer arm was removed from the *Ersatzheer*, both in the Reich and abroad, and put under his command.

In March 1944 another four tank divisions were hurriedly brought into being (9, 11 and 16), based on reserve training panzer formations: the *Panzerlehr* was formed from the *Panzer Schule II*. By the summer of 1944 there were fifteen panzer divisions in the east, seven in the west, one in Italy and one in Denmark.

In the late summer of 1944 the so-called panzer brigades were raised, although these were based on a single tank battalion together with a panzer grenadier battalion. They were later developed into much understrength panzer divisions, taking the numbers of earlier divisions that had been destroyed. Then came Guderian's belated attempt to rebuild certain panzer corps (24, *Grossdeutschland* and *Feldherrnhalle*) on the SS pattern, grouping two (understrength) panzer divisions with a panzer grenadier regiment under a single corps and amalgamating (and reducing) its fire and administrative support.

A 1938 *Abteilung* had three light (*Pz I*) companies and one medium (*Pz II*) company, in all eighty light and sixteen medium tanks, so that a panzer division had 340 light and sixty-four medium tanks in all. But each *Abteilung* left one company in the *Wehrkreis* on mobilization, so that the field establishment of the 39 panzer division was 324 tanks only. In May 1940 the real strength averaged 258 tanks, varying from divisions between a high of 300 and a low of 150. The 41 panzer division with only one panzer regiment should have had an establishment of about 160 tanks, but the actual strength in 1942 varied according to battle conditions and whether the division had a one, two or three battalion panzer regiment. The 43 panzer division had two battalions of four companies each of twenty-two tanks, so that it should have had an establishment of 176 tanks, but a count in the divisions in Army Group South in November of that year shows that with one exception (140 tanks) the strengths varied from twenty-seven to sixty-six tanks – and not all these were battleworthy. The 44 division had an establishment of 136 (dropping to 105), and the 45 division an establishment of sixty-four tanks. In 1939 the main battle tank was the Mk II (and sometimes the Mk I): these were steadily replaced until, in 1945, the Mk IV and Mk V were the main fighting tanks.

The effectiveness of a battle tank depends among other things on its fire power, its armour, its mobility and, according to the German school, its silhouette. The tank's main armament is usually a gun, since this has diverse uses, but if the gun is to kill other tanks it requires good penetrative power, and this will depend on projectile and gun design, particularly on muzzle-velocity (which may depend on the length of barrel) and bore. More powerful and bigger tank guns gave rise to bigger and more heavily armoured tanks, with new problems to maintain their mobility. Yet the slope of armour is more important than thickness. The development of a new series of attack weapons, the hollow-charge, the capped and the squash-head projectile, created other problems for the designers, but in the end the heavy tank and the big tank-gun still emerged triumphant.

ARTILLERY

In the Prussian Army the artillery arm was not held in great esteem, and artillery officers, in company with those of the engineer corps, rarely aspired to high command, although they might reach high rank in the general staff. In the *Reichsheer* particular attention was paid to the artillery in order to improve both its technical ability and the importance attached to that arm. But, as it transpired, the functions of the army artillery were severely restricted from 1933 to 1939 in that coastal artillery became the exclusive preserve of the navy, all anti-aircraft artillery defence was taken over by the *Luftwaffe*, and anti-tank artillery, as it developed, became the responsibility of the panzer arm. And the *Luftwaffe* and the panzer arm were to provide much of the close fire support, particularly in mobile operations, since the artillery at that time was unequipped for such a role. At the other end of the scale the infantry regimental commander found part of his own fire support from the infantry-manned guns and mortars.

Not until comparatively late in the war was any effort made to develop *Artillerieschwerpunkte*, as was the fashion in foreign armies, by the concentration of artillery regiments grouped as artillery divisions in army group reserve – it was in fact first attempted in October 1943 in Army Group Centre. Too often the limited artillery resources were frittered away by small scale near-static allocation, and the situation was not improved by the lack of mobility of the guns, for throughout the war most of them were horse-drawn.

The 1939 infantry division had two artillery regiments, one being of light 105 mm gun howitzers and the other of heavy 150 mm howitzers, four of the battalions being horse-drawn and one heavy battalion being motorized. This motorized battalion was later removed to form part of the corps artillery. From 1942 the infantry divisional artillery usually consisted of a single regiment of one heavy *Abteilung* of twelve 150 mm pieces and three 105 mm battalions, in all forty-eight guns, all of which were horse-drawn. Much Czech and Russian artillery equipment was taken into use.

Throughout the war there were variations dependent on the organization of the division concerned – static divisions on the beaches, for example, had no heavy battalion since they were to rely on the coastal artillery, and the two-infantry regiment divisions had only two 105 mm battalions instead of three. The category 29 grenadier divisions, having three infantry regiments, were restored to three light battalions (in addition to one heavy), but the light batteries had only three guns instead of four to the battery. By the end of 1944 however there was an attempt to return to the early war establishment with a single artillery regiment with three light *Abteilungen* and one heavy, in all fifty-four guns. These were usually 105 mm gun howitzers and 150 mm howitzers, although 75 mm anti-tank batteries were sometimes included.

The standard divisional artillery equipment was the *FH 18* 105 mm that fired a 30 lb shell a maximum range of 13,000 metres, and the 150 mm medium howitzer (*s. FH 18*) that fired a 90 lb shell about 15,000 metres.

The artillery of the panzer divisions was similar, except that it was motor-drawn, and not until 1943 were some of the guns mounted on tracked platforms, usually obsolete tank chassis, these being known as the *Wespe* (105 mm on Mk II), and the *Hummel* (150 mm on Mk III–Mk IV).

The artillery with their red piping arm insignia retained control and manned most of the medium assault guns (*Sturmgeschütze*) that were meant to provide close fire (and anti-tank) support for the infantry. This arm was not really developed until after 1941. *Sturmgeschütze* were, however, also introduced as part of the panzer regiments, and they were later to be part of the regular equipment for *Panzerjäger* troops (also manned by the panzer arm).

Whereas in the Prussian Army, artillery officers rarely aspired to a post beyond that of inspector of artillery, both Commanders-in-Chief of the Army in the Third Reich were artillerymen together with the first two chiefs of the army general staff; and among those field commanders of high rank, first commissioned in the artillery, were von Leeb, von Kluge, von Küchler and von Reichenau.

Notes and Sources

Titles have been included only if the quoted author has more than one work included in the bibliography of this book; in other cases the reader should refer to the bibliography for the full description of the source.

INTRODUCTION (pages xix–xxiv)

1. Kitchen, p. 15 *et. seq.*; Schmidt-Richberg, pp. 15–17.
2. Ibid., pp. 13–14, 18, 33–7.
3. Ibid., pp. 20–27.
4. Goerlitz, *The German General Staff,* pp. 118–30; Koller, p. 35.
5. Ibid., pp. 38–44; Gerhard Ritter's study condemned the Schlieffen plan as 'unrealistic and psychologically fatal for the future'. (cit. Haeussler, pp. 31–4); see also Beck, p. 143 *et seq.*
6. Schmidt-Richberg, pp. 38–41.
7. Ibid., pp. 41–2.
8. Groener's diary 6.10.17, cit. Groener-Geyer, p. 73.
9. Groener's 1936 description of von Ludendorff, cit. Groener-Geyer, pp. 372–4.
10. 'His serious defect was in his sharp underestimating of the enemy' – the official German press release of 21.11.18, cit. Groener-Geyer, p. 89.
11. Macdiarmid's biography of Grierson, cit. Kitchen, p. 19.

CHAPTER 1 (pages 1–20)

1. Groener-Geyer, p. 126 *et seq.*
2. Maercker, p. 12 *et seq.*
3. This was played upon in subsequent Nazi propaganda to the officer; 'When we [officers] came back home a wave of hatred rose up against us. Down with the cockade! Off with the shoulder badges! The officer had become easy prey!' Göring, p. 240.
4. Maercker, p. 65; Groener-Geyer, p. 129; Carsten, p. 21 *et seq.*; Craig, p. 326 *et seq.*
5. Gordon, p. 54 *et seq.*
6. Ibid., p. 85; Groener-Geyer, p. 167; Carsten, pp. 39–43; K-J. Müller, *Das Heer und Hitler,* pp. 17–19.
7. Faber du Faur, pp. 75–6.
8. Groener-Geyer, p. 184.
9. Carsten, p. 56 *et seq.*
10. Craig, pp. 372–9.
11. Gordon, p. 79.
12. Ibid., p. 149.
13. Ibid., p. 174 *et seq.*
14. Groener-Geyer, p. 244.
15. Order of 18.4.20; von Rabenau, p. 193; Craig, p. 384 *et seq.*
16. Schmidt-Richberg, p. 68 *et seq.*

17. Gordon, pp. 185–6.
18. Von Seeckt, *Thoughts of a Soldier,* pp. 86–7.
19. Schmidt-Richberg, p. 71.
20. See *Das Reichsheer und seine Altformationen.*
21. Müller-Hillebrand, Vol. 1, p. 17 and footnote.
22. Gordon, p. 309; Craig, p. 412 *et seq.*
23. Letter of 8.1.37 to von Gleich, cit. Groener-Geyer, p. 360.
24. Faber du Faur, pp. 76–7.
25. Von Seeckt, *Thoughts of a Soldier,* pp, 54, 62, 84, 86 and 94.
26. Cit. Carsten, pp. 104–7, 213–14.
27. Faber du Faur, pp. 125–6; Carsten says much the same and quotes the von Falkenhausen-Joachim von Stülpnagel correspondence that von Seeckt had only 'uneducated stereotyped yes-men' about him; and also General von Möhl, who said that von Seeckt cultivated 'Byzantinism and Cliquism'.
28. Maercker said that in 1919 minister Scheidemann was giving the *Freikorps* 'his heartfelt thanks': by 1920 he was telling the *Reichstag* that 'the officers should consider themselves lucky that they had been left with their shoulder-boards'.
29. Gordon, pp. 192–208; Craig, p. 388 *et seq.*
30. For example, von Manstein, according to his own account, was punished arbitrarily by von Seeckt to a loss of seniority for making a complaint.
31. Teske, *Die Silbernen Spiegel,* pp. 33–8.
32. Groener-Geyer, pp. 247–9.
33. Craig, pp. 141–2.
34. Faber du Faur, p. 146.
35. Groener-Geyer, p. 244 et seq. Groener, while insisting that the army should remain politically neutral, tried in vain to bring it closer to the people. (K-J. Müller, *Das Heer und Hitler,* pp. 28–9)
36. Groener-Geyer, p. 246.
37. Ibid., p. 247.
38. Carsten, pp. 299–304 and 389; as Carsten says, 'the commendation club of former foot guards were promoting each other'.
39. Ibid., p. 303 (the Marshall–Cornwall report of September).
40. Faber du Faur, p. 129.
41. Groener-Geyer, pp. 266–8.
42. K-J. Müller, *Das Heer und Hitler,* p. 76 and note 208; Reynolds, pp. 38 and 46.
43. Groener-Geyer, pp. 268–75.

CHAPTER 2 (pages 21–50)

1. Groener-Geyer, p. 283.
2. Ibid., p. 286.
3. Ibid., p. 289 *et seq.*
4. Ibid., p. 290–91.
5. Ibid., p. 296; also Carsten, p. 341 *et seq.*
6. Groener-Geyer, p. 301.
7. Ibid., p. 309.
8. Ibid., p. 325.
9. Von Papen, p. 116.
10. Ibid., p. 223.
11. Ibid., pp. 246–9.
12. Carsten, p. 393; also O'Neill, p. 9 *et seq.*
13. Müller-Hillebrand, Vol. 1, pp. 16–19.

14. Ibid., pp. 20–21.
15. Völker, pp. 149–65 and 213–21.
16. Ibid., p. 206.
17. Ibid., p. 205.
18. Ibid., p. 225.
19. Ibid., p. 188.
20. Müller-Hillebrand, Vol. 1, p. 13
21. Schmidt-Richberg, p. 73 *et seq.*
22. Müller-Hillebrand, Vol. 1, pp. 103–5.
23. Ibid., pp. 100–101.
24. Mann, pp. 421–6.
25. Bethe, *New Yorker (3.12.79)*, p. 94.
26. Faber du Faur, p. 129.
27. Deutsch, *Hitler and His Generals*, p. 14; Reynolds, p. 45; also K-J. Müller, *Das Heer und Hitler*, pp. 62–4.
28. Carsten, pp. 325–6; K-J. Müller, *Das Heer und Hitler*, p. 59; Reynolds, p. 23 *et seq.*
29. K-J. Müller, *Das Heer und Hitler*, p. 61 and note 131 (von Blomberg forbade his ministerial subordinates to visit von Hammerstein); cf. also Nehring, p. 78.
30. Von Papen, p. 288.
31. O'Neill, p. 23 *et seq.*
32. K-J. Müller, *Das Heer und Hitler*, pp. 76–7.
33. Messerschmidt, p. 81 and note 292.
34. St Antony's College Papers; the authenticity of von Fritsch's letter of 11.12.38 to Baroness von Schutzbar has been challenged, but, as K-J. Müller has said, the correspondence to Joachim von Stülpnagel is genuine: *Das Heer und Hitler*, p. 25 and note 52, and p. 82 and note 239.
35. Otto Wagener, cit. Reynolds and K-J. Müller.
36. Adam's *Erinnerungen*, cit. Reynolds, p. 46.
37. Beck, *Studien*, pp. 28–9.
38. Ibid., pp. 30–33.
39. Ibid., pp. 34–7, 53–4; Wetzell, *Die Deutsche Wehrmacht*, p. 64.
40. Beck, *Studien*, p. 30.
41. K-J. Müller, *Das Heer und Hitler*, p. 221 *et seq.*
42. Von Fritsch's 1938 deposition, cit. Hossbach, *Zwischen Wehrmacht und Hitler*, pp. 68–70.
43. Reynolds, p. 49.
44. K-J. Müller, *Das Heer und Hitler*, pp. 96–7, and notes 50 and 52.
45. Ibid., p. 74 note 197.
46. O'Neill, pp. 33–5.
47. Messerschmidt, p. 43 *et seq.*
48. K-J. Müller, *Das Heer und Hitler*, p. 94 and note 29.
49. O'Neill, pp. 37–8.
50. Ibid., p. 40.
51. O'Neill, pp. 43–4; K-J. Müller, *Das Heer und Hitler*, p. 100 and note 72.
52. Von Papen, pp. 307–10.
53. Bennecke, p. 85.
54. Ibid., p. 85 (von Kleist); also K-J. Müller, *Das Heer und Hitler*, p. 117 and note 182.
55. It has been said that the *Heeresleitung* may have been privy to the Röhm murders but no evidence has been seen that would support this statement: the Milch diary photostats (provided by the Imperial War Museum) certainly do not confirm the existence of such a conspiracy.
56. Goerlitz, *The German General Staff*, p. 288.
57. K-J. Müller, *Das Heer und Hitler*, p. 128.

58. Ibid., p. 123.
59. Groener-Geyer, p. 334.

CHAPTER 3 (pages 51–86)

1. O'Neill, pp. 54–5; K-J. Müller, *Das Heer und Hitler*, p. 134 *et seq.*
2. Deutsch, *Hitler and His Generals*, pp. 19–20.
3. Messerschmidt, p. 53.
4. Hossbach, *Zwischen Wehrmacht und Hitler*, p. 12.
5. Published as *Heeresverordnungsblatt*; see also O'Neill, p. 58.
6. K-J. Müller, *Das Heer und Hitler*, p. 155 *et seq.*
7. Foerster, p. 26 and Reynolds, p. 55.
8. Ibid., p. 64.
9. K-J. Müller, *Das Heer und Hitler*, p. 158.
10. Mann, pp. 435–7.
11. Foerster, p. 21; von Fritsch, cit. Hossbach, *Zwischen Wehrmacht und Hitler*, p. 70.
12. Müller-Hillebrand, Vol. 1, p. 103.
13. Tessin, *Formationsgeschichte der Wehrmacht 1933–39*, p. 19.
14. Ibid., pp. 20–22.
15. Ibid., pp. 108–12.
16. Ibid., pp. 112 *et seq.*
17. Ibid., p. 37.
18. Ibid., pp. 41–4.
19. Ibid., p. 91; also Koch, p. 17.
20. Tessin, *Formationsgeschichte der Wehrmacht 1933–39*, pp. 38–40.
21. Guderian, *Die Panzerwaffe*, pp. 167–70.
22. Nehring, pp. 41–57.
23. Ibid., p. 62.
24. Ibid., pp. 71–8.
25. Ibid., p. 59.
26. Tessin, *Formationsgeschichte der Wehrmacht 1933–39*, pp. 24–5.
27. Ibid., pp. 54–9.
28. Ibid., p. 56.
29. Guderian, *Die Panzerwaffe*, pp. 178–9.
30. Nehring, p. 90 *et seq.*
31. Müller-Hillebrand, Vol. 1, p. 61; Tessin, *Formationsgeschichte der Wehrmacht 1933–39*, pp. 23 and 56.
32. Nehring, pp. 95–6.
33. Ibid., pp. 115–23.
34. Müller-Hillebrand, Vol. 1, pp. 29–30.
35. Ibid., p. 32.
36. Ibid., p. 31.
37. Ibid., pp. 34–6.
38. Ibid., p. 37.
39. Völker, p. 254.
40. Tessin, *Formationsgeschichte der Wehrmacht 1933–39*, p. 71 *et seq.*
41. Koch, pp. 17–21.
42. Ibid., p. 24.
43. Adam's *Erinnerungen*, cit. Reynolds, pp. 89–90.
44. Kielmansegg, *Der Fritsch-Prozess 1938*, p. 103. Von Fritsch, on the other hand, who was naïve in his judgements, thought he was on good personal terms with both von Blomberg and Hitler (cf. K-J. Müller, *Das Heer und Hitler*, pp. 51 and 57 and note 109).
45. Ibid., p. 228 and note 113.
46. Nehring, Notes (13).

47. Erfurth, *Die Geschichte des Generalstabes von 1918 bis 1945*, p. 177.
48. Hossbach, *Zwischen Wehrmacht und Hitler*, pp. 94–6; also O'Neill, p. 88.
49. Stülpnagel, *Notizen zur Augenblicklichen Militärpolitischen Lage 11.4.35*, cit. Reynolds, p. 98.
50. Ibid., p. 99; Foerster, p. 31; also K-J. Müller. *Das Heer und Hitler*, p. 236 and note 151.
51. Cf. O'Neill, pp. 120–23
52. Ibid., p. 128; Hossbach, *Zwischen Wehrmacht und Hitler*, p. 97; Reynolds, p. 107.
53. Hossbach, *Zwischen Wehrmacht und Hitler*, p. 207 *et seq.*
54. Ibid., p. 121 *et seq.*
55. According to the Engel diaries (cit. Deutsch, *Hitler and His Generals*, p. 76) Hitler is said to have remarked at an earlier date 'that the time had come to part with von Blomberg'.
56. Von Manstein, *Aus einem Soldatenleben*, p. 300.
57. Keitel, pp. 47–54.
58. Cf. Wiedemann, p. 110; Warlimont, p. 13; Hossbach, *Zwischen Wehrmacht und Hitler*, pp. 125 and 133; O'Neill, pp. 143–7.
59. Reynolds, p. 136.
60. Von Manstein, *Aus einem Soldatenleben*, p. 303.
61. Adam's *Erinnerungen*, cit. Deutsch, *Hitler and His Generals*, pp. 265.
62. Goerlitz, *The German General Staff*, pp. 317–19.
63. Von Manstein, *Aus einem Soldatenleben*, p. 300.
64. Röhricht, *Pflicht und Gewissen*, p. 11.
65. Adam's *Erinnerungen*, cit. Reynolds, pp. 140–41.
66. Kielmansegg, pp. 114–16.

CHAPTER 4 (pages 87–112)

1. Müller-Hillebrand, Vol. 1, p. 52.
2. Ibid., pp. 57–61; Tessin, *Formationsgeschichte der Wehrmacht 1933–39*, pp. 26–7.
3. Müller-Hillebrand, Vol. 1, pp. 74–7.
4. Tessin, *Formationsgeschichte der Wehrmacht 1933–39*, pp. 21 and 26.
5. Ibid., pp. 20–24; also Müller-Hillebrand, Vol. 1, pp. 132–3.
6. Tessin, *Formationsgeschichte der Wehrmacht 1933–39*, p. 255.
7. Ibid., pp. 246 and 35.
8. Ibid., pp. 37 and 140.
9. Ibid., p. 239.
10. Müller-Hillebrand, Vol. 1, pp. 65–72.
11. Ibid., p. 61.
12. Ibid., p. 62.
13. Ibid., pp. 62–3.
14. Ibid., pp. 63–4.
15. Ibid., p. 65 *et seq.*
16. Tessin, *Formationsgeschichte der Wehrmacht 1933–39*, p. 36.
17. Müller-Hillebrand, Vol. 1, pp. 66–71.
18. Ibid., p. 82.
19. Ibid., p. 84 *et seq.*
20. Müller-Hillebrand, Vol. 3, *Anhang C*; and Tessin, *Formationsgeschichte der Wehrmacht 1933–39*, p. 19.
21. Müller-Hillebrand, Vol. 1, p. 87 *et seq.*
22. Schmidt-Richberg, pp. 81–2.
23. Müller-Hillebrand, Vol. 1, pp. 88–92.
24. Ibid., pp. 111–12; Schmidt-Richberg, pp. 88–91.
25. Hossbach, *Zwischen Wehrmacht und Hitler*, p. 14.

26. Müller-Hillebrand, Vol. 1, pp. 107 and 117.
27. Cf. Deutsch, *Hitler and His Generals*, p. 225.
28. Müller-Hillebrand, Vol. 1, pp. 100 *et seq*.
29. Ibid., pp. 123–5.
30. Ibid., p. 118 *et seq*.
31. K-J. Müller, *Das Heer und Hitler*, p. 45.
32. Faber du Faur, pp. 161–2.
33. Keitel, p. 58.
34. Foerster, p. 90 *et seq*.; K-J. Müller, *Das Heer und Hitler*, p. 308.
35. Ibid., p. 314; Hossbach, *Zwischen Wehrmacht und Hitler*, p. 148.
36. Foerster, p. 98 *et seq*.
37. Ibid., p. 103.
38. Ibid., p. 105.
39. Adam's and Weichs's *Erinnerungen*, cit. Reynolds, pp. 163–4; K-J. Müller, *Das Heer und Hitler*. p. 335.
40. Ibid., p. 338 and note 153; Keitel, p. 65.
41. Goerlitz, *The German General Staff*, p. 329 *et seq*.
42. 1 Army was a temporary mobilization cadre brought into being because of the crisis situation: Hitler had hinted that Beck was to have one of the *Heeresgruppenkommandos* when the war threat had passed. (Foerster, p. 131)
43. Hossbach, *Zwischen Wehrmacht und Hitler*, p. 130.
44. Cf. Reynolds, p. 171.
45. Jodl's Diary 10/13.9.38; Warlimont, p. 116.
45. Müller-Hillebrand, Vol. 1, p. 63.
47. O'Neill, p. 166.
48. Warlimont, pp. 22–3.
49. IMT documents PS1014 and PS798 reproduced in *KTB des OKW*, Vol. 1, pp. 947–9.

CHAPTER 5 (pages 113–30)

1. Greiner, p. 57.
2. Müller-Hillebrand, Vol. 2, pp. 16–22.
3. Greiner, p. 53.
4. Ibid., pp. 45–51.
5. Müller-Hillebrand, Vol. 2, p. 19.
6. Buchheit, *Hitler der Feldherr*, p. 58.
7. Greiner, p. 51.
8. Ibid., p. 9.
9. Von Lossberg, pp. 40–42.
10. Von Manstein, *Verlorene Siege*, p. 55.
11. Buchheit, *Hitler der Feldherr*. pp. 73–5.
12. Müller-Hillebrand, Vol. 2, p. 31 *et seq*.
13. Von Lossberg, p. 44.
14. Ibid., p. 45 *et seq*.
15. Greiner, pp. 55–6.
16. Ibid., pp. 59–60.
17. Ibid., pp. 58–9.
18. Ibid., pp. 61–3.
19. *KTB des OKW*, Vol. 1, p. 50E.
20. Greiner, pp. 66–8.
21. Guderian, *Panzer Leader*, p. 86.

22. K-H. von Stülpnagel, when briefing von Leeb at this time, said *'dasz Brauchitsch bei Hitler nicht mehr zu Worte käme, und vor dem Führer zusammenklappe'*. (K-J. Müller, *Das Heer und Hitler*, p. 508)

23. Greiner, p. 71.

24. Müller-Hillebrand, Vol. 2, p. 45 *et seq.*; Tessin, *Verbände und Truppen der deutschen Wehrmacht und Waffen SS 1939–45*, Vol. 1, p. 9.

25. Ibid., pp. 50–1; Müller-Hillebrand, Vol. 2, p. 36.

26. Ibid., p. 40; Tessin, *Verbände und Truppen der deutschen Wehrmacht und Waffen SS 1939–45*, Vol. 1, p. 112.

27. Müller-Hillebrand, Vol. 2, pp. 39–40.

28. Ibid., p. 41.

29. Ibid., pp. 42–4.

30. Buchheit, *Hitler der Feldherr*, p. 68.

31. Müller-Hillebrand, Vol. 2, pp. 27–9.

CHAPTER 6 (pages 130–44)

1. Greiner, pp. 74–6.

2. Ibid., p. 77.

3. Von Lossberg, p. 56.

4. Müller-Hillebrand, Vol. 2, p. 38.

5. Warlimont, p. 78.

6. Von Lossberg, pp. 56–64; Greiner, pp. 86–8. The able administrator Keitel, though later so 'unpopular and despised', protected his staff from Hitler's spite. Jodl, though he was to become entirely subordinate to the dictator, in the early days enjoyed the respect of most officers in the OKW and OKH – according to what Heusinger and Gehlen told the author – both for his ability and for his character.

7. *KTB des OKW*, Vol. 1, p. 60E *et seq.*; Buchheit, *Hitler der Feldherr*, pp. 105–6.

8. *KTB des OKW*, Vol. 1, pp. 174–80E (Jacobsen).

9. Greiner, pp. 90–91.

10. Halder, *Hitler als Feldherr*, p. 28; von Lossberg, p. 54; von Manstein, *Verlorene Siege*, p. 113; *'Blieb unklar, ob der ObdH Hitler überhaupt von unseren Vorschlägen gesprochen hatte.'*

11. Guderian, *Panzer Leader*, p. 89 *et seq.*

12. Von Manstein, *Verlorene Siege*, p. 118 *et seq.*

13. Greiner, pp. 95–6.

14. Ibid., p. 97.

15. Ibid., p. 100.

16. Müller-Hillebrand, Vol. 2, p. 45 *et seq.*

17. Nehring, p. 175.

18. Greiner, p. 101.

19. Müller-Hillebrand, Vol. 2, pp. 31 and 46.

20. Greiner p. 103; Guderian, *Panzer Leader*, p. 110.

21. Greiner, pp. 103–4; Buchheit, *Hitler der Feldherr*, pp. 114–15.

22. According to Halder's diary the meetings took place later in the day and only von Brauchitsch attended the 24 May meeting. *KTB des OKW*, Vol. 1, p. 158E.

23. Von Lossberg, p. 82.

CHAPTER 7 (pages 145–60)

1. Müller-Hillebrand, Vol. 2, p. 62.

2. Tessin, *Verbände und Truppen der deutschen Wehrmacht und Waffen SS 1939–45*, Vol. 1, p. 51.

3. Greiner, p. 111.
4. Ibid., pp. 112–14; Buchheit, *Hitler der Feldherr*, pp. 123–8.
5. Greiner, pp. 121–4.
6. Ibid., 125–6.
7. Ibid., pp. 126–7.
8. Halder, *Kriegstagebuch*, Vol. 2, p. 49, note 14.
9. Keitel, p. 122.
10. Halder, *Kriegstagebuch*, Vol. 2, pp. 45–6 and note 15 and p. 261.
11. Cit. Hillgruber, *Hitlers Strategie*, p. 512,
12. Müller-Hillebrand, Vol. 2, p. 66 *et seq.*
13. Buchheit, *Hitler der Feldherr*, pp. 144–7; Greiner, pp. 156–8.
14. Ibid., p. 161.
15. Ibid., pp. 165–6.
16. Ibid., p. 162.
17. Ibid., pp. 163–4; Müller-Hillebrand, Vol. 2, p. 73.
18. Greiner, p. 176.
19. Ibid., p. 181.
20. Ibid., pp. 182–3.
21. Ibid., pp. 205–6.
22. Müller-Hillebrand, Vol. 2, p. 74.
23. Greiner, pp. 214–23.
24. Ibid., p. 237.
25. Müller-Hillebrand, Vol. 2, pp. 76–9.
26. Ibid., p. 83 *et seq.*
27. Greiner, pp. 241–51.
28. Ibid., p. 253.
29. Müller-Hillebrand, Vol. 2, p. 78.
30. Tessin, *Verbände und Truppen der deutschen Wehrmacht und Waffen SS 1939–45*, Vol. 1, p. 175.
31. Nehring, pp. 126–30.
32. Tessin, *Verbände und Truppen der deutschen Wehrmacht und Waffen SS 1939–45*, Vol. 1, p. 52 *et seq.*

CHAPTER 8 (pages 161–75)

1. Müller-Hillebrand, Vol. 2, p. 93.
2. Ibid., p. 94.
3. Ibid., p. 95.
4. Ibid., pp. 95–7.
5. Halder, *Kriegstagebuch*, Vol. 2, pp. 32–3.
6 Marcks, *Operationsentwurf Ost*, 5.10.40.
7. *Fremde Heere Ost 20/001/geh Ausl. XXIb.* dated 17.10.40; and in particular the Secret German Handbook on the Red Army *Die Kriegswehrmacht der UdSSR, OKH Gen St d H O Qu.IV Abt. Fremde Heere Ost (11) Nr. 100/41g* of 15.1.41; also Köstring's briefing quoted in Halder, *Kriegstagebuch*, Vol. 2, p. 86.
8 Von Lossberg, pp. 105 and 113; Warlimont, p. 136; Greiner, p. 295.
9. *Die Lossberg Studie WF St Op H 905* of 15.9.40 cit. Bezymensky, *Sonderakte Barbarossa*, pp. 307–13.
10. Cf. *The German Campaign in Russia Planning and Operations 1940–2 (D of A No. 20–261a)*, p. 14.
11. Halder, *Kriegstagebuch*, Vol. 2, pp. 257–60.
12. Ibid., pp. 211–14; Halder, *Hitler as Warlord*, p. 41; *KTB des OKW*, Vol. 1, p. 981; Greiner, p. 322 *et seq.*

13. *KTB des OKW*, Vol. 1, p. 996; for English version see *Hitler's War Directives 1939–45*, p. 93 *et seq.*

14. Gehlen told the author that information about the east had been much hampered by Hitler's restrictions on German intelligence activity against the USSR after August 1939; an examination of the Kinzel edited 1940/41 handbook would appear to bear this out. On the other hand all German information services (and not merely military intelligence) were widely misinformed about the Soviet Union, having little conception of the extent of the changes there since the revolution.

15. Müller-Hillebrand, Vol. 2, pp. 80–1.

16. In a conversation with the author Heusinger was adamant that winter clothing was provided in good time, but only on a reduced scale. There appears to be no doubt, however, that it remained in rear depots and did not reach the front until early 1942. The files on winter equipment are not with the Freiburg Militärarchiv and appear to have been lost.

17. Cf. Nehring notes (3) on the *Panzer Gruppe*.

18. Halder, *Kriegstagebuch*, Vol. 2, p. 320; Picker, p. 270.

19. Ibid., pp. 335–8; Warlimont, pp. 160–1; von Lossberg, pp. 118–19; von Bock, Tagebuch.

20. Halder, *Kriegstagebuch*, Vol. 2, 6.5.41.

21. Army interests in the combat zones and immediate rear areas were taken care of by town majors and military commandants. Behind this line enemy areas were handed over to Rosenberg's civil administration for occupied territories with two Reich commissioners, Koch for the Ukraine, and Lohse for *Ostland* (the Baltic States and Belorussia). The SS (in accordance with a Keitel directive of 13.3.41) were generally responsible for police and most security and anti-partisan activities in the civil occupied territories and often in the army administered rear areas. In addition the German foreign office had its own *Oldenburg* staffs employed on the economic despoliation of the areas.

22. Greiner, pp. 247 and 249.

23. Ibid., pp. 268–9.

24. *KTB des OKW*, Vol. 1, pp. 368–71.

25. Greiner, pp. 275–6.

26. Müller-Hillebrand, Vol. 2, pp. 84–6.

27. Greiner, pp. 285–6; *KTB des OKW*, Vol. 1, pp. 397–9.

28. Müller-Hillebrand, Vol. 2, pp. 81–2.

29. See also Halder, *Kriegstagebuch*, Vol. 2, pp. 264 and 428; Erfurth, *Der Finnische Krieg 1941–44*, pp. 30–1; Mannerheim, *Memoirs*, p. 405; Keitel, p. 156.

30. Müller-Hillebrand, Vol. 2, p. 102.

31. Ibid., p. 103.

32. Ibid., pp. 103–6.

33. Ibid., p. 106.

34. Ibid., pp. 92–3.

35. Ibid., p. 99.

36. Ibid., p. 101.

37. *OKH Schematische Kriegsgliederung vom 27.6.41 (Gen St d H Op Abt III/Prüf-Nr. 16272* (reproduced *KTB des OKW*, Vol. 1, p. 1135 *et seq.*).

38. Zhukov, p. 250.

CHAPTER 9 (pages 176–98)

1. Halder, *Kriegstagebuch*, Vol. 3, p. 124.

2. Guderian, *Panzer Leader*, pp. 158–66; Hoth, pp. 51 and 62.

3. Cf. von Bock, *Tagebuch*, 26.6.41.

4. Halder, *Kriegstagebuch*, Vol. 3, p. 38.

5. Von Bock, *Tagebuch*, 25/26.7.41.

6. Directives 33 and 34 (Hubatsch, *Hitlers Weisungen für die Kriegführung*, pp. 140–7).

7. Von Bock, *Tagebuch*, 24.8.41; Halder, *Kriegstagebuch*, Vol. 3, pp. 194–5.
8. Wagner, p. 206; *Heeresgruppe Süd KTB II Teil Band 4 16.9.41 und Anlagen (24.9.41)*.
9. Hoth, p. 92.
10. Guderian, *Panzer Leader*, pp. 219, 227 and 230.
11. Gareis, pp. 125–30.
12. On 1.9.41, Halder was already advising the disbandment of twelve divisions to provide reinforcements. Halder, *Kriegstagebuch*, Vol. 3, p. 220.
13. Von Bock, *Tagebuch*, 30.10.41.
14. Halder, *Kriegstagebuch*, Vol. 3, p. 309.
15. *Heeresgruppe Süd KTB 30.11.41('Obd Hr Gr meldet hierzu die undurchführbarkeit dieses Befehls')*.
16. Halder, *Kriegstagebuch*, Vol. 3, pp. 319, 321–2.
17. Keitel, pp. 161–2.
18. Von Bock, *Tagebuch*, 30.11.41.
19. Cf. Müller-Hillebrand, Vol. 3, pp. 36–8.
20. Halder, *Kriegstagebuch*, Vol. 3, pp. 376–7; Guderian, *Panzer Leader*, p. 273; Keitel, pp. 156–7; Chales de Beaulieu, *Generaloberst Erich Hoepner*, p. 248.
21. Hoepner's *Laufbahn* and retirement record from Militärarchiv (1.8.69): Hitler removed Hoepner without even informing Bodewin Keitel.
22. Halder, *Kriegstagebuch*, Vol. 3, p. 401.
23. Müller-Hillebrand, Vol. 3, p. 38.
24. Ibid., p. 39 and note 64.
25. Zhukov, pp. 378–81; Vasilevsky, pp. 173–9; *Bitva za Moskvu*, p. 77.
26. *AOK 4 KTB Nr 11 3/8.1.42*.
27. Tessin, *Verbände und Truppen der deutschen Wehrmacht und Waffen SS 1939–45*, Vol. 1, p. 65.
28. Halder, *Kriegstagebuch*, Vol. 3, pp. 430–2; *KTB des OKW*, Vol. 1, p. 489; Müller-Hillebrand, Vol. 3, Table 65.
29. Ibid., p. 35.
30. Ibid., pp. 47–8.
31. Ibid., pp. 51–2.
32. Tessin, *Verbände und Truppen der deutschen Wehrmacht und Waffen SS 1939–45*, Vol. 1, p. 129 *et seq*.
33. Hubatsch, *Hitlers Weisungen für die Kriegführung 1939–45*, pp. 183–8.
34. Müller-Hillebrand, Vol. 3, pp. 56–65.
35. Halder, *Kriegstagebuch*, Vol. 3, pp. 470–6; Keitel, pp. 178–9.
36. Ibid., pp. 180–1; Halder, *Kriegstagebuch*, Vol. 3, p. 513; Warlimont, p. 256; *KTB des OKW*, Vol. 2, pp. 662–3.
37. Warlimont, pp. 256–8; Halder, *Kriegstagebuch*, Vol. 3, pp. 518–19 and 528; Keitel, pp. 180–4.
38. Müller-Hillebrand's discussion with the author and confirmatory notes 30.4.81.
39. Cf. Zeitzler, *Wehrkunde (März 1960) Heft 3*, p. 110; Heiber, p. 120.
40. Speer Interrogation Reports (Flensburg Papers); Heusinger's conversation with author.
41. Von Seydlitz-Kurzbach's views were in *51 Korps Nr 603/43g Kdos 25.11.42*. Arthur Schmidt wrote across this document: 'Wir haben uns nicht am Kopf des Führers zu zerbrechen und Gen. v. Seyd. nicht den des OB.'
42. Engel *Tagebuch*, cit. Jacobsen, *KTB des OKW*, Vol. 2, p. 83 and footnote.
43. *Tagebuch* von Weichs 23.11.42; *Akte AOK 6 – 75107/3*; Doerr, p. 73.
44. Hitler's speeches at Sportpalast 28.9.42 and the Munich speech of 8.11.42.
45. Von Richthofen, *Tagebuch* 24.11.42; Warlimont, p. 284.
46. Stahlberg, von Manstein's ADC, in correspondence with the author 4.6.74.
47. Nehring, p. 212; Goebbels' Diary 18.12.42.

CHAPTER 10 (pages 199–219)

1. Guderian, *Panzer Leader*, pp. 275–88.
2. Ibid., pp. 291–4.
3. Müller-Hillebrand, Vol. 3, p. 158 *et seq.*
4. Ibid., p. 124.
5. Klink, pp. 57–9; von Manstein, *Lost Victories*, p. 443.
6. *Operationsbefehl Nr 6 – OKH/Gen St d H/Op Abt (1) Nr 430/246/43g Kdos Chefs (15.4.43).*
7. Von Manstein, *Lost Victories*, p. 449; Guderian, *Panzer Leader*, pp. 306–8.
8. Von Mellenthin, *Panzer Battles*, pp. 213–16; Warlimont, p. 334.
9. Klink, pp. 197–8.
10. Müller-Hillebrand, Vol. 3, p. 125.
11. Von Manstein, *Lost Victories*, pp. 448–9; *KTB des OKW*, Vol. 3, p. 837.
12. The Soviet offensives *Rumiantsev* and *Kutuzov*; Shtemenko, Vol. 1, pp. 161–2; Bagramian, *Voenno-Istoricheskii Zhurnal* 11/67, p. 42; Vasilevsky, pp. 316–20.
13. Müller-Hillebrand, Vol. 3, Table 55.
14. *KTB des OKW*, Vol. 3, p. 832 *et seq.*
15. Ibid., p. 837.
16. Ibid., pp. 896–9.
17. Ibid, pp. 1082–98.
18. Ibid., pp. 1119 and 1124.
19. *Schematische Kriegsgliederung*, 4.10.43 cit. *KTB des OKW*, pp. 1160–1.
20. Heiber, p. 369 *et seq.*; von Manstein, *Lost Victories*, pp. 459–60.
21. Von Manstein, p. 461; much of this paragraph and the footnotes is taken from notes (4.6.74) given to the author by Stahlberg, von Manstein's ADC.
22. Fretter-Pico, pp. 114–19.
23. *KTB des OKW*, Vol. 3, pp. 933 and 983.
24. Ibid., p. 1083.
25. *OKH/Gen St d H/Op Abt (1 S/A) Nr 438586/43g Kdos Chefsache 4.9.43*; and Pickert, p. 57.
26. Fretter-Pico, pp. 123–5; von Mellenthin, pp. 247–8.
27. Heidkämper, pp. 27–8.
28. Ibid., p. 34.
29. *KTB des OKW*, Vol. 3, p. 1243.
30. Pohlmann, pp. 112–25.
31. Heiber, p. 532.
32. Von Vormann, pp. 46–51.
33. Heiber, pp. 486–7 and 493.
34. Stahlberg, von Manstein's ADC, in correspondence with the author (4.6.74).
35. Müller-Hillebrand in conversation with the author.
36. (And the footnote detail) one of von Manstein's staff officers in correspondence with the author (4.6.74).
37. *KTB des OKW*, Vol. 4, p. 858; Hillgruber, *Die Räumung der Krim* 1944, p. 72.
38. Müller-Hillebrand, Vol. 3, p. 132 *et seq.*
39. Ibid., p. 134.
40. Ibid., p. 136; also Tessin, *Verbände und Truppen der deutschen Wehrmacht und Waffen SS 1939–45*, Vol. 1, pp. 66, 67 *et seq.*
41. Ibid., p. 76.
42. Müller-Hillebrand, Vol. 3, p. 160.

CHAPTER 11 (pages 220–42)

1. *KTB des OKW*, Vol. 4, p. 255 *et seq.;* Speidel, p. 43 *et seq.*
2. Cf. von Rundstedt's intelligence appreciation 10.1.44, cit. *KTB des OKW*, Vol. 4, p. 258.
3. Ibid., Vol. 3, pp. 1091–2.
4. Hillgruber, *The Warlords*, p. 188 *et seq.*
5. Müller-Hillebrand, Vol. 3, p. 145.
6. Ibid., p. 144.
7. Huzel, pp. 80–120.
8. Tessin, *Verbände und Truppen der deutschen Wehrmacht und Waffen SS 1939–45*, Vol. 1, p. 16.
9. *KTB des OKW*, Vol. 4, pp. 255–7.
10. Ibid., p. 20.
11. Ibid., pp. 276 and 300.
12. Ibid., p. 288.
13. Ibid., p. 233.
14. Speidel, p. 112.
15. *KTB des OKW*, Vol. 4, pp. 366–7.
16. Mannerheim, pp. 481–3; Erfurth, *Der Finnische Krieg 1941–44*, pp. 241–2.
17. *KTB des OKW*, Vol. 4, p. 858.
18. Lange, pp. 110–13.
19. Müller-Hillebrand, Vol. 3, pp. 163–4.
20. Tessin, *Verbände und Truppen der deutschen Wehrmacht und Waffen SS 1939–45*, Vol. 1, pp. 76, 79, 87 *et seq.*
21. Cf. Guderian, *Panzer Leader*, p. 299.
22. Stahlberg, von Manstein's ADC, in correspondence to the author (4.6.74).
23. Boldt, p. 161; Messerschmidt, p. 438.
24. Müller-Hillebrand, Vol. 3, pp. 165–6.
25. Ibid., pp. 166–7.
26. Goebbels, *The Final Entries*, p. 103.
27. Ibid., p. 103; *Erlass Himmlers zur Errichtung von Sonderstandgerichten (26.2.45)*; cf. *KTB des OKW*, Vol. 4, p. 1163 (case von Bothmer).
28. Ibid., p. 858.
29. See Hitler's briefing of Westphal and Krebs 31.8.44, cit. *KTB des OKW*, Vol. 4, pp. 1633–5.
30. Ibid., p. 345.
31. Rendulic's critique to the author covering Finland and subsequent operations 31.7.70 and 21.8.70.
32. Faber said of Guderian that 'he remained a battalion *Jäger* officer and never conditioned himself to the traditions of the general staff'. Faber du Faur, p. 166.
33. Guderian, *Panzer Leader*, p. 351; but see also Messerschmidt, pp. 434–5 and in particular Guderian's open letter to all general staff officers dated 29.7.44, beginning 'Every general staff officer must be a NSFO.'
34. Friessner, p. 48 *et seq.*
35. Ibid., p. 57.
36. 20,000 men were still holding out on 29.8.44, and two days later a group of only 200 men were sighted from the air. *KTB des Ob Kdos der Hr Gr Südukraine, Band 4, Teil 1*, pp. 102–6.
37. Müller-Hillebrand, Vol. 3, p. 170.
38. Ibid., p. 171.
39. Milward, p. 93.
40. Speer Papers *FD2690/45 Vol. 10 (Flensburg Collection)*; also Jannsen, pp. 332–9.

41. Ibid., p. 374.
42. Müller-Hillebrand, Vol. 3, p. 172.
43. Tessin, *Verbände und Truppen der deutschen Wehrmacht und Waffen SS 1939–45*, Vol. 1, pp. 86–93.
44. Nehring, Notes (2).

CHAPTER 12 (pages 243–50)

1. *KTB des OKW*, Vol. 4, pp. 366, 367 and 395.
2. Ibid., p. 431.
3. Ibid., p. 450.
4. Ibid., pp. 444–6.
5. *Schematische Kriegsgliederung (26.11.44)*, cit. *KTB des OKW*, Vol. 4, pp. 1890–1.
6. *Führerbefehl über die Befehlsführung WF St/Qu 2 Nr 1409/44 (28.11.44)*, cit. Hubatsch, p. 299.
7. Müller-Hillebrand, Vol. 3, *Anlage 44*.
8. Nehring, p. 327.
9. Goebbels, *The Final Entries*, p. 247.
10. Guderian, *Panzer Leader*, p. 327.
11. Goebbels, *The Final Entries*, pp. 175 and 280.
12. Tessin, *Verbände und Truppen der deutschen Wehrmacht und Waffen SS 1939–45*, Vol. 1, listed '1944 Panzer Brigades'; also Müller-Hillebrand, Vol 3, *Anlage 41*.
13. *Gen St d H/Org Abt Nr 1/1600/45g Kdos (24.3.45)*.
14. Tessin, *Verbände und Truppen der deutschen Wehrmacht und Waffen SS 1939–45*, Vol. 1, p. 99.
15. Ibid., pp. 100–2.
16. Ibid., pp. 99–100.
17. Guderian, *Panzer Leader*, pp. 427–8; Boldt, pp. 98–100.
18. Keitel, p. 200; *KTB des OKW*, Vol. 4, pp. 1260–1.
19. Boldt, p. 122.
20. Goebbels, *The Final Entries*, p. 105.
21. *KTB des OKW*, Vol. 4, p. 1163.
22. Ibid., p. 1078.
23. Cf. Koller, pp. 88 *et seq.*
24. Ibid., p. 99; Dönitz, p. 440.
25. Cf. Deakin, Ch. 11; Kesselring, p. 418 *et seq.* glosses over these events.
26. Huzel, p. 181.
27. Speer, *Inside the Third Reich*, p. 657; cf. also Ellis, *Victory in the West*, Vol. 2 (events of 2.5.45).
28. Buchheit, *Les Généraux contre Hitler*, p. 199.
29. Speer, *Spandau – The Secret Diaries*, p. 192.

Bibliography

Official and Semi-Official Publications

Abwehrkämpfe am Nordflügel der Ostfront 1944–45. Herausgegeben vom Militärgeschichtlichen Forschungsamt, Deutsche Verlags-Anstalt, Stuttgart 1963.

Anhaltspunkte für den Generalstabsdienst mit Taschenbuch des Generalstabsoffiziers. Reichsdruckerei, Berlin 1914.

Das Deutsche Reich und der Zweite Weltkrieg (Volumes 1 and 2). Herausgegeben vom Militärgeschichtlichen Forschungsamt, Deutsche Verlags-Anstalt, Stuttgart 1979.

Das Reichsheer und seine Alttradition. Haus Neuerburg, Waldorf-Astoria u. Eckstein-Halpaus, Köln 1933.

Der Soldat im neuen Reich. O. Elsner, Berlin 1936.

German Air Force Airlift Operations (Morzik), *Operations in Support of the Army* (Deichmann), *German Air Force versus Russia* (Plocher). Department of the Army, Arno Press, New York 1961, 1962 and 1967.

German Campaign in Poland 1939 (Kennedy). Department of the Army Pamphlet No. 20–255.

German Campaign in Russia Planning and Operations 1940–42. Department of the Army Pamphlet No. 20–261a.

German Northern Theater of Operations 1940–45 (Ziemke). Department of the Army Pamphlet No. 20–271.

Handbuch der deutschen Militärgeschichte 1648–1939. Herausgegeben vom Militärgeschichtlichen Forschungsamt, Freiburg 1964.

Istoriia Velikoi Otechestvennoi Voiny Sovetskogo Soiuza (six volumes). Moscow 1961–65.

Kratkaia Istoriia Otechestvennaia Voina Sovetskogo Soiuza. Moscow 1964.

Le Operazioni Delle Unità Italiane. Ministero della Difesa, Stato Maggiore dell'Esercito – Ufficio Storico, Rome 1975.

Nazi Conspiracy and Aggression (eight volumes). US Government Printing Office 1946–48.

Nazi–Soviet Relations 1939–41. Department of State Publication 3023.

Operationsgebiet Östliche Ostsee. Schriftenreihe des Militärgeschichtlichen Forschungsamtes. Deutschen Verlags-Anstalt, Stuttgart 1961.

Ranglisten des deutschen Reichsheeres 1 Mai 1932. Mittler, Berlin 1932.

Stalingrad to Berlin (Ziemke). Department of the Army (Army Historical Series). *50 Let Vooruzhennykh Sil SSSR.* Moscow 1968.

Edited or Collected Works

Anatomy of the SS State. Collins, London 1968.
Bilanz des Zweiten Weltkrieges. Gerhard Stalling Verlag, Hamburg 1953.
Die Deutsche Wehrmacht 1914–39. Mittler, Berlin 1939.
Jahresberichte 1908–14. Löbell, Berlin.
Kriegstagebuch des Oberkommandos der Wehrmacht (four volumes). Bernard und Graefe, Frankfurt am Main 1961–65.
Wehrmacht und National Sozialismus 1933–39. Bernard und Graefe, München 1978.

Printed Books

Absolon, R., *Wehrgesetz und Wehrdienst 1935–45.* Boldt Verlag, Boppard am Rhein 1960.
Die Wehrmacht im Dritten Reich 1933–39 (Band 1–4). Boldt Verlag, Boppard am Rhein 1960.
Addington, L. H., *The Blitzkrieg Era and the German General Staff 1865–1941.* Rutgens UP, New Brunswick 1971.
Ahlfen, M. von, *Der Kampf um Schlesien.* Gräfe und Unzer, München 1961; and Niehoff, H.; *So Kämpfte Breslau.* Gräfe und Unzer, München 1960.
Baumann, H., *Die 35. Infanterie-Division im Zweiten Weltkrieg.* A. Braun, Karlsruhe 1964.
Beck, L. (ed. Speidel), *Studien.* K. F. Koehler Verlag, Stuttgart 1955.
Beinhauer, E., *Artillerie im Osten.* Wilhelm Limpert, Berlin 1944.
Bekker, C., *Angriffshöhe 4000.* Gerhard Stalling, Oldenburg and Hamburg 1964.
Benary, A., *Die Berliner Bären Division 257. Infanterie-Division.* Podzun, Bad Nauheim 1955.
Bennecke, H., *Die Reichswehr und der Röhm-Putsch.* Gunter Olzug Verlag, ·München 1964.
Bennett, E. W., *German Rearmament and the West.* Princeton University Press 1979.
Benoist-Méchin, J. G. P. M., *Histoire de l'Armée Allemande* (six volumes). Éditions Albin Michel, Paris 1964–6.
Bergh, M. van den, *Das deutsche Heer vor dem Weltkriege.* Sans Souci Verlag, Berlin 1934.
Bezymensky, L., *Sonderakte Barbarossa.* Deutsche Verlags-Anstalt, Stuttgart 1968 (orig. Moscow).
Bidlingmaier, I., *Entstehung und Räumung der Ostseebrückenköpfe 1945.* Vowinckel, Neckargemünd 1966.
Birkenfeld, W., *Geschichte der deutschen Wehr- und Rüstungwirtschaft (1918–45).* Harald Boldt, Boppard am Rhein 1966.
Blumentritt, G., *Von Rundstedt.* Odhams, London 1952.

Boelcke, W. A., *Deutschlands Rüstung im Zweiten Weltkrieg (Hitlers Konferenzen mit Speer 1942–45)*. Athenäum, Frankfurt am Main 1969.

Bor, P., *Gespräche mit Halder*. Limes Verlag, Wiesbaden 1950.

Boldt, G., *Hitler's Last Days*. Arthur Barker, London 1973.

Braubach, M., *Der Einmarsch deutscher Truppen in die Entmilitärisierte Zone am Rhein im März 1936*. Westdeutscher Verlag, Köln 1956.

Buchheit, G., *Hitler der Feldherr*. Grote, Rastatt (Baden) 1958.

Le Complot des Généraux contre Hitler. Arthaud, Paris 1967.

(Soldatentum und Rebellion. Grote Verlag, Rastatt (Baden) 1961.

Bullock, A., *A Study in Tyranny*. Harper and Row, New York 1964.

Buxa, W., *11. Division*. Podzun, Kiel.

Carroll, B. A., *Design for Total War*. Mouton, The Hague 1968.

Carsten, F. L., *The Reichswehr and Politics 1918–33*. Oxford University Press, Oxford 1966.

Carver, M. (ed.), *The Warlords*, Weidenfeld and Nicolson, London 1976.

Castellan, G., *Le Réarmement Clandestin du Reich 1930–35*. Plon, Paris 1954.

Chales de Beaulieu, W., *Der Vorstoss der Panzer Gruppe 4 auf Leningrad*. Vowinckel, Neckargemünd 1961.

Generaloberst Erich Hoepner. Vowinckel, Neckargemünd 1969.

Choltitz, D. von, *Un Soldat parmi des Soldats*. Aubanel 1964.

Craig, G. A., *The Politics of the Prussian Army 1640–1945*. Princeton and Oxford University Press, Oxford 1964.

Creveld, M. L. van, *Hitler's Strategy 1940–41 – The Balkan Clue*. Cambridge University Press, Cambridge 1973.

Deakin, W., *The Brutal Friendship*. Weidenfeld and Nicolson, London 1962.

Deutsch, H. C., *The Conspiracy against Hitler in the Twilight War*. University of Minnesota 1968.

Hitler and his Generals. University of Minnesota 1974.

Demeter, K., *The Officer Corps in Society and State 1650–1945*. Weidenfeld and Nicolson, London 1965.

Dieckert und Grossmann, *Der Kampf um Ostpreussen*. Gräfe und Unzer, München 1960.

Dieckhoff, G., *Die 3. Infanterie-Division*. Börries, Göttingen 1960.

Doenitz, K., *Memoirs*. Weidenfeld and Nicolson, London 1959.

Doerr, H., *Der Feldzug nach Stalingrad*. Mittler, Darmstadt 1955.

Erfurth, W., *Der Finnische Krieg 1941–44*. Limes, Wiesbaden 1950.

Die Geschichte des Deutschen Generalstabes von 1918 bis 1945. Musterschmidt-Verlag, Göttingen, Frankfurt, Berlin 1957.

Faber du Faur, M., *Macht und Ohnmacht*. H. E. Günther Verlag, Hamburg 1953.

Feuchter, G. W., *Der Luftkrieg*. Athenäum, Frankfurt am Main 1964.

Finker, K., *Stauffenberg*. Union Verlag, Berlin 1967.

Foerster, W., *Ein General kämpft gegen den Krieg*. Dom-Verlag, München 1949.

Förster, O. W., *Befestigungswesen*. Vowinckel, Neckargemünd 1960.

Förster, G., with H. Helmert, H. Otto and H. Schnitter, *Der Preussisch-Deutsche Generalstab 1640–1965*. Dietz-Verlag, Berlin 1955.

Forstmeier, F., *Odessa 1941*. Rombach, Freiburg im Breisgau 1967.

Fretter-Pico, M., *Missbrauchte Infanterie*. Bernard und Graefe, Frankfurt am Main 1957.

Friessner, H., *Verratene Schlachten*. Holsten, Hamburg 1956.

Gaertner, F. von, *Die Reichswehr in der Weimarer Republik*. Fundus Verlag, Darmstadt 1969.

Gareis, M., *Kampf und Ende der Fränkisch-Sudetendeutschen 98. Infanterie-Division*. Gareis, Tegernsee 1956.

Gehlen, R., *Der Dienst*. Hase und Koehler Verlag, Mainz-Wiesbaden 1971.

Gessler, O., *Reichswehrpolitik in der Weimarer Zeit*. Deutsche Verlags-Anstalt, Stuttgart 1958.

Gilbert, F., *Hitler Directs His War*. Oxford University Press, New York 1950.

Goebbels, J., *The Goebbels Diaries*. Hamish Hamilton, London 1948.
The Final Entries 1945 – Diaries of Joseph Goebbels. Secker and Warburg, London 1978.
Vom Kaiserhof zur Reichskanzlei. Zentralverlag der NSDAP, München 1938.
Der Steile Aufstieg. Zentralverlag der NSDAP, München 1943.
Reden und Aufsätze aus den Jahren 1941–42. Zentralverlag der NSDAP, München 1943.

Goerlitz, W., *The History of the German General Staff 1657–1945*. Praeger, New York 1953.
Paulus and Stalingrad. Methuen, London 1963.

Gordon, H. J., *The Reichswehr and the German Republic 1919–26*. Princeton University Press 1957.

Göring, H., *Reden und Aufsätze*. Zentralverlag der NSDAP, München 1938.

Greiner, H., *Die Oberste Wehrmachtführung 1939–43*. Limes, Wiesbaden 1951.

Groener-Geyer, D., *General Groener*. Societäts-Verlag, Frankfurt am Main 1955.

Grossmann, H., *Geschichte der Rheinisch-Westfälischen 5. Infanterie-Division*. Podzun, Bad Nauheim 1958.

Gschöpf, R., *Mein Weg mit der 45. Infanterie-Division*. Oberösterreichischer Landesverlag 1955.

Guderian, H., *Die Panzerwaffe*. Union Deutsche Verlag, Stuttgart 1943.
Panzer Leader. Michael Joseph, London 1952.

Haeussler, H., *General William Groener and the Imperial German Army*. University of Wisconsin 1962.

Haferkann, H., *Ostwärts bis Sewastopol*. Deutscher Volksverlag, München 1943.

Halder, W., *Kriegstagebuch* (three volumes). Kohlhammer, Stuttgart 1962.
Hitler as Warlord. Putnam, London 1950.

Haupt, W., *Demjansk*. Podzun, Bad Nauheim 1961.
Baltikum 1941. Vowinckel, Neckargemünd 1963.
Heeresgruppe Mitte. Podzun, Bad Nauheim 1968.

Hausser, P., *Soldaten wie Andere Auch*. Munin, Osnabrück 1966.

Heiber, H. von, *Hitlers Lagebesprechungen*. Deutsche Verlags-Anstalt, Stuttgart 1962.

Heidkämper, O., *Witebsk*. Vowinckel, Heidelberg 1954.

Held, W., *Verbände und Truppen der deutschen Wehrmacht und Waffen SS im Zweiten Weltkrieg*. Biblio Verlag, Osnabrück 1978.

Hess, W., *Eismeerfront 1941*. Vowinckel, Heidelberg 1956.

Heusinger, A., *Hitler et l'OKH 1933–45*. Berger-Levrault, Paris 1952.

Hilberg, R., *The Destruction of European Jews*. Quadrangle Books, Chicago 1961.

Hillgruber, A., *Hitlers Strategie*. Bernard und Graefe, Frankfurt am Main 1965.
Hitler, König Carol und Marschall Antonescu. Franz Steiner, Wiesbaden 1965.
Die Räumung der Krim 1944. Mittler, Berlin/Frankfurt 1959.
(Ed.) *Probleme des Zweiten Weltkrieges*. Kiepenheur und Witsch 1967.
and Hümmelchen, G., *Chronik des Zweiten Weltkrieges*. Bernard und Graefe, Frankfurt am Main 1966.

Hitler, A., *Mein Kampf*. Hurst and Blackett, London 1939.
Adolf Hitler Spricht. Kittler Verlag, Leipzig 1934.
Hitlers Wollen. (Siebarth). Zentralverlag der NSDAP, München 1941.

Hoffmann, P., *Widerstand Staatsreich Attentat*. Piper Verlag, München 1969.

Hossbach, F., *Zwischen Wehrmacht und Hitler*. Wolfenbütteler Verlagsanstalt, Wolfenbüttel und Hannover 1949.
Die Entwicklung des Oberbefehls über das Heer. Holzner Verlag, Wursburg am Main 1957.

Hoth, H., *Panzeroperationen*. Vowinckel, Heidelberg 1956.

Hubatsch, W., *Hitlers Weisungen für die Kriegführung 1939–45*. Bernard und Graefe, Frankfurt am Main 1962. (In English as *Hitler's War Directives 1939–45* edited by Trevor-Roper, Sidgwick and Jackson, London 1964 and Pan Books, London 1966)
Kriegswende 1943. Wehr und Wissen Verlagsgesellschaft, Darmstadt 1966.

Huzel, D. K., *Peenemünde to Canaveral*. Prentice-Hall, New York 1962.

Jacobsen, H-A., *Der Zweite Weltkrieg in Chronik und Dokumenten*. Wehr und Wissen Verlagsgesellschaft, Darmstadt 1961.

and Rohwer, J., *Entscheidungsschlachten des Zweiten Weltkrieges*. Bernard und Graefe, Frankfurt am Main 1960.

Janssen, G., *Das Ministerium Speer*. Ullstein, Berlin 1968.

Jenner, M., *Die 216/272. Niedersächsische Infanterie-Division*. Podzun, Bad Nauheim 1964.

Kahn, D., *Hitler's Spies*. Macmillan, New York 1978.

Keilig, W., *Das Deutsche Heer 1939–45* (three volumes). Podzun, Bad Nauheim 1956.

Keitel, W., *Memoirs*. Kimber, London 1965.

Kern, W., *Die innere Funktion der Wehrmacht*. Militär-Verlag der DDR, Berlin 1978.

Kesselring, A., *Soldat bis zum letzen Tag*. Athenäum, Bonn 1953.
Gedanken zum Zweiten Weltkrieg. Athenäum, Bonn 1955.

Kielmansegg, J. A., *Der Fritschprozess 1938*. Hoffman und Campe Verlag, Hamburg 1949.

Kissel, H., *Die Katastrophe in Rumänien 1944*. Wehr und Wissen Verlagsgesellschaft, Darmstadt 1964.
Der Deutsche Volkssturm 1944–45. Mittler, Frankfurt am Main 1962.

Kitchen, M., *The German Officer Corps 1890–1914*. Oxford University Press, London 1968.

Klatt, P., *Die 3. Gebirgs-Division 1939–45*. Podzun, Bad Nauheim 1958.

Klietmann, K. G., *Die Waffen SS*. Der Freiwillige, Osnabrück 1965.

Klink, E., *Das Gesetz des Handelns 'Zitadelle' 1943*. Deutsche Verlags-Anstalt, Stuttgart 1966.

Kloster, W., *Der deutsche Generalstab*. Kohlhammer-Verlag, Stuttgart 1932.

Koch, H. A., *Die Geschichte der Deutschen Flakartillerie 1935–45*. Podzun, Bad Nauheim 1954.

Koller, K., *Le Dernier Mois*. Payot, Paris 1950.

Krosigk, L. Graf Schwerin von, *Es Geschah in Deutschland*. Rainer Wunderlich Verlag Hermann Leins, Tübingen und Stuttgart 1951.

Kurowski, F., *Armee Wenck*. Vowinckel, Neckargemünd 1967.

Lange, W., *Korpsabteilung C*. Vowinckel, Neckargemünd 1967.

Lasch, O., *So Fiel Königsberg*. Gräfe und Unzer, München 1959.

Lemelsen, J., *Die 29. Division*. Podzun, Bad Nauheim 1960.

Leverkuehn, P., *German Military Intelligence*. Weidenfeld and Nicolson, London 1954.

Liddell Hart, B. H., *The Other Side of the Hill*. Cassell, London 1951.
The Rommel Papers. Collins, London 1953.

Lossberg, B. von, *Im Wehrmachtführungsstab*. Nölke, Hamburg 1950.

Ludendorff, E. von, *Vom Feldherrn zum Weltrevolutionär und Wegbereiter 1919–25*. Ludendorffs Verlag, München 1940.
Kriegführung und Politik. E. S. Mittler u. Sohn, Berlin 1922.
Mein militärischer Werdegang. Ludendorffs Verlag, München 1933.

Mackensen, E. von, *Vom Bug zum Kaukasus*. Vowinckel, Neckargemünd 1967.

Maercker, K., *Vom Kaiserheer zur Reichswehr*. Koehler Verlag 1922.

Malaparte, C., *The Volga Rises in Europe*. Alvin Redman, London 1957.

Mann, G., *The History of Germany since 1789*. Chatto and Windus, London 1968.

Mannerheim, C. G., *Memoirs*. Cassell, London 1953.

Manstein, E. von, *Aus einem Soldatenleben*. Athenäum-Verlag, Bonn 1958.
 Verlorene Siege. Athenäum-Verlag, Bonn 1955. (In English as *Lost Victories*, Methuen, London 1958)

Martens, H., *General von Seydlitz-Kurzbach 1942–45*. V. Kloeden, Berlin 1971.

Meinck, G., *Hitler und die deutsche Aufrüstung 1933–37*. Steiner Verlag, Wiesbaden 1959.

Meister, J., *Der Seekrieg in den Osteuropäischen Gewässern 1941–45*. Lehmanns, München 1958.

Mellenthin, F. W. von, *Panzer Battles*. University of Oklahoma Press 1956.
 German Generals of WW II. University of Oklahoma Press 1977.

Merker, L., *Das Buch der 78. Sturm-Division*. Kameradschaft der Division.

Messerschmidt, M., *Die Wehrmacht im NS-Staat*. R. v. Deckers Verlag, Hamburg 1969.

Metsch, F. A., *Die Geschichte der 22. Infanterie-Division*, Podzun, Bad Nauheim 1952.

Meyer, K., *Panzergrenadiere*. Schild, München-Lochhausen 1965.

Meyer-Defring, W., *Die 137. Infanterie-Division*. Kameradschaft der Bergmann Division 1962.

Milward, A. S., *The German Economy at War*. The Athlone Press, London 1965.

Morzik und Hümmelchen, *Die Deutschen Transportflieger im Zweiten Weltkrieg*. Bernard und Graefe, Frankfurt am Main 1966.

Müller, K. J., *Das Heer und Hitler*. Deutsche Verlags-Anstalt, Stuttgart 1969.
 Armee, Politik und Gesellschaft in Deutschland 1933–45. Ferdinand Schöningh Verlag, Paderborn 1979.

Müller-Hillebrand, B., *Das Heer 1939–45* (three volumes). Mittler, Frankfurt am Main 1954–69.

Munzel, O., *Die Deutschen Gepanzerten Truppen bis 1945*. Maximilian, Herford 1965.

Murawski, E., *Der Deutsche Wehrmachtbericht 1939–45*. Boldt Verlag, Boppard am Rhein 1962.

Nehring, W., *Die Geschichte der Deutschen Panzerwaffe 1916 bis 1945*. Propyläen Verlag, Berlin 1969.

Nitz, G., *Die 292. Infanterie-Division*. Bernard und Graefe, Berlin 1957.

Nuss, K., *Militär und Wiederaufrüstung in der Weimarer Republik*. Militärverlag der DDR, Berlin 1977.

Oesch, K. L., *Finnlands Entscheidungskampf 1944*. Huber, Frauenfeld 1964.

O'Neill, R., *The German Army and the Nazi Party 1933–39*. Cassell, London 1966.

Papen, F. von, *Memoirs*. André Deutsch, London 1952.

Philippi, A., *Das Pripjetproblem*. Mittler, Frankfurt am Main 1955. and Heim, F., *Der Feldzug gegen Sowjetrussland 1941–45*. Kohlhammer, Stuttgart 1962.

Picker, H., *Hitlers Tischgespräche*. Seewald Verlag, Stuttgart 1963.

Pickert, W., *Vom Kuban-Brückenkopf bis Sewastopol*. Vowinckel, Heidelberg 1955.

Platonov, S. P., *Vtoraia Mirovaia Voina*. Moscow 1958.

Pohlmann, H., *Wolchow 1941–44*. Podzun, Bad Nauheim 1962.

Pottgiesser, H., *Die Reichsbahn im Ostfeldzug*. Vowinckel, Neckargemünd 1960.

Rabenau, F. von, *Seeckt Aus seinem Leben* (two volumes). Hase und Koehler Verlag, Leipzig 1938–40.

Redelis, V., *Partisanen Krieg.* Vowinckel, Heidelberg 1958.

Rehm, W., *Jassy*. Vowinckel, Neckargemünd 1959.

Reitlinger, G., *The SS: Alibi of a Nation*. Viking, New York 1957.

Rendulic, L., *Gekämpft Gesiegt Geschlagen*. 'Welsermuhl' Wels, München 1957.

Reynolds, N., *Treason Was No Crime*. Kimber, London 1976.

Ritter, G., *Carl Goerdeler und die deutsche Widerstandsbewegung*. Deutsche Verlags-Anstalt, Stuttgart 1954.

Röhricht, E., *Probleme der Kesselschlacht*. Condor, Karlsruhe 1958. *Pflicht und Gewissen*. Kohlhammer Verlag, Stuttgart 1965.

Rossinski, H., *The German Army*. Praeger, New York 1966.

Rothfels, H., *The German Opposition to Hitler*. Oswald Wolff, London 1961.

Schacht, H., *Seul contre Hitler*. Libraine Gallimard, Paris 1950.

Scheibert, H., *Nach Stalingrad 48 Kilometer*. Vowinckel, Heidelberg 1956.

Schellenberg, W., *The Schellenberg Memoirs*. André Deutsch, London 1956.

Scheurig, B. von, *Henning von Tresckow*. Stalling-Verlag, Oldenburg und Hamburg 1973.

Schmidt, A., *Geschichte der 10. Division*. Podzun, Bad Nauheim 1963.

Schmidt-Richberg, W., *Die Generalstäbe in Deutschland 1871–1945*. Deutsche Verlags-Anstalt, Stuttgart 1962.

Schmitthenner, W. and Buchheim, H., *Der deutsche Widerstand gegen Hitler*. Kiepenheuer und Witsch, Köln und Berlin 1966.

Schramm, P. E., *Hitler als Militärischer Führer*. Athenäum, Frankfurt am Main 1962.

Schramm, W. von, *Aufstand der Generale*. Kindler Verlag, München 1964. *Beck und Goerdeler*. Gotthold Müller Verlag, München 1965.

Schüdderdopf, O. E., *Quellen zur Politik der Reichswehrführung 1918–33*. Norddeutsche Verlagsanstalt, Hannover, 1955.

Seaton, A., *The Russo–German War 1941–45*. Arthur Barker, London 1971.

Seeckt, H. von, *Thoughts of a Soldier*, Benn, London 1930.
Die Reichswehr. Kittler Verlag, Leipzig 1933.

Senger und Etterlin, F. von, *Die 24. Panzer-Division vormals 1. Kavallerie-Division*. Vowinckel, Neckargemünd 1962.

Senger und Etterlin, F. M. von, *Neither Fear nor Hope*. Macdonald, London 1965.

Shtemenko, S. M., *General'nyi Shtab v Gody Voiny* (two volumes). Moscow 1968 and 1973.

Speer, A., *Inside the Third Reich*. Weidenfeld and Nicolson, London 1970.
Spandau – The Secret Diaries. Macmillan, New York 1976.

Speidel, H., *Invasion 1944*. Henry Regnery, Chicago 1950.

Stalin, J. V., *Kratkaia Biografiia*. Moscow 1950.

Stets, H., *Gebirgsjäger in der Nogaischen Steppe*. Vorwinckel, Heidelberg 1956.
Gebirgsjäger zwischen Dnjepr und Don. Vowinckel, Heidelberg 1957.

Teske, H., *Die Silbernen Spiegel*. Vowinckel, Heidelberg 1952.
General Ernst Köstring. Mittler, Frankfurt am Main 1966.

Tessin, G., *Formationsgeschichte der Wehrmacht 1933–39*. Boldt Verlag, Boppard am Rhein 1959.
Verbände und Truppen der deutschen Wehrmacht und Waffen SS 1939–45 (Volumes 1, 2 and 3). Mittler und Biblio Verlag, Osnabrück.

Tippelskirch, K. von, *Die Geschichte des Zweiten Weltkriegs*. Athenäum, Bonn 1954.

Tornau, G. and Kurowski, F., *Sturmartillerie Fels in der Brandung*. Maximilian, Herford und Bonn 1965.

Trevor-Roper, H. R., *The Last Days of Hitler*. Macmillan, London 1947.

Vasilevsky, A. M., *Delo Vsei Zhizni*. Moscow 1964.

Vogelsang, T., *Reichswehr, Staat und NSDAP (1930–32)*. Deutsche Verlags-Anstalt, Stuttgart 1962.

Völker, K-H., *Die Entwicklung der Militärischen Luftfahrt in Deutschland 1920–33*. Deutsche Verlags-Anstalt, Stuttgart 1962.

Vormann, N. von, *Tscherkassy*. Vowinckel, Heidelberg 1954.

Wagener, C., *Moskau 1941*. Podzun, Bad Nauheim 1965.

Wagner, E., *Der Generalquartiermeister*. Günter Olzog, München 1963.

Warlimont, W., *Inside Hitler's Headquarters*. Weidenfeld and Nicolson, London 1964.

Westphal, S., *Heer in Fesseln*. Athenäum, Bonn 1950.
Der Deutsche Generalstab auf der Anklagebank Nürnberg 1945–1948. Hase und Koehler Verlag, Mainz 1978.

Wheeler-Bennett, J. W., *The Nemesis of Power*. Macmillan, London 1961.

Wiedemann, F., *Der Mann der Feldherr werden wollte*. Blick und Bild Verlag für politische Bildung 1964.

Wohlfeil, R., *Reichswehr und Republik 1918–33*. Bernard und Graefe, Frankfurt am Main 1970.

Zhukov, G.K., *Vospominaniia i Razmyshleniia*. Macdonald, London 1969.

Index

This index is in three parts: Name Index, Place Index, and General Index.

NAME INDEX

All entries of particular interest are accompanied by a few words giving titles, official positions and ranks. The ranks are usually those held in their final appointments although occasionally where a person was promoted through many ranks but still held the same appointment (e.g., Jodl and Schmundt) both the starting and closing ranks have been shown. As with the imperial army, the rank of colonel-general in the Third Reich was the next rank *above* that of general. It was customary to give the arm (e.g., 'general of artillery') only with the rank of general, although this has not been done with this index. All Luftwaffe generals have been so (LW) shown.

Adam, W., Col-Gen. (Chef
Truppenamt 1930–33,
Whrkr VII 1933–5, WM
Akademie 1935–8, Comd
West 1938); 18, 19, 30,
32, 38, 40, 49, 56, 75, 77,
84, 107, 113

Ambrosio, V., Gen (C of S
Comando Supremo from
1943); 207

Antonescu, Ion, Marshal
(Rumanian dictator
1940–44, killed); 156,
204, 236

Arnim, H-J., Col-Gen.
(Comd HGr Afrika 1943);
198, 266

Badoglio, P., Marshal (Head
Italian Government from
1943); 66, 207, 208, 209

Balck, H., Gen. (Comd
armies and then HGr G
1944); 259

Bayer, Gen (Comd Whrkr
XVIII 1939); 113

Beck, L., Col-Gen.
(Artillery, Chef
Truppenamt 1933–5,

Chief Army General Staff
1935–8, suicide July
1944); 19, 38, 39, 40, 41,
42, 43, 44, 45, 48, 49, 53,
55, 56, 60, 61, 63, 67, 68,
75, 76, 77, 78, 79, 80, 82,
83, 84, 93, 100, 103, 105,
106, 107, 108, 110, 111,.
113, 121, 231, 234, 275

Becker, Karl, Col to Lt-Gen.
(WaPrüf 11 1933–6, Chef
H WaA 1938–40, Chef
Wi-Stab OKW); 224

Bismarck, Otto, Fürst
(Prussian Premier
1862–90, German
Chancellor 1871–90); xxi

Blaskowitz, J., Col-Gen.
(Comd Whrkr II 1935,
HrGrKdo III 1939,
armies, and then HrGr G
1944); 56, 113, 114, 119,
140, 175, 227, 235, 259

Blomberg, W. von, FM.
(Infantry, Chef
Truppenamt 1927–9,
Whrkr I 1930–33,
Minister of Defence then
War 1933–8); 11, 13, 15,

18, 19, 25, 27, 31, 33, 34,
37, 38, 39, 40, 43, 44, 45,
46, 49, 51, 52, 53, 56, 63,
71, 73, 75, 77, 78, 79, 80,
81, 82, 84, 85, 101, 104,
121, 250, 272, 273, 274

Blumentritt, G., Lt-Gen. (C
of S HrGr D 1942–4);
194, 221

Bock, F. von, FM. (5 Foot
Guards, Comd Whrkr II
1933, GrKdo III 1935,
HrGrKdo I 1938, HrGr
Nord (B) later Mitte
1939–41, HrGr Süd 1942,
killed 1945); 5, 41, 56,
113, 114, 119, 120, 123,
125, 134, 135, 137, 138,
139, 140, 141, 142, 143,
144, 146, 149, 155, 164,
166, 168, 175, 176, 178,
180, 181, 182, 191, 192,
231, 232, 258, 260

Bodenschatz, K-H., Gen.
(LW) (Göring's LO with
OKW); 73

Bogatsch, R., Gen. (LW);
73

Bohnstedt, K., Col; 31

PLACE INDEX

303

m

Related Titles from MERIDIAN